FACE OF THE DEEP

Face of the Deep is the first full theology of creation from the primal chaos. It proposes a *creatio ex profundis* – creation out of the watery depths – both as an alternative to the orthodox power-discourse of creation from nothingness, and as a figure of the bottomless process of becoming.

The dogma of creation from absolute nothingness dominates the Western religious imagination as well as modern common sense. The *creatio ex nihilo* reflects the unquestionable presupposition of faith in an omnipotent Creator and Lord, and so in the pure and simple origin of our complicated world. Creative processes in matters natural, social and textual are thus also read as functions of power and order, upholding the transcendent power-structures of Jewish, Christian and Muslim orthodoxies. But the ancient scriptures, says Catherine Keller, imagine a messier beginning, with no clear point of origin and no final end. The heteroglossic Deep – the Hebrew *tehom* or primal oceanic chaos – already marks every beginning. It leaks into the bible itself, signifying a fluid matrix of bottomless potentiality, a germinating abyss, a heterogenous womb of self-organising complexity, a resistance to every fixed order. It sweeps away myths of abstract potency – of the paternal Word – in a tumultuous jumble of neglected parts whose creation is material and labored.

Voyaging through a hermeneutical sea mapped upon Moses and Moby Dick, Augustine, Derrida, Deleuze, Whitehead, Jonah's whale, Irigaray and feminist theology, *Face of the Deep* is more than a provocative deconstruction of fearful orthodoxies of nothing. It seeks to relate the maternal floods of primordial chaos to the swirling interdependencies of our embodied, interpretive beings. Engaging with the political and the mystical, the literary and the scientific, the sexual and the racial, it grippingly argues for the Deep as a dual symbol of denigrated marginality and of diffuse, metamorphic possibility, suggestive of the submerged faces within our culture and the gendered face of their suffering. The forgotten chaos struggles with ongoing creation; its turbulent indeterminacy nurtures our becomings. On its surfacing depths we catch a glimpse of our emergent selves.

From within a dangerous and crowded postmodernity, Catherine Keller's impassioned, graceful meditation opens up an ultimately hopeful space within the magnetic depths of cosmic origin. As a landmark work of immense significance for Jewish and Christian theology, gender studies, literature, philosophy and ecology, *Face of the Deep* stretches our originary story to profound new horizons, rewriting the starting point for western spiritual discourse.

Catherine Keller, Professor of Constructive Theology at Drew University, is a leading voice in contemporary constructive and feminist theology. Her books include *Apocalypse Now and Then: A Feminist Guide to the End of the World* (1997) and *From a Broken Web: Separation, Sexism and Self* (1986).

FACE OF THE DEEP

A Theology of Becoming

Catherine Keller

Routledge
Taylor & Francis Group

LONDON AND NEW YORK

First published 2003
by Routledge
2 Park Square, Milton Park, Abingdon, Oxon OX14 4RN

Simultaneously published in the USA and Canada
by Routledge
270 Madison Avenue, New York, NY 10016

Routledge is an imprint of the Taylor & Francis Group

© 2003 Catherine Keller

Typeset in Perpetua by
Keystroke, Jacaranda Lodge, Wolverhampton

British Library Cataloguing in Publication Data
A catalogue record for this book is available from the British Library

Library of Congress Cataloging in Publication Data
Keller, Catherine, 1953–
Face of the deep : a theology of becoming / Catherine Keller.
p. cm.
Includes bibliographical references and index.
1. Creation. 2. Feminist theology. I. Title.

BT695 .K45 2002
231.7′65–dc21   2002031703

ISBN 0–415–25648–8 (hbk)
ISBN 0–415 25649 6 (pbk)

To Jason—
in love
"Tiefer als der Tag gedacht"

CONTENTS

vii

ILLUSTRATIONS

ACKNOWLEDGEMENTS

This book has been written in gratitude for the relations that ebb and flow through every layer of its sentences. Their Deep overwhelms my capacity to name them—except for a few that have repeatedly influenced this text. Drew University has provided a chaosmos of support from the beginning: in the provocations of colleagues, the insights of students, the care of administrators. Among colleagues this book is especially endebted to Virginia Burrus for the sisterly spirit of her often quotable guidance in ancient history and timely rhetoric. Stephen Moore's creative interventions have been good news indeed, if not straight gospel. Dana Fewell has offered aid in the Hebrew Bible, Suzanne Selinger in Barth, and Bill Elkins in hermeneutics. Among doctoral students my research assistants have kept the manuscript on track: Marion Grau has since become a professor, and offered a last, invaluable loop of feedback; Sigridur Gudmarsdottir, with pastoral as well as scholarly skill, midwifed the final phase. Further afield, let me thank those scholars who read too much of this text: Kathryn Tanner, whose wry defense of the *ex nihilo* made her an especially sharp theological interlocutor; Mary de Shazer, wide-ranging scholar of women's literatures, whose willingness to slog through an early draft confirms the tenacity of friendship; Michael Lodahl, for the serendipity of his spirited reading. I also thank Tamara Eshkenazi for her generous comments, and long-time friend Bill Whedbee for his influence and interest. For Daniel Boyarin's interpretive forcefield—and the wording, over kosher wine, of *"creatio ex profundis"*—blessed be he. These three have encouraged the Judaizing tendencies to which this work has yielded, however liminally. To Kwok Pui Lan, who has graciously brought her decolonizing inquiry to bear on the text, I am grateful for growing theological solidarity.

I thankfully acknowledge the Lilly Foundation and A.T.S. for a faculty support scholarship, which in combination with a leave granted by Drew, freed time for writing. And I thank students, friends and family for bearing with me so I could write in unfree times. Thanks particularly to my St. Louis clan for their loving and incongruous aid during the final days—Gregory, Karen, John, Jennifer the graduate;

Jules lent his gifts, and Jane helped sound out the last syllables of what she says scientists are calling "chaoplexity." (She should know.) The marvelous women at Routledge, Julene Knox, Clare Johnson, Celia Tedd and Ruth Jeavons, injected grace into stress. And I would wish all writing friends a copy-editor with the wit and thoroughness of Jenny Overton.

It was "in beginning" with Jason Starr that this book was conceived, and with him that I daily take heart.

Catherine Keller
14 July 2002, NYC

I am painfully like a womanfish who has decided that now it is time to look the sea in its face. All flexed and anguished, she wrings her fins and spreads them wide–to no avail, she only surfaces between two waves and still has no wings.

(Helene Cixous, Promethea)

Thou hast thy mighty wings outspread
And brooding o'er the chaos shed
Thy life into the impregn'd abyss
Thy vital principle infused
And out of nothing's womb produced
The heav'n and earth and all that is.

(Charles Wesley)

Every person, place and thing in the chaosmos of Alle anyway connected in the gobbleydumped turkerey was moving and changing every part of the time.

(James Joyce, Finnegans Wake)

For it is now clear that in the sea nothing lives to itself. The very water is altered, in its chemical nature and in its capacity for influencing life processes, by the fact that certain forms have lived within it and have passed on to it new substances capable of inducing far-reaching effects. So the present is linked with past and future, each living thing with all that surrounds it.

(Rachel Carson, The Edge of the Sea)

PRE / FACE

When in the beginning Elohim created heaven and earth, the earth was tohu va bohu, darkness was upon the face of tehom, and the ruach elohim vibrating upon the face of the waters . . .

I

The undertow has gripped the wave. The salt washes the wound. We begin again, or not at all.

What if *beginning*–this beginning, any beginning, The Beginning–does not lie back, like an origin, but rather opens out? "To begin" derives from the old Teutonic *be-ginnan*, "to cut open, to open up," cognate with the Old English *ginan*, meaning "to gape, to yawn," as a mouth or an abyss (OED).

We gape back. We make brilliant machines for gaping. They inscribe a universe that appears to open endlessly. Indeed, its speed of expansion now seems, stunningly, to be accelerating–as though replaying the initial surge into materialization called the Big Bang.[1] Or more suitably: the Big Birth. A strange "dark energy" pushes the universe infinitely out. In a centrifugal expansion that is paradoxically without center, glamorous conflagrations of star death glide along on the same momentum with nurseries of nebulae incubating fetal stars. The galaxies interlace like a circulatory system: the nonlinear geometry of chaos is figured everywhere. Astronomers, who had once focussed upon "jewel-like lights that moved in eternally recurring patterns," must confront the possibility that the starry galaxies and their creatures are "barely more than flecks of froth on a stormy sea of dark matter."[2] Darkness upon the deep.

Do we–religious or irreligious–just gape a moment, yawn and look away? Does this sheer exteriority, this bounding boundlessness, wash out every signifier of human difference? At, say, a hundred billion galaxies times a hundred billion stars each, how should we empathize with these impossible quantities? Virtue–religious or irreligious–calls our gaze back to the streets, to meet a human scale of need with

PRE/FACE

humane projects. But then: behold the chaos of suffering that bursts from the margins. Just try to focus on a single issue. On ecology, economics, race, gender, sex . . . They all come flooding in. Difference multiplies difference. These Others refuse to stay faceless. Their eyes form galaxies.

We contract back into the cozy microcosms of a self, a love, a solidarity of spirit. Each one collapses into bottomless waters. We fail again to close off the infinite. Not the self-enclosed totality of an abstract infinity: "For me, it can never be one," says Luce Irigaray of this "fluid expansion." "Can never be completed, always in-finite [*infini*]."[3] Unfinished.

And darkness remains over the faces of *tehom*:[4] the deep, salt water, chaos, depth itself. Out there. In here. Meditating two centuries ago on "how everything begins in darkness," Schelling intimated that "most people turn away from what is concealed within themselves just as they turn away from the depths of the great life." So we "shy away from the glance into the abysses of that past, which are still in one just as much as the present."[5] Yet "most people" are not just cowards. We are trained to fear the darkness. "What terrifies you?" asks Irigaray of her masculine interlocutor. "That lack of closure," she surmises. "From which springs your struggle against in-finity."[6] What might happen if we ceased to fight, if we let the undertow draw us toward the depths?

The darksome deep wears so many denigrated faces: formless monsters, maternal hysteria, pagan temptation, dark hoards, caves of terror, contaminating hybrids, miscegenation and sexual confusion. Queer theories, groundless relativisms, narcissistic mysticisms. The collapse of difference. Excess, madness, evil. Death. Amidst the aura of a badness that shades into nothingness, how can we rethink the darkness of beginnings? This book is about that depth, its darkness, its face and its spirit. What kind of a subject-matter is that?

It is first of all a *theological* topic, indeed the first, *the doctrinal topos* ('place') *of "the creation."* Science quantifies the finitudes and the infinities of the creation, leaving it to theology to dwell upon their *quality*. Paradoxically, however, it is theology that taught the West to shun the *depths* of the creation. Christianity established as unquestionable the truth that everything is created *not* from some formless and bottomless something but from nothing: an omnipotent God could have created the world only *ex nihilo*. This dogma of origin has exercised immense productive force. It became common sense. Gradually it took modern and then secular form, generating every kind of western originality, every logos creating the new as if from nothing, cutting violently, ecstatically free of the abysms of the past. But Christian theology, I argue, created this *ex nihilo* at the cost of its own depth. It systematically and symbolically sought to erase the chaos of creation. Such a maneuver, as this book will suggest, was always doomed to a vicious circle: the nothingness invariably returns with the face of the feared chaos—to be nihilated all the more violently.

As a story and as the preoccupation and pre/text of this book, the chaos appears indelibly as the complex second verse of the Bible. So the present subject-matter

xvi

becomes at moments indistinguishable from *hermeneutics*. The author of Genesis, like virtually the entire ancient world, assumed that the universe was created from a primal chaos: something uncreated, something Other, something that a creator could mold, form, or call to order. But the Christian theology that early came to dominate the church could not tolerate this constraint upon God's power: for why should "He" have had to reckon with an Other? The prevenient chaos cramped the growing Christian imaginary of mastery—what we may call its *dominology*, its logos of lordship. I will argue that by the third century theological orthodoxy had defined itself by an unprecedented *nihil*. Classical theism created itself in the space of the erased chaos.

While critically engaging history and scripture, my argument remains a project of *constructive theology*. Offering like most theologies an account of "the creation," this one (unlike most) lets creation itself emerge from *the topos of the Deep*. I had *begun* elsewhere, *in medias res*, writing of relationality as a beginningless process; then of apocalypse as an endless dis/closure. So this becoming theology continues a *deconstruction* of the paradigm and presumption of linear time: the bottom line of origin, the straight line of salvation history, the violent end of the line of time itself. I mark "the beginning" instead as a beginning-in-process, an unoriginated and endless process of becoming: *genesis*. Here the figure of tehom answers—as deep calls to deep—to the watery chaos almost terminated in the Apocalypse: "there shall be no more sea." This theology continues an attempt, necessarily from the inside of the biblical tradition, to heal that desiccating hope. As constructive work, therefore, the present archeology of the deep becomes *ipso facto* a tehomic theology.

What *tradition* of theology is this? Just what inside does it occupy? Christian? Jewish? James Joyce named my own theo-familial circumstances nicely: you "semi-semitic serendipitist, you (thanks, I think that describes you) europasianised Afferyank!"[7] I think that describes the serendipitous hybridity of theology, too, whose promise would lie in the love of our own Afro/Asian/Euro/American complexity. But the *creatio ex nihilo* has occluded such initiating complexities. Perhaps it did not need to. When imposed, however, as the only possible, the original truth, it projects chaos and nothingness onto the non-Christian or sub-Christian Others. Yet those Others, inside and out, whisper to us "dark secrets" (Augustine) of our own complexity. That "our own" would perhaps be describable as a constructive mimesis, on the Christian side, of that "Judeo-Christianity," beyond both melting pot and identity politics, which Daniel Boyarin reads from "the twin birth of Christianity and rabbinic Judaism as two forms of Judaism."[8]

Not surprisingly, the aggressive nihilation of the chaoid otherness took the form of exacerbated, even divinized, masculinities. So for the foreseeable future a tehomic theology will be feminist in kind. But its feminism, like its religious identity, lacks purity. Indeed in the interest of dark beginnings it attempts to free itself from the "light supremacism" of Euroamerican ideals. The color code of light and dark will flicker throughout the present work, inseparable from and irreducible to what we call "race." The complexification of the movement of women through the contractions of race, economics, decolonization, class, or ecology, not to mention religion, comprises a primary context of the present theology: if we are to begin (again) we begin not with a unifying order but with the multiple movements of creativity. Such a multilateral theology ruefully (and not without amusement) acknowledges the double masculinity of *theos/logos* itself. Yet I wish not so much to stand outside of this tradition as to let its own lost waters liquefy its boundaries. Even in its formative orthodoxies, theology has not lacked those who—as Gregory of Nyssa read Moses—"had seen God in the darkness."[9] Who sang like Charles Wesley to a Spirit "brooding o'er the chaos", "nothing's womb"—no empty *nihil*, but "the impregn'd abyss."

Hidden from the glare of Christendom's triumphs, tucked inside of the margins of a text at once Jewish and Christian, might we write a new beginning upon the face of tehom? Here depth would no longer sink along a vertical axis, as a single dimension; it would no longer be containable within an interiority, a subjectivity; it would not function as the property of a soul, a mind, or a work. It would no longer serve to homogenize, to unify, the clutter of its surface. As Gilles Deleuze suggests, "depth as the (ultimate and original) heterogeneous dimension is the matrix of all extensity."[10] This depth insinuates not an undifferentiated chaos, but a chaos from which difference unfolds a cosmos. Thus the multidimensional surfaces of heaven-and-earth—its water, earth and atmosphere, its multiple species and societies—disseminate the deep. Fresh approaches from biblical studies will accompany this reading, where "by and large God does not work *de novo* or *ex nihilo*, but *ex voce* and *per collaborationi*."[11]

Face of the Deep labors to reclaim for theological reflection the tehom inscribed "in the beginning" itself. I do not pretend to construct its opening as it ever was, but as it might yet be: as it unblocks possibilities within, at least, a particular postmillennial context. I read these possibilities as divine gifts and graces. A tehomic theology will reflect in style the flows and eddies of its content. Its language crosses media, genres, disciplines, sexualities, economies, spiritualities—as theology always has. But a tehomic theology does so openly and affirmingly. Theological discourse, if it will live, will speak in the interstices between its historical densities of text and its creative creaturely hopes. For beyond the nostalgia for a premodern grandeur or the doomed utopias of modern reason, what is the actual work of theology—but an incantation at the edge of uncertainty? Let dogma then serve as heuristic device; let theory collect and connect conversations. In this gathering space, religious discourse as a spiritual and social practice offers a unique depth of history and future: but only inasmuch as we face our own grades and varieties of chaos. At its shore, the very edge of the tehom, the ancient oscillation of religious language between assertion and negation, utterance and silence, takes on a tidal rhythm.

II

A map of the book is in order, or at least a nautical chart. Part One not only introduces metaphors and methods, it also in a sense offers up the book in microcosm—but only in the form of its precipitating questions. What happened to the chaos of Genesis 1.2? Why did it disappear from Christian theology—at least on the face of it? Was it murdered? Was it a "she"? "Was" it at all? Is this a mystery that can be solved? Here certain tensions show themselves within contemporary theology, certain differences within which an emerging creation from chaos makes itself felt. The second chapter, beset by monsters, proposes a distinction between "tehomophobic" and "tehomophilic" approaches, both of which appear in the Bible. Furthermore, the distinction exposes a lasting correlation between tehomophobia and gynophobia. Yet a certain tehomic pluralism bequeathed by Aurelius Augustine leaves us an opening, perhaps even an ocean, within the classical tradition.

Part Two, "Orthodoxies of Nothing," undertakes a historical exploration of the doctrine of creation in its relation to the chaos. Chapter 3 traces the patristic construction of the *creatio ex nihilo*. Navigating through a thick and sexually charged fog of "nothingness," it analyzes the motives, moods and alternatives surrounding Irenaeus' and Athanasius' founding arguments. Then in Chapter 4 we read closely the creation from the "nothingsomething" (*nihil aliquid*) according to the *Confessions*, in which a trail of tears leads to an unexpected epiphany of the tehom. If the chaos was first repressed, then reopened and sublimated in Augustine's exegesis, it resurfaces in full horror as "*das Nichtige*" in Karl Barth. The fifth chapter, "Sterile Waters," studies his demonization of the chaos/nothingness, seen as the resurgence of a biblically certifiable tehomophobia. The deconstructive tendency of these readings of primary theological texts now requires hermeneutical explication.

Part Three thus investigates certain biblical and literary treatments of the primal chaos. Chapter 6 maps three registers of scholarly response to the twentieth-century discovery that scripture itself does not declare any *creatio ex nihilo*: two kinds of tehomophobia can now be distinguished, that of the mythic *chaoskampf* and that of an effortless omnipotence. But the beginnings of a third tradition, that of a tehomophilic exegesis, also become legible. Within the context of this tehomic hermeneutics—not just a hermeneutics of tehom—the dialogical intertextuality of Mikhail Bakhtin lets us reread Job's whirlwind (Chapter 7) as re-creation from chaos. Chapter 8 then picks up the trail of Job's Leviathan in Melville's *Moby Dick*. I read the parodic heteroglossia of these two tragicomic masterpieces as eco-spiritual code. Melville's "leviathanic revelation," breaching at the edge of the "heartless voids and immensities," prophesies its national future. These textual leviathans lead us back to the beginning, requiring a constructive theological response to the opening question.

In the interest and teaching of a *creatio ex profundis*, Part Four unfolds its vision from the iconic units of the first two verses of Genesis. Perhaps reminiscent of medieval commentaries, each of these six chapters recapitulates, from a different standpoint, the movement from deconstruction through hermeneutics to theological construction.

Bereshit, "in beginning," first of all distinguishes "beginning" from "origin." This chapter (9) will be the most theoretical section of the book. It considers the consequences for tehomic theology of the poststructuralist repudiations both of "depth" and of "origin." An early Said, Derrida and Deleuze, interwoven with some strangely fitting Whitehead, enable us to theorize a depth that can no longer be conceptualized in binary opposition to surface. Chapter 10 meditates on *bara elohim*, "created God," attempting to face up to the question of "the creation of heaven and earth." Drawing on the medieval Ibn Ezra and the current Gilles Serres and Luce Irigaray, it observes Elohim burst into a "Manyone" of elementals or angels. Next, in a modest offering to the interdiscipline of theology and science, Chapter 11 unfolds the *tohu vabohu* in the light of chaos and complexity science. Chapter 12 then plunges into the tradition of negative theology, considering the implications of its episteme at once for philosophical theology and for social liberation. An iconoclastic mysticism allows this wide loop, exposing tehomic theology to the test of race criticism. In Chapter 13, on tehom itself, I must at last articulate the difference of deep and divinity, of *tehom* and *elohim*, and so, by something like a panentheistic logic, of world and God. Here gender becomes the test, considering the natal metonymy of ocean and of womb. In conclusion, *ruach elohim* will vibrate into view, enabling such unlike trinitarianisms as those of Jürgen Moltmann, Elizabeth Johnson and Gilles Deleuze to interrelate: and more importantly, implicating us in a "dwelling place" or Shekhinah in which the spirit of the Deep might materialize.

To support articulations of such a space, to facilitate contemplations and activations of its possibilities, is the hope and love of this book. Outside of such a space the *creatio ex profundis* cannot take place. Its Deep faces us in confrontation or in attraction: but it faces us *amidst*—not below or above or beyond—the turbulent uncertainties within which every one of us is "moving and changing every part of the time."

Part I

CREATION NOW AND THEN

1

MYSTERY OF THE MISSING CHAOS

In the beginning, there can only be dying, the abyss, the first laugh.

(Helene Cixous[1])

I have heard what the talkers were talking,
the talk of the beginning and the end;
But I do not talk of the beginning or the end.
There was never any more inception than there is now . . .
Nor any more heaven or hell than there is now.

(Walt Whitman[2])

Beginning is going on. Everywhere. Amidst all the endings, so rarely ripe or ready. They show up late, these beginnings, bristling with promise, yet labored and doomed. Every last one of them is lovingly addressed: "in the beginning." But if such talk–talk of the beginning and the end–has produced the poles, the boundary markers of a closed totality, if "the beginning" has blocked the disruptive infinities of becoming, then theology had better get out of its own way.

In the beginning, theology starts again.

If something becomes, it is not what was before. Genesis–a becoming-text, a text of becoming, an unfinished narrative–is not a replication or a rearrangement. Always again there arises an element of the unprecedented. Does the new not come in this sense from nothing? Are we not created from this nothing–the bottomless shadow, tomb, or womb of ourselves? "We are created from *everything*!" exclaims a friend, gazing at his newborn child. He is thinking of the dust of stars, species, and genes, of histories and personalities, recycled in this unpredictable little *nova*, folded like a bud in his arms.[3]

In the face of the infinities of creation, then, the present work makes an infinitesimal move: to open up a possibility hitherto shut into the second verse of the Bible. Of course such a delicate maneuver can provide no prooftext. It does, however,

3

offer the original pre/text, the narrative of that which—in flagrant paradox—precedes any singular origin.

I Billowing deep, bellowing word

What could have been created from nothing? The first something? The first time? If there was such a time: the strange clause of chaos opens before us. Not a theological proposition, not even a *theo-logos*—but a theo-gram: a wisp of text, sent but never quite received. The *tohu vabohu*, the depth veiled in darkness, the sea over which the spirit pulses. Would this oceanic string of icons together signify nothing but—*nothing*? Or then: was the matter of verse 2 already *created* (from a prior nothing) before a word was said? So by the logic of *creatio ex nihilo*, either the biblical chaos really is *nothing*; or God wordlessly created a chaos. In the wake of the Christian—and subsequent Jewish and Muslim—solidifications of religion as orthodoxy,[4] these questions were not to be broached. So a theology of becoming begins more or less here, at the edges of a long silence. A silence vibrant with the unspoken Word.

One finds nowhere a full-fledged theology of creation from the deep. In a sense, the process theology spawned by Whitehead's cosmography comprises a family of exceptions. They postulate the creation from chaos explicitly, but as though in passing, and not as a theology of creation, with a hermeneutic of Genesis.[5] Perhaps for a beginningless and endless cosmos, where every novum takes place *in medias res*, creation is indeed best noted in passing—in process. Discourse of "the creation" does invariably reinscribe "talk of the beginning and the end." Likewise most feminist and ecological theologies jettison, with process theology, the omnipotent He-Creator and His linear salvation history. And they similarly move swiftly past this backwards-looking question.[6] Most other theologies, even liberal and liberation sorts, presume, as we shall see, the creation from nothing.

In other words, the *creatio ex nihilo* has reigned largely uncontested in the language of the church since the third century ACE. This doctrinal hegemony might not surprise us, but for the untoward fact that the Bible does not support it. As Jon Levenson summarizes the situation: "the overture to the Bible, Genesis 1.1–2.3, cannot be invoked in support of the developed Jewish, Christian, and Muslim doctrine of *creatio ex nihilo*."[7] Among biblical scholars there has existed on this matter a near, if nervous, consensus for decades. The Bible knows only of the divine formation of the world out of a chaotic something: not *creatio ex nihilo*, but *ex nihilo nihil fit* ('from nothing comes nothing'), the common sense of the ancient world. Yet theological orthodoxy has from nearly its own beginnings insisted on reading its *nihil* into the first chapter. Thus, for example, the fourth-century bishop Chrysostom performs an exegetical gesture that was becoming standard: he cites Genesis 1.1 for the desirable message and then simply ignores verse 2. "'In the beginning God created heaven and earth.' [Moses] well nigh bellows at us all and says, 'Is it by human beings

I am taught in uttering these things? It is the one *who brought being from nothing* who stirred my tongue in narrating them' [3]."[8] It is, however, Chrysostom himself, not Moses who "bellows at us all" what the text does *not* say—and so effectively drowns out what the next verse *does* say. Even among some of the least authoritarian revisions of the creation today, we will hear the echo of this bellow.

I want us to "hear into its own speech" (to cite a beginning-word of feminist theology[9]) the muted utterance of that next verse, the verse of chaos. But a theology of becoming can hardly go "back to the Bible," competing for the changeless authority of origin. It may, however, solicit the chaotic multiplicity of biblical writings, genres, voices and potentials. For within this *tohu vabohu* of signification—something like what Nietzsche (*not* returning to the Bible) called "infinite interpretation"—a peculiar space of beginning yawns open. To affirm rather than cover up its hermeneutical multiplicity is to hold a sacred space for all the multiples of which the trembling web of the creation is woven. A culturally potent text like Genesis 1—no matter how variously incongruous, archaic, or vicious its effects—can be ignored. But it cannot be erased. Instead of ignorance or orthodoxy, I argue for a defamiliarization of the first two verses. I insist that this is worth doing, that this algorithmic expansion of a hyper-familiar old text, the tiny text of the creation from chaos, is not a hermeneutical hysteria or a nostalgia for origins, but a strong socio-spiritual practice.

The tehomic practice emerges in metonymic proximity to the key principle of chaos theory: "*extreme sensitivity to initial conditions*." The "*iterations*" exhibited in fractal geometry comprise *interrelations*: it is a relational sensitivity, i.e. a responsiveness to an incalculable multiplicity of influences, that imports the "chaos" into a system. Through interrelation the iterations "amplify" the initial conditions. All theological interpretation (at least that which recognizes itself as interpretation rather than revelation) today exposes itself to an incalculable multiplicity of influences— movements, powers, protests, doubts, cultures, desperations, expectations. One pursues hermeneutical complexity. But one always risks chaos. Transcultural sensitivity to initial *textual* conditions iterates here the extreme sensitivity of the spirit hovering, or—in a century-old translation-tradition stemming from Gunkel— "*vibrating* over the face of the waters." So the butterfly effect of chaos theory intercalates its oscillations with the fluttering of the mother dove or brooding water-bird—as also with the interdiscipline of theology and science.[10]

A theology of becoming returns to talk of beginnings precisely to distinguish "beginning," which, as Edward Said has argued, is always relative, contested and historical, from "origin," which is absolute.[11] It does so as part of a decolonization of the space of "the creation." The term "creation" has the advantage of emphasizing the creative novelty, the mysterious event-character, of what comes to be (which is why astronomers like to use it). Thus we cannot simply exchange it for "universe," "cosmos," or "nature." In theology "creation" emphasizes an event in relation, and so

5

signifies a "Creator." The term therefore comes barnacled with stereotypes: of a great supernatural surge of father-power, a world appearing—zap—out of the void; a mankind ruling the world in our manly creator's image; a gift soon spoiled by its creatures' ingratitude. But despite the drag of original cliché, a theology of becoming can only begin in contestation of and relation to the classical tradition. For the creation from chaos rules out its own originality—if not its own creativity.

In as much as the *creatio ex nihilo* lacks biblical warrant, its *foundational authority* (not its possible *meaningfulness*) would be based on false pretenses. So this book cannot avoid deconstructing the doctrine. Indeed we will find a certain theological ancestry of deconstruction hovering upon the very face of the troubled waters. But deconstruction, as its founder has always been at pains to protest, is not the demolition but the destabilization of founding certainties, a "trembling" proper to a transition between epochs, "operating necessarily from the inside."[12] A tehomic theology operates with fear and vibration on the inside of a text whose interpretive boundaries have become more fluid than ever. The very use of scripture to determine what is "in" and who is "out" now trembles under the pressure of multiple inter-pretations. Even as the formative Christian-Jewish oscillations in their ongoing syncretisms with Greco-Roman, African, Asian and other local traditions shake into view, women open new floodgates of a Body that only queerly resembles a male Christ. "In the beginning", writes Derrida, "is hermeneutics."[13]

It is not the flimsy biblical case for the *ex nihilo* doctrine but a hermeneutical desire for a deeply resonant alternative that (in the beginning) provokes the deconstructive movement of the present writing. The gap between the *nihil* and the tehom provides an affirmative possibility: the chance for a creativity that does not confuse itself with control, for an order that does not effect homogeneity, for a depth that is not identifiable with subjectivity. Here, within a discourse of spirit, we may begin (again) to renegotiate the dominant *oikonomia*—the economics, the ecology, the ecumenism of order. Theology has not outgrown the subjection of the *oikos* to the *dominus*. The abiding western dominology can with religious sanction identify anything dark, profound, or fluid with a revolting chaos, an evil to be mastered, a nothing to be ignored. "God had made us the master organizers of the world to establish system where chaos reigns. He [*sic*] has made us adept in government that we may administer government among savages and senile peoples."[14] From the vantage point of the colonizing episteme, the evil is always disorder rather than unjust order; anarchy rather than control, darkness rather than pallor. To plead otherwise is to write "carte blanche for chaos."[15] Yet those who wear the mark of chaos, the skins of darkness, the genders of unspeakable openings—those Others of Order keep finding voice. But they continue to be muted by the bellowing of the dominant discourse. A tehomic discourse grows in the interstices of a maturing (but far from senile) tradition of unruly, disunited beginning-theologies (the liberation, political, feminist/womanist/ mujerista and ecological theologies, the postcolonial hermeneutics). These theologies clash as much as they conspire. They contour this topos of genesis, in which infinity becomes endlessly finite in our midst, as con/text.

If the tehomic infinite *exists*, it does so only in the materializing of its finitudes, its volatile and vulnerable interdependencies. The shifting limits of our shared embodiment mark the "edge of chaos." That trope, borrowed from complexity theory, signifies the "phase transition" at which a complex system organizes itself; and "order out of chaos" signaled the beginning of a new science.[16] The present text claims no quasi-scientific legitimations, only a systemic attraction to a range of scientific discourses and uncertainties Jean-François Lyotard dubbed "postmodern."[17] This postmodernism does inadvertently underwrite a quiet pneumatological transliteration: as complexity emerges at the edge of chaos, so the spirit of Elohim vibrates upon the face of the waters. In other words, a tehomic theology does not worship chaos. This trembling edge signifies at once the creative horizon of all our endeavors and the creaturely limits posed by our "extreme" sensitivity. The ethics of becoming must articulate itself in that borderland, where the flowing potentiality of each actuality, each creature, realizes itself in limitation. A creature signifies what Whitehead called "the decision amidst potentiality."[18] The decision may or may not involve consciousness. It partakes of the indeterminacy, or freedom, churning at the base of any observable order.

To decide for the most heterogeneous width of relations that I in my edgy finitude can embrace—is that my creativity in *imago dei*? To attend in whatever I decide to my interdependence with the others who embody that width—is that my responsibility in *imago dei*? The others in their singularity and their multiplicities will recurrently confront me with the face of the deep: the grin or grimace of chaos. Yet they demand my sensitivity and my justice. They flow to the surface as its own depth—in a limited analogy to what Emmanuel Levinas means by ethics: "The idea of infinity, the infinitely more contained in the less, is concretely produced in the form of a relation with the face."[19]

Deep will appear on the *face* or not at all. But the relation to the face, always most intensely focussed in the interhuman, now demands of us planetary practices which find "face" across the width of the world. These stretch us thin; our strategies can run shallow. So it is the argument of this work that the ethical remains high, dry, and perilously utopic, if not accompanied by a messier therapy: the healing of the systemic repression that I am calling tehomophobia. Theology can perpetuate the illness or it can *capacitate* the cure.

II Grammatology of beginning

Just those first two verses?

The more I meditate upon their iconic figuration, the more I hear them mutter a kind of Hebrew *koan*. Right there in the beginning, right at the mythic foundation of

7

1. Homer Wilson Smith, *Dragon*. Fractal Images provided by Art Matrix, www.artmatrix.com

the western world, there where we expect to hear the Word assert its original omnipotence—was installed a peculiar gap. A churning, complicating darkness was wedged right between the two verses which everyone knows with indelible certainty: between "*In the beginning God created the heaven and the earth*" and "*God said: let there be light . . .*" This interstitial darkness refuses to disappear. It refuses to appear as nothing, as vacuum, as mere absence highlighting the Presence of the Creator, as nonentity limning all the created entities. It gapes open in the text: "*and the earth was tohu vabohu, and darkness was upon the face of tehom and the ruach elohim was vibrating upon the face of the mayim . . .*" This void evinces fullness, its waters, viscosity. It is no wonder that this verse got systematically forgotten, its own flood drowned out by the amplification of the first verse.

So densely packed with its terse triune chaos, the second verse sends a mysterious tremor through the whole narrative of creation. Indeed its grammar unsettles the textual order, which otherwise is declaimed in tones of ceremonious triumph: in what Claus Westermann lauds as "that peculiar and effective monotony which enables it to articulate in characteristic fashion the utter transcendence of Creation."[20] But does the text itself belie the monotony? Did translation force the Hebrew syntax into a foreign over-simplification? Traditionally verse 2 is treated as an independent clause. But increasingly translators are coming under the controversial influence of a medieval Jewish translation. The form of the rare Hebrew *bereshit*— "in beginning"—fashions the first verse as a subordinate clause, not as a summary announcement; the second verse as an elaborate parenthesis; and only the third, where God speaks, as the independent clause. This was the argument of the eleventh-century French biblical and talmudic interpreter Rashi, based on multiple ambiguities of the grammar. The translation-tradition has been quietly shifting to the side of Rashi, who translated as follows: "*At the beginning of the Creation of heaven and earth when the earth was without form and void and there was darkness . . . God said Let there be . . .*"[21]

What happens here? Certainly this translation brings the chaos—if we may use that term to cover loosely the matter of the entire verse—into relief. Whatever it is, it precedes the work of creation. But at the same time this syntax throws off the sequential march of step-by-step commandment and fulfillment. While Rashi did not directly oppose the creation from nothing, he disputed any sense that the days signified a linear sequence: "the text does not intend to point out the order of the acts of Creation."[22] Indeed "you should be ashamed of yourself" for reading it chronologically. Rashi's "provocative statement" against chronological order invokes, according to Avivah Gottlieb Zornberg, "the gaps, the unexplained, the need to examine and reexamine the apparently lucid text, with its account of a harmonious, coherent cosmology."[23] The controversy continues to rage: independent or dependent clause?[24] That apparently minute grammatological nuance—the mere flap of a wing within the microcosm of a verse—hints at the whole point of the present work: that in form as in context the chaos is *always already there*. Verse 2 differs from an absolute origin; it inserts its otherness—neither "Creator" nor "creature"—*into* the origin. Let light differ from darkness; upper tehom from lower, solid from fluid, fish and winged things from the water, earthlings from the earth . . . Let there be differences! But difference itself will have preceded its Word.

Theologies have tried to draw the line at "God," to say that, whenever the creation starts, it is preceded by absolutely nothing—nothing but the pure and simple presence of God the Creator. Certainly this "nothing but" of a nonnegotiable starting-line lends a useful sense of foundation. It offers protection from the tidal waves of a chaos for which we are never prepared; and from the slow lapping erosion of meaning. Is it possible, however, that the foundationalisms themselves have proved more dangerous than that which they have dammed and damned? Does their danger become apparent only when they mobilize crusades, holy wars, market reforms and other mobile extensions of their uncompromising truths? Admittedly that *tehomic alterity* which has been relegated to the outer darkness threatens to flow back monstrously: the *flux*, repressed, returns as *the flood*. I am arguing that the genuine threat that chaos poses is no better reason to patch up the failing foundations, than to tear them down with nihilistic abandon. But does such nihilism "originate" in the modern denial of a foundational origin, as is generally supposed—or rather in *the doctrine which produces the* nihil *in the first place*? For as will become evident, that *nihil* did not "exist" in the Bible or in its neighboring myths and ideas. *The* ex nihilo *doctrine constructed as orthodoxy itself the pure dualism of originating* Logos *and prevenient Nothing*.

Would a third way, neither nihilism nor *ex nihilism*, lie in the affirmation of a difference—a difference bursting into supernovas, squalling infants, turbulent texts—that is not preceded by its logos? Then the difference released in the deconstruction of origin as the pure *nihil* signals an impure alternative. The affinity of tehom to Derrida's *différance* lies there where the latter leaves its "trace" in writing. Might we read its elusive "always already" in the salt water deposited in the second verse of the Bible? We might then track this precreation trace back out through the prolific play of difference flooding "the creation," unfolding in its light and dark, its swarming multiples, its "creeping things innumerable." Spurred on by the more recent grammatology of Derrida's beginnings, we need no longer derive these swarming, fluttering, bifurcating multiples from the undifferentiated Origin of a simple Creator. Difference marks an originative and *originated* beginning. It gives rise to aqueous sayings: "that the origin did not even disappear, that it was never constituted except reciprocally by a nonorigin, the trace, which thus becomes the origin of the origin."[25] In other words the attempt to discover the true origin is doomed. It only brings us to the boundary of our own language, to *originating conditions that have themselves originated*: an infinite regress, that which Derrida calls the "bottomless," opens abysmally at the beginning. Derrida, as we shall later investigate, denies the "bottomless play of the signifier" any *depth* at all.[26] Still we might wonder: might not this bottomlessness—on the *face* of it—signify the Deep itself?

10

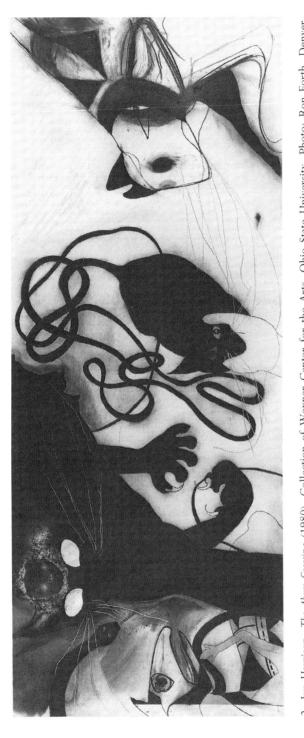

2. Jan Harrison, *The Abyss Crossing* (1980). Collection of Wexner Center for the Arts, Ohio State University. Photo: Ron Forth, Denver, Colorado. Reproduced by kind permission of the artist.

If we discern a third space of beginning–neither pure origin nor nihilist flux–its difference translates into another interstitial space: that between the self-presence of a changeless Being who somehow suddenly (back then) created; and the pure Nonbeing out of which that creation was summoned, and toward which its fluency falls. That alternative milieu, neither being nor nonbeing, will signify the site of becoming as *genesis*: the topos of the Deep. Can we tell the story this way: that tehom as primal chaos precedes and gives rise to the generative tensions of order and disorder, form and formlessness? Might tehom henceforth suggest the chaoid (so not necessarily chaotic) multidimensionality of a bottomless Deep: the matrix in which the creation *becomes*? In which the strange inter-fluencies of creatures–in ecology, predation, genetics, cultures–crisscross the abyss of difference?

III Lubricitous conjunctions

Within this counterdiscourse of creation interstitial words become the carriers of revelation: signifiers that can signify only "within the fire, the cloud and the thick darkness" (Deuteronomy 5.22).[27] Thus "the chaosmos" coined in the thick darkness of *Finnegans Wake* offers itself as a transcription of "the creation." "Every person, place and thing in the chaosmos of Alle anyway connected."[28] Joyce's chaosmos hosts the infinity of allusions–"moving and changing every part of the time"–of a non-linear grammar, an open text, a creativity without origin or end; or rather originality *ever after*, after loss, after end.

"The lubricitous conjugation of the first with the last . . ." The felicitous tehoms of Joycean language itself reveal (to those who have ears to read) not nonsense but an excess of sense, in which every word of the book, like every unit of the universe, comes webbed in unpredictable, multiply allusive, interfluencies. Joyce's chaosmos has been said to foreshadow the sciences of chaos, as they learn to conjugate the uncountable multiplicities of iterations, the relations between the flap of a butterfly's wing, a breeze, a river, an ocean, a distant storm.[29] At the same time, the trope of the chaosmos has political significance: *Finnegans Wake* has been dubbed "the most formidably anti-fascist book produced between the wars," performing "an active transnationalism, disarticulating, rearticulating and at the same time annulling the maximum number of traces–linguistic, historical, mythological, religious."[30] Theology, however, cannot long linger within the style of a Joycean "polyhedron of scripture," the "collideoscope," or the "meanderthale"[31]–certainly no more than it can sustain positivist scientific or political discourse. Religious language meanders along the borders between proposition and invocation, theory and literature; there it generates an open order, a changing text; its scriptural polyhedron refracts the colliding hopes of a history that threatens closure, but has not ceased to begin. "If *Finnegans Wake* is a sacred book," writes Umberto Eco, "it tells us that *in principium erat Chaos*."[32] Quite apart from the religious status of the text, it does read as a colossal midrash, a "semisemitic serendipity," on our quavering little verse. The genesis of chaosmos, and so *the chaosmos of Genesis*, articulate a code of epochal transition, a significance–and in this like unto the language of negative theology–verging knowingly into the unknowable.

De docta ignorantia: this is the knowing, indeed the sacred ignorance, as Nicholas of Cusa–who with Giordano Bruno had a profound impact upon James Joyce–defined "negative theology." The iconoclasm of the infinite shatters any claim of the finite to fix, name, or enclose an ultimate meaning.[33] That knowing ignorance seems almost to anticipate the third space of postcolonial theory–at least as articulated in Trinh Minh-ha's spiritually resourced "critical non-knowingness."[34] The iconoclastic infinity, always offered as a *theological* cure for the insufferable certainties of theology, unfolds under the very "cloud of unknowing." Its uncertainty covers the relativity of our relations. I am wondering if it is that cloud, the darkness, which lies upon "the face of the deep." The creation that emerges from that cloud would then come to be within the third space of the chaosmos; indeed it would *be* the chaosmos. So creation comes to be *as an open* infinity not just of relational signs but of signifying relations.

Those relations form the matrix of possibilities. The creatures actualize these possibilities as their own. Whatever they become adds potentialities of the matrix. At least this is a possible transcription of Whitehead's "principle of relativity": "it belongs to the nature of a 'being' that it is a potential for every 'becoming.'"[35] Like Derrida half a century later, he has returned to Plato's myth of creation from the *khora*, the unformed matter; or, in Whitehead's words, the "aboriginal disorder, chaotic according to our ideals;"[36] or the "third kind" that would deconstruct from within the (platonic) dualisms that shaped thought ever since. So perhaps in this wide philosophical loop we may bring into unlikely rapport, or oscillation, the discourses of Whiteheadian metaphysics and Derridian antimetaphysics.[37] Indeed khora belongs among Derrida's "nonsynonymous substitutions" for *différance* and trace–his strategic alternatives to ontotheology, or the amalgam of platonic metaphysics and classical theism dominant according to Heidegger in western thought.

"Khora reaches us, and as the name. And when a name comes, it immediately says more than the name: the other of the name and quite simply the other, whose irruption the name announces."[38] As *triton genon*, third genus, "neither 'sensible' nor 'intelligible'," "the name of khora seems to defy that 'logic of noncontradiction of the philosophers' . . . that logic 'of binarity, of the yes or no.'" Khora signifies "the opening of a place 'in' which everything would, at the same time, come to take place and be reflected (for these are images which are inscribed there)." Analogously, tehom at once opens a place of all becoming and reflects upon its "face."[39] And Derrida hints that this, the place of a deconstruction, an *abyss* or *mise en abîme*, might *make* a difference: it "affects forms of a discourse on places, notably political places, a politics of place entirely commanded by the consideration of sites [*lieux*] (jobs in the society, region, territory, country), as sites assigned to types or forms of discourse."[40] This politics of khora finds an echo in the theoethics of tehom. It carves a place in which the defaced depth of the others can register as spiritual demand.

As to the femininity of the platonic "third kind"–receptacle, nurse, mat(t)er: Derrida has begun to dislodge her from her passive function within the "holy family" of intelligible forms/khora/sensible things (Caputo). Her quasi-feminity, like that of the womb-watery tehom, will not in the present context be wasted by an anti-essentialist irritation. Even as place itself, she does not define the "place of women." She may, however, wash out its boundaries. These topical tropes are "moving and changing every part of the time." For a theology of becoming, they ripple metonymically through the topos of the deep. In its archaic "scriptural polyhedron" we are reconsidering the difference creation *makes*.

IV The unfathomable body

Within the first century and a half of the Common Era, the biblical tehom and its companions of verse 2 had been assimilated to the philosophical version of creation from an unformed matter. Myths of creation from a chaos, or from a primal ocean charged with the signifiers of birth, had provided common cosmogonic currency. Traces of a pre-Hellenic Pelasgian myth intimate the goddess Eurynome–Night– dancing upon the dark ocean; from her movement the north wind is made, who twines round her as a snake. The world-egg comes forth from her womb.[41] "Verily first of all did Chaos come into being, and then broad-bosomed Gaia," chants Hesiod. Sometimes the chaos is oceanic, sometimes dry, sometimes female-associated, sometimes neutral. The causal lines of its amalgamated metaphoricity cannot be fixed in any linear path of transmission. For instance, much further to the east, the poems of the *Tao te ching* were composing of the primal waters a "nothingness" that is a "cornucopia that never runs dry. / It is the deep source of everything–it is nothing, and yet in everything."[42] The Tao invokes a flowing, formless infinity that "nurtures all things without lording it over anything."[43] This nothingness, far from the abysmal shadow cast by a disembodied Lord, does not evoke fear:

> Before the world was
> And the sky was filled with stars . . .
> There was a strange, unfathomable Body.
> This Being, this Body is silent
> And beyond all substance and sensing.
> It stretches beyond everything spanning the empyrean.
> It has always been here, and it always will be.
> Everything comes from it, and then it is the Mother of Everything.
> I do not know its name. So I call it TAO.[44]

14

No One rules or precedes this ineffable All-Mother. But the Tao cannot, however much the west appropriates its scriptures, make the tehomic passage *for* us.[45] Yet it suggests how widely *possible* it has been to imagine the primordial matrix in positively nonpatriarchal language, language that would play lightly, with whimsical reverence, upon the nameless.

In the west the shift toward a chaos-negative view develops slowly. In the *Metamorphosis*, composed as Christianity begins, Ovid opens his epic of mutability with a chaos cosmogony: "Before sea or land, before even sky / Which contains all, Nature wore only one mask–Since called Chaos. A huge agglomeration of upset. / A bolus of everything–but / As if aborted."[46] Chaos–under pressure from the Roman sense of order–has taken on the persona of a frightful mess, an abortive birth; but certainly not of nothing. Poets ever after will ambivalently crave this sexy chaos of beginnings: even the doctrinally correct Protestant Milton invokes the "Spirit" who from the first

> Wast present and, with mighty wings outspread,
> Dove-like sat'st brooding on the vast abyss,
> And mad'st it pregnant . . .[47]

V Doctrine *ex nihilo*

Until the late second century, Jewish and Christian interpreters seem to have assumed that the Creator formed the creation from some depersonalized version of this primordial stuff. For example, the Palestinian philosopher known as Justin Martyr wrote in the mid-second century: "that He in the beginning did of His goodness, for man's sake, create all things out of unformed matter."[48] In the definitive study of the historical emergence of the *creatio ex nihilo*, Gerhard May notes that through the second century, classically educated teachers like Justin interpret the creation as *world-formation*; they map the "cosmogony of Moses" upon the *Timaeus*. "In Justin's thinking," argues May, "there is already clearly a tension between the idea of world-formation and the conviction of the unconditioned omnipotence of God, but only in the following generation is an adequate clarification of the idea of creation achieved."[49] Yet May's reading, as we shall see, itself destabilizes the "adequate" outcome, of which Justin's creation from chaos falls short. Only in the next generation will the model of world-formation be overcome, and the doctrine of *creatio ex nihilo* "formulated as a counterproposition, which as early as the beginning of the third century is regarded as a fundamental tenet of Christian theology."[50]

What Christianity first presumed was the idea not of the *ex nihilo* but of a Creator effecting "in the beginning" irreducibly new and contingent reality. The idea of a creation from nothing rather than a formation from formlessness only gradually ensconced itself in Christian common sense. Along with it settled the dogmas of omnipotence: not just of the biblical lord of great if somewhat unpredictable power, but an immutable, unilateral All-Power clothed in the attributes of a single male Person (or two; or . . .). Is it then the orthodox postulate, rather than the universe, which got produced from nothing? In the next chapter we will read closely certain formative texts of the *ex nihilo* logic. But we inherit that logic through its fuller-bodied fourth-century Augustinian form.

Augustine's two-stage creation provided a major solution to the problem that the verse of chaos posed for classical Christianity: how can the omnipotent Creator of all things depend upon some preexistent material from which to form the universe? In the last three books of the *Confessions*, Augustine obsesses lovingly over the exegetical puzzle posed by this text. Having embraced a Catholicism that brooked no uncertainties as to the founding omnipotence of the Creator, he wrestles, at once fascinated and exasperated, with the implications of this one verse. For a moment, just a moment, unnerved by its irreducible ambiguity, he must assure himself that the presumed author of Genesis was not, well, underendowed. "I cannot believe that to Moses . . . you would grant a lesser gift than I would will and desire from you for myself."[51] Surely such a strategically placed verse cannot be a bit of sloppy logic . . .

How then within the platonic ontotheology by which Christianity was converting the intelligentsia, a theology that equates changeless, intelligible *form* with the Good, can a good God, to create a good world, make first an inferior matter, a runny "*bolus* of stuff"?[52] Yet nothing can exist that God does not first create (except God): *non de deo sed ex nihilo*. The chaos cannot be eternally with God; but neither can it be part *of* God. So: God must have nonetheless created the primal matter first, like a clay from which to fashion the rest. Yet the text itself refuses to deliver the proper message. The rhetoric of *Confessions* is far more persuasive than dictatorial. Here, however, he resorts to simple assertion of dogma: "if Genesis is silent as to anything that God made—and that God did make it neither sound faith nor sure reasoning doubts—*no sober teaching will dare to affirm that these waters are coeternal with God*, merely because we hear them mentioned in the book of Genesis but we do not find when they were made."[53] Thus the bellow of orthodoxy echoes in the gapped logic of scripture text. "Why should we not understand, with Truth teaching us, that also formless matter, which Scripture calls earth invisible and unformed and darksome deep, was *made by God out of nothing, and therefore is not coeternal with him, although this narrative may omit to state when those things were made?*" What Augustine closes into a rhetorical question, we may reopen as an urgent and real one: the question of becoming itself, of *genesis now*—even if the question lurches off in a direction he would judge unsound and unsober.

Before, however, I can expect current readers to experience the gaps and tensions of this ancient cosmological quandary as their own, let us consider the grip of the *ex nihilo* upon a wide spectrum of recent theology. All theologies that claim orthodoxy posit the *creatio ex nihilo*. But it would be misleading to equate the doctrine with theological conservatism. Some of the most progressive theologies of the twentieth century, which bring their confession to bear upon social injustice and ecological trauma, firmly reaffirm the doctrine.

VI Hope *ex nihilo*

Jürgen Moltmann, whose work with rare effectiveness calls the church to political responsibility, takes the normative doctrinal stance: "*The beginning has no presuppositions at all*" (my emphasis). He knows that the Genesis accounts fail to deliver the desired message. This gap only sharpens his claim: "the later theological interpretation of creation as *creatio ex nihilo* is therefore *unquestionably* an apt paraphrase of what the Bible means by 'creation.' Wherever and whatever God creates is *without any preconditions*."[54] In other words the origin has no further origin: the origin is pure and absolute. No salty trace. God enters into relations with what He [*sic*] has already created. Creation is a unilateral act. When this template dominates the Christian imagination, "an apt paraphrase" becomes the "unquestionable." To endow an extrabiblical proposition with biblical authority, he repeats the classical gesture we saw in Chrysostom: he swerves abruptly, ignoring verse 2, from the comfortable "God created heaven and earth" of the story to the authoritative abstraction of the metanarrative. Not that Moltmann's tone rings authoritarian. On the contrary, he battles the classical theism that claims "God is the Creator, Lord and owner of the world; and in the same way the human being had to endeavor to become lord and owner of the world."[55]

As long as the *ex nihilo* premise remains unquestioned, however, I fear that the dominology he unmasks with one hand will be blessed by the other. When the Jewish mystical *zimsum* ("contraction") captivates Moltmann's doctrine of creation, it seems to promise a less conventionally unilateral, masculinizing creativity: "In a more profound sense he 'creates' by letting-be, by making room, and by withdrawing himself. The creative making is expressed in masculine metaphors. But the creative letting-be is better brought through motherly categories."[56] Given his neoorthodox context, I welcome the feminizing signal.[57] It emits his long-standing critique of the merely active Lord of classical theism, who cannot suffer. Yet this version of divine androgyny reinscribes stereotypes of masculine creation vs. the feminine passivity. Men create, women procreate. This gender dualism comes hitched to the binary of transcendence and immanence. Moreover he defines that transcendence against the foil of process theology's brief utterance of the creation from chaos.[58] When he develops his own pneumatology, Moltmann articulates the fruitful third space of an "immanent transcendence."[59]

For a theology of becoming, it is precisely the dichotomy of "making" and "letting be" that Genesis precludes. How else does Elohim *make*—but *by* letting be: "And God said: *let* there *be*. . ."? Through this dichotomy the *ex nihilo* doctrine keeps control of Moltmann's exegesis. He then appropriates the kabbalistic *zimsum* as tool of Christian dogma: "The nihil in which God creates his creation is God-forsakenness, hell, absolute death."[60] Yet kabbalah–whose first divine principle is the *Eyn Sof*, the Infinite, also named the *Nothing*–hardly affirms such a dogma. The consequences for Moltmann's courtesy to feminism are disappointing: the space in which we are let-be morphs into this hollow, hellish *nihil* within God. For what is his "literally God-forsaken space" but that of the hinted-at divine maternity? Such horror can only, if inadvertently, resonate with a familiar history of feminized abysses, from Tertullian's "devil's gateway" to Sartre's "dark hole." Indeed the epic intertext of all maternal monstrosity will soon swim out of Babylon into view.

I am suggesting that quite apart from authorial intention, the nothingness of the *ex nihilo* produces its own nihilating effects. In Moltmann's earlier *The Crucified God* "Creation, new creation and resurrection are external works of God against chaos, nothingness and death."[61] In this strict exteriority echoes Karl Barth's "creation on the frontier of nothingness;" which, like the Wild West, is "continually confronted by this menace."[62] This version of "nothingness" does not square with the *zimsum*, a space, abyss or fissure which opens (*ginan*) within God. As Scholem interprets kabbalah, "creation out of nothing means to many mystics just creation out of God."[63] The *zimsum* is a "nothingness" *interior* to God. Yet Moltmann continues to reaffirm the Augustinian postulate–*non de deo sed ex nihilo*. The doctrine brooks no ambiguity: God creates from nothing; and not from *within* the divine self (as by a self-unfolding, a neoplatonic emanation or later kabbalistic *sephirot*). So despite Moltmann's radical affirmation of divine omnipresence, we must admit that the creation from nothing requires a space–outside or even within God–where God most definitely is *not*. Perhaps such incoherencies–of a pure God-forsakenness *within* God, or of a *within* that is after all *outside*–need only be transmuted into complexities. Then they point to the need for an unapologetic expansion of Moltmann's own trinitarian perichoresis: a sociality of rhythmic interrelations in which inside and out would no longer bifurcate. The present book will end in this divine vicinity.

VII A feminist disruption

For a mere nothing, the deep poses quite a threat. How could *nothing* be so malevolent? So *out* there? *Where?* These dilemmas will in Chapter 5 send us back to Barth's doctrine of the chaos as nothingness, "*das Nichtige*." Unlike Moltmann, more attentive on this point to biblical scholarship, Barth never quite affirms the classical creation from nothing. He does it one better: the fathers were too soft on the chaos. God would not create *from* such horror. Barth endows *das Nichtige* with the personality of a rebellious, death-dealing monster of chaos: "Nothing good can or will emerge from this primeval flood. Already in the Tiamat myth it is the evil mother, the enemy of all life who must first be killed so that from her members the world may be constructed." The face of the goddess is stripped of the mysterious intertextuality that has been tempting to German romantics, Old Testament exegetes, or feminist theologians. There can be no rebirth from (or of) her God-forsaken womb: "The Old Testament and the present text know absolutely nothing of any such 'Die and become' with reference to *tehom*. Nor do they know anything of a motherhood of *tehom*. They give it no such chance."[64] What Moltmann ambivalently recuperates through "contraction," Barth deprecates as the "monstrous world" of the "sterile waters."

Nor has the God of the philosophers opposed by Barth given her any such chance. "She is left with a void, a lack of all representation . . ." writes Irigaray of western ontotheology; with the "nothing, no/thing" of the lacking phallus. "But let us say that in the beginning was the end of her story, and that from now on she will have one dictated to her: by the man-father."[65] Revealed or reviled, penetrated or abandoned, contracting in creation or in hell, womb or tomb, evil mother or "impregn'd abyss."[66] The specter of a flushed-out femininity haunts the paradoxes. Orthodoxy raised the Father to the one *unsubstitutable* name of the Creator. How could this have taken place without first establishing His capacity to create without a Mother? So the tehom had first and always again to be sterilized. And yet how can the name Father be sounded without its instantly summoning its own ghost of a Womb–and so of a terrifying, an evil Mother? Could the Word of the Creator, as Son of the Father, only unify itself over *against* the feminized chaos?[67] Nothing new under the Son? Just one exceptional incarnation, mirroring a once-for-all creation?

What if we begin instead to read the Word from the vantage point of its own fecund multiplicity, its flux into flesh, its overflow? As "the mystery of a word that seeks its incarnation . . . In excess of every existing language"?[68] Inversely to Barth's logocentric doctrine of the creation, a tehomic theology derives the incarnation from the chaosmic width of the creation. A chaosmic Christ would represent the flow of a word that was always already materialized, more and less and endlessly, a flow that unblocks the hope of an incarnation, in which all flesh takes part. But this new creation will not come forth *de novo ex nihilo*. It takes place within the shared, spatiotemporal body of all creatures.

VIII Liberation dis/orders

However justly gendered, theology does not come down to "boys vs. girls." Or girls vs. boys, more recently. The question is whether the theology of creation keeps the future wide and *opening*. The biblical interest in beginnings served a unique passion for the *new*: a historicizing passion moving not in the cyclical return of myth, not along the line of modernity, but in a rhythmic, irreversible process, an oscillation of land and nomadism, of exile and exodus. The novelty of this promise lay in novelty itself: God would do a "new thing." The future would be locked into the terms of the past—and so the past itself, from its inception, must display that open process. The prophetic symbol of the New Creation organized that hope. Christianity learned to center the temporal flux from creation to new creation, what Irenaeus called, after Paul, the *recapitulatio* in Christ. Thus one can say the irreversibility took the form of a recapitulative, helical temporality.[69] Faithful to this motion, Moltmann has rethought creation eschatologically. The present text—like all theology circulating within the liberation orbit of the New Creation—shares this privilege of hope.[70] Yet when Moltmann trades his hope upon the transcendent power of the Creator, who *guarantees* the new creation—as *novo creatio ex nihilo*—the foundational force of *an absolute origin* is transferred to *an absolute future*, beyond time and transience.[71]

Similarly, the *future* of the *ex nihilo* partly undergirds the hope of Latin American liberation theology.[72] In this regard an important essay by the Brazilian liberation theologian Vitor Westhelle rewards a close reading. His invocation of "vital space"—a dwelling space for planting, living, being again at home in a world that the landlords have appropriated—helps to concretize a chaosmology of place itself. Deftly linking the politics of place to the doctrine of creation, he explains the reticence of liberation theologians to engage creation at all: that doctrine has provided the foundation of western conservatism.[73] Western theologies of creation ground themselves upon "the order of creation." Of the Eurocentric "sacralization of order" Westhelle writes: "Creation language has been permeated by language that stresses order." But "in Latin America nature is not seen as ordered and 'order' is not a positive concept;" order is "most often an ideological disguise for domination, repression and persecution." For "where order is the result of the demiurgic work of the 'invisible hand' of capitalism, where order is the patriarchal hierarchy, the stability and control of the whole society is guaranteed."[74]

Ironically, right at the heart of his incisive critique of the Christian privilege of "order," Westhelle invokes the traditional creation doctrine as the foundation for liberation theology. "In the experience of total negation, *creatio ex nihilo* is the affirmation of hope in a God who will not succumb to negation."[75] But if the deification of order is oppressive, does the *ex nihilo* not accomplish that order by the suppression of chaos? He argues from II Maccabees 7.28, where the Maccabee mother urges her seven sons to *martyrion* against Roman oppression, in faith that the God who could create the world "out of non-being" will (be able to) resurrect their bodies. Identifying the colonization of the Latin American poor with that of persecuted Jews—legitimately—Westhelle follows the old Christian dependency upon that single verse to legitimate the *ex nihilo* doctrine. Yet that Hellenistic Jewish text uses the Greek phrase that elsewhere designates *procreation*—very much a creation, however contingent and new, from the *something* of the parents.[76] Westhelle imagines a "liberation granted by the power of a creator God and sustained by a faith assured that the maker of heaven and earth can make all things new *and is not bound, even by what already exists*."[77]

A tehomic theology also works in hope of radical renewal. But does not Westhelle's formulation–omnipotence will finally step in to make things right–show itself bound by the discourse of oppressive dominance? One wonders (as must the disenchanted poor) whether it is not at any rate a bit late in history for such an unconstrained divine agent to show up? The gap between such poignant guarantees of final justice and the suffering of present oppression opens, indeed gapes, into the old conundrums of theodicy. How can a good God who is all-powerful permit evil *to start with*? Unless He [*sic*] is in cahoots with the powers that be after all, who seem to receive all the rewards? Theodicy is not a problem to be solved by theological abstraction. But the uncritical repetition of the *ex nihilo* abstraction will continue to import the template of omnipotent–total–order. Conflicts within the movements of liberation suggest that its homogenizing, paternalist tendencies vis-à-vis its chaoid Others of gender, race and religion are not innocently linked to the dominological tradition it has powerfully challenged.[78]

Westhelle rightly reclaims the topos of "the creation" as a "vital space." Certainly the Genesis narrative emanates from a historical context not anticipating that of the colonized and oppressed poor of Latin America today. But I wonder whether precisely the Genesis *tehom*–which implies neither pure evil nor total victimization but something more like the matrix of possibilities in which liberation struggles unfold–would not serve the current context better than the orthodox *ex nihilo*. Of course the dissident liberation mimicry of dogma has exercised its own menace.[79] But as liberation theology navigates postmodern waters–proudly declaring itself "postmodern before Europeans thought of postmodernism"[80]–its own internal tensions, theological and sociocultural, may stimulate new waves of liberation.

IX Living waters

Might those who do not hope for a final, omnipotent intervention, hope for a "new creation" modeled not on a dry *ex nihilo* but on a fluid process that will "make all things new"? In another flavor of Brazil, *Longing for Running Water*, activist and nun Ivone Gebara has complained more gently of the "anthropocentric and androcentric character" not just of official but also liberation Catholicism. She challenges the dualistic stress on epistemological "distance" or "discontinuity" between God's life and that of the creation.[81] Instead she pours forth a Latin American ecofeminism, borrowing from process theology and Sallie McFague the metaphor of "the universe as God's Body."[82] She articulates a full-bodied panentheism of God in the world and the world in God, but not as the intersection of two entities. In an accessible language, she overthrows the ontotheology of God as "a pure essence existing in itself; rather, God is relationship." In view of our species' devastation of the relationships of which "heaven and earth" are woven, she laments "that our hope is ailing, that our Sacred Body is ailing." Even as she lives and works among the favelas of the poorest humanity, she moves beyond the anthropocentrism of liberation discourse. The growing recognition that justice for the poor cannot be imagined apart from what the World Council of Churches (WCC) calls "the integrity of creation" bodes well for a chaosmic coalition.

The striking trope of God's sick body–or rather that of the ailing, sacred body, coming free in her writing from the separative edges of the "God"-word–infuses the very site of creation with unbearable loss. Yet she judges this loss "not a fatal illness, one that is bound to end in death; rather, it is a serious ailment that brings with it the gravest of risks."[83] Writing theology as a therapeutic lament for the earth, she wastes no time in apologetic equivocations. "We no longer speak of God as existing before creation, but, in a way, as concomitant with it. *We no longer think of God first and creation later, because this sort of gap between atemporality in God and temporality in creation does not make sense to us*."[84] (That may be all I'm hoping to say.) She offers in the gap "a 'con-spiracy,' a 'breathing with' by one who wants a 'new heaven and a new earth' to spring from this very ground."[85] This rhythmic, breathy eschatology lovingly and firmly dislodges God from within the patriarchy of liberation theology and its power–almost in passing. Any theo-politics of omnipotence, left or right, will gravitate toward a theology of machismo–which lays itself open (indeed exposes itself) to gender analysis.

X Indecent theology

As liberation theology, or that which it is becoming, conspires ever more with those who speak not just for women, for the indigenous peoples, for the human body, for all the nonhuman bodies, it conveys ever less the straightforward hopes of the *ex nihilo*. Far indeed from "straight," Marcella Althaus-Reid's "indecent theology"–her queer and postcolonial term of approbation–confronts liberation Catholicism less politely. She reads it for its "(hetero)sexual idealist theology, based in the systematic tradition of the West." Granting that there were some salutary "traces of indecency . . . in the genesis of Liberation Theology," she investigates the effects of "the insertion of Liberation Theology in the Western theological market." This insertion, she complains, accrued at once power and order–"decency"–to an otherwise more promising heterogeneity. "The poor" got cleaned up and homogenized as the saintly martyrs and victims of liberation eschatology, suffering in faithful and solidaristic anticipation of God's new creation.

She reads them instead in their chaotic carnality and carnivals, dancing down shantytown streets carrying "a transvestite Christ accompanied by a Drag Queen Mary Magdalene kissing his wounds, singing songs of political criticism."[86] With Maria Mies, she suggests that inasmuch as "all forms of capitalism are patriarchal derivatives," the liberation struggle cannot achieve its own ends without a more profound emancipation from its own (hetero)sexism.[87] Given the proportion of "*homo*phobia" within "*teho*mophobia," a tehomic theology can only concur (though in my paler context I would continue to find late capitalism a more suitable opponent than liberation theologians guilty of limited strategies—for though all capitalism derives from patriarchy, all patriarchy is not capitalist). A theology of becoming explores the resonances of an alternative sexual economy of creation. Its chaosmos articulates a queerly erotic universe—no private property of a proper Lord.

Indeed Althaus-Reid, like Westhelle, recognizes the indelible linkage of the various capitalisms with "a cultural political platform based on Creation Theology." Hence most liberation theology has, as we noted, avoided "the creation." Yet, like Gebara, she finds that liberation theology rests upon "a modern conception of (Western) linear time." Indeed does not all "progressive" thought do so, as well as that Christianity from which it seeks to progress? But does the progressive linearity itself not derive from the *ex nihilo* origin? Althaus-Reid's carnivalesque spatio-temporality begins to enflesh the recapitulatory spirals of a liberative countercreation. Theologically she hints at a sacramental in/carnationality: "every text carries with it a subversive version, and in communion there is an example of intertextuality or intersexuality with God who becomes (transsubstantiation or not) our bodies and shares our complex sexualities." Her festive iconoclasms make the current tehomism seem wintry: nonetheless it gladly receives this improper revelation: "And God becomes chaos: the smell of our bodies when making love, our fluids and excretions, the hardening of muscles and the erectness of nipples."[88]

Let me offer a less transgressive, indeed dogmatically impeccable, transcription: a God who is ubiquitous cannot be absent from any molecule, membrane or mucus of the creation. Not only the Christian mystics but, for instance, John Wesley preached that "God is in all things," indeed "pervades and actuates the whole created frame, and is in a true sense the Soul of the Universe."[89] I am not trying to tidy up Gebara's panentheism or Althaus-Reid's divine chaos, but to give credit where it is due: even the Christian mainstream has not kept itself altogether decent.

As God becomes our bodies, as our bodies relax, breathe and bleed into the Sacred Body of all bodies, let the formal question of the relation of "God" to "chaos" begin to take flesh as well. From the yearnings of sky-and-earth, mud-and-mucus creatures, irrupting not only in sickness but in festival, gush waters still turbulent with tehom. Sometimes we may calm them. We undertake this pneumatic conspiracy not to make a mess but to make *better* orders. But even amidst their more abysmal uncertainties—the chaos that cannot be controlled, the mystery that cannot be solved—appear "monsters of grace."[90]

Is it a coincidence that two such different styles of feminist theology from within the Latin American context both happen to overturn—again, almost casually, *in media res*—the *ex nihilo* doctrine? If a counterdiscourse of creation begins to percolate up "from below"—from a dark underside readily woman-identified and racially inflected—this assures no facile correlation of the below of theologies from the social bottom with the tehomic bottomlessness. Both social location and its perpetual dislocation in theory may obstruct solidarity. But the political coalition for the eco-social justice of the third Christian millennium may be re-creating its selves from a chaos that can never be conquered.

2

"FLOODS OF TRUTH"

Sex, love and loathing of the deep

See now how stupid it is, amid such an abundance of true meanings as can be taken out of these words [Genesis 1.2], rashly to affirm which of them Moses chiefly meant.

(Augustine, *Confessions*, XII.26)

In order to open an interpretive forcefield in which tehomic meanings of "the creation" may be affirmed, this chapter articulates the difference between tehomo-phobic and tehomophilic registers within scripture itself. It sets the biblical difference in the context of the ancient slaughter of the sea-she-monster as well as of a recent feminization of the flux. Finally it draws the question and the difference of the Deep back into the framework of a constructive enquiry: does the icon of the marine chaos convey a *theologically* meaningful depth–such as that which we will sound in the tehomic hermeneutics of Augustine's *Confessions*?

I Leviathanic sightings

Emissions of the flux, the flood, splotch the landscape of scripture. If the creation from absolute nothingness poses neither a biblical nor an ethical prerequisite for theology, we may now consider the hermeneutical options. Scripture, as Chapter 6 will document in the literature of the biblical discipline, knows only a formation of something new from something–*else*, something yet unthinged, unformed, some sort of marine chaos not identical with the literal sea but not separable from it. Can we, however, generalize about a biblical attitude toward that chaoid something? By itself the second verse of the Bible, however nonjudgmental toward the chaos, however free of any implication of evil and nothingness, can do little more than magnify–like a tiny well-ground lens–our fears and longings. I will argue that the Bible in general hosts two radically distinct attitudes toward the tehom. A brief comparison of two psalms will suggest the difference.

Psalm 74: a desperate lament: "O God, why do you cast us off forever? Why does your anger smoke against the sheep of your pasture?" (74.1f). The psalmist attempts to redirect YHWH's rage, embodied in Israel's enemies, back towards *them*: "the enemy has destroyed everything in the sanctuary . . . Why dost thou hold back thy hand?" The rages of the enemy, of the people, and of YHWH violently amplify each other. They foment the mythic sea of chaos–even while hoping to quell it:

> Yet God my King is from of old,
> Working salvation in the earth.
> You divided the sea by your might;
> You broke the heads of the dragons in the waters.
> You crushed the heads of Leviathan.
> (Psalm 74:12–14a)

Collating the liberation theogram of Moses' dividing the sea by his "rod" with the "dividings" of creation (as of upper from lower waters), this psalm displays classic motifs of the divine warrior tradition. Its dependence upon pagan mythologies of theomachy–creation by battle–is typical of its genre.[1] The Near Eastern prototype of theomachy resides in the *Enuma Elish*, in which the lord Marduk slaughters his grandmother Tiamat, the oceanic chaos.[2] It has multiple Mid-Eastern parallels relevant to the biblical material, especially those of the warrior god Baal conquering Rahab. In the Bible, we can read Leviathan–however the monster gets evaluated–as the created embodiment of the uncreated chaos.

Let us characterize this attitude toward the oceanic immensity and its monstrous bodies as an incipient *tehomophobia*. It faces the prevenient chaos as evil, and God therefore as its powerful, if disappointing, conqueror. Phobia does not mean a simple fear, which has an object–such as the real, historical threats to which the psalmist alludes. Fear transmutes into phobia when it obsessively repeats itself, coding its dread and loathing in a symbolism that may in fact make it more difficult to face real threats. The tehomophobic imaginary, however, does not entail but prepares the way for the *creatio ex nihilo*. Indeed the major resistance to the *ex nihilo* doctrine over the past century comes from the unearthing of multiple polytheist traditions for this divine warrior combating the sea. Numerous Near Eastern traditions depicted the waters as sinister, a "metaphor for social threat."[3] Jon Levenson's *Creation and the Persistence of Evil* offers a potent theological hermeneutic of this struggle with chaos, in which God "masters" but does not eliminate the chaos.[4] A theology of dominance emanates from the tehomophobic iconography. Psalm 74 echoes Genesis' imagery of creation by division (of upper from lower waters, etc.). But it generates an entirely different atmosphere. On Genesis' "fifth day," "the great sea monsters" (*tannin* [1:21]) make their appearance as the culminating creatures of the "swarming" sea. And Elohim–having commissioned the sea to "swarm forth" creatively–warmly pronounces them "good." But this psalmist appeals to a Lord who does not bless the sea monsters but bashes their heads.

Yet the "polyhedron of scripture" disobeys any uniform sense of order. Indeed the psalmic tradition offers its own cure for tehomophobia. The creation template of *tehom / mayim / sea monster* can also manifest a wildly pacific mood and meaning. Psalm 104, a hymn of creation, brims with a great enthusiasm for the universe and its fluids.

> O YHWH, how manifold are your works!
> In wisdom you have them all:
> the earth is full of your creatures.
> Yonder is the sea, great and wide,
> creeping things innumerable are there
> living things both small and great.
> There go the ships,
> and Leviathan that you formed to sport in it.
> (Psalm 104.24–6)

The rabbis have emphasized a certain ambiguity of the Hebrew: the last verse can be translated "Leviathan that you formed to sport with you." Of course one could with Jon Levenson or Bernhard Anderson read such cosmogonic celebrations–including Genesis 1 with its divinely affirmed sea monsters–as demonstrations of the Lord's mastery of all His [sic] creatures.[5] Only He can play around with Leviathan: "YHWH's rubber duckey."[6] But does the power paradigm not squelch the playful spirit and distinctive insight of the psalm–which reads after all as one long doxology of shared divine / human delight in the pluriform beauty of creation? To make its Leviathan stand for evil is to ignore the entire hymn. So another Jewish tradition lies beside that of the tehomophobic mastery.

> The day consists of twelve hours: during the first three hours the Holy One, blessed be He, is occupying Himself with the Torah, during the second three He sits in judgment on the whole world, and when He sees that the world is so guilty as to deserve destruction, He transfers Himself from the seat of Justice to the seat of Mercy: during the third quarter, He is feeding the whole world, from the horned buffalo to the brood of vermin: during the fourth quarter He is sporting with the leviathan, as it is said, There is leviathan, whom Thou hast formed to sport therewith . . .[7]

In other words the Holy One spends one quarter of every day joking and playing with the monster! It is this tradition within the chaosmos of scriptural effects that we might as well call *tehomophilic*. To love the sea monsters and their chaos-matrix is consonant with affirming their "goodness" within the context of the whole. It doesn't make them safe or cute. They also get poetically "rebuked," i.e. bounded, held back, so that the orders of creation may emerge; so that any creative work may be wrested, as it must be in all our creations, from chaos. But this tradition cannot be reconciled with the identification of chaos and its wild creatures as *evil*.[8] And even less, as *nothing*. In the psalm, tehom is not "created" like the earth. Rather YHWH "covered the earth with the deep as with a garment." The tehom lies here depersonified but preexistent, as a layering or enveloping matrix.

This playful tehomophilia has gained a formidable if inadvertent ally in natural science: "Chaos, once viewed as something uncontrollable and terrible, is becoming friendlier," writes physicist Heinz Pagels. "Out of chaos comes order, and out of simplicity emerges complexity."[9] Chaos theory thus does not simply map the chaos which (*à la* Psalm 74) threatens the orders of creation with randomness or dissipation; but (*à la* Psalm 104) is learning to recognize everywhere the life-sustaining and -enhancing functions of an alternative order that had been so long mistaken for disorder.

II The heart of the monster

The face of the deep was first—as far as we can remember—a woman's. Tiamat, "salt water, primal chaos," lay in primordial bliss with Apsu, "sweet water," "abyss." From their mingling waters precipitated a beginning. Tiamat migrates into Hebrew as tehom. Moreover, Genesis 1.2, while ascribing no personality to the deep, does use the feminine noun tehom as though it is still a proper name. "The tehom signifies here the primeval waters which were also uncreated. Significantly, the word always appears without an article in the singular and is feminine in gender."[10] The biblical scholarship that noted the dramatic residue of the oceanic female deposited, depersonalized, in Genesis 1.2, comprises the same trajectory that concedes the biblical creation from chaos. Behind Genesis 1.2–in a contested background lineage of Babylonian, Ugaritic and Caananite sources–lies not the Leviathan but the oceanic all-mother Tiamat. Preserving the destruction of Tiamat as epic achievement, the *Enuma Elish* portrays the creation of the world from the hero's slaughter of the first goddess. Sanctifying the new imperial politics of Babylon, creation by war efficiently supersedes the trope of cosmic procreation. To this end the epic poet presided over the production of a most unfriendly face for the chaos. The *Enuma Elish* narrates the dramatic metamorphosis of Tiamat from loving mother of the gods to their direst enemy. The gender politics of the Bronze Age transition to an ever more central and patrilineal order provide a transparent enough motive. But the means? How does a religion manage to vilify the goddess it still recognizes as cosmic parent of all that is?

Monotheistic erasure was not yet a possibility. This anxiety of influence poses epic problems: how within the living memory of a female God discredit her creation–which her discreditors continue to inhabit? The strategy is familiar: accuse her of betrayal. But with disarming honesty, the poet exhibits the reconstruction of the oceanic divinity as monster-mother. The poem retains a vivid portrait of the earlier character of Tiamat. Her primal mate Apsu had found intolerable the noisy disorder of the divine grandchildren, running around inside of them. "Their way was not good,"[11] admits the poet. But "Tiamat was silent in regard to their [behavior]." So Apsu came to her and said "in a loud voice"–gender registered in decibels:

> "Their way has become painful to me,
> By day I cannot rest, by night I cannot sleep;
> I will destroy them and put an end to their way,
> That silence be established, and then let us sleep!"[12]

Sleep-deprived parents may sigh in sympathy. But Tiamat does not.

> When Tiamat heard this,
> She was wroth and cried out to her husband;
> She cried out and raged furiously, she alone.[13]

This sounds like every woman who has ever tried, with aching deliberation, to protect children from abuse. Her cry protests the betrayal of life itself. Her own beloved "Abyss" wants to silence the turbulence and return to equilibrium. She, the oceanic chaos, *suffers* the children to come into their own. In the lull before epic power conquers its own lyricism, the goddess voices an ethic anticipatory of Ghandian *Satyagraha*:

> She pondered in her heart the evil (and said):
> "Why should we destroy that which we ourselves have brought forth?
> Their way is indeed very painful, but let us take it good-naturedly!"

Let us borrow her utterance as a proposition for any tehomic ethic: *to love is to bear with the chaos.* Not to like it or to foster it but to recognize there the unformed future. Ignoring her impassioned wisdom, Apsu gets reinforcements from the second generation (the exasperated parents), his plans leak, and the young gods kill him first. The goddess now falls into psychic disarray: "Disturbed is Tiamat, and day and night she restlessly hastens about." So the gods of the middle generation guilt-trip her for not standing by her man: "when they slew Apsu, thy spouse, thou didst not march at his side, but thou didst sit quietly . . . disturbed is thine interior, and we cannot rest." The manipulation is effective. Persuaded to exteriorize her depression

29

as anger–or in the gods' preferred jargon, to "go to battle and requite"–Tiamat now begins to breed monsters with which to war on her own grandsons.

Marduk emerges as the great hero who will slaughter her, and thus save his generation and all future ones from terror: he has his mission and his moment. "It is only a female thing you fear," he sneers. In exchange for getting to be Lord of the universe, he offers to cure their tehomophobia. We will reexamine the slaughter, the founding teho/matricide of western civilization, later, within a more developed hermeneutical context. Her living chaos waters become the primal stuff of which he forms his universe: a total solution. Except that she would not stay dead. But why did the poet want the audience to remember her caring face–this politically inexpedient, friendlier face of chaos–before it would be distorted forever? Is it precisely for protecting children from the father's betrayal–even when the father is betraying the sons for whom the story is told–that the female is branded a traitor by those she protects?[14] Apparently Tiamat's metamorphosis into the Great Horror of Babylon had to be managed carefully. The vestiges of her lovable face were incorporated into the tale of her demonization.

"As the text is the transformation of a signifying system and of a signifying practice," argues Daniel Boyarin, "it embodies the more or less untransformed detritus of the previous system."[15] His reading of midrash as intertextuality, defined as the way that history records its struggles within textuality, will offer a key to a chaosmic hermeneutics. As the epic records a conflict between signifying systems (for example, between Babylon and the subjugated symbolisms of less patri-lineal, hierarchical and misogynist peoples), so the cosmogonic drama with its matricide seems to be "embodied" in Genesis; which in turn is a product of a people colonized by Babylon. But Genesis neither reinscribes the same power-arrangements nor simply reverses them. Like Chinese boxes, the biblical intertext of Tehom/Tiamat opens into yet more ancient conflicts, prior to and formative of writing itself. The gender turbulence fissures the *Enuma Elish* even as its watery chaos–its "more or less untransformed detritus"–leaves a gaping uncertainty in the second verse of Genesis. Whatever her function in the *Enuma Elish*–nostalgia for the womb, safety valve in the shift to slave state, warning to insubordinate women and their men–the trace of a positive chaos has not been erased within the epic or its biblical iteration.

A question has haunted me through decades: does Genesis' allusion to the theomachy reinscribe, subvert or simply side-step the warrior matricide? What these traces might have *meant* (to "P," the so-called "Priestly writer" to whom this strand of scripture is attributed) has gone down the discursive drain; the fluid chaos was long ago flushed out of the basin of cultural assumptions that hold water. What they might yet mean remains–promisingly–open. This much can be asserted: Genesis 1 betrays no fear of the dark, no demonization of the deep, of the sea, its she and its dragons No trace of divine warrior or cultural misogyny appears on the face of the text of the first chapter. Does the contrast to the Babylonian epic, which we read as mythological intertext of Genesis 1.2, not begin to appear dramatic, deliberate, almost parodic? We will return to this question in Chapter 6.

III Floods of female

Yet it is the tehomophobic imaginary that has energized western civilization and its heroic subjects: to master the chaos, perchance to destroy it, to flush it from the universe. In the Bible, curiously, its femininity would virtually disappear. We cannot retrace the biblical and theological routes of this fearful vitality without first recognizing more clearly its inscription upon the seascape of modern sex. Rather than attempting to remap that well-traveled space, let me offer two graphic, indeed sexual, cases, one from a feminist art historian, the other from a feminist artist.

1

The aquatic female does not only recur as a grandmotherly monster. She has sex appeal. Indeed she has always managed more sinuous, local incarnations. But these did not make her less frightening. The dread female flesh of the deep would return, in all its mythic citationality, to provoke the modern imagination. Tehomic iconography—as oceanic, as turbulent, as natural, as below, as dark, as womb or as abortion—outfitted an entire western legion of shadowy femininities. For example, in his catalogue of *fin de siècle* fantasies of feminine evil, Bram Dijkstra demonstrates a voluminous output in painting and literature inspired by the specter of the whirling, dissipative, watery femininity. A vast nineteenth-century visual vocabulary of mermaids, sprites, nixies, sirens is drawn from the *Odyssey* and regional folklores, to express "very modern cultural concerns."[16]

It is the New Woman, Dijkstra argues, who provokes the preoccupation of water-nymph paintings like John William Whiteley's *A Sail!* (1898). "Living under clouds and surf that seem like steam rising from the boiling cauldron of the elemental sea, these women represent that unabashed independence and elemental sense of freedom the men of 1900 feared, and found most fascinating, in the viragoes of their day." For many men, he suggests, the apparent—and unnatural—activity of these "viraginous women" only masks the passivity with which they will engulf the creative powers of the male. "In the popular lore of the years around 1900, the sea was ultimately passive, and woman was the creature of the sea, water being her symbol: totally yielding, totally flexible, yet ultimately all-encompassing and deadly in its very permeability. Her predatory sexuality was the tool with which nature tried (?) to 'draw back by cohesion and [refund] into the general watery surface' of the ocean of undifferentiated instinctual life the individualized 'drop' representing the male intellect."[17] Recall that simultaneously Freud is disciplining the individualized drop of oedipal ego to resist its "oceanic feeling," a concept that fails to differentiate between undifferentiated narcissism and any feminizable, fluid experience of relatedness. Edward Burne-Jones's *The Depths of the Sea* exemplifies this tehomophobic phantasm in the gratified smile of his water-woman, as she pulls her man under.

2

Eve Ensler's *Vagina Monologues*, a play that spawned a national movement, takes the form of a set of soliloquies responding to two rather droll questions: "What would your vagina say if it could? What would it wear?" "The Flood" soliloquy is offered by an elderly Jewish woman from Queens. She responds first with outrage at the question. Then she ruminates on her "down there." "It's very damp, clammy. You don't want to go down there. Trust me."[18] She recalls a humiliation half a century old. When she was kissed on her first date, her body had responded. "I couldn't control it. It was like this force of passion, this river of life just flooded out of me, right through my panties, right onto the car seat of his new white Chevy BelAir." Appalled at possible damage to his upholstery, he called her a "stinky weird girl" and never spoke to her again. She promptly withdrew all feeling from "down there." She remained a dry virgin. But she has a recurrent dream:

> Burt Reynolds. I don't know why . . . We'd be out. Burt and I. It was some restaurant like the kind you see in Atlantic City, all big with chandeliers and stuff and thousands of waiters with vests on . . . We were very happy together. Then he'd look into my eyes and pull me to him in the middle of the restaurant—and just as he was about to kiss me, the room would start to shake, pigeons would fly out from under the table—I don't know what they were doing there—and the flood would come straight from down there. It would pour out of me. It would pour and pour. There would be fish inside it, and little boats, and the whole restaurant would fill with water, and Burt would be standing knee-deep in my flood, looking horribly disappointed in me that I'd done it again, horrified as he watched his friends, Dean Martin and the like, swim past us in their tuxedos and evening gowns.[19]

At the end of the monologue she answers the question: "What would 'down there' wear?" "It would wear a big sign: '*Closed Due to Flooding.*'" A grandmotherly hysteric has unconsciously somatized the slaughter of the grandmother Tiamat. Her own frozen sex iterates the tehomophobia as self-loathing. The subject subjects herself, requiring no external lord. Unlike the "new women" who thawed, who opened up a flow of resistance, who were marked as whores, witches and viragoes, these tame women incarnated the closure. Such stereotypes of monster mother, mermaid and

3. Sir Edward Coley Burne-Jones, *The Depths of the Sea* (1887). Courtesy of the Fogg Art Museum, Harvard University Art Museums, Bequest of Grenville L. Winthrop. Photo: Katya Kallsen. © President and Fellows of Harvard College.

shriveled virgin no longer enclose the horizons of women's becoming. But the tehomophobia they symptomatize still marks, I am arguing, the boundaries of most Christian thought.

IV Re/monstrating feminism

At the transition from a tehomophobic modernity to the unknown, feminism has de/monstrated its own icons of new creation. Into the frame we whittled signs of a cosmogonic transition: "new woman/new earth." For the patriarchal cosmos presumed throughout the premodern western mythologies has been provisionally dismembered. Not so long ago, we began to recognize amidst the misogynist graffiti of western theology our appropriated energies, our "stolen goddess power," our "elemental passions," our defaced bodies. Feminism set out with mythic energy to "reverse the reversals." We began "in the beginning." The dismembered corpse of Tiamat was exhumed: "deep memory," indeed "Tidal Memory" itself became sacrament: the re/membering of Tiamat. She roared out a tidal wave of creativity, scorning the tidier femininities. "I am a monster," we chanted. "And I am proud." We ate from the monstrance of a willfully imagined past, origin that never was. Rosemary Ruether worked this radical feminism into Christian theology: "God/ess who is primal Matrix, the ground of being-new being, is neither stifling immanence nor rootless transcendence."[20]

A later feminism has been wont to dismiss the prior wave, in its embarrassing over-generalizations, as "essentialist." Many women, no longer noticeably oppressed, have returned to academic *terra firma*, irritated by the epic grandiosity of these "foremothers." Others of us, less trustful of linear progress (and its cutting edge), feel that Tiamat's insurrection has barely begun. We share the impatience with the simplified dualisms of oppressor and oppressed. Indeed in its mythic self-invention, any oppressed group romanticizes its lost, original purity; it looses a utopic vision, invariably exclusive, against the invincible Marduks.[21] I have argued that a certain neo-apocalypticism better describes such radical oppositionalism (in feminist as well as in liberation discourse) than does "essentialism"[22]–a term itself deployed with crypto-apocalyptic negation. A tehomic theology recycles the grand creativity of these beginning-feminisms counter-apocalyptically.[23] It is less important to count the "waves" of feminism than to practice the wave-action of our *movement*.

This is not a matter of coming full circle–another dream of closure–but of narrating the recapitulatory, iterative dynamic of becoming itself. Within this feedback loop, gender analysis risks a certain leakage. For it is precisely the attempt to theorize the complexity of our relations that results in an increasingly queer, postcolonial, polymorphous and possibly perverse feminism. In this case, however, the diffusion resembles the "dissipative system" of chaos theory:[24] greater complexity amidst chaotic turbulence. So the dissipation of the "original" movement does not warrant any posture of postfeminism. The present work—as a feminist theology—confesses the privilege of its own indirection, its elliptical politics and its conflictual, overlapping and celebratory solidarities. This complexity takes place in the interest of a depth that issues upon the face, even in its dissipation, the surface of the social "issues."

The topos of the deep suggests not the depth of a single dimension, a verticality, but rather a layered dimensionality. Thus Irigaray's ironic mimicry of Nietzsche[25] invokes, for all its risk of an essential—"elemental"—depth of femininity, a reverse repristination of the watery virago, the subject location of a theology of becoming:

> Deep, deeper than anything you could dream of taking or giving beneath the surface of my skin, that is where I am. And because of forgetting that darkest life, if you come close, you retreat into yourself again.[26]

Yet the "I" remains female, the "you" male (the prophetic male, subtle in his misogyny, indeed lovable in his radicalism). At this twenty-first-century moment I confess that I find (post)feminist women as likely as men to forget that darkest life; to retreat into a pale and professionalized subject-location; to neglect at once the race and soul of that flowing dark. So in the very interest of that "deep," the present diagnosis of the systemic forgetfulness will often interpellate the "we" of a less dyadically divisible gender; a sex "which, always pouring out liquid, blurs boundaries."[27] Not only between "the sexes," but between their sexualities. Between their wider solidarities. Between the finite creature and the in-finite it embodies. To remember the dismembered Tiamat—and other occasionally and differently female figures—exposes the spatiotemporal construction of the gender boundaries. It need not bound our possibilities now within a fixed "gender fidelity."[28] Ellen Armour poses an astute question: "Can the cracks marked by these female figures be held open, or will the patriarchal onto-theo-logic that surrounds them reseal them?"[29]

Feminist theology will remain a *sine qua non* of any theory of radical becoming: recognized or not, the He-God powers every ontotheology. Getting rid of "God" won't solve the problem. It only leaves "Him" unaccounted for. But conversely: only at the theological depth sounded by the tehomic tropes will feminism as theology and theology as feminism continue to become. The relationalism of feminist theology requires an ever wider scale of iterative differences. But we will have to leave feminist Sunday School: getting rid of "Him" only puts God in drag. The proposed tehomism necessarily implicates us anew in "the tradition," that is, in the iteration of texts in which "she" left hardly a trace. But if "she is left with a void, a lack of all representation," as the "nothing, the no/thing" of a lacking phallus, this does not mean she ever disappeared. If tehom turned into the nothingness of the Christian tradition, this does not mean that the sign matrix of the originary chaos evaporated. We seek out those she/sea traces among massively male texts not to reassure ourselves that Christianity was or is really OK for women. But whatever beauty and justice we may now articulate–we who read as and with women–will not flow from a new supersession, a new *ex nihilo*.

V Adam's womb

> All things are beautiful because you made them, but you who made all things are inexpressibly more beautiful. If Adam had not fallen away from you, from his womb [*uterus*] there would not have flowed that salt sea water, the human race, so deeply active, so swelling in storms, and so restlessly flowing.
>
> (Augustine, *Confessions*, XIII.20)

In Augustine's reading of Genesis 1, the poetic tensions still spurt ambiguously from the text. He must as a Christian affirm the goodness of creation. And yet he cannot manage any celebration of the creatures without an immediate qualifier–we are to love the creation only as a means to the Creator. Sure all things are beautiful. But he only cares now for the beauty of the Creator. He wants only to flow molten into the immortal embrace. The beauty of everything else has been badly disfigured by sin. So he can here construe tehom–"that salt sea water"–as the turbulent *product* of human sin. And he thereby installs that sin, whose collective transmission is engineered by human sexuality, within the "uterus of Adam."[30] Otherwise, as a closer reading will later divulge, Augustine exegetes tehom as God's first creation, the creation of that matter from which both the heaven and earth would be then secondarily created. In the above figure, he rechannels the tehom as a wild uteral efflux, queering Adam as sinner and storming the creation.

Without all this disorderly human conduct, this revolting flood from "down there," the creation would have remained beautiful. In this, Augustine's Greco-Roman aesthetic of order determines his creation theology. The harmony of the creation would reflect a dry, unmoving, sun-bleached beauty. Until the irruption a century ago of indeterminacy, chaos and complexity, this symmetrical sensibility ruled even the scientific sense of the universe, which could therefore–even astronomically– never quite match the perfect Euclidean circles and time-symmetries of the mind.[31] It is as though the tehomic emissions threw everything into a disappointing state of flux, lacking the beauty that could be attributed to a (properly hellenized) divine Being. The creation itself had caught our disease. It suffers the hysteria of an infinite "lack."

Augustine, however, cannot be so simply diagnosed as an ontotheological tehomo-phobic. He craves, he loves, "depth." When he can dislodge the deep from the flesh, the womb, the material cosmos, when he can resituate tehom in *language* he enjoys an ecstatic tehomophilia:

Wondrous is the depth of your words, for see, their surface lies before us, giving delight to your little ones. But wondrous is their depth, O my God, wondrous is their depth! It is awesome to look into that depth: an awe owed to honor, and a trembling arising from love![32]

Augustine seems almost stubbornly to delight in the surface beauty, not merely the abstract depth, of the text. It is not coincidentally our verse of Genesis 1 to which Augustine is riveted in this passage. Characteristic of the ontotheological tradition would be the subjugation of the surface multiplicity to the single truth of a hierarchy of being. Depth would comprise an intellectual reflection of the heights of pure Presence. Indeed Augustine's "depth" will ultimately withdraw from its textual surface, to be contained as a rational interiority to which only the hermeneutical elite–as opposed to "your little ones"–will have access.[33] The little ones, the literalists, will then be left with the mere surface text, while the wise transcend the letter in the spirit. Only the allegorical reader of scriptures will "penetrate their depths."[34] Augustine sternly sublimates upward: he seeks in his own depths the heights of Being, the eternal changelessness of God. It is within this theological interplay of depth, height and surface that poststructuralism poses a challenge to the foundational Pauline identification of "the letter," *liter*, with the fleshly minded, superficial and indelibly Jewish literalist.[35] It does so in honor of the textual surface. Yet the *Confessions*–unlike *On Christian Doctrine*–cannot be read as simply advancing a hierarchical scale of allegorical readings. Indeed he has not yet peeled the shimmering surface of the text off its "depth." On the contrary, it is precisely in this fascination with the fissures on the skin, the vellum, of our very text of Genesis 1.1 –2 ("like a book . . . stretched over us like a skin".[36]), that this pneumatic trembling arises.

Must a tehomic theology accommodate then some strange confluence of two opposed and powerful streams of signification: of "depth" and "*différance*"? Does such a confluence remain possible, even necessary, to the extent that the deep is read upon its "face"? To that extent it breaks like facets of sea into an irreducible multiplicity. Here we cannot expunge the trace of a tehomic potentiality–"trace of a trace"–even within a self-avowed western orthodoxy.

In a certain sense I share the concern of radical orthodoxy for "depth." John Milbank, rereading Hamann, suggests that "we must reckon with an immense depth behind things;" and that "we trust the depth, and appearance as the gift of depth."[37] This movement distinguishes a related, "faithfully perceived" indeterminacy, which "may hover close to nihilism," from a "baptism of nihilism in the name of a miscon-strued 'negative theology.'" This book will reconstrue that supposed misconstrual, code for "Derrida," in terms that elude this polemical binary. Yet *radical* ortho-doxy, like any other, cannot distinguish between the *nihil*, the chaos and "the flux." Or, as Catherine Pickstock puts it, read the "skeptical postmodern subject" as announcing–oxymoronically, as though facing something "present to it"–"the flux of nothing."[38] Thus this orthodoxy proposes "an indeterminacy that is not impersonal chaos but infinite interpersonal harmonious order"–of a sort derived comfortably from Augustine's hellenism.[39] Though its taste for an infinite and trustworthy depth flows close to a tehomic theology, radical orthodoxy identifies that depth with the stability of a foundation, and so depends upon shallow dichotomies of order vs. chaos, solidity vs. flux, behind vs. face, One vs. nothing–and, of course, Christ vs. atheism.[40]

By contrast, we are exploring–with a less orthodox sort of support from Augustine–the possibility that *this theologically originary indeterminacy generates order not in opposition to but upon the face of the chaos.* That face expresses an infinite interrelationality that at once negates and proliferates metaphors of finite personality. Having gone so far as to theologize the indeterminate, why retreat into a tidy neo-classicism–as though only an unchanging order can save us from a chaotic *nihil* of meaning? The text of the *Confessions*, so much more attractive, more permeable, than all the orthodoxies it inspires, reads as an ancient estuary bubbling with a still suppressed potentiality. Here we may with Augustine, if only in passing, take delight in the surface; indeed, in its billowing multiplicity.

VI Augustine's hermeneutical flux

In tehomic refraction depth continually filigrees–at the edges of difference–into multiplicity. In the course of struggling with our very couplet, Augustine not only repudiates a fallacy of authorial intention, he invents that almost unheard-of thing in Christendom: *a pluralist hermeneutic.* He had pointed out the futility, indeed the stupidity, "amid such an abundance of true meanings as can be taken out of these words, rashly to affirm which of them Moses chiefly meant . . ."[41]–and so of privileging any single articulation of meaning at all. In his need to uphold Moses' authoritative truth while allegorizing his way free of it through Genesis 1, Augustine claims the validity of his own interpretation of scriptural signs, not in spite of Moses' intention but in addition: "even though he [Moses] through whom they were spoken perhaps had in thought but a single meaning among *the many that were true!*"[42] It is his discernment of multiple possible readings of Genesis 1.1f that produces in him a passionate defense of interpretive pluralism.

This hermeneutic of multiple truths is irreducible to allegory. That is, he is not invoking here multiple *levels* of truth, but alternative and lateral meanings: *less a multitiered than a multilateral matrix of meaning.* Augustine himself would abandon such dissemination in his subsequent battles with heresy. Indeed his development of what would become the standard theory of religious language leaves this generous "play of difference" in the dust of the literal sign.[43] Multiple levels of a single truth rather than multiple truths would characterize medieval scriptural exegesis. It founds itself upon the Word identified as the changeless, single and invisible–inherently unwritable–divine truth. For the later Augustine, the multiplicity of language morphs from gift into sin. Of him Susan Handelman avers, "linguistic multiplicity is the condition of the fall." Augustine would perpetrate a hierarchy of meaning, in which the deepest reading mirrored the highest–the one, non-fluent, and immaterial–Truth. The sign as such, the letter, was thus said to be "stubbornly adhered to by the Jews."[44] Allegory thus cuts against a rabbinic tradition of argumentative multiplication, in which interpretations gather multilaterally *around and about* rather than *above* the text (*literally*, in the graphics of the midrash). The sign in the ontotheological tradition points purely beyond itself, to the stabilizing truth of the "Transcendental Signified."[45]

The erection of the heights/depths hierarchy would soon erase the trace elements of an oceanic multidimensionality. Just for that reason I am arguing that the pluralism of Augustine's earlier thought–indisputably founded in a neo-platonic eternal unity–should not also be erased. *Confessions* actually exults in linguistic, and also cultural, multiplicity: "Consider sincere love of God and neighbor, see how it is expressed corporeally in many holy rites, and in innumerable languages, and in each language by innumerable turns of speech. Thus do the offspring of the waters increase and multiply."[46] In this passage the fluency and multiplicity of language are not only free of any taint of sin, but are collated with "various kinds of true interpretations."[47] This disseminative metaphor runs deep, its waters carving a channel right through his exegesis of the tehom, whose multiple possible meanings he cannot reduce to *one*: "*out of a small amount of words pours forth floods of clear truth.*"[48]

A butterfly effect of the text: from simple initial conditions cascades an unpredictable complexity. In the struggle with the strange waters of *beginning*, Augustine temporarily comes as close to a midrashic multiplicity of meanings as any text of the classical Christian tradition. As for this Augustine, so for a tehomic theology: *many* truths do not mean *any* truths. The many must bear their truths in resistance to those for whom truth is either One, or None.

VII Chaosmology

If an open flow of signification got clogged up "in the beginning," theology may find its own circulation improved by deconstruction.[49] Yet it cannot rest with anti-metaphysics or feminist denunciation. It lives at "the limits of a demystification."[50] At the edge of the specific chaos where we negotiate language about what endlessly precedes and exceeds our language–theologos–the unfinished infinity, the Deep, is never simply identifiable with "God" or " Creator." God-talk–theist or atheist, sexist or feminist–remains almost, but not necessarily, in thrall to ancient habits of pseudocertainty, stereotype and reaction. It may transcend its own doubts by dissociating from the matter at hand: the body and then the world. Or it falls into a demoralized indecision. Even when it takes responsibility for the suffering inflicted by the church's self-contradictory indifference to the world (for the church never in fact transcended the creation), it has rarely learned *to bear with* its own chaos.

Theologies of creation have followed the orders of various orthodoxies and run almost dry.

Under the sign of a *creatio ex profundis*, we release the *matter* of language into its own materialization; into the dark and dazzle of the spacetime known as "the creation." The logos of a becoming-in-relation will here fold continuously in and out of the chaos, producing the complications of a light shining *in* the dark: neither of a new nonbeing, a mere absence, a worship of disorder, nor of a delusional solidity of Presence. What appears first as formless, a dense shadow shot through with spectral afterimages, may be incubating the form you need. Brood a while longer.

In case there is anything to my hunch—that the monsters of chaos pose a hermeneutical question that we must no longer avoid; that the mystery of the lost depth is encrypted on the feminized surface of its repression; that the chaosmos of Genesis can yet sustain the shimmering, resilient Earth our dominion has so badly damaged—we turn to the early Christian creation of the *creatio ex nihilo*.

Part II

ORTHODOXIES OF NOTHING

Man provides a foundation for himself on the basis of reducing to nothingness that from which the foundation proceeds.

(Luce Irigaray, *Forgetting of Air*)

3

"TEARS OF ACHAMOTH"

The fathers' *ex nihilo*

They do not inquire whence were supplied to their Mother . . . so great an amount of tears, or perspiration, or sadness, or that which produced the remainder of matter.

(Irenaeus[1])

The fact that she may have served, may still serve, as mirror of every kind does not solve this remainder: extra, deep. Which upsets the whole thing.

(Irigaray[2])

I Much ado about *nihil*

Having opened the dark matter of Genesis 1.2, let us now ask: what was historically at stake in the exclusion of the chaos, the waste, the liquid remainder? What desire–beyond repression–produced the novel, post-biblical postulation of a pure and single origin? The doctrine certainly does not arise effortlessly, as though from an omnipotent Word; it churns up a turbulent wake of conditions, a storm path of altercations and bifurcations. In this chapter we investigate the historical tumult of alternative beginnings generated by the hermeneutical forces of biblical, platonic and gnostic exegesis. Gerhard May, upon whose historical analysis this chapter often depends, designates the late second-century Theophilus and Irenaeus as "the specific founders of the church doctrine of *creatio ex nihilo*."[3] With Irenaeus' *Against Heresies*, the doctrine "took a settled form" (iv).[4] If Irenaeus hammers out the full logic of the church's doctrine–and this chapter will read his moves closely, within their own conflictual matrix–it is Athanasius in the early fourth century who lays it into the foundation of Nicene orthodoxy.

I will argue that it is not a latent biblical logic but the polemic against "heresy" that crystallized earlier narratives of beginning into the "orthodox" doctrine of origin; that this absolute origin extrudes the Christian metanarrative as a single line stretching from the beginning to the end of history; and that this rhetorical extrusion draws its driving omnipotence from a drama of gender. Cosmology, indeed "the creation," matters in these *original* arguments only as the arena of salvation—as the eschatological theater of patristic Christianity. As it hardens, this narrative of omnipotent origin vaporizes any residual, female-tinged chaos. We will, for instance, overhear Irenaeus decry the gnostic myth of "a formless substance," "such a nature as a woman could bring forth," as an "abortion . . . boiling over in places of shadow and emptiness."[5]

Why return to these old paternal cosmo-polemics? I suggested that theology has no choice but to return recurrently and critically to its originative discourses—unless it wants to create theology *ex nihilo*. If we do not content ourselves with an ahistorical origin, historical beginnings matter. According to the key principle of chaos theory— that of the "extreme sensitivity of initial conditions"—beginnings repeat themselves. But always with a difference. If their fractal, complex iterations become readable, their homogenizing power dissipates. A turbulent process such as that of early Christian thought, "far from equilibrium," exhibits a multiplicity of initial conditions felt as unruly, even monstrous, by those attempting to unify them under their leadership. That anxiety of order remains relevant as long as our own cultures, wrought of a new, corporate genre of cosmopolitan imperialism, echo the Greco-Roman superpower within which the church fathers organized their complex discourses and communities. If a patristic tehomophobia still shapes the patrimony of the church, shall we continue to conceal the chaos of the doctrine's own origins under the banner of an inspired consensus?

Or, in response, shall we erase the fathers who nihilified the (m)others? Here the hope is for more rather than less legibility. So I am patristically aided by the subtle feminism of Virginia Burrus' historiography of early Christianity. "If the particular masculinizing 'theory of the subject' that was erected in late antiquity has come to seem numbingly familiar, we must push back behind boredom," she pleads. We must "learn again to feel surprised that the ongoing construction of a 'neutral subject' should have been underwritten by the doubled and linked repressions of materiality and of the female."[6] The early Christian patriarchy claimed its gender neutrality, its "neither male nor female," as the sexual foundation of its unifying order. So any exhumation of such doubled and linked repression demands a gender analysis of the mat(t)er and the fathers of its original nihilation. Will that feeling, that surprise, partake of the affect of a teary, sweaty, matter-making "Mother"?

We will find richly ambiguous motives amidst the "sensitive initial conditions" of the fathers' Christianity. What, for instance, is going on, when they construct a heretical, hysterical Sophia-goddess at the very site of the chaotic matter of Genesis?[7] And even if we could find her face again, amidst the gnostic and anti-gnostic denigrations, what would we want with this lachrymose, oversensitive "Mother"?

II The matter of creation

If biblical scholars cannot situate the *ex nihilo* proper within Hebrew, Hellenistic Jewish or Christian scripture, historians find it within the theological debates of the second century. It takes the form of a critique of the platonic idea of *world-formation* from the formless matter, which had seemed (as we noted in Justin) so readily reconcilable with the Genesis creation from tehom. "Only in the second half of the second century does the theology of the Church develop, in opposition to philosophical cosmology and to Platonising gnosis, the doctrine of *creatio ex nihilo* in the strict sense, which in the Catholic Church very quickly attains an almost unquestioned validity."[8] May himself never questions that "unquestioned validity," judging it the inevitable consequence of a "biblical" view of the divine. But he staunchly peels off layer after layer of standard hermeneutical attribution. Thus he refutes the conventional appeal to Hellenistic Judaism for evidence of a Semitic source of the *ex nihilo*, such as II Maccabees 7.28 (ibid., p. 7).[9] That "text implies no more than the conception that the world came into existence through the sovereign creative act of God, and that it previously was not there." In fact, he insists, "the Hellenistic Jewish theology says nothing in a principled anti-Greek sense about creation 'out of nothing', so that arguing back from the formal turn of phrase to an underlying theological tradition is ruled out" (7).

Similarly, Philo speaks of God as creating "out of non-being" or even "creating non-being." But despite his knowledge of the platonic ontology, Philo never refutes the idea of the uncreated matter. Rather he presupposes it: "God did not himself form the formless material, since it is unthinkable that he should touch the endless confused matter."[10] (Would He have been contaminated by this feminine impurity?) May diagnoses a failure to "reflect on the problem of how the omnipotence of the biblical God could be united with the view of a mere formation of the world" (ibid., p. 12). But the "failure" may lie in May's apologetic concern. Daniel Boyarin's discovery of the "Jewish birth of the logos" suggests that Philo's logos theology, rather than that of a "Christian avant la lettre," may reflect a pre-Nicene view of divine complexity that could have developed quite differently (ibid.).[11]

The New Testament likewise fails to reveal the *ex nihilo*. John's prologue, a midrash on Genesis 1 that according to Boyarin belongs among the Jewish texts of the *logos/sophia*, certainly replaces tehom with *logos* as the only eternal Other of God. According to Rudolph Bultmann "it is emphatically said that everything without exception was created through the Logos; but reflection on the How and the When is totally lacking." Then he takes a doctrinaire liberty with that scriptural loophole: "The Greek view, that wants to understand the world as a correlation of form and matter, is also excluded: the creation is not the arrangement of a chaotic stuff, but is the *katabole kosmou* (17.24), *creatio ex nihilo*."[12] The sleight of hand whereby the Greek phrase for "world-founding" is rendered synonymous with *creatio ex nihilo* symptomatizes a modern form of the anxious Christian need to find the doctrine amidst the founding texts. Other New Testament passages (Romans 4.7; Hebrews 11.13), traditionally invoked in support of the *ex nihilo*, similarly fail to exclude world-formation.[13]

Justin was the most important Christian thinker of the first half of the second century (apart from the gnostics) to take the platonic tradition seriously. In his interpretation of Christianity as the true philosophy, he was indebted to Hellenistic Judaism and its *logos*.[14] It is he who seems to have first displayed the parallelism between the biblical creation story and that of the *Timaeus*. With some hermeneutical *chutzpah* he speculates that Plato got the idea that God made the cosmos from the khora by reading Genesis.[15] Given the powerful apologetic impetus to bond biblical metaphor with Greek cosmology, Justin's resourceful synthesis provided a context-congenial, ecumenically inviting hybrid. It resonated with the common *ex nihilo nihil fit*, while revising platonism with some Hebrew historicism. To read this sort of platonic mimicry as mere assimilation (*à la* Harnack) would miss its radicalism. Thus classicist Rebecca Lyman grants Justin, martyred by Rome, the status within "the creative space of the second century," of a subversive colonial "hybrid."[16]

How did the *ex nihilo*, lacking this sort of resonance–neither biblical nor Hellenistic, nor yet a hybrid of the two–prevail? Justin's student Tatian was the first to argue within the proto-orthodoxy at mid-century that the matter itself was created by God.[17] For Tatian it was the logic of omnipotence that would demand this critical shift. But these abstractions did not arise in a rhetorical vacuum. Several different Christianities are by the second century competing with the patristic theology. The themes of cosmogony were raised with increasing speculative scope by the great Christian gnostics of the early second century. The platonic myth of world-formation, often refracting Genesis motifs, underlay their complex narratives. Yet Tatian, like Justin, shared much of the gnostic-platonic matrix of thought.[18] With Theophilus, a bit later than Tatian, the argument turns not just against gnosticism, but against *any* overt use of platonic cosmology.[19] And now the open space of the Christian philosophical imagination begins to shut down. Irenaeus would soon give the doctrine of creation "its essentially permanent form"[20] within the context of his protracted argument *Against Heretics*.

In other words, the patristic *ex nihilo* formula, indubitably a *possible* paraphrase of the biblical text, reads as a reaction against other hermeneutical options. It comes consistently framed as a polemical anti-gnosticism. While the orthodox position depended upon platonic metaphysics, it did so ever more by force of habit, while actively inhibiting the platonic spectrum of lively variations. Thus, ironically, it locked into dogma a clean and simple form of Hellenistic dualism, lacking the pagan aroma and evading autocritique; that between the changeless, impassionable eternity of God and the dissolute mutability of the material world. So as the (platonic) pre-existent chaos and its ambiguous "third genre" came under fire, the (platonic) dualism

THE FATHERS' *EX NIHILO*

was amplified—indeed lent an unprecedented omnipotence. The discourse thus produced would later be interrogated under the heading of "ontotheology." Does the simplicity of its story of origin, combined with the security emanating from the now total omnipotence, account for its persuasive power?

Another factor must be added to the account of this success. Here comes May's own *coup de grâce*: the first theological proponents of the full doctrine are themselves gnostics. "The idea of *creatio ex nihilo* is already found in Basilides a generation before Tatian and Theophilus."[21] Gnostic schools shared, indeed exacerbated, the Hellenistic disdain for the material world. So some could not tolerate the co-presence of some material preexistence as a first principle along with the purely spiritual first principle of God. It is the renowned gnostic teacher Basilides who was the first Christian thinker "to controvert explicitly the Greek model of the formation of the world and to formulate the thesis of *creatio ex nihilo*." No one before Basilides seems to have made the founding argument: that any uncreated something existing alongside God would detract from God's divinity; "his creation cannot merely consist, as in the case of a human artist or craftsman, in the shaping of a stuff previously" (ibid., p. 84).

In other words, we owe the invention of the *creatio ex nihilo* to a strong form of gnostic monism. It is then within the wide, shared matrix of "heretical" and "orthodox" discourse that the new *ex nihilo* found its resonance. "Is it anything more than a curious accident of history, that the doctrine of the *creatio ex nihilo* first meets us in ambiguous form in the work of a gnostic theologian?" asks May (ibid., p. 83). His answer is a gingerly "yes." In the face of his own excavation of the gnostic *ex nihilo*, he struggles to dispel its implications: the "attempts of the great gnostics to explain the origin and nature of matter hardly influenced in a direct way the inception and general prevalence of the church doctrine of *creatio ex nihilo*, for the general systematic conceptions with which they were bound up had to be regarded as *unacceptable by correct theology*" (ibid., p. 117; my emphasis).[22] May, with theological correctness, performs the ritual anti-gnostic antagonism of historical theology. This "t.c." cyclically renews the orthodox myth of origin, which is at the same time the myth of the origin of orthodoxy. What would happen if church history (in the spirit of Burrus' plea) shook off this weight of settled rightness? However dreary when cooked down to the repeatable formulae, theological discourse boiled passionately as gnosticism and orthodoxy wrestled and mimicked each other. Turbulence, according to chaos theory, is produced by such iterations—repetitions that differ. Has the repression of that turbulence concealed the startling extent of the dependency of orthodoxy upon its heretical Other?

III "A born heretic, he is, further, a turbulent man"

The case against Hermogenes, a philosophical theologian of the last decades of the second century, will help to diagnose that turbulent moment of transition. In his doomed opposition to the *creatio ex nihilo* and its omnipotence, an alternative path made itself briefly available. He rejected both the gnostic and the patristic *ex nihilo*, in favor of a biblically based doctrine of world-formation. His works are known to us only through Theophilus and Tertullian, who composed treatises against him.[23] He wrote against the gnostics and advanced a biblical Christology with the help of mid-platonic cosmology. He parsed the options lucidly: God creates either (1) out of Godself; or (2) out of nothing; or (3) out of something. If (1), then the world would be a part of God–but God is indivisible into parts. If (2), then God created evil too. A God who creates everything from nothing is responsible for evil. Theodicy therefore drove Hermogenes to the third option–that of creation from a preexistent matter. But he very carefully argued that matter is not in itself evil (as in Marcion): rather in its unformed state it is neither good nor evil, but requires the act of divine formation to bring forth its potential good. But also therefore it has the capacity to resist God and go bad.

Tertullian pounces: "you ought to have declared yourself unequivocally–that matter was either good or evil." Since one cannot have it both ways, he submits, Hermogenes must *really* mean that matter is evil, and so violates the "it is good" of Genesis. Hermogenes is further accused of "declaring that matter is partly corporeal and partly incorporeal," or "neither corporeal nor incorporeal." Indeed Hermogenes seems to have been intuiting a "third genre," a development of the *Timaeus* khora as primal energy or potentiality. But Tertullian–avowed enemy of "Athens," righteously oblivious to the Hellenism of his own dualism–scorns this nonbinary logic: "for, if I am not mistaken everything must necessarily be either corporeal or incorporeal . . . at all events, besides the corporeal and the incorporeal there is no third class of things."[24] Calling for a *triton genos*, Hermogenes may have been anticipating a poststructuralist reading of the khora. But his subtle logic did not stand a chance before the aggressive new either/or of the *ex nihilo*. However painstakingly Hermogenes insisted that the chaos did *not* limit God–that, *au contraire*, its freedom protected God's supreme goodness from a morally inferior notion of omnipotence– Tertullian could retort: "I lay down against him the rule that what is eternal and unborn does not admit of any diminution and humiliation." He drips sarcasm (ibid., p. 37): "Great indeed is the service which matter rendered God, that to-day He should have something whereby He can be known and be called the Almighty, save that He is no longer almighty, if His might did not extend to this also–to produce all things out of nothing!" Here Tertullian seems to be heading all future process theology off at the pass. He bristles at the notion that God might *need* anything. One who depends on "another's property" is *ipso facto* inferior, "powerless and all too little adapted to make out of nothing what He wanted." Hermogenes, who made his living as a painter, may have understood matter less in terms of ownership than of aesthetics. At any rate he did not consider the metaphor of formation *from* matter as inferior to that of the creation *of* matter.

According to the logic of *ex nihilo*, one is either good or evil, corporeal or incorporeal, eternal or temporal, almighty or powerless, propertied or inferior. One need not argue that this grid of dualisms necessarily accompanies the *ex nihilo* argument–only that historically it has done so.[25] Within the context of the late second century, the reaction against all philosophical speculation rigidified the binarism of orthodoxy. "In this historical situation," notes May, "a synthesis of Christianity and platonism, such as Hermogenes was attempting, could no longer be pursued; to undertake it was, in the atmosphere of anti-gnostic theology, immediately to incur the verdict of heresy." He comments that the "controversy with Hermogenes no doubt contributed to a further clarification of the concept of creation and eased the way for the adoption of the doctrine of *creatio ex nihilo*,"[26] and he approves the verdict. By contrast, David Griffin spots in Hermogenes a fellow process theologian. He notes that the classical adoption "of *creatio ex nihilo* was made without due regard to the warning by Hermogenes about the threat to Christian faith implicit in this doctrine–the threat to the perfect goodness of God."[27] To render the biblically "all-powerful" deity formally omnipotent was to close out the primal space, the khora or chaos, of creaturely spontaneity. Without that space, human freedom and natural chance are themselves directed by a Lord–who is thereby responsible for the havoc they wreak. A tehomic theology seeks with Hermogenes (and Griffin) a theological alternative to the dangerously unavowed amorality of omnipotence. The Hermogenean trace indicates a pathway by which the biblical creation from chaos *could* have been developed. This would be the imaginary of a divine power that "lures" goodness from freedom rather than imposes right by might; a third way between gnostic monism and orthodox dualism. But the method of multiple "third ways" was itself dismissed as a symptom of the chaos.

With a sharp satiric stroke, Tertullian paints the painter out of the picture: "And thus, in as far as it has been established that matter did not exist before the creation . . . in so far is it proved that all things were made by God out of nothing. I would add only that by delineating a condition of matter quite like his own–irregular, confused, turbulent, with a disordered, rash, and violent motion–Hermogenes has put on exhibition a sample of his art: he has painted his own portrait."[28] Such *ad hominem* caricature is the rhetorical fuel of orthodoxy. If it has not practiced the orderly dispassion it preaches, it did successfully censor any alternative to the *ex nihilo*.

IV Of nonsense and nothing

Within the pressure cooker of the late second century, Irenaeus, Bishop of Lyons, wrote his multivolume *Against Heresies* in the guise of a letter to an unnamed friend. "Thus, having learned of these mysteries yourself, you can make them clear to all your people and warn them to be on guard against this profundity of nonsense."[29] This is a cunning quip: he is about to introduce the Valentinian system of Aeons, or divine emanations, of which Bythus, "Profundity"–the deep–is the first principle. Tehomo-phobic ridicule seems to have become a standard weapon of heresiology.[30] Irenaeus will lay out in what he rightly calls "tedious" detail the narratives of several varieties of gnosticism before proceeding to refute their "miserable and baseless fables." He fashions himself as hunter: "that I may not only expose the wild beast to view, but may inflict wounds upon it from every side."[31] Echoes of the divine warrior battling the monster of chaos?

He opposes to the gnostics, point by point, the first comprehensive biblical theology. Indeed, comments Burrus, "Irenaeus invents 'the Bible' at the same time!"[32] His hermeneutic distinguishes him plausibly as "the creator of the Christian view of history."[33] Thus heresiology becomes historiography. Foundational to this model is its new account of the origin. Irenaeus infuses the *ex nihilo* formula with its "decisive and unambiguous clarity." Now it will stand as a "fundamental tenet of Christian theology."[34] A tehomic theology cannot treat this achievement as mere loss: in his protection of the goodness and entirety of the creation from the gnostic second god and evil matter, Irenaeus arguably evinces the first postbiblical case of "the emergence of the ecological motif."[35] Given the fragility of this motif in Christian history, I hope we can protect its antique stirrings–which would mean learning to distinguish the matter-affirming intention of the *ex nihilo* from its own matter-nihilating dualism.

One God now unambiguously produces the one world, ordering it on a time-track running from one origin to one end. This construction–later known as *Heilsgeschichte*, "salvation history"–has become so habitual that we forget it had to be *made*. It underlies all western views of history as a movement from origin toward goal.[36] Thus Irenaeus' interest in the creation is always soteriological rather than cosmological: the creation founds and guarantees a final salvation. Yet Irenaeus' time-line, forged in the heat of his heresiology, slices like a sword against the complicated speculations of the gnostics. Clearly, growing numbers of Christians found in gnostic allegory an absorbing and transforming exegesis of scriptural metaphors. To counter its permissive reading practices, which multiplied narratives along with divine emanations, Irenaeus asserts the single, public and simple truth of "the Bible." May lauds this simplification: "Where the gnostics distinguished a plurality of divine beings, relying on quite arbitrary interpretations of the Holy Scriptures and appealing to all sorts of secret traditions, which could not be checked for the truth of their content, Irenaeus points out that the Old and New Testament Scriptures, which agree among themselves and also with the generally similar church tradition, bear witness unanimously to the action in history of the One true God, which runs from the crea-tion to the incarnation of Christ and then on to the eschaton."[37] Oddly for a historian, May unquestioningly reinforces this ahistorical homogenization of scripture. Irenaeus' turbulently reactive coherence comes to frame and be framed as the truth of church history, its simple unity forever defeating the arbitrary chaos of the heretics.

Irenaeus' own reading strategy thus mirrors the "simple, uncompounded Being" of "the Father."[38] Thus the objectionably complex allegorical style of the heretics likewise mirrors a "compound" supreme deity. This One, the perfect first Aeon, was variously named "First-Being, First-Beginning, First-Father and Profundity." Irenaeus intends "to put an end to . . . Bythus himself, and thus to obtain a demonstration that he never existed" (ibid., p. 117).[39] Irenaeus does not discuss the gnostic identification of this Bythus with the Deep of Genesis 1.2b. So we witness in Irenaeus' anti-depth the incipient gestalt of a systematic tehomophobia. The dismissal of the profound— and by ready association the mystical, the complex, the fanciful and, as we may soon see, the female—as heretical disorder, as a nonsensical chaos in form and content, is becoming normative. Depth appears in this interplay as a heterogeneous, layered flux, not a pristine void but a "dirty gap."[40]

Irenaeus, however, is performing something very like a deconstruction: he offers a "manifest subversion of their entire argument." "We may remark in the first place," he comments upon the Valentinian narrative, "that the whole of it marvelously falls to ruin on both sides, that is, both as respects defect and excess."[41] The grand narrative of a unified history gleaned from a unified text ironically composes itself as a subversive reading of defect (flaw, fissure, gap) and excess (supplement, transgression, remainder) in gnostic exegesis. Irenaeus is (dis)counting the excessive emanations, each one of which both divides and exceeds the simple Oneness of the Father. The thirty Aeons of Valentinian philosophy appear dramatically as male, female and androgynous personifications meant to account both for the fall through passion of spirit, as Sophia, into matter and for redemption from the latter. Irenaeus defends the incorporeal simplicity of God against "their compound and corporeal Being."[42] For they divide the One rational and indivisible Creator into a monstrous hybrid, materializing in multiple, sensual and emotional figurations: an excess of divine manifestations productive of the defective creation they describe.

Irenaeus' critique runs deeper, however, than his disgust with the chaotic multiples. In the process of multiplication, the emanations distance the good creation from the good Creator. Citing John ("all things were made by him . . .") he seeks to eliminate all mediations between God and world: not the gnostic *Pleroma* ("Fullness") beyond the creator but the Pleroma *of* the Creator "should contain all things in His immensity."[43] Here roots that ecological motif. God as Pleroma *is* the ultimate environment of the material universe.[44] An earthly-minded Christian theology will not want to trade this immanence of the world to the divine, this intimacy of the infinite, for a gnostic hierarchy. Irenaeus' God does indeed, through "his hands" Logos and Sophia, reach out and touch matter. In this sense Irenaeus deconstructs a certain neo-platonic idealism. Before relaxing into some eco-apologetics for orthodoxy, however, we note that this hands-on immediacy strengthens the imaginary of unilateral, linear and masculine dominance.

V Sex and power *ex nihilo*

Without trying to recuperate the "subjugated knowledge" of gnostics, one may follow how their creation narratives provoke the *ex nihilo* reaction. All of the Aeons that emanated from the first unfathomable *Bythus* want to know this unknowable Depth, which is the root of their own existence. This desire grips Sophia, the twelfth Aeon, as a passionate suffering. In this yearning she parthenogenically conceives a daughter, her own Intention (*Enthymesis*)—and has a miscarriage, birthing "a formless substance . . . such a nature as a woman could bring forth" on her own. In ancient biology, the male seed provides the form for the female material. So Sophia's passion is now rent by grief. Finally the Father is able to emit, as a redemptive device, the androgynous figure of Limit. Limit separates Sophia from her passion and her formless Intention. Her aborted intention (like our own?) does not simply disappear, but continues "boiling over in places of shadow and emptiness." Christ the Aeon takes pity on Enthymesis and lends her the missing masculine form. She is then called Achamoth, a plural form of the Hebrew Hochma, to designate her relation to—indeed multiplication of—her mother Sophia. Now, intelligent and conscious, she yearns for that Word, that light, which gave form to her chaos. But she comes up against Limit. So "left outside alone, she fell into every kind of varied and different passions that exist": sorrow in loneliness, delight in remembering, bewilderment at her condition. How shall we not imagine these affects as symptoms of the distress of an intelligent woman trapped inside, and therefore outside, the patriarchal cosmos? Her passions, rendered in a cosmological poetry that prosaic Irenaeus takes literally, give rise to the material world. Her tears become water; her smile, light; her sorrow, solid bodies; and her terror, motion. Such an emotional and sensuous creation myth, though it presumes the superiority of the male mind to the bodily passions of females, provokes Irenaeus' derision: "For, when they tell us that all moist substance proceeded from the tears of Achamoth, all lucid substance from her smile, all solid substance from her sadness, all mobile substance from her terror, and that thus they have sublime knowledge on account of which they are superior to others,—how can these things fail to be regarded as worthy of contempt, and truly ridiculous?" The gnostic speculation invests Christian narrative in an ambiguous, originative matrix of libidinous world-mothers.

However down and abject on the divine hierarchy of mediations, "ridiculous" perhaps even from a feminist viewpoint, Achamoth appears as female body, still divine, and mattering. The universe ("good" also for this non-Marcionite gnosticism) springs forth from her fluids and her feelings. This materiality of creation matters also to Irenaeus. Indeed it matters so much that there must be no gap, no hierarchy of mediation between God the Creator and the creation. Instead of the chaos effected by Sophia's passion, Irenaeus offers the immediacy of divine presence. He finds "incredible, infatuated, impossible, and untenable" the logic by which these other

Christians imagine that the Aeon's "passion and feeling . . . became matter." Matter must come from the immaterial Creator, not from an erotic, maternal matrix already vaguely embodied. Irenaeus' hands-on making thus competes with the "vision of the erotic foundations of creating" shared, according to classicist Patricia Cox Miller, by these "diverse feminine figures."[45] It is in this very writing of the feminine chaos, glaring right at this leaky Mother, that Irenaeus gives birth to the full logic of *ex nihilo*: "They do not believe that *God (being powerful, and rich in all resources) created matter itself*, inasmuch as they know not how much a spiritual and divine essence can accomplish."

In other words, scorn at the matrilineal creation defines for the future of Christianity the nature of the Creator and thus of His act: a creation not *from* matter but *of* matter. "But they do believe that their Mother, whom they style a female from a female, produced from her passions aforesaid the so vast material substance of creation . . . They do not inquire whence were supplied to their Mother . . . so great an amount of tears, or perspiration, or sadness, or that which produced the remainder of matter." The gnostics lack the true origin, which can only be explained as the product of the resource-rich and powerful He-God. He needs no body of his own, no co-eternal, unoriginate mat(t)er like the platonists, no mediating Aeons and Intentions like the gnostics. All that is needed is "the power and will *of Him who is God of all*."[46] Thus the Father's gift of immediacy is packaged as proof of His omnipotence. It is by defeminizing and decorporealizing the activity of creation that he can articulate the full logic of the doctrine: "While men, indeed, *cannot make anything out of nothing*, but only out of matter already existing, yet God is in this point pre-eminently superior to men, that *He Himself called into being the substance of His creation*, when previously it had no existence" (ibid., p. 146; my emphasis).

What is at stake in the doctrine now becomes explicit: "He, who is God above all, formed by His word, in His own territory, as He Himself pleased, the various and diversified works of creation inasmuch as He is the former of all things, like a wise architect, and a most powerful monarch."[47] These are biblical images, metaphysically solidifying into attributes of the omnipotent God. "Wise architect" certainly alludes to Proverbs 8, in which the personified Hochma/Sophia is the conduit for all future creation, and all too suggestive of a divine emanation. If Irenaeus also articulates (after Theophilus) a trinity of Logos and Sophia as the two hands, the polemic against gnostic Sophia mitigates against any bi-gendered complexification of the divinity.

The Father needs nothing but his own logos to create. This is a rhetoric of sheer power. I hope I am elucidating how a specific cluster of signifiers–of masculine supremacy, of female abjection and of unilateral domination–form the metonymic links of the new doctrine. I am not arguing that its intentions were primarily dominative and misogynist. On the contrary, Irenaeus means to prove, as Kathryn Tanner interprets him, that "God's presence and influence are unrestricted in their range; there is nothing that exists apart from God and nothing that is not subject to God's direct influence."[48] But that "direct influence" takes the form of a consistent and masculinizing dominology. In what May recognizes as "astonishingly radical formulations" Irenaeus states flatly: "The will of God must rule and dominate in everything, but everything else must give way to it, be subordinated to it and be a servant to it."[49] Indeed the Christian God thus not only gets to be superior in power to any platonizing comers, but also to the Jewish God, i.e. to the "wholly unsophisticated image of God in the Old Testament."[50] In this orthodox historiography, "the total coherence and impregnability of Irenaeus' theology" rests on his recognizing that "*creatio ex nihilo* is a necessary fundamental proposition" (ibid., p. 177f.). Thus Christian orthodoxy originates in a symbolic misogyny in which it cashes in the complex mediations of cosmogony for the property rights of the dominus. Who does, it must be admitted, maintain an appreciative, hands-on relation to his possessions. But who must keep his women in hand.

VI Wisdom and the silly woman

> But what is primal repression? Let us call it the ability of the speaking being, always already haunted by the Other, to divide, reject, repeat . . . Why? Perhaps because of the maternal anguish, unable to be satiated within the encompassing symbolic.
>
> (Julia Kristeva[51])

The paradigm of power cleanses the divine pleroma of passion and femininity. Power becomes omnipotence in precisely the place, or khora, where the feeling female body has left its trace, its cosmogonic remainder. Into the darkness of theology will soon disappear even the Irenaean reminder of this vivid "intention" of Sophia. But lumpy layers of citation and counterdiscourse are still tucked into the seams of Irenaeus' argument. Her repression, as therefore she herself, is still active and visible. Like the Kristevan "abject," she appears divided, deformed, incomplete, neither quite subject nor quite object, moist, lucid, voluminous, monstrously "a female from a female." Repressed and expelled, but poignantly–and to orthodoxy menacingly–alive and intelligent, drenched in tears and sweat, her passion narrative inscribes a tehomic matrilineage.

Irenaeus warns against the "infatuations" of real women, too, and the dangers of woman-identified men. Women are prone to be seduced, literally, by those men who let women consecrate the cups of a magical communion service, men who teach of the Mother.[52] He denounces supposedly philandering gnostic teachers, like Marcus, who "devotes himself especially to women, and those as are well-bred, and elegantly attired," men who "have deceived many silly women, and defiled them."[53] "Emanating" beyond the bounds of a proper, simple, impassive God, emitting jouissance and anguish, a figuration of foolish femininity flickers through his text.[54] Irenaeus takes pains to set boundaries around a still leaking, ambiguously gendered origin. Abjection results, in Kristeva's words, from "what disturbs identity, system, order. What does not respect borders, positions, rules. The in-between, the ambiguous, the composite. The traitor, the liar . . ." The mystic, the heretic, the single mother. If the dissociative dynamism of biblical tehomophobia here grows into a systematic abjection, the chaotic Other becomes "the nurturing horror" that classical theology both repels and locates "by purifying, systematizing, and thinking; the horror that they seize on in order to build themselves up and function." But as Kristeva insists, this abject is always *"edged with the sublime."*[55]

If a current Intention may revise a text of origin, we may imagine her resisting this sublime repression by both gnostic and orthodox systems. The former uses her, the latter loses her. These great theological opposites were shadow-boxing over the humid body of a woman. Their boundaries blur: Irenaeus argues for the *ex nihilo* against gnostics who had already invented it. But in the specter of the gnostic goddess we are coming to recognize the "primordial repression" comprising the boundary of the metanarrative of salvation–a "constitutive exclusion" (Judith Butler) that has lent the logic of *ex nihilo* its hugely productive power. A boundless omnipotence stepped into the dirty gap left by the deficient femininity. All the more reason, having touched the excess and the defect of its logic, to widen its own opening.

VII Irenic epitome

> For the Creator of the world is truly the Word of God: and this is our Lord, who in the last times was made man, existing in this world, and who in an invisible manner contains all things created, and is inherent in the entire creation, since the Word of God governs and arranges all things and therefore he came to his own in a visible manner, and was made flesh, and hung upon the tree, that he might sum up all things in himself.[56]

This is Irenaeus' famous doctrine of the "summing up," the *recapitulatio*, offered as a gloss on Ephesians 1.10. Do we glimpse here, in the Christological climax and center of Irenaeus' order of salvation, the discursive potentiality for a nondualistic and nonlinear theology, long since smoothed out of view by his heirs? He offers a precise statement of panentheism: all-in-God, and God-in-all. The "invisible" panentheism becomes visible and therefore accessible through the recapitulative dynamism of the incarnation. Irenaeus then doubles the biblical symbols of historical alienation (disobedience, sin) with redeeming analogues from Jesus' life: "[T]hat the Lord then was manifestly coming to His own things, and was sustaining them by means of that creation which is supported by Himself, and was making a recapitulation of that disobedience which had occurred in connection with a tree, through the obedience which was exhibited by Himself when He hung upon a tree, the effects also of that deception being done away with." Does such doubling suggest a notion of "saving" less wasteful than a sheerly linear dissociation from the sinful past? "For in the same way the sin of the first created man (*protoplasti*) receives amendment by the correction of the First-begotten, and the cunning of the serpent is conquered by the harmlessness of the dove, those bonds being unloosed by which we had been fast bound to death."[57]

Such recycling of the first-created in the first-begotten, of Adam in Christ, of Eve in Mary, of serpent in dove, intimates the "positive feedback" of fractal iteration. What better image than a tree for the bifurcation characterized in chaos theory as "branching"?[58] As with Irenaeus' Christology, so with Ilya Prigogine's nonlinear dynamics: each actualization of one rather than another possibility, i.e. each bifurcation, recycles in itself, in microcosm, the previous history of bifurcations. "Thus the dynamics of bifurcations reveal that time is *irreversible* yet *recapitulant*."[59] If the iterations of chaos theory form recapitulatory loops within unfurling spirals, their repetitions figure not sameness but difference. Just as sin had spread through the mythic interactions of Adam and Eve, the Christic microcosm produces a difference that iterates, by a dynamic of panentheistic interconnection (divine love), through Jesus' community. So will any oppression or liberation radiate through the constitutive relationality of our creatureliness. While the vocabulary of sin and grace dominates Irenaeus' theology, salvation entails a new creation of all things: "when also the creation, having been renovated and set free, shall fructify with an abundance of all kinds of food, from the dew of heaven, and from the fertility of the earth."[60] This is a still material eschatology. As Paul Santmire insists, the Irenaean God "does not dominate the earth as some alien, despotic other. Accordingly, human dominion over nature is a muted, not to say scarcely visible, theme for Irenaeus."[61]

If *recapitulatio* rather than *ex nihilo* be taken as the primary trope—as seems appropriate to the Irenaean priority of soteriology over cosmology—a helical, recapitulatory sense of history begins to arise at the very site where the linear time of *ex nihilo* had been installed. The time/space of the universe then matters theologically as the very dynamism of incarnation. Incarnation could become rule rather than exception in the grammar of creation. Theology might be (again?) "drawn into the mystery of a word that seeks its incarnation . . . in excess of every existing language."[62] In this way we protoplasts may affirm the irenic anticipation of "those bonds being unloosed by which we had been fast bound to death." Summing up all things in its liberating body, the divine would assume the language of our bodies. Its Logos would touch every defect. Its Sophia would convey a love spread—excessively—across the material universe.

VIII The nothingness of creation

> God will be on their theory a Mechanic only, and not a Creator out of nothing; if, that is, He works at existing material, but is not Himself the cause of the material.[63]

The reading that quells the second verse, the clause of chaos and breath, has been well rehearsed by the time Christianity takes official form. Athanasius, the mid-fourth-century architect of Nicene orthodoxy, perfects in *De Incarnatione* the normative exegetical practice. Building on prior heresiological work, he sums up the erroneous views of creation, making short shrift of each: that of the epicurean, self-generated matter; that of the gnostic demiurge; that of platonic preexistent material. As to the latter—whose possible affinity to Genesis 1.2 he does not mention—he argues that it makes God "weak," dependent upon stuff already there, like a craftsperson: "the wood must exist ready at hand for the carpenter, to enable him to work at all." Athanasius characterizes as "weakness" the demiurge's inability to "produce anything He makes without the material, just as it is without doubt a weakness of the carpenter not to be able to make anything required without his timber." The argument is circular, already presupposing that the standard of excellence—power—is this ability to make something from nothing. Yet the strength of any craftsperson is measured by the ability to work with what is available. Athanasius proclaims with impatient tautology that "godly teaching . . . brands their foolish language as godlessness." (Of course the gnostics, hardly godly in his book, had long made this same anti-mechanic *ex nihilo* argument.[64]) The world is created neither "spontaneously" nor "weakly." Creation means command.

"*But that out of nothing, and without its having any previous existence, God made the universe to exist through his word*, as He says firstly through Moses: 'In the beginning God created the heaven and the earth' "; secondly, in the most edifying book of the Shepherd, thus he bestows upon the doctrine its fixed and final form. To drive home the scriptural authority of such a move, he has to turn to the extracanonical shepherd of Hermas. Then he backs up the *ex nihilo* with a quoteless allusion to "Hebrews 11.3." That text reads: "the world was created by the word of God, so that what is seen was made out of things which do not appear."[65] (No, again, not *ex nihilo*.) Athanasius merges the creativity of the Word with creation from nothing, "things which do not appear" with "absolutely nothing."

Amidst the bellowing negations, assertions and prooftexts, one might miss the omission: he makes no reference to the second verse. Again we learn to leap from a pure statement of the *ex nihilo* doctrine, via an authorizing allusion to Genesis 1.1, right back into a supposedly unified theological tradition. He offers no argument for his apparent contradiction of the second verse. I have been arguing that theology in the orthodox tradition (as we read in Moltmann) still performs this sleight of hand:

the fathers' Word deliberately conceals the chaos of scripture. By the fourth century the problem of the verse's compatibility with pagan mythologies and the platonic *khora*, was widely known. For instance, Athanasius' western contemporary and anti-Arian cohort, Hilary of Poitiers, lists Genesis 1.2 (because darkness appears to be coeternal with God) as one of the texts causing special difficulty for the expounder.[66]

Yet for Athanasius, as for Irenaeus, there is more than repression of the chaos at work. There is an affirming desire. Athanasius means to lift up the goodness of God, the generosity of its power enhanced by the foil of the *nihil*: "grudging existence to none, He has made all things out of nothing." Certainly the Christian intuition of a lovable source of all life struggles hard against classical visions of God's cold indifference to the world, or of hot caprice within it. One may infer that Hermogenes' question still worries the orthodox: would an all-powerful Creator not put the lie to His own goodness? For an irresistible omnipotence must then bear the responsibility for the evil in a fallen creation. In Virginia Burrus' analysis of the Nicene period, the divine attributes of beneficence and omnipotence in combination lay quite a burden upon the new doctrine. "Although initially meant to affirm both God's omnipotence and the goodness of a cosmos of purely divine origins, the forced concept of a creation eked out of nothing quickly begins to show symptoms of stress, bearing as it does unprecedented explanatory weight in Athanasius' text."[67] The strain upon the theological carpentry of the church registers precisely in the attempt to nail that divine goodness to the omnipotence founded upon an absolute Origin.

The Logos is at once the word of the Creator and the victim of "His" power. But the paradox now solidifies into the unquestionabilities of Nicene Christology. At this point something resembling Derrida's "logocentrism" becomes discernible—"the full presence summed up in the logos," the Transcendental Signified to which all signifiers ultimately refer, is stabilizing history in terms of a beginning and an ending that meet in the unchanging Logos of Being.[68] The pre-Nicene logos/sophia, unlike Derrida's somewhat generic, Transcendentally Signified Logos, was always both signifier and signified, revealer and revealed. Now, as its Hellenistically derived immutability hardens into the "only begotten" son, "very God of very God," same substance with the Father, the interdimensional oscillations of a more mobile incarnation freeze. Western salvation history tightens its line from protology through Christology to eschatology: a trajectory driven, or pulled, from the origin by the end. Centering time in Christ, the time-line at once lurches forward toward the end—and is pulled back by the power of the origin itself. "The creation" now serves less to open up a universe than to limit its significance to the timeless logos, or rather the dehistoricized past tense, of the Christ event.

Creation itself, with its nonhuman multiples and materialities, continued to lose whatever intrinsic value it might have been granted, had the Church retained a greater sense of cosmological and hermeneutical diversity. Another quite formidable tendency takes over. Whatever dualism was overcome within the discourse of eternity–by eliminating any preexistent matter or chaotic Other–returns to electrify the boundary between eternity and time. The uncriticized binary of eternal being vs. spatio-temporal becoming now gets dramatized in the dominion of the purely eternal and unchanging Creator over and above the perishable world He created. But this world-stuff, as it turns out, is terribly unstable. It is constantly dissolving back into the nothing from which it came. For inasmuch as we are created out of nothing, we are creatures, and this condition is one of mortality, the "corruption of death": "for man is by nature mortal, in as much as he is made from nothing."[69] Human mortality had been problematized in the ancient world without recourse to an *ex nihilo*.

But mortality now limns the goodness of God with the shadow of nonbeing. If it was by creating from nothing that Athanasius' God displayed his superior power over all other models, was this great gift of life not all that it seemed? God "has pity . . . on the race of men . . . having perceived its inability, by virtue of the condition of its origin, to continue." But the "condition of origin" comprises the foundation of this theology. So this nothingness against which was displayed the Creator's unrivalled power now sadly shows up as a defect in His product. Athanasius therefore announces that "He gave them a further gift, and He did not create man" like the other creatures, "but made them after His own image, giving them a portion even of the power of His own Word."[70] This second generous act gets destabilized as well. "Death having gained upon men, and corruption abiding upon them, the race of man was perishing; the rational man made in God's image was disappearing, and the handiwork of God was in process of dissolution." As Burrus reads it, "Athanasius' all-powerful God–boasting, in essence, that only weaklings use pre-existent matter–can barely keep his handiwork from unraveling, and the good cosmos seems destined for a bad end."[71]

How to save it? For now death had a "legal hold over us," due to our willingness to slip into corruption. Athanasius judges that the "result was in truth at once monstrous and unseemly."[72] Monstrosity again: a nothingness designed to *occlude* the chaos is behaving like the chaos. The returning repressed, like the leviathan, threatens to swallow up the finest work of the Creator. Thus Athanasius invokes the final, the Christological, solution. Otherwise we will keep slipping sinfully back into our chaotic "condition"–neither quite being or unbeing. The divide between the incorruptible God and the corruptible gapes wider than ever. Only the ultimate gift of the incarnation of God's son, born of flesh and sacrificed to death, will do the trick: it will spare God the double monstrosity of "the work being ruined;" and of God, who had to sentence us to corruption (for our corruption), coming off as "a liar for our profit and preservation."[73]

Along his dramatic journey–through city and desert, political foray and ascetic retreat–Athanasius would succeed in defeating the Arians and solidifying the homoousic Christology of Nicaea. The desired same-substance consensus was itself prone to slip into difference, much to the emperor's dismay: to slide toward chaos. Gradually, however, the creed that most Christians receive still as simple truth locked into the unquestionable. Christ is the Son of God who is begotten not made; he is begotten without sex by the bodiless Father, and not created like bodily things. But he will "put on flesh," like clothing. It is a clean body, free of the chaos transmitted by sex, but a mortal body just the same. Even in undergoing the nothingness of death he avoids "monstrosity" and "unseemliness." Only the "clothes" die. For the naked Word, of the same essence as the eternal and immutable Father, could not "suffer death, being immortal." This salvation story in one sense closed the distance between God and creation; but by the same token it closed the boundary between them. Only so could an eternal future be guaranteed to beings with rotting bodies. Only by participation in the God-Man, the eternal Logos robed in a mortal body, can we (sons of the Son) be assumed into his immortal life. That life promises eternal freedom from change, multiplicity, difference: the Logos as "life without *différance*: another name for death, historical metonymy where God's name holds death in check."[74] And where "woman" incarnated difference itself?

IX Chaotic default femininity

What does the establishment of the high Nicene orthodoxy of Christ as "begotten not made" mean for the sign matrix of female-matter-multiplicity? According to Burrus, Athanasius pioneers "a newly crystallizing doctrinal orthodoxy that would eventually both fix the masculine terms of a theological language and pull down the cosmic veil that decisively separated the fully transcendental heavenly triad of Father, Son and Spirit from the realm of material creation."[75] If the *creatio ex nihilo* closes the border between immaterial Creator and material creation, does it simultaneously lock into Christian symbolism the corollary classically gendered cosmos of immaterial male and material female? "Pre-cultivated 'nature' is characterized (as we have seen repeatedly) by the instability, fragmentation, and flux that has nonbeing as its matrix; materiality's chaotic default femaleness must be stabilized, simplified and sublimated in the ascetic production of the divinized self as a virtual–though never quite a 'real'–man." A productive proposition: the feminized chaos which cannot be permitted to *be* before the creation characterizes all the more intensely the materiality of creation itself. This is a radical move. Irenaeus had protected the physical world from just such a conceptual degradation. Theology now pushes toward an eschatology of personal, end-of-the-line resurrection. The saving work of the (once) creative Word defines the divine Sonship, for which only our personal salvation as "sons" is of interest. All the rest of the first corruptive creation drops back in importance, into the near-nothingness of nature, the natal *mater* that cannot matter in the End.

For the newly empowered ascetic masculinity, the sex/gender difference marks the site at which that materiality must be controlled in the course of our natal, mortal lives. Kristeva's insight into the formation of the firmly bounded subject through the repression of a maternal anguish that becomes the abject suggests what tension guards the classical boundary of divine and material. The newly politicized self-interest of the ecclesial hierarchy extrudes an unprecedented chain of desexualized fathers. Ejaculating their heresiological Word with relentless oppositionalism, they produce a potent new theo-political order. Guided by poststructuralist and feminist interrogations of the subject, Burrus stages this order as the formation of a new style of self: its "sustained dichotomy" of Creator/creature "helps structure a subjectivity that paradoxically both inscribes a sharp cosmological opposition between the human and the divine and reassigns 'divine' status to men–disowning the messes made on the earthly plane, which are swallowed up by the 'great maw' of the salvivic Word."[76] The dualism both produces and nihilates its own chaos. The "Logos," a now desperately needed mediator between the upper and lower planes (a century after Irenaeus' resistance to all mediation) becomes ever more monotonously, as Burrus demonstrates, in Athanasius' later writings, the "Son." But she simultaneously examines Athanasius' own formidable power-plays. Within an ecclesial culture in which new forms of celibate father-right vie with the classical *pater familias*, the father–son relation catalyzes tremendous socio-symbolic energy.

Unlike Irenaeus, Athanasius cites no salty traces of the animate tehom, no sweat and tears of a lost goddess. His defining opposition is with the manly and monotheist Arians, not with the polymorphically perverse gnostics. Athanasius may object to the Arian "pollsters in the market-place" querying "little women" about their births–as though such corrupt natality had anything to do with the begetting of the Son.[77] But the sex/gender dynamics of the *ex nihilo* are already established. Therefore they can be successfully repressed. "Maternity's stubborn particularities are what finally come to 'nothing,' disappearing almost entirely from Athanasius' text, while a paternity wholly sublimated–pure culture, one might say–lays claim to what is essential, giving the name of Father to an identity more natural than nature itself" (ibid., p. 54). The deceptive neutrality of the western subject is advancing, hollowed and shaped by an ever emptier nothing. "By denying sexual difference, the Fathers affirm the difference of divinity; by making maternity invisible, they privilege fatherhood on the very basis of its invisibility . . . by suppressing materiality, they push the spirit to new heights" (ibid., p. 190). Ascetic masculinity, unlike the classical, is now free to express its androgynous or feminine proclivities. But this new spiritual freedom produces new perplexities.

X Queering the chaos

> Perversion means sexual chaos.
> (Suzie Bright[78])

A spirit "more natural than nature"? This "more" means both divine supernature and sinful hyper-nature. On the one hand Athanasius argues that "nature"–tilted toward non-being both as evil and as mortality–is that *from* which we need salvation. But "as corruption ran riot" within a dissipating human nature, we became evil "to an even more than natural degree." In yielding to our corruptible created nature, we exceed nature. *On the Incarnation*'s discussion of creation from the chaos-tainted nothing immediately yields a list of natural excesses: the usual line-up of adulteries, thefts, murders, injustices, wars. But only to his final example does Athanasius give serious attention: "crimes contrary to nature." "Their women changed the natural use into that which is against nature; and the men also, leaving the natural use of the woman, flamed out in lust toward each other."[79] Suddenly, in this citation of Romans, "nature" signifies not what sin succumbs to, but what sin sins against. Nature may be corrupt, but at least it's straight.

In the matter of our sexuality, "nature" is suddenly rehabilitated. The chaos of a lawless nature, the unnatural nature, goes to such an extreme, symptomatized in the abject bodies of those whom we now call lesbians, gay men, or bisexuals, that "nature" flips around to signify the unambiguously good, lawful work of the Creator. The major Christian denominations as I write still largely impose this incoherent "biopower" (Foucault) as the straight and narrow; and some are drowning in the tidal wave of this self-contradictory sexual "nature." The boundary of death/evil/ nothingness is indelibly inscribed–beyond gender difference–as sexual chaos: where gender order breaks down. On this classical homophobia hinges Athanasius' text. Structurally this passage happens to comprise the transition from the Creation to the Incarnation. It is in the face of the nothingness thus queerly epitomized that he postulates the Incarnation as the only solution to such sinful monstrosities. Thus Judith Butler's notion of the "founding repudiation," designating the social function of homosexuality as the "constitutive outside to the domain of the subject,"[80] flames into anachronistic relevance. Within the ascetic revolution inaugurated by Paul, it would seem that the sublimations required in a single-sex community weakened the procreative heterosexual norm in such a way as to infuse the same-sex boundary with special threat: not so much sex itself as the chaos of a polymorphic diversity of Christian subjectivities. "Athanasius appears to have lacked a concept of an essential self or given personality," suggests David Brakke. "Rather conformity to some model defined a human being's character, for good or ill."[81]

Tehomophobia never exceeds its constitutive *homophobia* by much. If Nature is good, its inherent wobble and emptiness, its defect and excess, its bizarre, nay queer, capacity to resist the One who created it, demands the utmost vigilance. The phantasm of creation from a nothing that at every moment threatens to break into chaos charges the designated order with a dangerous sexual tension: irresponsible because repressed, explosive because closed. The circulation of the Logos Spermatikos through its all-male orders could not fail to produce confusion at the edge of its rationality. "That Spermatic Word," suggests Althaus-Reid, "is the word of origins, the word and embodiment of God the Father who produces praxis (actions and thoughts) by a process we may call 'Spermatogenesis.' "[82] Creaturely hybrids and their sexual variations threatened from the beginning to "out" the disorder of the order of (spermato)genesis; more embarrassingly, to out the (te)homophilic propensities of the Body of Christ.

Thus did the chaos take up its dwelling as the queer within the closet of creation.

XI Present in all things

What if the Body of Christ opens up? Into its own tehomic indeterminacy? Does the doctrine of the incarnation, precisely in its ancient collusion with the logos of creation, not finally–late indeed–push toward a chaosmic dis/closure? Do the moist uncertain zones of our bodies, of every body, not still flow into and from the unfinished entirety of "nature" itself, the nature of a not so tidy–if brilliantly organized–cosmos? To heal the logogenic traumas of western social bodies, then, it matters whether an imprint of the materiality within God and the God within materiality can still faintly be read from the Nicene origin. And surprisingly it can. Even at the hardening heart of orthodoxy, a classical panentheism still modulates the ontotheology.

God incarnate as the Word "was not, as might be imagined, circumscribed in the body, nor, while present in the body, was he absent elsewhere; nor, while he moved the body, was the universe left void of his working and providence."[83] Here, within a recrudescence of classical panentheism, this Logos embodies a spatiality already healed of what Whitehead would diagnose as the modern "fallacy of simple location."[84] The intuition of a complex commingling of creator and creature has not yet fully dissolved into the hypostatic union of two separable and simple natures in Christ. It has not yet cashed its cosmic promise into christological exceptionalism. Athanasius continues:

> Rather, but thing most marvelous, Word as he was, so far from being contained by anything, he rather contained all things himself; and just as while present in the whole of creation, he is at once distinct in being from the universe, and present in all things by his own power–giving order to all things, and over all and in all revealing his own providence, and giving life to each thing and all things, including the whole without being included.[85]

This giving of order does not necessarily imply a totality of control. As long as interest in "all things" and in "the whole of creation" still remains, so does the possibility of a full-bodied panentheism: this God-in-all and all-in-God suggests a divinity irreducible to unitary simplicity or self-contained triunity.

Athanasius himself would translate Logos almost exhaustively into the fully anthropo/andro-pomorphic "Son." But the Logos of *De Incarnatione* still expresses–"thing most marvelous"–an intimate cosmological immensity.

XII *Recapitulatio*

Could this panentheistic path lead us back and forward to the forbidden shores of tehom? I have offered no single cause for the *ex nihilo* doctrine. I might want to say–*this* is its origin, *this* is what it "comes down to." (As the one Logos came down . . .) Yet a monocausal explanation (feminist, political, sexual, psychoanalytic) will reinscribe a founding exclusion as surely as does the *ex nihilo*. Instead, in honor of the patristic incarnation, we might recapitulate. We have traced the rise of a logos of creation that could no longer brook the prior chaos. Tehomophobia is not novel–its texts of evil sea and theomachy dot the Bible. But unlike the Bible, the fathers rule out the preexistent chaos. Tehomophobia, its fear of death and femininity cooked into a serene habit of abjection, will in the tradition of the fathers rarely need to face its own chaos, its Others. In their triumphant logos we have read a logic whereby the creation doctrine guards God's unity against gnostic complexity; unconditional omnipotence against constraining conditions; masculine symbolic privilege against the affective, sensual and unruly femininity; the prestige of the disembodied Father against all maternalized chaos; a Creator who "begets" against any who procreate; the monosexual celibate elite against same-sex temptation; the closure of canon against uncontrolled textual multiplication; the ascendancy of the imperial narrative of a single Logos against the confusion of competing narratives.

To summarize the doctrinal development traced in this chapter formulaically: Genesis 1 + omnipotence + ontology = *creatio ex nihilo*. As, however, that Athanasian "whole of creation" communicates ever more clearly its mysterious, chaos-edged *infini*, it begins to shake off the onto-logos of an original control. For all its anxiety in the face of non-being and femininity, the patristic theology articulated a divine wisdom pervading the universe. If we can recapitulate the ancient God-in-All without (re)capitulating to the accompanying dichotomies of power, theology might (re)gain a certain indispensable depth: that of a history folded and wrinkled into the polemics of old texts, of a temporality that unfolds even in the sophic spiral of our reading.

4

"MOTHER MOST DEAR"

Augustine's dark secrets

A hearing engaged in by the whole body that evokes speech–a new speech–
a new creation. The woman had been heard to her own speech.

(Nelle Morton[1])

Hear me as I cry out of the depths. For unless your ears are present with us
in the depths, where shall we go?

(Augustine[2])

I The deep's *double entendre*

De profundis. Is it possible that the Augustine of *Confessions* cares as much to sound
those depths as to found a theology? This writing is crying, this crying is praying: its
first person calls to the second person. Who, you? (No, *you*.) Of course we readers
are just listening in. He can't be praying to us. Or not? "One who does not know you
might call upon another instead of you" (I.1). But how would one avoid this risk of
writing, the risk of an open-ended call? In this enunciation of the private, or rather
this production of the private by its publication, "must you rather be called upon so
that you may be known?" How would this "you" not flow, oscillate, between you-the-
reader and you-God?

"Unless your ears are present . . . in the depths," why write? Why read? *Which*
depths? *Which* ears? Their orifices open into–more depth. More waters. Infinite
waters: "as if there were a sea, one single sea, that was everywhere and on all sides
infinite over boundless reaches." The creation, imagined the African, floats in this
sea like "a sort of sponge, huge indeed, but yet finite, and this sponge was filled in
every part by that boundless sea." Which boundless sea? Within the parable the
implication is unambiguous: "Thus did I conjecture that your finite creation was filled
by you, *the infinite*."[3] We read these drops in a time in which "the creation" is getting
squeezed dry. The divine ocean breaches the surface of the text and plunges quickly
out of hearing. A mirage? A tehomic opening?

65

I will read *Confessions* as neither tehomophobic nor tehomophilic, but as rhetorically fluctuating between both currents. Less propositional than psalmic, its answers iterate into questions, its creed into quest. *Confessions* is a saturated text. Its metaphors open into "the boundless sea." Yet it presumes, indeed it strengthens, the boundary-setting proposition of *creatio ex nihilo*. It does not echo the combative furies of anti-heresy (unlike the later anti-Donatist and anti-Pelagian Augustine). It *sublimates* rather than *suppresses* the biblical tehom.[4] And startlingly, the second half of *Confessions*, the drier half, where the juicy autobiography ends and the hermeneutical-theological work takes over, turns out to be little more than an exegesis of the first chapter of Genesis. Indeed it is Augustine's fascination and frustration with the second verse and its chaos that, following his meditation on time, define the final three books. Most surprising of all: what I will designate his "tehomic ambivalence" discloses another ambivalence, the tensions of which arguably lend the *Confessions* as a whole its otherwise missing structural continuity.[5] As his readers often complain, the book divides into an autobiography (1–9) and a cosmography (10–13), with little to justify their lying under the same cover.[6]

Confessions may be read as a quest for Wisdom: "to love Wisdom herself, whoever she might be, and to search for her, pursue her, hold her, and embrace her firmly–these were the words that excited me and set me burning with fire."[7] This eroticized quest therefore drives the above rhetorical question–"Where shall we go?" The confession of its answer brings the reader to a Wisdom sexually sublimated but hardly desexualized: to a *Sophia / Sapientia* whose femininity, I will argue, mirrors with uncanny precision that of Augustine's mother. Monica's portrait in Book 9 brings the autobiography to its end and climax. While the literal woman vanishes in the second half, the very face of tehom will take on an unpatristically, lovably maternal aspect. It will display a split, doubled and displaced femininity: that of both Sophia and his own mother.

II The great ear

> Hearing in this sense can break through the political and social structures and
> image a new system. A great ear at the heart of the universe–at the heart of
> our common life–hearing human beings to speech–to our own speech.
>
> (Nelle Morton[8])

Speaking of women. What does the ancient "cry out of the depths" have to do with this already old cry of feminist theology? What does the whole body's hearing have to do with that of the classical God? Nelle Morton's "divine ear" with Augustine's? Late in the second Christian millennium, the cry from the depths welled up in a woman's voice: "I hurt . . . I hurt all over . . . but I don't know where to begin to cry." The flood of tears, she fears, might drown her. She talked on and on, and no one interrupted. "Finally she finished," writes Morton. "After a silence, she looked from one woman to another. 'You heard me. You heard me all the way.' Her eyes narrowed. She looked directly at each woman in turn and then said slowly: 'I have a strange feeling *you heard me before I started*. You heard me to my own story."[9] In retrospect Morton read in this episode a parable: "A complete reversal of the going logic in which someone speaks precisely so that more accurate hearing may take place" (ibid., p. 127).

This hearing effects a beginning-narrative in the creation of feminist theology.[10] "This woman was saying, and I had experienced, a depth hearing that takes place before the speaking–a hearing that is far more than acute listening. A hearing engaged in by the whole body that evokes speech–a new speech–a new creation." It is in this eschatological context that Morton's most "original" line–itself a citation–is uttered: "The woman had been heard to her own speech."

Did Augustine's God-ear hear him to *his* own speech? Augustine was paraphrasing the psalmist: "Out of the tehom I cry to you, O Lord. Lord, hear my voice! Let your ears be attentive to the voice of my supplications." (Psalm 130.1). Augustine amplifies the psalmist's *chutzpah*: *Listen* to me when I speak! And the African not only cries *from* the depths; he installs, like Morton's "depth hearing," an Ear *within* the depths. For Morton, however, "the powerful old maleness in deity had been superseded by the new reality coming audible in woman speech."[11] This bodily language of women would also supersede (if it could) the disembodied He-ness of the Christian imaginary.

To juxtapose his venerated classic with Morton's patchwork *Journey Is Home* is anyway something like comparing a Roman basilica to an Appalachian quilt; the "great wealth of style" of a patrician rhetor to the rough "new speech" of a race, gender and church activist. Augustine's episcopal eloquence resounds with the genius of the imperial Christendom *against* which western struggles for social justice have had to direct their new speech. But just for this reason we may wish to hear him to another speech: his own tehomic fluctuations, heretofore inaudible to most Christian theology, may open a certain deconstructive path *within* his quest, the very trail of which connects the two dissociated halves of the *Confessions* itself.

III "Dark and fluid inner being"

> How shall I find words to explain how the weight of concupiscence drags us down into the sheer depths and how the love of God raises us up through your Spirit, who moved over the waters?
>
> (Augustine, *Confessions*, XIII.7)

At one level the book's binary form precisely manifests the bifurcations of its content–of *autos* from *cosmos*, of the soul from its own body and from the creation, a severance repeating the dichotomy of a divine, disembodied interiority and the material outside of creation. Yet the subjective interior in which Augustine finds God is the interior in which sin itself metastasizes. Let me suggest that "depth" encodes the tension, the ambivalence, indeed the duplicity of that interiority; that historically speaking it is here that the tehom itself gets *interiorized*. Is it the very Deep of creation that is here (re)published as the inaudible, or divinely audible, privacy of a heart or soul? It becomes *my* depth. Others "cannot lay their ears to my heart, and yet it is in my heart that I am whatever I am" (Augustine, *Confessions*, trans. Pine-Coffins, X.3). Augustine reports the emptiness of "seeking God outside myself." The pretty display of the creation remains empty: for he had not found "the God of my heart." "For the light was within, while I looked on the world outside" (ibid., VII.7). This privilege of the inward self differs from the psalmic intertext, which calls the community to "hope in the Lord," who will "redeem Israel from all its iniquities." The depths from which the psalmist cries flow from the situation of a community and its political vulnerability. This Hebrew subjectivity, however heart-felt and soulful, situates itself inextricably in its eco-social context. Morton's ear, hearing "from the heart of our common life," in this more nearly resembles the psalmist's. The depths out of which Augustine cries do not bleed from injustice.[12] They report, they cultivate, an inner anguish. If it is Augustine who lends the subsequent western subject its textual "depth," it is nonetheless not as a serene and self-sufficient interiority. In this his "soul" diverges from that of Stoic and neo-platonic alternatives.[13] His ability to "enter the inner regions" never yields a unified self-presence. Rather, despite the conversion and ecstatic graces granted on its way, the interior quest only provokes new struggles.

Indeed it reopens the waters of the deep. Tehom now appears under a new face: that of "*our dark and fluid inner being*" (Augustine, *Confessions*, XIII.14). The spirit "was mercifully borne above" this inner chaos. Unlike his heresiological antecedents, Augustine does not erase the primeval waters. He does not repress their dark chaos. Rather he channels those depths into a public narrative of private shame: "not for nothing have you willed *that these dark secrets be written on so many pages*" (my emphasis). Not just sexual secrets: his confession secretes its sexuality into the depths of soul; the *autos* soaks up an eroticized universe as temptation and squeezes it out as confession. In the final books of the *Confessions*, he writes (between the lines of Genesis 1) multiple meanings of the "darkness over the waters." The erratic multiplicity of the world can be signified, and therefore sublimated, as little more than theater for the drama of "God and the soul." Yet it gets under the skin, leaks *in*, enturbulates the dark waters.

The autobiographical Christian self excels in its capacity to transcend its bodily, social and ecological contexts. But its ascetic withdrawal does not yet redeem it from suffering. Detaching itself even from the creaturely warmth of its own body, it endures the shocks of its own passions all the more intensely. The dissociation reverberates in a widening social vacuum. Thus the ontological breach between Creator and creature reinscribes itself *within* the "friend of God."[14] Augustine, unlike Athanasius, insists that this capacity to struggle through to victory over one's own mutable, creaturely sensuality occurs by grace only. Indeed, while Athanasius marked the sensory creation wrenched from nothing as the turbulent Other of the Creator, Augustine writes the fleshly passion of his own soul as the Other. It is not then the dualism that is new to Augustine but its complex internalization: this split subjectivity has inspired the self-preoccupation of the Christian soul ever since. In its deep fissures flow the ambiguous waters of tehom itself: sometimes the ocean of divinity, sometimes the very "flood of sin" (*Confessions*, XIII.7) from which God lifts us. The double signification of "depth" signals the productive force of this tehomic ambivalence.

IV "A cauldron of shameful loves seethed and sounded"

"Who can untie this most twisted and intricate mass of knots?" writes Augustine of his youth. "It is a filthy thing: I do not wish to think about it; I do not wish to look upon it." This chaos of his own beginnings conveys a dark and liquid heat, a trace infecting even the state of grace, a complication in what yearns for purity. The *Confessions* is the most influential discourse of shame ever written. It begins in infantile greed and the theft of the pear: "I, so small a boy and yet so great a sinner, was not unworthy of punishment." Memory tallies evidence for the originality of sin. Youthful escapades testify (not without a wince of humor) to the peril of sociality. We yield to mischief not from desire for "gain or for vengeance, but merely when someone says, 'Let's go! Let's do it!' and it is shameful not to be shameless!" (*Confessions*, II.9). The shame, oscillating into shamelessness, iterates and dissipates in its very writing. Augustine, suggests Burrus, "deliberately makes much ado about almost nothing. His purpose, it seems, is to cut moral transgressions down to their ordinary, non-heroic size while at the same time restoring a sense of their modest complexities."[15]

The magnetic center of the shame-narrative lies in sexual desire, in the uncontrollability of youthful—and with the exception of his concubine, homoerotic—passions: "to love and be loved was sweet to me, and all the more so if I enjoyed my loved one's body. Therefore, I defiled the very source of friendship by the filth of concupiscence, and its clear waters I befouled with the lust of hell" (*Confessions*, III.1).[16] The rhetoric of confession boils over. But its chaotic intricacy remains *legible*. The distinctiveness of the Christian "technology of the self" *vis-à-vis* that of Greek ethics lay in a shift of ideal: "now self-examination takes the form of self-deciphering." Foucault wrote of this confessional development that "the problem is to discover what is hidden inside the self; the self is like a text or like a book that we have to decipher, and not something which has to be constructed by the superposition, the superimposition, of the will and the truth."[17] Indeed Augustine forms the self as a text to be "written on so many pages," cleansed by confession until finally transparent, "purged and melted clear" (*Confessions*, XI.29). The mass of knots must be untied through writing, the mess deciphered through confession. By what Peter Brown calls Augustine's "relentless introspection," a salvageable subject is cultivated within the fluid medium of the interior. The *Confessions* does not resort to a sword of Damocles. But that "intricate" mass will later mutate into a greatly simplified lump of perdition (*massa perdita*), the sin-infected or sin-infested sociality that will exclude the human majority, including its unbaptized infants, from salvation. What Burrus calls the "relatively forgiving, almost Apuleian eye that Augustine casts on his own past" nonetheless inscribes in the autobiographical tangles of the self a rat's-nest of shameful, hellish egotism.

Shame has been psychoanalytically defined as "that feeling of self-castigation which arises when we are convinced that there is something about ourselves that is wrong, inferior, flawed, weak, or dirty."[18] In her important mapping of U.S. racial identifications upon this psychology of shame, the theologian Thandeka describes a "pitched battle by a self against itself in order to stop feeling what it is not supposed to feel: *forbidden desires and prohibited feelings that render one different*."[19] By contrast with shame, guilt is "a feeling that results from a wrongful deed." Guilt can be redressed or recompensed. Shame issues not from wrongs done but rather, continues Thandeka, "from something wrong with oneself." One accumulates shame-scenarios as humiliating memories, forgotten when possible: "I do not wish to look upon it." "Looking at these uncomplimentary mug shots, one feels shame as in the feeling that 'I am unlovable,'" writes Thandeka (whose Swahili name, the gift of a twentieth-century African bishop, means "lovable"). She derives from the fifth-century African bishop the origin of a "theology of shame." His "original sin" "blames the victim for its own brokenness rather than the social order that assaulted it."[20] Because Augustine makes no distinction between guilt and shame, he compounds humiliation with judgment. The Augustine of *The City of God* would indeed stretch that judgment onto the history of "the city of man"—a history in itself irredeemable. The subjects of the city of God would be redeemed *from* history. "The shame theology Augustine bequeathed to the Christian West," continues Thandeka, "is a doctrine that had made peace with a Roman world of pervasive human suffering framed by a profound sense of personal alienation."[21] Such a theology of shame effects a historical realism "without an edge of social criticism" (ibid., p. 119). I have argued elsewhere that this Augustine helped to purge the newly imperial church of its revolutionary–apocalyptic–social potentialities. Indeed the heaven of *The City of God* eerily mirrors the ordered hierarchy of the Roman state.[22] Sin—understood as the *internal* resistance to the ordained order—requires *external* dominance. Due to the unruly darkness of our disordered nature, any order—however unjust—would count as superior to any chaos. The psalmist in his cry from the chaos presumed a *differently* collective sense of self. Sin meant a deforming injustice for which members of a community stand responsible before each other and therefore God: closer in the operative distinction to guilt than to shame.[23]

Does the gradual shift from socially framed guilt to pervasive personal shame then mirror the shift from a creation out of chaos to a *creatio ex nihilo*?[24] Without over-investing in a forced dichotomy of shame and guilt (shame may be a cultural universal, and inasmuch as Christianity infuses its new "structure of existence" [John Cobb] with shame, Paul has already made the constitutive moves), we may now state more clearly the relation of the *ex nihilo* to the shame theology. Augustine presupposes, indeed sharpens the view that the formless waters were created: "you made the matter entirely out of nothing" (*Confessions*, XIII.33). He does not invent, he *deepens* the *ex nihilo*. When he radicalizes the story of the fall as the originality of sin, it will correspond, as in a shadow-negative, to the founding originality of the creation. But original sin is not articulated in *Confessions*—only its seething cauldron of sinful potentials. Augustine's trope of Genesis 1.2 as "our dark and fluid inner being," as the very tehom of shame, *interiorizes the creation*. It creates a new subjectivity. By displacing the cosmic chaos into the individual soul, he not only renders moot the *ex nihilo* presupposition (for of course human confusion does not precede the creation itself); he produces the engulfing drama of the inner being: the gradual triumph of the God-in-depth over the dark depths of shame. An ambivalent confluence indeed, with enough textual energy to exercise its oceanic magnetism for millennia.

Our shames blush across the face of the Augustinian deep. Shame, according to Heinz Kohut, shows upon "the exhibitionistic surface of the body-self, the skin" as "a heat and blushing side by side with pallor," a "disorganized mixture of massive discharge (tension decrease) and blockage (tension increase) in the area of exhibitionistic libido." Augustine's writing of libidinous defilement charges the *Confessions* with narrative tension. But from the beginning floods also what Kohut considers the healthy alternative: "the pleasant warmth of successful exhibitionism."[25] Augustine has spread out his life and then the life of the creation for a display more joyful on the whole than damning, its self-display boiling with more pleasure than censure: "we see all these things, and we see that they are very good, because you see them in us, who have given to us your Spirit, by whom we might see them and in them love you" (*Confessions*, XIII.34).

Augustine confesses jubilantly to "the last remains of my darkness, until my infirmity be swallowed up in your strength" (*Confessions*, XI.2). So his dogma of creation from nothing swallows up the precreation waters. But not quite. *Confessions* holds its water. So then a tehomic theology recognizes that we can never excise the Augustinian subjectivity. We—western Christians at least—have swallowed Augustine willy-nilly. We have internalized the gesture of internalization itself, in its dissociative dualisms, its ecosocial indifference—as well as its gifted complexity. It *becomes us* still. It harbors our own psychic complexity. Right where he/we try to cut free of materiality, maternality, mortality. But a loss can heal rather than fester. If it wells up as grief?

V T/ears

> I closed her eyes, and a mighty sorrow welled up from the depths of my
> heart and overflowed into tears. At the same time, by a powerful command
> of my mind, my eyes drank up their source until it was dry.
>
> (*Confessions*, IX.12)

The depth surges up irrepressibly: transmitted by touch from the mother's eyes to the son's eyes, from death to life, from heart's depth to body's surface. A flood defies his self-control. The tears condense in themselves the salt water of the primal tehom. Luckily he masters the waters before anyone notices: as Moses parted the sea with his rod, so Augustine commands the waters with his mind. He deciphers this paradigmatic act of manhood with phenomenological precision. The organs are not puppets. Eyes and heart have wills of their own. The body can collude with the disorderly deep, it rebels against the mind's authority. Only with pain can he suppress the conspiracy of body and tehom: "Most ill was it with me in such an agony!" The scene is her funeral, situated at the end of the autobiographical half. When his son Adeodatus "burst out in lamentation," he is immediately shamed into silence.

To mourn the dead is unbecoming in a man; all the more in a Christian. Suppression of grief testifies to faith in eternal life. He resents the vulnerability but glories in narrating its suppression: "But in your ears, where none of them could hear, I upbraided the weakness of my affection, and I held back the flood of sorrow." The flood vies ferociously with his self-control. " I was again swept away by its violence, although not as far as to burst into tears, nor to any change of expression" (*Confessions*, IX.12). No outward hint of affect: a moment of classically male triumph. The private turbulence of this interior tehom is successfully kept locked behind floodgates. He who surrenders to the fluid and the mutable fails to imitate the divinely unmoved, the impassionable One. Weeping eyes cannot host visions of the immutable One.

"So the mother's child is engaged in stripping away the membranes, the inheritances that he finds too material. Subject to fading and death." Nothing like a flash flood to turn the eyes material and membranous, to occlude their specular distance. "And if this enlightened gaze was already rising above baser and darker attractions," continues Irigaray, "it must also be purified of overly terrestrial sights, and equally he must give up his trust in so finite an organ as the eyes."[26] While Augustine struggles against the mortal materiality of his maternal bond, the oceanic imaginary deluges the text: "I fought against the wave of sorrow and for a while it receded but then it swept upon me again with full force." Yet his introspective analysis exceeds (and so is deficient in) Stoic terms: "but I knew well enough what I was stifling in my heart. It was misery to feel myself so weak a victim of these human emotions, although we cannot escape then . . . and so I had the added sorrow of being grieved by my own feelings."[27] With psychological fidelity he captures his entrapment in this "twofold agony." "Human emotions" of grief belong to the same continuum as lust: tehomic revolt–of himself against himself and against the divine order. Yet his stance is not that of simple judgment, but of knowing ambivalence.

Tears–microcosms of the deep–after all mirror his mother, who had been praying for his conversion for years "with her piteous tears and groans;" and for him, in his conversion, when he "probed the hidden depths" of his soul and "wrung its pitiful secrets from it." At that moment when he had aggressively deciphered the interior flux, "a great storm broke within me, bringing with it a great deluge of tears."[28] The psychic tehom repeatedly challenges his command–but in the case of his conversion, the challenge is divine. These secretions of conversion were "the sacrifice that is acceptable to you." So a tehomic ambivalence seems to shadow his maternal ambivalence. If the unacceptable waters are those that flow from feelings of attachment to a creature (especially to a woman) rather than to the Creator, none-theless, these acceptable tears wash away the great obstacle to intimacy with his mother.

After her funeral, finally alone, he gives vent to his sorrow. Now he acknowledges that he grieves for his own loss, thinking "about her sweet and holy care for us, of which I was suddenly deprived." In a wonderfully unstoic moment of auto-compassion, he writes that now he "took comfort in weeping in your sight over her and for her, over myself and for myself." He finally gives way "to the tears that I had held back, so that they poured forth as much as they wished. *I spread them beneath my heart, and it rested upon them,* for at my heart were placed *your ears, not the ears of a mere man*, who would interpret with scorn my weeping" (*Confessions*, IX.12).

In other words the divine ear, in its fluid receptivity, liberates him from the discipline of masculinity. The You does not do to Augustine what Augustine did to his son. It does not suppress his emotions. The divine ear sprouts in the moist visceral deep "beneath my heart."[29] Like a wise counselor, it listens to the sorrow–all the way down. Thus does it bless the mourner. Prehending–feeling the feelings of–the heart floating restfully upon a tehomic waterbed, Augustine momentarily embodies (here at the heart of the *Confessions*) the heart's rest in God, the eschatological image that opens and ends the *Confessions*. When the Deep floods through the armored *apatheia* of elite Christian masculinity, he momentarily defies the male scorn. But does this exceptional male only prove the rule? Not of the crude patriarchy of his abusive father, but of the spiritual patriarchy exalted by his mother? His relationship to Monica remains exceptional. Augustine writes the personal mother as a dimensional human being, visible, articulate, emotional, imperfect and lovable. Not simple encomium, yet almost hagiography, his portrait of Monica provides, as Burrus writes it, "a vehicle for conveying a deviously complex eschatology–a potent signifier of the mysteries of God's will at work in a fallen world, her performance always flawed and yet somehow redemptive."[30] He shamelessly confesses both her failings–as when she has wrongly shamed him–and his affection.[31]

73

Structurally, it is as though in his narrative return to his mother's life and death he takes heart for the task at hand: the birth of his own theology. This for him meant returning to the origin, to solve the problem of origin itself. This is a hard nut to crack: he had been struggling since his conversion to believe in the *ex nihilo*, with its omnipotent yet good God (*Confessions*, VII.5). What "dark secrets" for a hermeneutic of Genesis 1.2 might be hidden in the subcardiac waters? If mourning lets the Deep gush through his eyes, the waters will well up afterwards in his hermeneutics. No autocratic, dispassionate point of view, but a passionate, indeed bodily theology begins to take form, attentive to his own volatile fluctuations.

VI A heavenly nothingsomething

"I both shudder and glow with passion: I shudder, inasmuch as I am unlike it; I glow with passion in as much as I am like to it." "It" is "Wisdom, Wisdom itself which shines through me." And precisely here comes the beginning move that neither requires nor rejects the *ex nihilo*. He cites Psalm 104, that poem of the tehomophilic creation: "You have made all things in wisdom!" (104.24); and then by midrashically splicing it with Genesis 1.1, he can announce: "That wisdom *is* the beginning, and in that beginning you have made heaven and earth" (*Confessions*, XI.9). This sapiential beginning threatens to destabilize the founding, linear narrative. But its tehomic potential is constrained by the curve of the Augustinian passion toward the timeless: away from the wetter and wilder reaches of that cosmic Sophia.

So when Augustine at last turns to the creation narrative, we should not be surprised that his real concern is not with the material and mortal creation but rather: how can I be sure of my own immortality? "The lowliness of my tongue confesses to your highness that you have made heaven and earth, this heaven which I see, this earth on which I tread and from which comes this earth I bear about with myself" (*Confessions*, XI.4). Sure they are good. But: "compared to you they are neither good nor beautiful nor real." Even the prelapsarian earth feels so burdensomely bodily. "Where is the heaven that we do *not* see?" The universe, however pretty, interests him only if it contains the *immaterial* heaven which God has–surely–made to house us beyond death: the goal of our earthly pilgrimage. "Where is that *heaven of heaven*, O lord?" Augustine here uses a "hebraicism found in Latin versions of Scripture, 'the heaven of heaven,' to name God's dwelling place in contrast to the term 'heaven' as meaning the sky, which is, of course, as material as the earth."[32] But this yearning poses an exegetical dilemma: he must find this "heaven of heavens" within the Genesis narrative of origins, which never mentions any heaven separable from "sky." Indeed the Bible remains parsimonious in its allusions to an immaterial heaven or afterlife.[33] So how will he be able to locate the true "heaven" within the founding narrative?

He presumes that God created not from any preexisting other, as in the *Timaeus*, nor out of any aspect of the divine selfsame, as with Plotinian emanations. *Non de Deo sed ex nihilo.*[34] Therefore "heaven" must be created. But more. "Doubtless that heaven of heaven, which you made in the beginning, is some kind of intellectual creature" (*Confessions*, XII.9). Heaven has its own mind? Yet Genesis 1.1, which contains the crucial "heaven"–the one he must endow with this intellect–serves as an introduction to the rest of the chapter, whose only subsequent reference to "heaven" is the definitely material "firmament" of the second day.[35] Augustine takes up the challenge with gusto. He will need to argue that the "heaven" of the first verse is something altogether different from the "heaven" of the second day. So he suggests that the phrase "heaven and earth" in verse 1 signifies a still undifferentiated mix of both corporeal and spiritual potentiality. Then he can argue that the materially formed stuff of the sky (firmament) derives from this "heaven and earth;" but so does the invisible, incorporeally formed stuff of the "heaven of heaven."

Why does this stuff matter to *us*? Patience, I pray (you): for in his restless quest for an eternal resting place he will also produce an unexpected set of tehomic gender effects. In order to pull off this exegesis, he now solicits the tehom of verse 2. "Lord, have you not taught me that before you formed this unformed matter and fashioned it into kinds, there was no separate being, no color, no shape, no body, no spirit?" Almost the hypothesis of *formation from* primal matter (rather than *creation of* all matter) recurs.[36] "Yet there was *not absolutely nothing*: there was *a certain formlessness* devoid of any specific character" (*Confessions*, XII.3; my emphasis). It is Augustine's preoccupation with the "certain formlessness," his pluralist meditation upon the complexity of this tiny text, which distinguishes his exegesis.

Between the purely absent *nihil* and the finished present of creation, he spots it "in the *transition* from form to form." First he had been repelled: "my mind turned over forms foul and horrid in confused array, but still forms." These monstrous forms struck him "as something strange and improper" (*Confessions*, XII.6). But he realized that these were still *forms*. Only when he fixed his thought *"on the bodies themselves, and peered more deeply into their mutability,"* did this chaos begin to morph into a third genre, neither formless nor formed: "If it could be said, a nothingsomething [*nihil aliquid*] or an is/is-not [*est non est*] I would say that it is such" (XII.6). For a moment, in the space of this nothing full of something, a counter-ontology seems to emerge, a phenomenology of becoming akin to Whitehead's notion of "transition."[37] But after tantalizing us with this tehomic voyeurism (after long exhibitionism), Augustine leaves us in its dark. His "heart" retreats into a "hymn of praise for those things which it cannot dictate." He refuses to publish *this* dark–and apparently shame-free–secret. He tells us he is sparing us readers "all the knots which you [God] have untied for me concerning this question."

A knotty mystery. He leaves us guessing. This much he does divulge: *the almost-nothing of the tehom is the stuff of the heaven of heaven*: he interprets "'darkness above the deep' as spiritual matter before any restraint was put upon its almost unbounded fluidity" (*Confessions*, XII.17). What, or who, is this "stuff"? Does it have a mind of its own?

VIII God's wife, the heavenly tehom?

The Heaven of Heavens, we learn, partakes "of [God's] eternity, and because of its most sweet and happy contemplation of you, it firmly checks its own mutability" (*Confessions*, XII.9). That is, this incorporeal creature "checks" its instability by "clinging fast" to God. It needs to: its instability is bottomless. For Augustine derives *the Heaven of Heaven of verse 1 directly from the tehom of verse 2*.[38] The instant it was created, this Heaven of Heavens grabbed hold of the Creator and clung for dear eternity. Thus it never became subject to mutability, to transience. It is as if this unbounded fluidity freezes on contact. Therefore it is suited to offer Augustine's soul an eternal abode. His logic is knotted indeed: already in its state of formlessness, he avers, there can be no change—for change means a contrast of *forms*. So the formlessness of "heaven" allows him to argue cunningly for its immutability—an attribute otherwise reserved for God alone, as the eternal Being of form and order itself ("for in you there is no change, of form or motion" [XII.11]). The implications are curious: a changeless God would be *ipso facto* a *formless* God? *Ergo* God is chaos? Needless to say Augustine does not go there. (No more than the ocean of divinity let him identify God as tehom.) But he is able to argue that the "heaven" of verse 1 *is* "the first heaven, the heaven of heaven"[39] which he had identified with the tehom.

Realizing the eccentricity of his exegesis, he supplies fully five alternative interpretations of the verse pair. With the pluralism that he will later abandon, he admits a certain undecidability: among Catholic Christians, reasonable objections and alternatives to his interpretation will obtain. Indeed it is while considering the verse—"the earth was without form and invisible, and darkness upon the face of the deep"—that he bursts into delight rather than frustration at the tehom of textuality itself: "Wondrous is the depth of your words" (*Confessions*, XII.14). Heaven, partaking in immutable eternity, while yet created as tehom, as the chaotic, the aboriginal potentiality, echoes his joy. "Oh happy creature, if there be such, for cleaving to your happiness."

Who is this tehomic "creature"? This "certain sublime creature that cleaves with so chaste a love to the true and truly eternal God" (*Confessions*, XII.15) now shows her face—and it is redoubtably, indeed doubly, feminine. It is here that she is unveiled as the Wisdom of Proverbs 8: "a created wisdom was created before all else, the rational, intellectual mind of God's pure city, *our mother, the heavenly Jerusalem, a city of freedom, which lasts eternally in heaven.* Can this be any other than the Heaven of Heavens?"[40] So the invisible "*heaven*" is the created tehom—is the created *Hochma / Sophia*—is the *New Creation*, or the *City of God*. The female Wisdom as "heaven of heavens" signifies at the same time, in this mobile metonymy, its *mind*. Here at last the goal of his quest becomes visible: "May my pilgrimage sigh after you!" An iconography of heavenly femininity pulses momentarily into view, intellectual, incorporeal, and indubitably erotic: "I will enter into my chamber and there I will

76

sing songs of love to you, groaning with unspeakable groanings on my pilgrimage" (*Confessions*, XII.15).[41]

As this female subject merges with the traditionally feminine New Jerusalem, erotic and filial yearnings become romantically fused. "Jerusalem my country, Jerusalem my mother, and you who over her are ruler, enlightener, father guardian, spouse, pure and strong delight, solid joy, all good things ineffable, all possessed at once . . . I will not be turned away until out of this scattered and disordered state you gather all that I am into the peace of her, the *mother most dear*" (*Confessions*, XII.16; my emphasis). Augustine, notes Eugene Rogers, "did not have to read Freud to mix the yearnings of the spouse and the child that the Bible refuses to separate."[42] What may be unique in this conflation of Lady Wisdom with the bridal/maternal New Jerusalem is the manifestation of either as the primordial waters.

By personifying heaven as an intelligent female, he is able to project onto this unfading face of tehom the unmistakable traits of his own mother. After her death at the middle of the book he rewrites her as the very corpus, the matrix, the *place* of all resurrection. Monica's best traits—her intelligence, fidelity and "sweet and holy care"—are iterated and amplified in the icon of the Deep. Monica most dear is not just revised but raised. She who adhered to a base husband now clings joyously to the ultimate bridegroom. Having blessed his dead mother to heaven, Augustine idealizes her attributes as those of heaven itself. It is this poignant sublimation of the mother as "sublime creature" that swaddles in maternal sweetness his obscure correlation of the Christian heaven with the tehom. Thus is eschatology cradled in the waters of protology.

VIII Mother of ice

Yet this rhapsodic identification of tehom as the immutable heaven remains unstable: the waters continue to signify the shameful, "dark and fluid inner being" (*Confessions*, XIII.7). Fluidity, as mutability itself, denotes the very opposite of the eternal stability he seeks. In order to move from first to second verse in such a way as to save heaven and his soul from materiality, he needs the waters to signify incorporeal, "spiritual matter." So he has the "earth without form and invisible" signify the "corporeal matter" from which the earth and the firmament were produced. "'The earth invisible and without order' would be understood as corporeal matter before being qualified by any form, and 'darkness above the deep' as spiritual matter before any restraint was put upon its almost unbounded fluidity" (*Confessions*, XII.17).

Still: how can the *waters* cease to be fluid? How can the "unbounded fluidity" of the primal sea become the eternally bounded and bonded stability of Mother Most Dear? His emphasis upon her luminosity and stability, as participating in her High Husband's eternity, seems to cure her chaotic origin. But the following passage confirms that the strange identification of tehom with heaven is not (just) the product of a perverse reading: "I have had much to say of the *Heaven of Heavens, of the earth invisible and without form, and of the deep, showing how its darkness was in keeping with the spiritual creation*, which in its formlessness, had no cohesion or stability." Of course this passive, incoherent femininity–while glowing in its darkness without shame–is utterly dependent upon the masculine deity for its in/formation. "Such it would have remained unless, by being turned to God . . . it had received beauty as well as life by the reflection of his glory."

The dividing of the upper and lower waters by the firmament effects this extraordinary hermeneutical sublimation: "In this way the Heaven of Heavens came into being, that is, the heaven of the heaven that was later created [firmament] between the waters above and the waters below" (*Confessions*, XIII.5; trans. Pine-Coffin). So then: the upper waters, at the moment of the dividing, become separated as the heaven of heavens, the mother; while the lower waters beneath the firmament become the earth's seas.[43] The "unbounded fluidity" is thus precariously congealed, its darkness radiated with divine light. Heaven awaits the restless soul, which like a child snuggles up to Mom, who has *her* arms around Dad.[44] A cozy trinity. (What room could there be for Christ, who barely appears in the *Confessions*–except as hermaphroditically camouflaged in the "principium" of the beginning, the Sophia (ibid.)? She abides forever the same, clinging to her husband, mirroring in her unfading beauty his omnipotence–and thus wraps our finitude in immutable immortality. The most stable of families.

From the violent fountain of tears for Monica has cascaded an epiphany of the upper waters. And what are nonfluid waters–if not a simple oxymoron–but *ice*? *La mère de glace?* Her "almost unconstrained fluidity" gets immobilized, frozen in glory. Sophia, refashioned as the New Jerusalem, becomes a bodilessly feminine figure of speech for the City of God–a supernatural heaven, not a transformed earth; eschatology checks its "edge of social criticism" at her door.[45] Sublime, subjected, sublimated, and female: this hope (as he admits, ceding multiple true readings) treads on thin ice. Separated from her wilder materializations, from the watery "down there," from the known filth of bodily femininity, she cleaves to the higher masculinity. She offers embrace, comfort, home. Yet at the same time she absorbs–like many an idealized woman–the immobility to which she clings. No wonder she will excite ambivalence. Frozen, her fluidity denied, she reroutes desire itself. An ice queen attracts the subject to his own ultimate rest.

"In other words, man does not get out of the maternal waters here but, by freezing the path that would lead back to her, he gazes at himself, re-producing himself in that paraphragm."[46] So Irigaray, in her exploration of Plato's cave, tracks an earlier version of the frozen femininity. The very path by which the masculine subject flees from the mother, i.e. from his own fleeting creatureliness, *is* the frozen form of "her." Simply to nihilate her is to risk the flood. The dry wit, the absracted vision of his immaterial and tearless eyes, require the mirror of her unmoving surface, her speculum. He does not see her face, her *panim*. He sees his own. Yet as this freezing act repeats itself in the *Confessions*, these waters appear in a far fuller cosmogonic dignity. Albeit under strictly patriarchal conditions, they are celebrated as female. In his passion for wisdom—"I glow and shudder"—Augustine almost melts down the ideal of the unchanging Same. Only to freeze the future in the eschatological embrace of the mother.

A woman without flux. Her issues are not ours. This is no mother of feminism, no adequate ear for those still struggling into speech. Nonetheless, tehomic possibilities survive in frozen form, like textual embryos that would otherwise, in a more straightforward *ex nihilo*, have been simply eliminated. Do they matter? Will they materialize?

IX Habit of harm

> If Adam had not fallen away from you, from his uterus there would not have flowed that salt sea water, the human race, so deeply active, so swelling in storms, and so restlessly flowing.
>
> (*Confessions*, XIII.20)

Now the tehom reappears as the elemental medium of human sin, sin not just internalized but tending here toward originality. Augustine's initial revulsion to "something strange and improper" seeps into this hermaphroditic "down there" of the *lower* waters. He textually hollows out, "distends," liquifies, Adam's body, lending it a uterus (Gk *hysteros*, "lack"). The ancestral hysteria of Genesis is reproduced genetically. As the issue of this invaginated Adam, our species today appears ever more dangerous in its turbulence. Self-destructive and all mixed up. Together. In *deep* trouble. Nonetheless, a theology of becoming finds grace within, not outside, that very flow, that "deeply active" passion and flux. It diagnoses the *blockage* of the flow, not the flow itself, as primary cause of our collective ills. To freeze off our dark fluidities only further swells the storms. Thus the neo-imperial orders of late capitalism foment a consuming hysteria, a greed, which indeed never rests—and which requires for its temporary satisfactions the objectification of dark peoples, the blockage of their freedom, and the extinction or commodification of the other species of creation. Of course such an anachronistic gloss strangely mirrors Augustine's own ambivalence. For the Augustine who attended to "the bodies themselves," having "peered more deeply into their mutability," implicitly counters an already classic tehomophobia. Like the spirit itself, like no other theologian in history, he hovers over this verse of the primeval chaos. He reports years of intellectual uncertainty. The contradiction of divine omnipotence and the goodness of creation had tied him into theological knots. Mainstream Christianity has not yet disentangled them. If all that the good God makes is good–"where then is evil? What is its origin? . . . How did it steal into the world? What is the root or seed from which it grew? . . . Can it be that there was *something evil in the matter from which he made the universe?*" (*Confessions*, VII.5). In that chaos, in other words? But surely not, if God made it? So finally he simply affirmed like a good Catholic that God created the matter itself first. Creation required two stages. Only then does evil as a deformation of free will worm its way into a good creation–as a mere *privatio boni*, a hysteria, a lack, of goodness.

In a sense a theology of becoming also finds in the "deeply active" swells of tehom the *source* of sin. For we read the tehom as the chaosmic spontaneity of all becoming; as analogous to what Whitehead called the "substantial activity," or later the "creativity" of which all creation is an articulation. It is the indeterminacy of a freedom to actualize good or ill. So we too may, with Augustine, locate evil in a deformation of freedom. From this perspective "sin" appears not as disobedience but as *discreation, that is, creaturely relations that deny and exploit their own interrelations*. Sin is in this sense "original": it co-originates us. I did not choose my ancestors' slaveholding, my nation's aggressions. Yet such preconditions have shaped, privileged and deformed "me"–like a contagious disease, as Augustine would say (yes we are all connected). If one earthling falls into alienation, into greed, into domination–that sin will infect its relations and thus *in part* constitute all who follow. A relation is a repetition: *recapitulatio*. As Augustine does *not* say: this flowing relationality is for good as well as for ill. I experience myself as created not from nothing but from this ambiguous mix of preconditions. Also he would not say: I stand *not guilty* for the patterned chaos of relations preforming me–but *responsible*.[47] I become guilty if I do not take responsibility for the effects of past relations upon me now, as I affect the future. Curing my shame thaws the flow of response.

For this sense of recapitulation we require Augustine's notion of sin as "force of habit": "For the law of sin is the force of habit, by which the mind is dragged along and held fast, even against its will, but still deservedly so, since it was by its will that it slipped into the habit" (*Confessions*, VIII.5.12). We go along, we do not resist, we seek to secure our existence. The repetitions become habitual, often compulsive, carried along by global patterns of assumption–economic, sexual, racial, religious. Amidst these structures, our agency may be unconscious. But it is never simply absent–we slip "by our will." Sin is a matter not just of bad choices but of the *capacity* to choose. (This would later come to mean for Augustine that we deserve damnation from birth. But at this point his logic has not become bitterly rigid.) This insight alone, crucial to any systemic analysis of injustice, makes it impossible to dismiss the Augustinian sense of collective, preconscious "sin" in favor of a simple doctrine of specific sins.

With and against Augustine's ambivalence, the tehom begins to emerge as icon of a primal freedom that "is" neither good nor evil but comprises the potentiality for the whole gamut of creaturely choices. So a tehomic theology transmutes "original sin" into something less original, if still productively systemic: the habit of dis-creation. While it results from endless harm, abuse, *han*, its blockages have become their own conduits of the chaos. The chaos–not the good, not the evil–but the potential for good or ill. The habit of discreation is healed, inasmuch as it can be healed, not by a one-time, unmoved incarnational solid, but by the *capacitating* flux of what for us mammals is an ever carnal grace. Which we may address. As *you*.

X This boundless sea

We might take the African's hint and keep our minds fixed on the bodies. Not as objects, not as substances or fixed points, but, in his language: as mutabilities. Dying, Jean-François Lyotard read in the body of the *Confessions* not the shamed and steaming flesh, but this rare grace: "To deliver the soul from its misery and death, grace does not demand a humiliated, mortified body; rather, it increases the faculties of the flesh beyond their limits, and without end. The ability to feel and to take pleasure unencumbered, pushed to an unknown power–this is saintly joy."[48] What inspired this postmodern, postmortem textual "delivery"? Remarkably it is none other than Augustine's most tehomophilic trope, that of the cosmic sponge. In its incom-prehensible immensity, its still finite quantity radiating in all directions, this universe is saturated with divinity:

> I pictured you, O Lord, as encompassing this mass on all sides and penetrating it in every part, yet yourself infinite in every dimension. It was though there were sea everywhere, nothing but an immense, an infinite sea, and somewhere within it a sponge, as large as might be but not infinite, filled through and through with the water of this boundless sea. In some such way as this I imagined that your creation, which was finite, was filled by you, who were infinite.[49]

The divine ocean, the Infinite, permeates all finitude, utterly soaks and saturates the creation: God-in-All, All-in-God. To be sure, this imaginary of divine immanence subsides in Augustine's thought. (Indeed from this very passage he launches into his above perplexity about theodicy: how if God is everywhere is there space for anything but goodness?[50]) Yet within this God-soaked topos of creation *the deity flows freely*. As such this space echoes the potentiality of a postmodern khora, neither intelligible nor sensual, neither abstractly infinite nor "simply located."[51] "To conceive of these transformations of space," writes Lyotard, "Augustine cannot rely on Dedekind and Poincare geometry."[52] But Lyotard, who can, translates the divine ocean into the spatial matrix figured in the fractal geometry of chaotic attractors: "An n-dimensional space-time folds around the naturally three-dimensional volume of the body" (ibid., p. 10). The infinite- and *inter-dimensional space* of chaos theory offers a relational, nonsubstantial logic unavailable to classical Christianity. Headed toward the perfect immortal body on its rigid hierarchy in the City of God, the flesh of *Confessions* nonetheless enfolds such tehomic possibilities.

As the sponge-like body of the creation is thus encompassed, so also it is penetrated. By the same principle each finite body is thus surrounded and permeated by infinity. "Such is flesh visited, co-penetrated by your space-time." Shaken and confused, the frail body is nonetheless "steeped in infinity, impregnated and pregnant with your overabundant liquid: the waters of the heavens, he says. The body, sponge-like in its permeability to the other space-time, exceeds its sensoria." In this reading of a sublimated and overabundant eros, these beginning-waters of creation flow again as birth waters, in which even a dying body may find grace. "If the human, thus bestowed with grace, is declared to be inner, it is simply because the secret of such an ecstacy remains kept, because the words to express it are lacking" (ibid., p. 11). The African's dark secret (verging on but never quite revealing the shame-free darkness of apophasis) comes to speech on the edges of ineffability. The lack, the hysteresis, of language itself–known all the more acutely where the gift is great–keeps opening into the *n*-dimensional space. If the Augustinian interiorization of the *creatio ex nihilo* has written itself into the western self, indeed written itself as the subject of that self, the writing of it appears still pregnant with post-Augustinian possibilities–with a fluidity that burst the bounds of any frozen subjectivity.

XI The new, the pneuma and the natal

This is the spirit which from the beginning "moved upon the face of the waters." For neither can the Spirit act without the water, nor the water without the Spirit.

(Augustine[53])

Augustine would thus set the Johannine baptismal formula, "whoever is not born of water and the spirit, cannot enter the kingdom of God," in tehomic terms. In the liturgical collation of the waters of rebirth with the waters of chaos, the *ruach* of Genesis almost disrupts the *ex nihilo*. The Spirit *depends* upon water. No dry-handed birth will do. For persons or for universes: "let the sea too conceive and give birth." Did this sacramental birth *have* to supersede the mothers of flesh? One professional and feminist midwife, who coincidentally happens also to be literate in theology finds the Augustinian discourse on beginnings, "both spiritual and corporeal," to be satisfyingly "saturated with images of birth. The theologian labours with fear and elegance through the formless waters, the deep dark seas, the multiplications, figurative and literal, of sentient life and religious expression."[54] If women still hear an echo of their own search in his writing, this suggests no protofeminism on his part, but perhaps a possibility shunned, a road not taken, frozen within his brilliance. Thus Hannah Arendt credits his doctrine of creation with her revolutionary notion of "natality" and "plurality" in public life.[55] Natality challenges the western philosophical focus on mortality as the source of both anxiety and action. Arendt privileges "the fact of having become" over the fact that we will die. She having written her political philosophy as a German Jew during and after the Second World War, her intuition into this liberating natality cannot be taken lightly. She situates human freedom and thus the *political* freedom with which to resist totalitarianism in the notion of "beginning." "This very capacity for beginning is rooted in natality" (ibid., p. 147).[56] Beginning and birth are thus together radicalized: "Beginning, before it becomes a historical event, is the supreme capacity of man [sic]; politically, it is identical with man's freedom." She frequently cites this text: "*Initium ut esset homo creatus est*, 'that a beginning be made, man was created,' said Augustine. This beginning is guaranteed by each new birth."[57]

Might a theology of becoming not need to incorporate elements of this politics of natality?[58] Her hopeful reading of Augustine, who showed little interest in "each new birth" except as a locus of sin and immediate baptism, may be a bit forced. But her definition of our creaturely finitude through birth rather than death opens a new reading of the *ex nihilo*. Against Plato, in whom the lack of a definitive beginning serves conservative ends, she reads the Augustinian *initio* as a new beginning for thought.[59] While Arendt does not note the gender play around the sophic Mother, we glimpse in her political philosophy after all a certain Augustinian edge of social critique. Arendt does not interest herself in Augustine's birth mother or in modern feminism. But if we position the doubled mother Monica/Wisdom as the hinge of the two halves of the *Confessions*, Arendt's reading gains further plausibility. Thus the link between autobiography and cosmography proves to be a womb not only of spiritual inception but of political promise–the promise not of a beginning from nothing but from it *all*.

The divine Wisdom we follow does not now simply discard her antique visage, captured in the brilliant mirror of the upper waters. In carnal grace she changes faces. May the ice of paradise melt into a parched earth. May it flood without apocalypse into our restless species.

After too many tears we are still beginning. In *Your* hearing.

5

"STERILE WATERS"
Barth's nothingness that is

In that monstrous sphere even the Spirit of Elohim . . . is condemned to the complete impotence of a bird hovering or brooding over shoreless or sterile waters.

(Karl Barth)

I Nothing good

Of Genesis 1.2, Karl Barth writes that "this verse has always constituted a particular *crux interpretum*—one of the most difficult in the whole Bible." He finds it "small comfort to learn from Gunkel that it is a 'veritable mythological treasure chamber'" (III.1.102).[1] Barth's doctrine of creation registers the newly discovered mythic contamination of the Bible—especially by the material of the *Enuma Elish*—as hermeneutical emergency. If the early fathers repress the dark waters, if Augustine more indulgently sublimates them, Barth's opus performs their demonization. The biblical chaos floods again into view, after centuries of frozen invisibility. But now it returns as that which God has from the beginning "negated, rejected, ignored and left behind." In other words Barth's desublimation is not a nihilation but a repudiation. If the sparkling treasures of the tehom begin to lure us into the depths, here is a voice warning against the siren call of the waters: "Nothing good can or will emerge from this primeval flood" (III.1.105). If its cloak of primeval darkness seems to promise some renewal, to emit some luminosity of its own, Barth decries all poetics of the night: "Just as nothing that is good can come out of *tehom*, nothing that is good can come of darkness."[2] The Barthian deep is not nothing, but worse than nothing.

Needless to say, a tehomic theology will find "small comfort" in the *Church Dogmatics*. It is tempting to react in kind: to frame Barth as mere foil for a theology of becoming, even as he frames *tehom* as mere adversary for a theology of God's "absolute superiority and lordship." I do not promise to overcome the temptation. But merely to ignore or caricature this hugely influential dogmatics of the church, its sexism almost as famous by now as its anti-fascism, would be to miss a chaosmic

84

opportunity. Here the stakes of a *creatio ex profundis* become clear. In Barth's exegesis God creates not *from* nothing but *against* the "nothingness"–which is the chaos. Not only does a recognizable biblical creation motif reappear in this primal antagonism, but also Barth provides a kind of countermodern limit case for any tehomic deconstruction. For there is real peril in the deep. A tehomophilic exegesis can flood out the very difference it approaches.

II The new wave Barth

Barth meant to honor the creation-complex of finite and uncertain relations precisely by proclaiming the "infinite qualitative difference" of its Creator. But it is a postmodern Barth, a Barth read from within the semantic forcefield of Derrida's *différance*, who demands a tehomic hearing. This Barth is written by certain theologians whose acute sense of otherness–at once ethical and poststructuralist– seems at odds with the unrepentant patriarchy, biblicism and positivism of "the neo-orthodox Barth."[3] In his originative contribution to this Barthian new wave, Walter Lowe gleans from his Derridian reading of Barth a nuanced critique of the homogenizing Reason of modernity. Lowe acknowledges the oppositionalism of Barth's language of darkness vs. light, and the tendency for the "qualitative difference"–even after Barth had subtracted from it the "infinite"–to fall into oppositionalism. But he reads from Barth "with a final nod toward Derrida, an analogy of difference;" this difference–as he argues against Barth's critics–would not sacrifice creaturely distinctions to the one transcendent difference. On the contrary it interrupts the rendering of any finite reality as infinite and so as dedifferentiated. It frees creation from idolatry to "be what it is: various, many-faceted, a festival of innocent difference."[4] Barth's negation of the dark deep would then guard against "the night in which all cows are dark" (Hegel's ridicule of Schelling–to whom not coincidentally the present work is partial). Lowe reads this anti-dark by way of a "thematics of dimensionality." In Barth's *Roemerbrief* "'the wisdom of the Night' issues in folly 'because it holds firmly to a two-dimensional plane,' a plane persistently contradicted by actual occurrence."[5] This plane occludes "the new dimensional plane which is the boundary of our world and the meaning of our salvation." Indeed Lowe's dimensional commentary suggests the odd affinity between a tehomic multidimensionality and Barth's anti-tehomic polemic. So we remember with Barth that "to accept a contradiction and rest in it" (III.1.40) defines faith itself. But this rest can be only temporary: for to link a theology of creation from the chaos with its main opponent would comprise from his perspective the kind of contradiction that is "not hope, but a sorrowful opposition." Bearing in mind then the many historical oppositions–to Nazi paganism, a compromised German religious liberalism and the looming revolt of women–that distinguish Barth and his context from the postmodern, we return with him to the biblical text.

III The third possibility

The doctrine of creation according to Barth must secure the confession that "God is before the world in the strictest sense that He is its absolute origin, its purpose, the power which rules it, its Lord. For He created it" (III.1.7). So what to do with verse 2, which seems to undermine just that absolute origin? Barth unflinchingly repudiates Augustine's solution to verse 2–that God created the chaos as the raw material or first stage of creation–as too soft on the chaos. He then rejects Luther's version of this "desperate expedient." If there were any merit to this two-stage notion, with its "raw and rudimentary state" of creation, "it is inconceivable that he [the biblical author] should have remained silent about it" (III.1.103). He would have included it in "the work of the six days." "Such a silence", writes Barth, "could only spread great confusion not only over v. 1 but also everything that follows; the confusion into which we actually stumble." So any ambiguity about the chaos is strictly out of order. This chaos, this "glaring opposition to what is later described as God's good" (III.1.104), cannot serve as the material of creation.

Contrary to orthodoxy, however, including the neo-orthodoxy he spawned, Barth will not solve the problem by any return to the *ex nihilo* doctrine. "It may well be that the concept of a *creatio ex nihilo*, of which there is no actual hint in Genesis 1.2, is the construct of later attempts at more precise formulation." He is too faithful to the biblical text to have recourse to the classical formula. "But its antithesis–the mythological acceptance of a primeval reality independent of God–is excluded in practice by the general tenor of the passage as well as its position within the biblical context." So Barth seeks "a third possibility" (III.1.104).

As does a theology of becoming: it must also reject the alternatives of either a nonbiblical *ex nihilo* or "a primeval reality independent of God." The latter would not characterize a *creatio ex profundis*, which derives from the chaos of verse 2 an alternative to this very dualism of independence/dependence. Yet even if a tehomic third possibility may seem diametrically opposed to Barth's, we agree with him that "the dilemma in which we find ourselves by refusing both interpretations [*ex nihilo* and primeval independence] is not inconsiderable."

IV The intimacy of domination

Just as Barth suspected, the mythic intertextuality of verse 2, tucked microcosmically into a few mysterious metaphors, gives succor to those of us seeking a biblical starting-point before and beyond orthodoxy. He warns against its seductive sparkle: "the primeval waters and darkness, the *tohu wa-bohu*, can become to [the creature] an acute and enticing danger" (III.1.109). One notes the proximity of Barth's exegesis to the turn-of-the-century German painterly paraphernalia of mermaids, nixies and other watery feminine enticements. Admittedly a tehomic theology does take a certain risk of regression, the wrong-way womb, the tomb of difference, the in/difference that swamps excessive complexity; or, in Barth's words, "the darkness in which man cannot be man or can be only sleeping, intoxicated, dreaming man" (III.1.105). Sleep, dream and the altered state nonetheless remain sources, not enemies, of a tehomic creativity. If, however, Barth means "only" the darkness adrift in impossible possibilities, addictive desires or soporific peace, a kind of primary narcissism or dissolution of all boundaries, then even—or especially—feminist sensibility shares a related concern.

In a romanticism of chaos woman cannot be woman, even more surely than "man cannot be man." Any idealization of chaos as such threatens us with the peculiar cruelties of the Dionysian dissolution,[6] with a Great Mother of masculine projection and feminine essentialism; or with dispersal and indecision, the feminine sin diagnosed early in feminist theology over and against the sin of pride (Saiving, Plaskow, Nelson). The distinction of chaosmos from chaos, like that of connection from fusion, guards against the dedifferentiation or dissolution. It seeks to protect the difference of the other from self as well as of self from loss in the other. But if such protection is sought through the erection of a boundary against all chaos, a symbolic apparatus of domination will be required to maintain it. And that domination will produce its feminine Other as complement and threat.

In a limited sense Barth sought what feminism has since found: a radical relationalism, or intersubjectivity, in which difference is not swallowed up by the self, but enhanced. Serene Jones argues in a feminist poststructuralist register that Barth resembles Irigaray in situating himself "within language in such a way that it breaks open and internally subverts the traditional rules of reference that ground the 'logic of the same.'"[7] She finds the trinitarian reality of his God "radically multiple, radically relational, and infinitely active."[8] Sooner than most theologians, Barth sought to overcome the individualism of Enlightenment reason by means of a Reformation faith developed into a relational anthropology. Similarly, Suzanne Selinger has argued that he absorbed significant elements of the "dialogical personalism" of the 1920s, of which Buber was the most influential spokesperson. "Barth understood Buber thoroughly," she writes, "when he wrote in [*Church Dogmatics*] III.2: *Ich bin indem Du bist* ('I am in that thou art')." Barth can write persuasively of the correlation of the "being in relation to God" (*Sein in der Beziehung zu Gott*) and the "being in relation to cohumanity" (*Mitmenschen*).[9] Thus his reinscription of the *imago dei* as relational rather than an ontological endowment, mirroring the trinitarian interdependence of the Persons, signals his part in a hopeful shift of western thought. The present book continues that shift toward a difference *always* mixed up in relation.

Yet how can we receive Barth's supposed privilege of difference, when he marks the difference as "absolute" (i.e. "absolved" of relation): "absolute superiority" and "absolute origin"; and names as its enemy the very tehom which we had begun to read as difference itself—difference that precedes any sameness of origin? For us the mythic chaos articulates not so much a monstrous indifference but–in analogy to Derrida's *différance*, Whitehead's pluralist creativity, Ruether's "divine Matrix"–the differential matrix of all relations. How can we accept Barth's warning, agonistically hardened as it is against seduction by the dark waters, against, indeed, the vestiges of feminine divinity he would flush from faith? Any attempts "to find in it [tehom] more friendly images like those of a world-egg or a mother-womb which bears the future, forget that the author [of Genesis 1] undoubtedly knew this mythical conception but that his only possible object . . . is to contest it" (III.1.104). It is becoming evident that the reduction of female divinity to an idolatrous and chaotic matter underlies all orthodoxies. Indeed Barth's hypermasculine God imagery–intensified beyond that of much patristic discourse by his elimination of philosophical epithets such as Being, Logos, the Infinite, Wisdom–cashes all too readily into his systematic argument for the subordination of women. When he declares the tehom to be worse than nothing, does he not echo the gnostic abjection of Sophia's monstrous abortion more than the patristic *ex nihilo*? For the Barthian tehom designates "the barren, monstrous and evil cosmos."

V Dominating intimacy

What, according to Barth, does a tehom-positive hermeneutic put in jeopardy? Is it "the proposition that God created heaven and earth and man," and so the assertion that "this whole sphere is from God, willed and established by Him as a reality which is distinct from His own" (III.1.7)? Certainly without a radical distinction between the creatures and the divinity who desires them, the symbol of "creation" begins to implode. But Barth is not content with *distinction*–unless it means "that God is before the world; that *He is an absolutely distinct and individual being in relation to it*." In others it is the nature of God that is at stake: "*that* unlike the world *He belongs to Himself and controls Himself*; that He is *completely self-sufficient* because established and determined by Himself" (III.1.7; my emphases). Why is God's self-control in question? Does the chaos of the world put God's orderly nature in doubt?

Barth's attributions emanate from the foundational logic of metaphysical theology: that of the aseity, the independence or self-sufficiency, of God. Barth never suspends, not even in the depths of his Christology, the property of classical aseity. Barth wants this discourse to smash the idols of the modern self: *divine* self-control heightens in direct proportion to the mounting arrogance of *human* self-sufficiency (epistemo-logical, anthropological, ontological, political). Therein lies its "postmodern" work. But does this divine aseity–derived not from scripture as Barth presumes–not reinscribe precisely the ontotheology that funds modernity? Does the Creator, thus determined, not reinscribe at the origin of Christian faith the God of the philosophers?

The first article of the creed tenders, in Barth's rendition, "a knowledge which no man has procured for himself or ever will, which is neither native to him nor accessible by way of observation and logical thinking, for which he has no organ and no ability; which he can in fact achieve only in faith" (III.1.3). We might paraphrase sympathetically: our observations, indeed our selves as observers, remain perspectival constructions. Therefore any certainty, lodged in some property of my identity or some mastery of my universe, remains delusional. In this move Barth joins the critique of modern epistemological absolutes. But the tehomic affinity may not run much deeper than the overlapping criticisms of Modern Man. These Barthian negations of our "native" knowledge all shake out of his "*nein*" to natural theology, and enable the positivism of his supposedly credal and therefore *unnachfraglich*, "unquestionable," assertions of the classical attributes.[10] He can assert with certainty, "indeed as absolute and exclusive truth" (III.1.22), that the creation is what "comes first," that "all the things distinct from God begin with it," "excluding God Himself and His purpose, anything prior to this beginning, cannot even be imagined" (III.1.43).

Upon this exegesis rests his construction of the creation as "the external basis of the covenant;" and so of the covenant as "the internal basis of the creation." In terms of this foundational western logic of "external" and "internal," Barth presents the creation as a mere stage for the drama of salvation: "man and his whole universe as the theatre of the history of the covenant of grace." We–the external world, its creatures–have merely instrumental value, value *for* the creator. We are created for "His good-pleasure," from the fullness of his [*sic*] love. Yet this love reduces, in Reformation style, to the Father's love of the Son, who "covers" us. In order to reinforce our "absolute dependence," Barth returns to our Owner any properties that modern Man [*sic*] had tried to filch for himself. Thus–echoing Irenaeus' argument from nothing–the doctrine of creation secures first of all God's right of possession: "in the humanity and universe which are *God's creation and therefore His property*, and as such the object, scene and instrument of His acts" (III.1.44). Thus the dogma of creation as a relationship of "grace," i.e. unilateral dependency, rests upon the identification of God as absolute Owner and Origin.[11]

Is the (self-)possessive modern subjectivity that Barth denounces merely displaced upward, projected onto the propertied Lord in heaven? In an attempt to guard against both projection theory and the *analogia entis* (both of which rise from an improper "below") Barth insists upon the downward thrusting *analogia fides*.[12] How can human language speak thus from above? Because God is not only land-lord, but word-lord: even "our words are his property" (II.2.229); "in His revelation *God controls His property*, elevating our words to their proper use, giving Himself to be their proper object, and therefore giving them truth" (II.2.230). In other words God guarantees (in writing?) His property's proper theology. Against the certainty claims of human rationality, Barth pits–absolute certainty. "We are dealing with a faith that claims it does not have merely a relative certainty, but the *absolute, simple and indisputable certainty of God Himself*" (II.2.180). In the attempt to put Modern Man in his place,

Barth seems to have transferred to the Lord's account our most modern claims to certainty and property. Of course he does this to widen the difference between Creator and creature, so that the latter can finally be freed of "his" pretenses.

As, however, Lowe stresses, the post-*Romans* Barth drops the "infinite" from Kierkegaard's "infinite qualitative difference." The wholly Other incarnates in intimate proximity to the creature. Does this nuance lessen the dominological force of the continuing Barthian absolutism? Surely Barth is wrongly understood as maintaining a mere transcendence. Though "Jesus Christ" comprises the only point of divine immanence, "at this point we are *secured on all sides*" (III.1.25). It is God's Otherness that distinguishes "him" from finite creatures and thus *enables* "his" omnilateral presence in Christ. Does this version of total Presence mitigate the Greek ontology of divine self-sufficiency, however? Or does it intensify its ontotheology–and thus its potential for dominological abuse? Certainly we need not read Barth–or most mainline theology from the fathers on–as the mouthpiece of a merely absent Father, totalitarian Ruler, or distant infinity. But then it is not the specter of a detached transcendence that would pose the problem for justice. The problem would lie rather in the very *intimacy of domination*–in the "condescending" lordship inscribed in Christ's fully human and immanent love. The Barthian Lord is all-powerful in the possessiveness of this love. "God has in this other being an opposite, *a partner, who is completely subject to His lordship and under His control*" (III.1.25; my emphasis). This is *intimacy without reciprocity*. The He-God does not stay aloof, but through the incarnation consummates his loving control. He penetrates but is not penetrated.[13] He enters into relation freely and from above. This is "the unity of God with man effected in Jesus Christ." If He had not been absolutely alone *before* creation, then his unilateral rule over His creation now and in the future would be jeopardized. Did an eternity of solitary self-contemplation render him incapable of mutuality?

What "difference" does this discourse of dominance guarantee but that "complete subjection" for the subjects of the Lord above? If I may add an analogy "from below," indeed from "down there": it is domination up close, in the name of loving, jealous control, not domination at a distance, that drives women to the shelters.

VI The risk of creation

To secure this Lordship "on all sides" the power-point of origin cannot be allowed to leak. A leak could become a flood. A point as such has no "space" for a fissure. Thus the credal statement–*creavit*, "He created"–"encloses an event, a completed act" (III.1.13). There is no possibility here of a process with ambiguous beginnings and endings: its grammatical tense is that of an "incomparable perfect." Nothing can preexist the creation besides the cleanly bounded, self-sufficient Creator.[14] But the troubling grammatology of verse 2 remains. Barth will face its chaos manfully.

Barth reads the *tohu wa-bohu* as "the earth which is nothing as such, which mocks its Creator and can only be an offense to the heaven above it." Here is Barth's definition of the stuff: "It is that which is excluded from all present and future existence, i.e., chaos, the world fashioned otherwise than according to the divine purpose, and therefore formless and intrinsically *impossible*" (III.1.102; my emphasis). Is this "threatening curse" that God rejected from the start just a bad idea he conceived and rejected? Or more like a kind of parallel universe, a shadow world, "the reality of a creation that might be neutral or hostile to Him"–not nothing, but something real, the road not taken, the creation not created: not of an actuality but "the *possibility* which God in His creative decision ignored and despised"–which is at the same time "*formless and intrinsically impossible*" (III.1.102; my emphasis)? Thus we have here, after all, an anticipation, but in reverse, like a photo negative, of Derrida–for whom the impossible is the messianic, the promise, the Yes, the "impossible possibility." Barth struggles with his own anti-ontology in Volume III, in the context of the rejection of what is not elect (III.3.351). "Nothingness is not nothing . . . It 'is' nothingness" (III.3.349). Thus it "has as such its own being, albeit malignant and perverse" (III.3.352). If we could–which we cannot–free up this chaos from the weight of this demonization, its ontic paradox, its "being not being," would resonate not only to Augustine's nothingsomething but to the tehomic difference. In the meantime it displays the impossibility of the pure *nihil* of *ex nihilo*. For the nothingness always returns as the chaos–but then as the repressed.

Barth's reading of the chaos brings forth–along its way, the way of a *theologia viatorum* opened up precisely within this ambiguity–a further important dimension of the tehomic Other: "to posit the creature as such is undoubtedly a risk, since it is to posit a freedom which is distinct from the freedom of God." (III.1.109). From its freedom grow the evils, the malignancies which exploit life-supporting systems. When he gleans from verse 2 the risk for God, the risk of creating free creatures who "can reject their own creatureliness," I concur. All creativity entails the risk that the creature will turn malignant, indeed will turn against its creator. Even our own writings, loves, technologies, might turn against our intentions. The haze of indeterminacy surrounding every event includes the uncontrollable futures it stimulates–and some will sport hydra faces of ingratitude and betrayal, mockeries of our best efforts. But I read the tehom not as the evil, but as the active potentiality *for both good and evil*. So the capacity to resist any order, even a divine order, belongs to its indeterminacy. It gives rise to the destructive chaos in the universe as surely as–with divine wisdom–it gives birth to the beauties of complex order. Even a tehomophilic reading of verse 2 does not declare the chaos itself "good."

And so in proximity to Barth we may symbolize this risk as divine. Barth acknowledges the risk, but only to master it: "This is the undeniable risk which God took upon Himself in the venture of creation–but a risk for which He was more than a match and thus did not need to fear." Echoes of divine warrior and the *chaoskampf*?

Thus when Elohim first speaks, Barth hears "the radical crushing of the sovereignty of the element of chaos." This sounds like the Leviathan-busting God of Psalm 74, not the monster-loving God of Psalm 104 *or* Genesis 1. Barth thus finds here that "the infinite waste of waters is revealed as the . . . death of every possibility of life" (III.1.133). How does he then, in the face of the text, contrive to dam(n) these deadly waters? With the exegetical ingenuity of Augustine, but with far more tehomic panic, he makes of the sky itself a dam: the firmament that separates the waters now "forms the unbreachable wall between the waters. It breaks their infinity" (III.1.133). The idea of an infinite universe, for which Bruno burnt at the stake, threatens always to break the conceptual walls of a nice, controlled creation. Barth cannot conceive of the finitude of creatures nesting within an open infinity–the creation would not then comprise a finished and enclosed event. For the most part, however, Barth's God does not need to fight. The imaginary of a sovereign Lord more powerful than the warrior Marduk prevails. He dominates not with sword but word.

Barth's theology thus stands with one foot in the scriptural tehomophobia (the chaos is real) and the other in the effortless sovereignty of the *ex nihilo* (the chaos is nothing). Without the "freely uttered and freely repeated Word of the grace of God, the cosmos has no real guarantee against precipitation into chaos" (III.1.109). Does faith then demand a guarantee? Does the guarantee override the risk? Barth situates a risk in verse 2 that seems–appropriately–continuous: "It is not by the use but the misuse of this freedom that man can look back and return to that past and *conjure up the shadow of Genesis 1.2*, thus enabling that past to defy its own nature and to become present and future" (III.1.109; my emphasis). This "shadow" of our text threatens to trap time into its past. Just to read the text sympathetically is to be drawn into its hermeneutical hex: "God will not allow the cosmos to be definitively *bewitched and demonized* or His creation totally destroyed, nor will he permit the actual realization of the *dark possibility of Genesis 1.2*" (III.1.109; my emphases). He thus resorts to the rhetoric of witch-hunt to mark the face of the deep. "That chaos can also become present and future cannot alter the fact that it is essentially the past, the possibility negated and rejected by God." What is this strange temporality of chaos, which sucks us toward a feminized, paganized past? In an appealing reflection on the goodness of created time, Barth affirms mutability itself. It has its "own grace" as the time "which does not flee but flows" (III.1.75). But chaos renders the flux a flight, having "no real present and therefore no real past and future, no center and therefore no beginning and no end" (III.1.72). By defining chaos as the "essential past," Barth interprets the P-narration of an uncreated preexistence of the chaos. "Genesis 1.2 speaks of the 'old things' which according to II Cor. 5.17 have radically passed away in the death and resurrection of Jesus Christ. It tells us that even from the standpoint of the first creation, let alone the new, chaos is really 'old things,' the past and super-seded essence of this world." So the "essence" of the creation, the creation before Christianity, is this superseded evil? Marcion casts a long shadow indeed.

Yet despite the tortured effort to lock the chaos into a "non-recurring past," God is still out there battling it volumes later as *das Nichtige*. Now we read that it "is *always present*—as it were on the frontier of the cosmos to which He has given being. It continually calls this cosmos in question" (III.3.76; my emphasis). This shift to present struggle has potent biblical and contextual resonances.[15] However, Barth inadvertently but irresistibly reinscribes two violent aggressions of western modernity (perhaps straining Lowe's hopeful reading of the Barthian cure for modern violence): the "frontier" of European colonization of dark chaotic peoples; and witch-hunts. War against the people of chaos: perhaps I should not read his metaphors according to the letter. What then of "the spirit"?

VII The impotent spirit

What, indeed, of the divine spirit who seems in Genesis 1.2 content to oscillate intimately upon the dark waters? Recognizing the threat to the total divine sovereignty posed by any tolerance (even that of Augustine and Luther) of the biblical chaos, he takes extreme measures:

> Our only option is to consider v. 2 as a portrait, deliberately taken from myth, of the world which according to His revelation was negated . . . and to which there necessarily belongs also the "Spirit of *Elohim*" who is not known in His reality and therefore hovers and broods over it *impotently because wordlessly*. (III.1.108)

"Impotently because wordlessly." Barth bravely unmasks the Spirit of verse 2 as a hoax. Impotent because speechless. "How could this be the God who is seen to speak and act in v. 3ff.? How could we recognize in Him, even vaguely, the God of the rest of the Old and New Testaments? Where in the Bible is there any suggestion that this *passive-contemplative* role and function is ascribed to God?" (III.1.107). Indeed this quiet, listening, spirit, this rhythmic entrainment of Elohim with the waters, does not conform to the bellowing meta-narrative of the Word. For Barth this is the nonnegotiable: that the *Holy* Spirit cannot be quiet. This God hears no others to their speech: He is to be heard and obeyed. The medium of creation is purely verbal. Such countertextual logocentrism—yes, in the full Derridean sense of the transcendental privilege of the oral over the text—should perhaps not come as a shock. For the Protestant mainstream, prayer is speech, silence liturgically wasteful, and Roman Catholic contemplation suspiciously heathenish (let alone Asian meditation!). "This God who for His part has become a caricature" is for Barth the God of this monstrous, rejected, tehomic world.

And so Barth proposes his "third possibility"—that these caricatures of the good world and its Creator are themselves being caricatured; that the author is cleverly mocking that which mocks the Creator. "If what is characterized at the start is the utter irrelevance and untrustworthiness of the god of myth, in conscious and cutting contrast to the real God of creation and His work and in a picture of devastating irony, at once everything becomes clear" (III.1.108). One must admire Barth's audacity: he has outed the Spirit of God as an impotent monstrosity. He can now read verse 2 as an intentional parody of paganism. But it is mainly "myth" (perhaps given its dangerous repristination through Bultmann's form criticism of biblical mythology) which he fights here with biblical "irony." In the same chapter he had insisted that myth is ironic, whereas "the biblical creation saga speaks . . . without irony." But Barth does not let contradictions quiet him. Preoccupied like Calvin with the endless religious production of idols, Barth finds the writer of Genesis posting a preemptive warning. Thus we are to imagine that the priestly narrator inserted a one-line parody into the first words of the otherwise solemn creation narrative.

Intriguingly Barth's solution to the exegetical emergency of verse 2 releases a flood of sexual imagery. Biblical criticism has given credence to "the idea, known already to the apostolic fathers," Barth observes, "that this hovering and fluttering bird is 'brooding,' and therefore to the ancient and widespread myth of a world-egg from which heaven and earth originally emerged" (III.1.107). The gender of the bird itself slides menacingly between mother and male: "In that monstrous sphere even the Spirit of Elohim . . . is condemned to the complete impotence of a bird hovering or brooding over shoreless or sterile waters . . . This God who for His part has become a caricature would be the God of this world" (III.1.107). So the impotent bird hovers over sterile waters: Barth bats a double-whammy for Protestant virility. An inadequate masculinity "flutters" above an abortive femininity.[16] As to the queer *motherhood* of the bird, Barth admits unhappily that the text does seem to allude to "the ancient and widespread myth of a world-egg from which heaven and earth originally emerged" (III.1.107). Such a maternity of the mother bird over the waters would suggest the view that "by reason of God's faithfulness chaos has the opportunity and capacity to develop from within into the cosmos." This is what Barth cannot tolerate: from the rest of the chapter, he argues, building upon Gunkel, that "the existence of the cosmos is not in any sense effected by a *development from within*, but by the will and deed of a God who disposes and acts *without any presuppositions*" (III.1.107; my emphasis). Without conditions–from outside. Any maternity of spirit or its waters would veer far from the theater, performing instead more evolutionary theories of emergence, theories that might now emphasize the self-organizing complexity of creation. As such it would relativize God's omnipotence.[17] As for most theists still: God is *either* omnipotent *or* He is impotent. No relational third space can be admitted. Any concept therefore of a generative chaos, a spontaneous natality, must be sterilized.[18] As to any God who demonstrates queer male or any female propensities–Barth kills both birds with a single stone

VIII Her contempt for order

"He" will continue to empower the icons of masculine supremacy, and *ipso facto* of an absolute and so absolutely defeminized origin. If Barth's doctrine of creation evinces such an iconic sexual intensity, then his doctrine of "Man and Woman" can regrettably not be by-passed like some embarrassing, time-bound accident. "A precedes B, and B follows A. Order means succession. It means preceding and following."[19] Does Barth's gender logic only make explicit and literal motives that otherwise remain metaphorically indirect, to be teased out of the small print of bigger matters? "It is here that we see the order outside which man cannot be man nor woman be woman" (III.4.169). Within his gender-doctrine the language of "order" dominates the text: "The woman as behind and subordinate to man, ordered, related, directed to man and thus to follow the initiative which he must take . . . properly speaking, the business of woman, her task and function, is to actualize the fellowship in which man can only precede her, stimulating, leading and inspiring" (III.4.171). To this rule "the only alternative is disorder" (III.4.169). In other words in the subordination of woman to man lies the social template of chaos-control: the very bottom line of the Creator's dominance and defeat of tehom.

This "order" that he repeatedly appeals to (not to be identified, presumably, with "the order of nature" of natural theology) must be read in the context of his own relationalism, with its trinitarian and anthropological openings. But when it comes to opposing the women's movement,[20] *the order* takes precedence over any other understanding of relationship. It is "the true order which God the Creator has established, succession, and therefore precedence and following, super and subordination." The imaginary of *Ordnung*, like masculinity not overtly divinized in his doctrine of creation vs. chaos, seems to have been provoked by feminism into uninhibited display. Yet its logic hardly represents an anomalous gesture. It flows from his doctrine of revelation. The difference of our "knowledge of God" from all other knowledge "is that the position of the knowing man in relation to this object is the position of a fundamentally and irrevocably determined subsequence, of a *subsequence* which can in no way be changed or reinterpreted into a *precedence* of man. It is the position of grace" (II.1.21; my emphases). In other words, God is to Man (the species) as Man (the sex) is to Woman. Woman is written anew in Barth's text as object of a man's knowledge. The "position of grace" for women only redoubles her position of "irrevocable subsequence."

With cunning Paulinism, Barth clarifies that the "inner equality" that this order of creation confers–that of Galatians "neither male nor female"–means that the order "demands subjection and obedience, it affects equally all whom it concerns." In other words woman's duty of subordination is *equal* to man's duty of superiority. Without any disavowal he draws the Pauline analogue to the spiritual "equality" of slave to master (III.4.164).[21] He recognizes what is at stake: "every word is dangerous and liable to be misunderstood when we try to characterize this order. But it exists. And everything else is *null and void* if its existence is ignored" (III.4.169). He does not want to gird up a crude misogyny. But the very order of creation–its ability to withstand the void, the nothingness of tehom herself!–is on the line.

He addresses male abuse. Such a male, Barth judges, is himself violating the order. But the woman violates the order if she protests the violation. "It may well be that *her protesting and rebelling spring from the same source of contempt for order* with which man offends her so deeply." So under abusive circumstances she should continue to obey the order–by obeying the disordered man. The oppressive undertones of intimate Power thus reverberate through the entire *Ordnung* of creation. Within the "freedom in community" that he advocates, one's main obligation is to "be together" as man and woman. But Barth's relationalism snags on his (hetero)sexism as surely as upon his classical theism.[22]

Barth's understanding of love transfers from God to humanity via his *analogia relationis*. In developing his idea of creation, he asserts that "Love wills to love. Love wills something with and for that which it loves" (III.1.95). Surely. But Barth discerns no vulnerability in that desire. *Au contraire*: "He cannot have set a limit to His glory, will and power" (III.1.95). Thus the signifiers of sex/gender run continuously through the symbolic apparatus of His power. The unlimited He-will sets clear limits for "man and woman." Man is to woman as Creator is to creation, as God is to Israel and church. So of course woman herself does not represent the chaos–*except when she gets out of order*. Then chaos becomes incarnate as the woman who rebels, who makes "gender trouble" (Butler); it unhinges the heterosexual dyad of our creation in the image of God; and the *straight* a-to-b order of creation threatens to break up. The linearity of its time is to be neatly reproduced in the "succession" of A to B.

"We must be clear that relationship does not mean transition and dissolution." Relationship for Barth presupposes and must reproduce clear boundaries. I had myself argued that the dissolution of self in relation was for woman a special peril.[23] Yet his identification of dissolution with transition–implying that the boundaries are to be fixed–goes elsewhere. Relationship "does not mean a denial of one's own sex or an open and secret exchange with its opposite. On the contrary, it means a firm adherence to this polarity and therefore to one's own sex, only insofar as such adherence is not self-centered but expansive, not closed but open . . ." Does "gender fidelity" (Irigaray) require polarity? What kind of "openness" is this, in which no exchange, no equal force, no reciprocity of influence, is possible? An expansion that purges the dark residues, the traces of oceanic wombs and fluttering bisexuals, from its frontiers? Once again–to characterize the master paradigm as much as to single out Barth–the (te)homophobic boundary patrol is guarding at once divine omnipotence and heterosexual potency.[24]

IX *Creatio* vs. *nihilo*

Still, perhaps, Barth's dialogical personalism, in its (almost) postmodern attention to difference, pressures this order of phobic boundaries. According to Selinger's feminist assessment, Barth's notion of "the I–Thou relationship of male and female" includes also a "compelling, mature theology of relationality." This is not mere apologetics. "As I address [the other] I allow myself to unsettle and distrust him/her by drawing attention to the fact that I am there too."[25] Appealing to postmodern readers, she points to a "vocabulary that persists" in *Church Dogmatics* "when he evokes the God who is not genial and affirming but radically questioning and abrogating of the certainties of human existence. It is the vocabulary of decentering, of the overwhelming encounter with the wholly Other."[26] In the relations between "the sexes" no one who wishes to live humanly "can escape this unsettlement, this criticism and tension." Nor, as he well knows, can any human theology.

Barth's occasional bouts of self-critical irony keep the tension alive. He notes the "temptation" of a vicious circle, "*circulus vitiosus*," just where he thinks–and he does think–he is moving in the *circulus veritatis Dei*. He calls (praise God) for a theological "deassurance" (cf. I.3), wondering whether in fact he has been "chasing a shadow." For "we may certainly have represented and understood the veracity of cognition, but not the veracity of cognition of God."[27] Thus "the final consolation and security," he writes, may "consist in a simultaneous insecurity and destruction." The postmodern Barth stands within this insecurity. Reading here an omen of Derrida, Graham Ward delights in this "rhetorical strategy presenting both the need to do and the impossibility of doing theology." Where "the Word stands in utter contradiction to words," writes Ward, "it is allowed to stop the text."[28]

Such an interruption would be welcome. The Other of the text might get a Word in edgewise. Another postmodern heir of Barth, Joerg Rieger, wonders if theologians remain "unaware that they might have substituted their own words for the Word and confused the two."[29] Rieger attributes to Barth (following Lacan) "the discourse of the master." Admiring Barth's critique of the modern self, Rieger nonetheless suspects that by presumptively doing away with the self, "the discourse of the master merely seems to repress its own troubles" (Barth's acknowledged "temptation"). The object of its repression inevitably then "comes back to haunt us." Is that returning object the very shadow Barth chases? A shadow that turns and menaces the theologian? The chaos that could not be expelled as mere nothing roars back as a revolting Nothingness; the Nothingness morphs from the nonrecurring past tense to a threatening and persistent present. Confusingly, this tehom is first declared "not an adversary to God;" but then, *doch*, "it is His enemy no less than ours."[30] This (chaotic) slippage of the signifiers, this unacknowledged flux, suggests perhaps the dilemma of every project of dominance: divine or human, it must produce the monsters that at once justify its control and mock its mastery.

So there are a couple of dominological apologies that do not work for me. First, that by asserting *God's* dominance, faith breaks the idols of *human* dominance. Such a claim merely spins the vicious circle of language. Theologies of analogy have this right: since we will use anthropomorphic God-talk, we should at least use the best possible images. Would this not require of us metaphors arising from non-hierarchical, democratizing visions of sociality, not metaphors of totalizing economic and political order? The second apology might suggest that a violent context justifies the demonization of chaos. One might explain the case at hand in terms of the Nazi demolition of civil and humane orders. Barth's willingness to invest his international prestige as a churchman in a risky public confession may have saved the possibility of a morally legitimate Protestantism. But I would have thought that his protest against National Socialism would have sharpened his suspicion of the high value of order: the terror of Nazism once it achieved state power lay not in anarchy but in its use of "chaos"—especially as Jewish contaminant of racial purity—to justify its unprecedented, its total, *Ordnung*. Should the European experience of ungodly orders not have put into question the assumption that order is always better than chaos?[31]

In the love-coated Christian dominology evil continues to be identified with chaos, disruption and revolt. We may thank Barth for rendering the logic of order honestly. So honestly, in fact, that he inadvertently initiates its own deconstruction. If the omnipotent self-sufficiency of the classical deity had originally established the *creatio ex nihilo*, that same God performs in Barth a *creatio anti nihilo*. And here the paradigm frays along its frontier. For if "from the standpoint of the first creation, let alone the new, chaos is really 'old things'" (III.1.110), how could the Nothingness become "His adversary"? "How, then, can it still assail, oppose, resist and offend Him? How can it concern Him? But we must not pursue this thought to its logical end" (III.3.356). Indeed. For the fissure in the fantasy of this self-sufficient omnipotence must prohibit critical thought at just this point: the chaos of theodicy shows its face, the threat of an impossibility not of the tehom but of the purely good, purely dominant creator. Is the notion of an independent chaos merely the shadow cast by the independence of the classical Creator from nothing? If so, no wonder Barth seeks (as we do) a third option.

X *Theologia viatorum*

As in his doctrine of sex, so in his doctrine of God, an ineradicable boundary cuts against the possibility of a true interdependence. Despite his powerful trinitarian, Christological and anthropological motions toward a radical relationalism, Barth remains surprisingly captive, I claimed, to the God of the philosophers: there can be "no other person or thing conditioning Him standing in relation to Him. God is *a se*" (I.1.179). He staples the personal attributes of the biblical God to that aseity. Despite the pressure both from the chaotic nothingness on His bad side and love for the creature on His good side, this deity remains unconditioned, therefore unmoved and unaffected, by His (ever graciously condescending) relations to His dependants. But Barth's creation vs. nothingness recaptures the vibrancy of the biblical *chaoskampf*, which in its belligerent patriarchy at least immersed God in the struggles of history. Unlike the biblical tehom, however, Barth's chaos, its bizarre "sovereignty" liquidated on "the second day," became a creature: "It threatens and will threaten. It is and will be a sign that creation could have been the catastrophe of the creature; that the creature had no power to avert this; and that it was God alone who averted it. Itself a creature, it cannot and will not be again a catastrophe to its fellow-creature" (III.1.133). Perhaps in a time of terror, some will find comfort in this promise. A tehomic theology would in this sense concur: our catastrophes are only relative to the infinite life of the creation.

I have read Barth's ridicule of the *ruach elohim* as an autodeconstruction of the *ex nihilo* tradition. Barth's desublimation of the chaos demonstrates from within the logic of orthodoxy itself the instability of the *ex nihilo* doctrine. Thus tehom–albeit only as monstrous–does at least breach the surface of the Barthian signifiers. And it is in the very context of this breach, this turbulent, unthinkable aporia, that Barth offers to a theology of becoming a way through the waters: a "theology on the way." For it is precisely on the threshold of analysis of the problem of nothingness–and so of theodicy and its "contrast between God's holiness and His omnipotence"– that Barth articulates an alternative to his own positivism. In the face of this tehom, "we soberly acknowledge that we have here an extraordinarily clear demonstration of the necessary brokenness of all theological thought and utterance. There is no theological sphere where this is not noticeable. All theology is *theologia viatorum*." I do not read this admission as another prohibition of thought, an evasion of self-contradiction. "[Theology] can never satisfy the natural aspiration of human thought and utterance for completeness and compactness" (III.3.293). The humble recognition of this brokenness, this running breach and fissure, will lead him down a different path than that of the tehomic wake. Nonetheless for us the deep remains the very name, place and open end of that brokenness.

In the meantime it sends us back to biblical hermeneutics to negotiate a "third possibility" that, with Barth, rejects both the *ex nihilo* and an independent preexistence of chaos. For the very concept of such *independence* belongs not to "myth" but to the separative work of the dominological order. The divinization of independence–as aseity–casts this chaotic independence as its own shadow, its fear and its female. How little has this nightmare of nothingness to do with the sensitive interdependence of the spirit vibrating upon the waters. Does the lost treasure, the pearl of great value, lie buried not beneath the text of Genesis (as in some antique "treasure chamber") but rather within it: in the surface and on the way of its lost and despised Deep?

Part III

MONSTERS OF HERMENEUTICS

When Leviathan is the text, the case is altered.
(Herman Melville, *Moby Dick*)

6

"SEA OF HETEROGLOSSIA"

Return of the biblical chaos

Rabbi Yehuda the son of Simon opened: "And He revealed deep and hidden things" (Daniel 2.22). In the beginning of the creation of the World, "He revealed deep things, etc." For it says "In the beginning God created the heavens," and He did not interpret. Where did He interpret it?

(Bereshit Rabbah[1])

Rather has the world become "infinite" for us all over again, inasmuch as we cannot reject the possibility that it may include infinite interpretations. Once more we are seized by a great shudder; but who would feel inclined immediately to deify again after the old manner this monster of an unknown world?

(Nietzsche, The Gay Science[2])

I Hermeneutical haggling

Hovering close to the field of biblical criticism, might theology negotiate not just a hermeneutic of the tehom but a tehomic hermeneutic? I have argued that the presumption of *creatio ex nihilo* pretty much kept the lid on Genesis 1.2 after the second century ACE. But the late nineteenth-century recovery of mythic antecedents injected a new interpretive potentiality into the study of scripture. We observed in the last chapter how the opening of the "mythological treasure chamber" seriously disturbed the most influential Protestant theology of the twentieth century. But theology has largely disregarded the mounting biblical case against the *ex nihilo*—a case that as we shall see, however, does not represent any simple consensus within its own discipline. Indeed the hermeneutical ruptures and divergences themselves intimate "this monster of an unknown world." In this chapter, we negotiate a theological pathway through the bifurcating history of recent biblical interpretations.

"Negotiation," as not only Derrida but also the new historicists and postcolonial theorists deploy the term, retains a useful taint of political interest, engagement, bargaining.[3] Graham Ward transacts its theological significance as "the economy of textuality itself": "negotiation suggests suspicion of intentionality (one's own and the other's); it suggests that each participant in any encounter comes heavily laden with presuppositions and previous contexts; it suggests that the movement in the transfer being performed is slippery and not necessarily progressive."[4] Suspicion of intentionality does not abrogate intentionality; it complicates it. Because we are so deeply mired in contexts that bottom into innumerable overlapping contexts, the politics of our textual transactions lacks purity. An engaged hermeneutics negotiates not from a fixed identity (as, for instance, of Christian/woman/white) but from the slippery strength of an enlarged politics (a Christianity enmeshed in Judaism and in resistance to the biblical patriarchies, which themselves resist imperial patronization while enmeshed in ethnicities and universalisms among which "whiteness" is a late and devastating mutation; etc.). In this way the interpretive situation multiplies its relations, its perspectives and therefore its truths logarithmically, like the fractals of chaos; or Nietzsche's infinite: "once more we are seized by a great shudder."

By contrast to a tehomic hermeneutic–which negotiates whenever possible with monsters, those called or calling "monsters"–the warrior-hero modeled civilization on the violent purity of nonnegotiation. Indeed Marduk's power is predicated on his constituency's confessed fear of negotiation with the monstrous mother. In the foregoing chapters we have seen the chaos waters repressed, sublimated and diabolized. But they have not stopped moving. We are beginning to discern in their movement the motion of another theology: another *theologia viatorum*, one that has given up the straight path for an endless labyrinth of interpretation. It would be "moving and changing every part of the time: the travelling inkhorn (possibly pot), the hare and turtle pen and paper, the continually more and less inter-misunderstanding minds of the anticollaborators" (Joyce). But isn't *understanding* not only the skill of negotiation but the keystone of hermeneutics? Is the possibility of a tehomic hermeneutic then already, like Tiamat, dead in the water?

II Tehomic regress

> Thus the "object" is not as massive, as resistant, as one might wish to
> believe. And her possession by a "subject," a subject's desire to
> appropriate her, is yet another of his vertiginous failures . . . The quest
> for the "object" becomes a game of Chinese boxes. Infinitely receding.
>
> (Irigaray, *Speculum*[5])

So I realize that an espousal of the hermeneutical tradition may jeopardize the present endeavor. Inasmuch as biblical interpretation shares the hermeneutic theorized by Schleiermacher, Dilthey, Bultmann, Gadamer and perhaps Ricoeur, the desire for "understanding" suggests the subject's "need to know" its object.[6] The very project of understanding signals a certain Enlightened respect for the discourse of the Other, originatively framed as the Jewish Other of the ancient biblical text. But at the same time, and within the ongoing context of western modernity, understanding readily translates as *appropriation*. The theological discipline of hermeneutics largely stems from Schleiermacher's attempt to situate theology within the modern university as belonging to a cluster of religious *Wissenschaften*. Without his attention to communal standpoints, epistemic relationality, and the priority of affect, Christianity might not have undergone a hermeneutical conversion at all. Yet he nonetheless relies upon a recognizable, modern rationality: thus hermeneutics means "to understand as well as and better than the author."[7] Gadamer, likewise, defines the goal of understanding as "the assimilation of what is said" in the textual tradition "to the point that it becomes one's own." Indeed he concludes in no uncertain terms: the hermeneutical practice of "questioning and research," while unlike the methods of science implicating the "knower's own being," is "a discipline that guarantees truth."[8]

Does hermeneutics thus secure the property rights of the knowing subject? The object is found and fixed–emancipated from a chaos to which it often ungratefully returns. (Such an understanding gesture would thus modestly mirror the *ex nihilo*, by which we have seen the Creator's ownership of the creation routinely reaffirmed.) Appropriation, at any rate, shuts down negotiations; the hermeneutical circle would then close what it opens. Thus the poststructuralist revolt against what Nietzsche had criticized as the "timeless knowing subject" opposes the *différance* of writing itself to what Derrida (haggling with Nietzsche over "the question of the woman") called "the hermeneutical project." This style of interpretation "postulates a true sense of the text."[9] That is, the interpretive process aims at its own closure. But in the interest of reopening the text would we cease to try to understand–and thus to understand the resistance of the Other to being known? Indeed, if in order to avoid appropriation we posit the text as an incommensurable alien, its alterity protected by a metaphysical abyss, do we not exercise an inversion of the same fixative reason? Does the separative gesture not merely complement the inclusive and appropriative reason?

Let me suggest that another option exists, implied within both traditions. It insists upon hermeneutics as always first of all *interpretation* and only secondarily and tenuously *knowledge*. Understanding then takes place as a relational, therefore relativizing, effect of interpretation. Nietzsche called not for ignorance but for a perspectival knowledge. Such knowledge is generated by an incessant interpretive process: "so that one knows how to employ *a variety of perspectives and affective interpretations* in the service of knowledge."[10] Without disciplining itself to Nietzsche or his *Uebermensch*, this project presumes such an endless and affecting play of perspectives. No feat of understanding can terminate its motion. Inasmuch, then, as hermeneutics secures its objects, Nietzsche's repudiation obtains: when "'to understand' means merely: to be able to express something new in the language of something old and familiar." The qualifying "merely" matters–a theology of becoming does not dissociate from the old either in its strangeness or its familiarity. Otherwise we perpetrate a modernist originality. Interpretation pursues understanding as a creative negotiation with the past, not as novelty *ex nihilo*.

"In the beginning is hermeneutics." Interpretation as *process in infinitum* requires of theology an immense, haggling recoil back into its ancient writings. Only so do we spring forward into our current interactivities. The chaos of our verse may open up unfamiliar understandings. But how would they not escape the "vertiginous failure" of a history that nihilates what it cannot appropriate?

III In the beginning was murder

> The evil wind he let loose in her face.
>
> (*Enuma Elish*)

By slaughtering the salt-water goddess, "she who gave birth to them all," the splendid young Marduk rises to supremacy. Since the *Enuma Elish* served not just to commemorate the cosmogonic deed, but to justify therewith the political hegemony of the city-state of Babylon, we are not surprised to read its raw will to power. His heroic deed was based on a negotiation to end all negotiation:

> If I am indeed to be your avenger, to vanquish Tiamat and to keep you alive, convene the assembly and proclaim my lot supreme . . .
>
> May I through the utterance of my mouth determine the destinies, instead of you. Whatever I create shall remain unaltered.[11]

Here, before monotheism proclaims its own lot supreme, a warrior God claims the prerogatives of a creator, *by word alone*, of *an unchanging order*. Scholars after Gunkel's *Schöpfung und Chaos in Urzeit und Endzeit* (1895) assumed multiple parallels between Genesis 1 and the *Enuma Elish*, including the derivation of *Tehom* from the Semitic root for *Tiamat*.[12] Many follow Von Rad, however, in insisting that "the actual mythical meaning . . . has been long since lost in our text."[13]

One wonders how many meanings can get "lost in our text"? Where do they go? "Down there?" Into the zone that Von Rad wishes to purge from the signifying field of the text? "We must reject even the assumption that the Priestly document necessarily had to fall back on strange and half mythological ideas to make clear the chaotic primeval state." Referring this primeval state to the fecundity of the waters, Albright has to admit that "the *ruah elohim* was evidently still thought of as exercising a 'sexual' influence upon the tehom." He was rejecting the view that "the *ruah* corresponds to the winds which Marduk sends against Tiamat."[14] Sex and violence leak into the text. An oneiric, mythically coded chaos permeates the creation texts of the Bible. Why would important prehistories—however disturbing—of the signifier so conveniently "get lost"? Is it perhaps more likely, given the context of the priestly narrator under the colonizing power of Babylon, that the mythic intertext mediates something of a "political unconscious of the text" (F. Jameson)?

Especially disturbing to a tehomic theology would be the possible parallel to Genesis 1:2c of the wind, Marduk's doomsday weapon. "He created the *imhullu*: the evil wind, the cyclone, the hurricane, the fourfold wind, the sevenfold wind, the whirlwind, the wind incomparable."[15] Confronting Tiamat amidst her entourage of newly spawned monsters, he accuses the creator of the universe of having criminally usurped the authority of her sons. As she opens her mouth in fury:

> He drove in the evil wind, in order that [she should] not [be able] to close her lips.
> The raging winds filled her belly;
> Her belly became distended, and she opened wide her mouth.
> He shot off an arrow, and it tore her interior.[16]

A traditional medium of insemination, the wind is blasted into her mouth, causing her belly to balloon out in a deadly parody of pregnancy.[17] The epic proceeds with gory details of her slaughter, his victory and his construction of the cosmos from her oceanic carcass. The power of prepatriarchal goddesses must yet have posed some ideological resistance to Babylonian goals. Marduk mocks both Tiamat and those who fear her specifically with her gender: "What man is it who has brought battle against thee? Tiamat, who is a woman, is coming against thee with arms!" (Tablet II, 110f.).[18] Thus an older creation imaginary, that of birth from the salt-waters of a goddess, must be denigrated. The new masculine creation is performed as satiric aggression against the mother's body, to be replayed annually at the festival of the new year. I had earlier characterized such cosmological matricide as "the theological psychology of the West"[19] and left the question open as to how to read the Genesis parallel. The question, undecidable in purely historical terms, still opens wide as Tiamat's mouth.

Must we, for instance, decode the *ruach* vibrating over the deep as the monotheistic version (whether borrowed or shared) of the vile wind breaking in the face of a disfigured mother? Von Rad suggests that *ruach elohim* "is better translated as 'storm of God,' i.e., terrible storm."[20] This tradition transparently distances the *ruach* from God "Himself," protecting God from its materiality and reducing Spirit to an inanimate emission. But within the text itself, does the biblical storm provide cover for a silent reassassination of the goddess, all the more efficient because the original matricide was already neatly taken care of by the Babylonian enemy? Is the patriarchal supersession (of what? surely no matriarchy, not even an egalitarianism, but perhaps a matrilineage capable of constraining the warriors?) so total as to require just such subliminal reminders? Does a mere glint of the sword behind the word suffice to preserve the nonnegotiable, immaterial masculinity of God?

As, however, Von Rad observes, "Genesis, Ch. 1, does not know the struggle of two personified cosmic primordial principles; not even a trace of one hostile to God can be detected!"[21] This is a crucial absence. Yet neither does Von Rad find a trace of the "mythically objective world dragon, Tiamat." He insists that "the tehom has no power of its own; one cannot speak of it at all as though it existed for itself alone, but it exists for faith only with reference to God's creative will, which is superior to it."[22] Of course neither does one find within the biblical text any trace of these disclaimers. They record the anxiety of the Christian interpreter more than the theology of the Hebrew priest. Such standard textual control almost seems to echo the nervous closing incantation of the *Enuma Elish*:

> May he subdue Tiamat, may he distress her life, and may it be short!
> Until future (generations of) [people], when the (present) days have
> grown old,
> May she retreat without hindrance, may she withdraw forever![23]

It seems that this she-chaos can never be dead enough. Such apotropaic verses justified the annual Babylonian ritual of world-renewal through matricide. The sacred and habitual violence against "our bearer, who hates us"[24] produces a new sociomythical order. Out of various tribal confederations, agricultural villages and cyclic nomads the hypermasculinized slave-state of Babylon forges "civilization." So the question must continue to haunt the interpretive process: did this evil wind really get "lost" within the *ruach elohim*, and *Tiamat* behind *tehom*? Or does the *Enuma Elish* (or some Canaanite analogue) lie "within" the text as its prototype? What sort of *within*—concealment, consumption, pregnancy, entombment—would the text embody? Might a tehomic hermeneutic entertain another option, reflective perhaps of the complex relations of Israel to its neighbors?

IV Deep detritus

> Intertextuality is, in a sense, the way that history, understood as cultural and ideological change and conflict, records itself within textuality. As the text is the transformation of a signifying system and of a signifying practice, it embodies the more or less untransformed detritus of the previous system. These fragments of the previous system and the fissures they create on the surface of the text reveal conflictual dynamics which led to the present textual system.[25]

Boyarin's analysis of midrash as intertextuality designates an alternative historical "within" of the text. The cumulative tensions and transformations do not in this view dissipate into nothingness. They layer, they build up, they stratify within the tense composite of the text. They wrinkle its surface. The text is not a void into which prior meanings disappear; nor is it a container carrying prior truths intact. It thus resists any hermeneutical appropriation of its meanings by an interpreting subject. It suggests rather the interdimensional folds, registered on the surface as incongruities, that "the transformation of a signifying system" produces. By this account, the forces of historical transformation leave their mark. A prepatriarchal signifying system seems to have left its trace in the *Enuma Elish*; and then later, by the same process, the polytheist patriarchy has pre-marked Genesis 1.2. Whether as gap, contradiction, or monstrosity, it recalls that which it repressed. But the recall occurs within a particular, always contemporary, interpretation. Thus a current theological reading can only implicate the reader in the text and thus further complicate its field of effects. Indeed Boyarin's notion of intertext fissures the boundaries by which an interiorized subjectivity would protect itself, its significance, from its own conflictual context.

Thus the differences of interpretation and of context (including those registering on *Face of the Deep*) may be read as developments of Genesis 1.2's own intertextuality. We only approach the biblical mythologoumenon through the history of its effects. "Since Genesis 1.1–3 belongs to the heart (*Herzstuecken*) of Christian (creation) theology," avers Michaela Bauks, "it must be read against the background of a long *Wirkungsgeschichte*, which extends to contemporary Old Testament studies."[26] I am trying to read the heart-beat of that modern history in both its dependence upon and its resistance to Christian doctrine.

V Dogmatic hermeneutics

> But the pathos of Genesis, Ch. I, is not primarily that of reverence, awe, or gratitude, but that of theological reflection. The sober monotony of the account, precisely because of this radical renunciation, emphasizes what faith is capable of declaring objectively.
>
> (Von Rad[27])

I want to return for a moment to Von Rad's exegesis, as typifying the first of three main strategies for reading the tehom in the light of the mythic interest. We noticed in Von Rad's biblical theology of Genesis a tense maneuver around the Babylonian antecedent: he recognizes and discounts it.[28] He reads the priestly narration's "sober monotony" as a rejection of the mythos of formation from chaos. This "radical renunciation" of a more dramatic style "mediates aesthetically the impression of restrained power and lapidary greatness".[29] Von Rad's Heidelberger successor Claus Westermann echoes this tonal inference: "The same order of sentences recurring through the whole chapter gives it that *peculiar and effective monotony* which enables it to articulate in characteristic fashion the utter transcendence of Creation over any other event."[30] In this argument from style, these influential commentators solemnly repeat the phenomenon Nietzsche named "monotonotheism."

Like Von Rad, however, I read these verses as a "theological" and "careful distillation of everything mythological."[31] Yet he happens to find in P a proto-Protestant neo-orthodoxy, stressing "what faith is capable of declaring objectively." Von Rad rejects out of hand the notion that "the Lord of the world" would produce a chaos, or even subject "a pre-existing chaos to his ordering will!" Thus like Barth he frames the topos of the chaos as "temptation": "Man has always suspected that behind all creation lies the abyss of formlessness, further that all creation is always ready to sink into the abyss of the formless, that the chaos, therefore, signifies simply the threat to everything created; and this suspicion has been a constant temptation for his faith" (ibid., p. 49). Von Rad forthrightly admits that the Genesis document moves "not so much between the poles of nothingness and creation as between the poles of chaos and cosmos." In spite of this abyss between the text and the necessary theology, he heroically stays the classical course: "That does not mean, however, that one must renounce establishing quite definite and unrelinquishable theologoumena."

The reader may guess which nonnegotiable theologoumenon he means. "It is correct to say that the verb *bara*, 'create,' contains the idea both of complete effort-lessness and *creatio ex nihilo*, since it is never connected with any statement of the material. The hidden pathos of this statement is that God is the Lord of the world" (ibid., p. 47). The original foundation of Christian orthodoxy is at stake. So if the myth of the "material" got lost, what is *found* is this "hidden pathos" of the verb *bara*–as though the fact that this verb is rhetorically reserved for God proves the creation from nothing.[32] When Von Rad claims that the verb is "never connected" with materiality, he does so in the face of such matter in the very next verse. Does the pathos lie rather in the hermeneutical anxiety of such a strained argument? Even the Assyriologist Alexander Heidel, who also insists that, in contrast to the *Enuma Elish*, Genesis "predicates a creation out of nothing (*creatio ex nihilo*)" does not believe it can "be deduced from the Hebrew verb *bara* as it has been done."[33]

Von Rad admits that "the sequence of particular declarations in verses 1–3 comprises a theological wealth of reference whose fullness is scarcely to be comprehended." But if we are teased by the trace of an interpretive infinity, the dogma slams it shut. One might have expected of the *Alttestamentler* more solidarity with the text *against* the "unrelinquishable theologoumena." But it is precisely his insistence on reconnecting theology to exegesis–a reconciliation that after all the present theology also pursues–that reproduces the standard repression of the mythological intertext. Biblical scholarship cannot in itself rule out the repristination of the *ex nihilo* doctrine.[34] Hence transdisciplinary collusion may be needed in the formulation of alternative avenues for a "biblical theology." For the question is not *whether* theology will shape hermeneutics, but *which* theology.

VI Warrior hermeneutics

Most exegetes after Gunkel have resisted the authority of the *ex nihilo*, however. The major alternative mines the Mesopotamian, Canaanite and Egyptian texts of the *Chaoskampf*. It highlights the sense of profound historical struggle signified by the mythico-political intertext of the chaos. Marduk's battle with Tiamat was framed as "perpetual conflict," argues Bernard Batto; and the priestly author, writing during the "dark days of Babylonian exile," "manipulated his primeval story to express the same basic concept."[35] Taking the myth-affirmative stance of archetypal inter-pretation, Batto makes a strong claim on behalf of P. Against the J-document's "naive Yahweh God who only gradually learned how to make his creation work" (p. 98), P "found in the Semitic myth of the battle against chaos the theological emphasis he was looking for." At least Batto found it. "That myth affirmed that the world was ruled by an intelligent and all-powerful creator who would never permit it to disintegrate into meaninglessness or succumb to the nihilistic force of evil at work in the world" (p. 98).

By reading the chaos through the warrior traditions of neighboring cultures and of other biblical texts, such an exegesis finds a narrative of divine power that at once takes evil seriously and has the manly muscle to combat it. This tradition lifts up "YHWH's combat with the sea," pushing free of the intellectual omnipotence of the *ex nihilo* tradition to a recognizably biblical persona. We discussed earlier a great inspiration of the *Chaoskampf* exegesis, the dragon-bashing deity of Psalm 74. He appears also in the so-called Isaianic apocalypse (Isaiah 24–7), which culminates in the most potent theomachy of the Bible, short of John's Apocalypse:

> In that day the Lord
> with his hard and great and strong sword will punish
> Leviathan the fleeing serpent,
> Leviathan the twisting serpent,
> And he will slay the dragon that is in the sea.
>
> (Isaiah 27.1)

Leviathan the dragon (*tannin*) issues from the Canaanite and Mesopotamian combat myth, with YHWH cast in the role of Baal. Cosmological and cosmogonic motifs are here transposed eschatologically onto the desired historical future: "*Endzeit gleicht Urzeit*" (Gunkel). The gender of the dragon in Canaanite myth has become masculinized, as befits a worthy opponent for the Lord of the universe. Bernhard Anderson suggests that this proto-apocalyptic rhetoric centers on the "victory of the Divine Warrior over the monster of chaos."[36] The wake-up call of Isaiah 51 then erupts from an anguished sixth-century BCE nostalgia for the miraculous interventions of yore, of Genesis and Exodus combined:

Awake, awake, put on strength,
O arm of the Lord;
awake, as in days of old,
the generations of long ago.
Was it not you who cut Rahab in pieces,
who pierced the dragon?
Was it not you who dried up the sea,
the waters of the great deep;
who made the depths of the sea a way
for the redeemed to cross over?
(Isaiah 51.9–10)

The Leviathan, in the guise of a wicked and elusive serpent, embodies the churning tehom which appears as the rebellious medium of monsters, the *tehom rabba*, "Great Deep." Second Isaiah has interwoven the creation and Exodus traditions, generating a potent poetics of hope. This hope, however, marks the "movement from prophecy to apocalyptic."[37] Anderson argues that Israel's interpreters now "grappled with the radical power of evil at a different level" than the prophets, "who preached repentance and spelled out the consequences of covenant infidelity. Historic injustice now becomes a massive, 'demonic' force, it becomes 'Babylon': manifest 'typically as a colossal military power that sweeps inexorably over small peoples . . . and . . . in structures of power that crush the poor and helpless in society'" (ibid., p. 206). Thus the apocalyptic imaginary of a "sinister force of evil that corrupts human history," a force too great for humans, arises here in the fusion of the liberation tradition with the mythic *Chaoskampf*.

In the Jewish mimicry of a Babylonian hero-myth, Babylon is turned into its own demon Tiamat: but by the same "colonial mimicry" (Bhabha), YHWH has become Marduk. For a theology of nonlinearity, this subversive/subverted transmutation provides quite a clue: the symbol of the creation as battle against chaos depends upon the apocalypse. Isaiah fairly explodes with an uninhibited poetry of mythic teho-mophobia. But with the intertext of the divine warrior develops also the troubled theology, in which belief in divine interventions must suffer their repeated and horrifying absence. Yet this belief entails no doctrine of God's omnipotence. It is rather His impotence that seems to be at issue. YHWH has already retired to the life of a dozing old warrior, whose prophet frantically seeks to rouse him–even using the symbols of the enemy, indeed amplifying them to a universal drama of good and evil. The recycled *Chaoskampf* encodes a poignant hermeneutical conflict: that of an already disappointing patriarchal mythos operating within a collective psyche uniquely gifted with the lure of the future. Rhetorically, of course, it is the community who is actually being called to wake up, to remember, to keep faith even under great stress and confusion.

Jon Levenson has made the preeminent theological case for a hermeneutics of *Chaoskampf*. Invoking the Jewish history of suffering, he challenges the failure of the *ex nihilo* doctrine to recognize the depth, the complexity and the indeterminacy of the divine struggle with evil. Levenson cuts to the quick: "properly understood, the overture to the Bible, Genesis 1.1–2.3, *cannot be invoked in support of the developed Jewish, Christian and Muslim doctrine* of *creatio ex nihilo*."[38] In the face of the uncertainty and injustice of history, he does not politely let God off the hook. He establishes a strict binary of order/chaos: "Creation is a positive that stands in pronounced opposition to the harsh negative of chaos. *The world is good; the chaos that it replaces or suppresses is evil*" (ibid., pp. 121, xx; my emphases). Thus the opposition of order/chaos is no longer fudged by the superimposition of nothingness/creation, but rather sharpened to a high pitch of moral dualism. For Levenson the "Jewish drama of divine omnipotence" is that of the Isaianic cry, the hope—occasionally gratified, often disappointed—that God will exercise "his omnipotence" on our behalf. God's omnipotence is not in question, only "his" will to use it. Levenson defines "creation" in equally unambiguous terms: "The affirmation that God is the creator of the world is directed against the forces that oppose him and his acts of creation—the forces of disorder, injustice, affliction, and chaos, which are, in their Israelite worldview, one" (ibid., p. xix).

Does the "Israelite worldview" really offer up such oneness—either of theology or of evil? "Order is now a matter of the maintenance of boundaries, and even when the forces of chaos pose no threat to the creator, they still persist, and their persistence *qualifies—and defines—his world mastery*" (ibid., p. 65; my emphasis). In other words mastery entails subjugation. Tehom functions openly in this oppositional paradigm as indispensable Other, indeed as defining enemy. The ideal of mastery rules Levenson's theology: no effortless divine sovereignty, but an invigorating, often tragic struggle with a persistent chaos. Levenson calls his own readers to subject themselves willingly to the regime of omnipotence: "Though the persistence of evil seems to undermine the magisterial claims of the creator-God, it is *through submission to exactly those claims that the good order that is creation comes into being*" (ibid., p. 16; my emphasis). Any resistance to such submission (and so to his argument) places the reader in the subject-position of the defiant chaos. As we noted in Barth's unavowed *Chaoskampf*, such hermeneutical unfalsifiability necessarily surrounds claims of omnipotence. But is not submission to the "magisterial claims" of a benign and just omnipotence, despite the evidence of all unnecessary suffering, precisely what the *ex nihilo* faith demands? And does not then a hermeneutical mastery of the text extend the *Chaoskampf* well beyond those texts in which it is clearly attested, to those—such as Genesis 1, Psalm 104, and, as we shall see, Job—in which a less Manichean, more self-implicating sense of the divine struggle with the chaos might be read?[39] As the classical doctrinal boundary of order vs. nothing thins out hermeneutically, the mythic and modern frontier of order vs. chaos snaps into its place.

I have traced how biblical hermeneutics bifurcates into the creation from nothing and the creation vs. chaos; indeed how the rediscovery of the primal *chaoskampf* produces within biblical studies a reassertion of the *ex nihilo*. This difference enacts a tension between dogmatic theologoumenon and scriptural mythologoumenon; between sovereign creator by word alone and strident creator by the s/word. But for the present meditation, this difference between masterful masculinities–between verbal nihilation and violent annihilation–cannot satisfy. As soon as the intertextual chaos appeared in modernity, she/it was fought back all the more ferociously by the divine warrior who pops out of antiquity at the same time; and, less dramatically, by the scholars in his retinue.

Are we then doomed to the "effective monotony" of this double-edged dominology? Between the theological tehomophobia of a repressive transcendence and the biblical tehomophobia of a cosmic belligerence, the tehom does, however, show her face. This is no small matter. This is the matter of the infinite. With this biblical difference, one can negotiate.

VII Creation out of line: Rashi's revolution

Just a bit of translation pried open the possibility, the tradition, the negotiating space, of a tehomic hermeneutics. As I noted in the first chapter, it is at the bifurcation point of two possible translations of *bereshit* ("in beginning") that the leak springs. The grammatical minutiae of how to interpret its role in the syntax of the first three verses, of the absence of an article and the deferral of masoretic points, set off a butterfly effect of translation.[40] E. A. Speiser, who retranslated *Enuma Elish* and also wrote a commentary on Genesis, quietly mainstreamed the controversial position that originates in the Genesis commentary of Rashi, the eleventh-century French Jewish grammarian and hermeneut. Rashi had argued that the first verse of the Bible is not a sentence but a dependent clause. The first three verses thus comprise a single compound sentence. Speiser argued that "a closer examination reveals that verse 2 is a parenthetic clause," whose independent clause comes only as verse 3. This syntax is precisely echoed in the opening of the Yahwist creation narrative Genesis 2.4b–7; more disturbing, it mirrors the structure of Mesopotamian creation stories.[41]

So the schematic structure of the three-verse sentence would parse roughly as follows:

(1) *When Elohim began to create heaven and earth*
(2) *–at which time the earth was* tohu vabohu, *darkness was on the face of the deep and the* ruach *was moving upon the face of the waters–*
(3) *then God said, "Let there be light . . ."*

This complex and unfamiliar structure has won over enough scholars to shift several major translations to the new opening syntax. Given the evident wobble injected into this founding text, the trend of course generates powerful opposition.[42] Rather than the grand opening proposition of a serial monotony (*He said . . . He created . . . He affirmed*), a different grammar, a grammar of difference, is insinuating itself into biblical scholarship.

Rashi reads the first sentence as "crying aloud for interpretation." His brief exegesis has further radical implications: "*the text does not intend to point out the order of the acts of Creation*–to state that these (heaven and earth) were created first."[43] As the first verse announces not a first action but the subject-matter of the chapter, so according to Rashi the entire "order" of creation breaks up: it falls out of line. Thus: "you should be ashamed of yourself," says Rashi, if you believe this is a chronology of creation. To read the first chapter of Genesis as a linear sequence of events, is to contradict the first verse–which announces the appearance of earth and waters on days two and three. Rashi thus dislodges the foundation stone of "Judeo-Christian" linear time. Midrashic methods seem to have allowed an opening both of form and of content that has hardly made its appearance within Christian theology. Avivah Gottlieb Zornberg hints that the "mystery that inheres in the very first word"–*bereshit*–stands in tension with the "benevolent clarity" of the narrative.[44] In historical context it encodes resistance against the crusading hegemony of Christian doctrine and its assimilation by Judaism.[45]

Building on Rashi, Speiser departs from the *chaoskampf* for exegesis. He finds in P "a recognition of pertinent Babylonian sources as well as a critical position toward them."[46] Though criticized for the implication that parallelism proves borrowing,[47] Speiser's key move should not be lost: he finds P repudiating *not* the assumption of a preexistent chaos, but rather the belligerent and politically oppressive *chaoskampf itself*. He concludes with a diffident double negative: "The present interpretation precludes the view that the creation accounts in Genesis say nothing about coexistent matter . . . At all events the text should be allowed to speak for itself." I don't know how a text "speaks for itself"–especially one subject to such massive ventriloquism. But we can give it a chance.

The Jewish delinearization of the time of creation opens up space for a biblical theology of creation, in which the chaos is neither nothing nor evil; in which to create is not *to master the formless but to solicit its virtual forms*. Such solicitation, when expressed as divine speech, may sound less like a command than a seduction. At the level of hermeneutical form, Rashi's subtle nonlinearity threatens to scramble the entire line of command: from the omnipotent lordship down to the hermeneutics of mastery. Westermann admits that a command given to that which does not yet exist is "beyond our understanding." But he explicitly refuses Rashi's option, preferring to undergird "utter transcendence" with the language of dominance.[48] For if the first verse is not a sentence (to be read as a simple announcement), neither, implied Rashi, does the third verse lead off the whole unilateral series of the days. If "Let there be light" belongs to the complex syntax of creation from chaos, then the metric regularity of the whole order has been perturbed—from the beginning—by another rhythm. How might we characterize this emergent third option?

VIII Dialogical hermeneutics

If this divine speech no longer blasts royally into a vacuum, how would we then interpret the iterative utterances of the "let there be"? Less, perhaps, in the monotone of command than in the whisper of desire? Might the imperatives metabolize into such suggestive theograms as John Macquarrie's divine "letting be," John Cobb's "lure" to creative transformation, Rita Nakashima Brock's "divine Eros"? Staying closer to the discipline of exegesis, I find the dialogical approach of William Brown, inspired by the sociological poetics of Mikhail Bakhtin, especially fruitful. For Bakhtin, texts are inherently dialogical. They produce meaning only with the intertextual dynamics of literary-social construction, i.e. rhetorically. Interpreting Genesis 1 in terms of the "art of persuasion," Brown discerns in the imperatives to the earth and the sea—that *they* should bring forth—a rhetorical artistry unequaled in each case by the parallel fulfillment reports ("and God created . . ."). Elohim engages in almost flirtatiously alliterative wordplay: verse 11, the earth "produces" (*tadse*) vegetation (*dese*); verse 20, the waters "produce" (*yisresu*) sea creatures (*seres*) (p. 24). Already Genesis had opened with the alliteration of be*re*shit *bara* and the rhyme of *tohu vabohu*.

   "Such a creative process", writes Brown, in a swerve from form into content, "does not thereby imply a God who simply imposes order on unruly matter or creates everything *ex nihilo*."[49] Far from unilateral commands, the admonitions to the earth and the waters can be read as "invitations to enter into the grand creative sweep of God's designs" (p. 28). Brown proceeds to challenge the notion of the elements as inert matter: "their role in creation is one of *positive participation*" (my emphasis). He then makes the rare move to recognize the preexistent chaos without summoning the warrior. "*Any attempt to read into Genesis 1 some motif of conflict or conquest is entirely mistaken*" (my emphasis). In response to the classic concern for transcendence, he asks whether such a reading, suggestive of an eternal coexistence of the tehom, implies "an elevation of chaos" at the expense of "God's transcendent character." For as Barth made clear, if the chaos is read as an eternal first principle existing independently of God, it would produce a primordial dualism or ditheism. Brown's alternative puts on a firm hermeneutical footing the logic with which I had replied to Barth. The label "autonomy of chaos," which is often used to characterize the coexistent matter, "is arrived at only by presupposing its logical opposite, *creatio ex nihilo*," which Genesis 1.1–3 "neither rejects nor endorses, and thus does not address" (p. 31). Reading the creation imperatives as "rhetorically nuanced speech," a speech that acts by inviting rather than controlling, Brown moves toward a convincingly relational theology: "God chooses and implements noncoercive ways of creating, thereby allowing the elements to share positively in cosmogony" (p. 32). In a more recent work, Brown continues to resist the notion of matter as inert mass or rebellious alien: in creating "order out of 'chaos'" God draws from "its own creative dignity."[50] We may thus read such *dialogical cooperation* between Elohim and the elements as preceding the dualism of Creator/creature (the dualism whereby classical Christianity *fought* the dualism of Creator/chaos). An icon of Creator/creature synergy now anticipates the co-creativity of evolution–against which an *ex nihilo* creationism fitfully continues to pit itself.[51] Could what scientists call "self-organizing complexity" now be read as an articulation of divine creativity? To this possible interface of religion and science we turn in Chapter 11.

Unleashing rhetorically a cascade of nonlinear interactions into genesis–the book and the process–already insinuates a hermeneutics of chaosmos. The interaction between Elohim and Tehom effects, we might say, a *creatio cooperationis*. Thus, for example, the productive capacity of tehom has through its differentiation into the lower waters become that unambiguously "good" sea which Elohim invites in untranslatably artful Hebrew to "swarm forth" with "swarming creatures" (verse 20). Then the sea's untamed creations are confirmed, indeed repeated, as also the product of the divine *bara* (verse 21), and declared "good"–especially "the great sea monsters–*hattanninim haggedolim*" (verse 21)!

Beyond the significantly shared presumption of the chaos of beginnings, how could this pacific vision be reconciled with that of Isaiah's evil leviathan? Indeed what resemblance remains to the grim Babylonian slaughter of the mother ocean and her wild brood? Perhaps a pointed one: similarity enough in sequence and allusion to intensify difference; to mimic ironically its warrior lord and his gynocidal omnipotence? While I do not wish to join the biblical commentators hygienically cleansing the biblical text of pagan influence, there is something to the notion of this particular "anti-mythological polemic" (Hasel).[52] Or rather more specifically–a polemic against creation from matricide.[53]

Might we read the difference between P and the *Enuma Elish* as an intentionally disarming parody–as Barth did? But if the latter sought to neutralize the chaotic female, we read P disarming her killer. According to Bakhtin "every parody is an intentional dialogized hybrid. Within it, languages and styles actively and mutually illuminate one another." Do the *tannim*–swimming about in what Boyarin called "the untransformed detritus of the previous system"–pantomime within the topos of creation "the transformation of a signifying system and of a signifying practice"? Certainly in their midst the exegetical incongruities of the creation push beyond the hermeneutics of tehom to a tehomic hermeneutic.

IX The sea resists

A polytonal co-creativity could take the place of the monotone of absolute transcendence. Might such a *creatio cooperationis* find its hermeneutical infrastructure within an open interactivity of interpretation? Augustine, in the face of tehom, hinted at a hermeneutical multiplicity of "true meanings." A more developed pluralism emerges from Boyarin's midrashic hermeneutics.[54] He employs the poststructuralist trope of the "gap" to signify "any element in the textual system of the Bible which demands interpretation for a coherent construction of the story;" gaps, contradictions and repetitions "indicate to the reader that she must fill in something that is not given in the text in order to read it." In other words it is not a matter of dredging, explicating, or returning to what was already present in the origin. As "a native rabbinic saying" invoking this sense of gap, he cites Rashi's very expletive on verse 1–"this verse cries out, 'interpret me!'" (ibid., p. 41). The intertextual pressure of conflictual memories has fissured the already sedimented surface of the text. The intertext *is* the gap. A midrashic reading "is founded on the idea that gaps and indeterminacies in one part of the canon may be filled and resolved by citing others." He formulates "the essential hermeneutical moment" thus, citing the sixth-century Rabbi Yehuda: "This is a verse made rich in meaning by many passages," i.e. the verse is impoverished in meaning when read only in its context (ibid., p. 27f.).

The notion of intertext, derived by Kristeva from Bakhtin's "hybridity" of languages, renders every text "a mosaic of quotations." Might we then construe midrash as an "intentional dialogized hybrid"–with ever parodic potential? For according to Boyarin "The biblical narrative is gapped and dialogical." The fissures invite interpretation; they make room, indeed they invite, they "let be," relationship. "The role of midrash is to fill in the gaps" (ibid., p. 17). Of course one might infer that the gap could be finally plugged, the dialogue closed, or according to the more orthodox, confined within ungapped, well-sealed boundaries. Indeed the midrashic *inter*textuality can restrict itself to *intra*canonical conversation, in a rabbinically circumscribed (not to say circumcised) "mosaic." To that extent, a midrashic hermeneutic cannot be transposed to a wider feminist conversation, in which interpretation would include Christian, nonbiblical and anti-canonical "passages," without at one and the same time violating the limits of the genre and the aims of gender analysis. The gesture of gap-filling will at any rate hardly satisfy feminists of any tradition. Yet the method Boyarin develops, even here before he had learned to write *with* feminism, drives beyond a strictly bounded midrashism, toward a differential filigree of the boundary itself. If, in other words, it is "these gaps in the text which the midrash reads," then we have to do not with a nothing–which ever wants plugging–but with a *legible matrix of virtual meaning*.

Does the potentiality burbling between the cracks suggest already a tehomic Deep? Not as a backwards or downwards pushing interiority of the text, but as a dialogical potentiality? Boyarin challenges the historical school of modern Jewish hermeneutics (an analogue to the Christian hermeneutical mainstream). Both privilege the truth of the original and so seek to return. Boyarin's "story of midrash quite reverses the narrative of hermeneutic that is presupposed by the historical school." The latter assumes that "the text is clear and transparent at the moment of its original creation, because it speaks to a particular historical situation, and it becomes unclear, owing to the passing of time and that situation." In contrast to this, Boyarin's midrash lets "the text make its meaning in history." But do we make meaning–from nothing? Boyarin–midrashically–finds his hermeneutic of the gap anticipated in a key text in the midrash on Genesis:

> Rabbi Yehuda the son of Simon opened: "And He revealed deep and hidden things [Daniel 2.22]. In the beginning of the creation of the World, 'He revealed deep things, etc.' For it says 'In the beginning God created the heavens,' and He did not interpret. Where did He interpret it? Later on, 'he spreads out the heaven like gossamer' [Isaiah 40.22]. And the earth, 'and He did not interpret.'"
>
> (*Bereshit Rabbah*[55])

God, it seems, has left interpretive gaps in the universe itself, and therefore also in the Torah. The world and the text await interpretation. Thus the text cannot mirror an original, transparent–and apparently nonexistent–meaning. It will make meaning through a cooperative interaction in history–meaning not from nothing but from everything preceding. That meaning lives only in the relationships constituting the present signifying process. Boyarin's rendition of this dialogical practice is at once textual and psychoanalytic (so doubly Jewish). "History is not a one-way street. Older formations remain. They manifest themselves in the social body as dissident groups, in the individual as hidden and partly repressed desires, in the texts of the culture as intertextuality" (ibid., p. 104).

How fortunate it is that when Boyarin psychoanalytically amplifies his theory of midrash, he happens to choose a midrash on tehom-Tiamat it/herself. Developing an analogy between dream-work and text-work, he explores how "partly repressed desires" carried within the text appear as a *mythic* intertext. In Exodus 14.21, "the sea began to resist." Moses, who has lifted his rod and commanded the sea to part, is the object of this resistance. This the rabbis found in need of interpretation. For though Moses was empowered to part the sea–here is the gap–it is only a direct divine intervention that gets the sea to "flee." The midrash, Boyarin suggests, has stumbled upon *the lost personality of the sea*, concealed but not lost in the biblical text. Its place is marked by the gap in coherence. The Exodus text was composed within a context in which polytheism, with its animate elementals and oceanic deities, was a living option. If the monotheism that defined Israel's fragile identity over and against the cultural wealth of the polytheist powers needed defense, this would have been the case for the priestly composer of Genesis 1. But for the later public of the midrash, polytheism no longer posed a temptation. So when the rabbis draw upon Psalm 114 ("the sea saw and fled") to fill the gap, the latent personality of an animate sea becomes manifest. The Bible "records openly the conflict in its culture between paganism as the old religion of the people and the new religion of the Torah and the Prophets." But it registers the conflict as a crack in the text: a gap which the interpreter (far from glossing over it as "incomprehensible") gently–as if handling gossamer–widens.

The waters, like the repressed, return. But now they wear again their mythic persona. Thus midrashically emboldened, they will not and need not subject themselves to any human "dominion." Thus we witness a "revivification of the mythic universe" (ibid., p. 100) of the animate, proud and productive waters.[56] Might we then analogously speak of the tehom of Genesis 1.2 as a *repressed but recorded mythological intertext*, depersonalized by the biblical text in the struggle to neutralize the polytheistic worldview? Not accidentally, it is in reading the sea's resistance that Boyarin finds traces of noncanonical material in the midrashic intertext, traces which also lead toward gender enquiry. If the recovery of the animate *tehom/ mayim* opened for the twentieth century the "mythic treasure chamber"–its topos previously mapped by little more than the X of a *crux interpretans*–that cross marks the Christian dumping ground of a heterogeneous, bodily and Jewish "detritus."[57] Gunkel's chamber couldn't be locked up again. Surely the lack of a midrashic tradition makes the return of the repressed all the more traumatic among Christian interpreters.

Boyarin's irenic reading of the sea's resistance does not avoid conflict but allows us to *attend* to it. Then both the repressed female of the cosmos and its materiality come back into play. While Boyarin does not here consider the genders of the protesting sea and of Moses' "rod," his recent work develops a hermeneutics queer enough to compass the sexual fluidities of the sea and its/her monsters. But he does not miss the cosmological significance of this tehomic revivification: "It is hard for me to imagine precisely what it 'felt like' to live in a world peopled by a personal earth, a personal sea, and a personal desert, but it is not hard to imagine in general how different an orientation to the world this provided." He underwrites the ecological meaning of a nature which can resist. "Certainly it is difficult to see people who have such a consciousness acting toward nature as if it were only there to be exploited and spoiled for human purposes–as if it had *no ontological importance of its own.*"[58]

From a tehomic perspective, it is this importance "of its own"–resembling what process theology refers to as the *intrinsic value of all actualities*–that the *ex nihilo* and the warrior together erase. The animate earth and sea go dead with the evaporation of the deep. For its influx signifies the potentiality for ongoing co-creativity. As I write, however, virtually no eco-hermeneutics has found voice amidst the cutting edges of theory. Yet do not textual and ecological contexts, hermeneutics and ontology, culture and nature, lap and overlap endlessly? Like waves?

In this section we have practiced a hermeneutic with which to read the she/sea buried within the biblical Deep. This is not to say, for instance, that I could write midrash. Within its communal and canonical boundaries, midrash cannot harbor the eclectic idiosyncrasy of the present construction. This theology understands itself not as midrash but as a quasi-midrash, as a midrashically *inflected* polytonality. It follows Boyarin's hermeneutic into a *gaping* intertextuality, resisting every andrographic rod. It churns up in solidarity those many and shifting Others marked as the chaos–like the Jewish detritus of a superseded testament, "unheroic" contaminant of an otherwise masculine and Europeanized Christianity.[59] (Still, Tehom as *Jewish mother?*)

X The good-natured chaos

Just what do we *face* there, as the text splits open–the tehom opening back into the personified sea, the sea back into its mythology, and myth into the figure of the first mother turning monster? If she comes at us teeth bared and raging, returning to us the repressed infinity of interpretation, or even arms outstretched–would we want to declare her our goddess? "Who again would want immediately to deify in the old manner of an unknown world? And to worship from this time on the unknown (*das Unbekannte*) as 'the Unknown One' (*den Unbekannten*)? Nietzsche's allusion to Paul's missionary ploy among the Athenians forestalls an indubitable temptation. "Alas, too many *ungodly* possibilities of interpretation are included in the unknown, too much devilry, stupidity, and foolishness of interpretation–even our own human, all too human folly, which we know."[60] In other words, pluralism cannot be controlled. Will the recognition of our perspectives *as such*–without "decreeing from our corner that perspectives are permitted only from this corner"–prevent us from deifying our own folly? Is it when the infinite is theologically cornered that it turns ungodly?

Back to the story then, where we can practice facing the monster head-on. The *Enuma Elish* begins, however, not with a monster but with a benevolent, somnolent mother mingling her salt waters with the fresh waters of her mate. Inasmuch as Genesis 1.2 recycles the Babylonian text–or some shared mythic *prima materia*–does not the vibratory proximity of *ruach* upon the waters suggest that intimate co-generativity? If, as Boyarin suggests, the intertext emblematizes a repressed desire, does the Babylonian intertext offer itself as the site at once of the repression and the recollection of desire? Of a desire that sinks below the heterosexual mating of Tiamat and Apsu, into an infinite intimacy; the desire for a mothering matrix, where we can romp and risk?

"She pondered in her heart the evil . . . 'Why should we destroy that which we ourselves have brought forth? Their way is indeed very painful, but let us take it good-naturedly!'" At any rate the poem records the conflict between signifying-systems in such a way as to preserve "untransformed" the irenic tolerance of a more matristic wisdom, *even as* it morphs into that (m)other to be mocked as female and slaughtered as enemy. This is quite a "gap." Thus the "detritus of past signifying systems" lies side by side in the text with the new system, which contradicts it. So the biblical text absorbs an already self-contradictory narrative into its own gap, thus generating the bifurcating pattern of fissures. But they are at the same time connections. In Tiamat's "heart-pondering," may we not receive a clue for a hermeneutics that would let her live: her, the primal creativity, where children run wild, where the new is granted a costly permission by its antecedents; the body of all that is silenced or slaughtered so that the new order need not negotiate its claims? Such a tehomic hermeneutic, haunted by the dead goddess but not worshiping her, would not find the chaos waters always pacific. It would tune its texts to a universe that puts up with a lot of painful noise. It would teach its insecure traditions that turbulence, though it may have ill effects, cannot be excluded without murder.

All-too-humanly, Tiamat could not, after too much loss, maintain her good-naturedness. But chilling and telling in the *Enuma Elish* is the admission on the part of the grandsons that they were too afraid to try to speak with her. They had been advised to "go stand before Tiamat that her heart may calm down": another "peacemaking proposition."[61] But instead no negotiation was attempted. So out of cowardice, not courage–*coeur/age* after all must risk the heart-to-heart–the warrior paradigm prevailed. She who "in her heart" perceived the evil and in anguish tried to prevent it, can go into a grief-driven rage; those who have been objectified, commodified, subdued, slaughtered can become violent. She can be blamed by the children she protected. Then enters the knowing warrior, who can work fear to his advantage.

If we read the layered deep of Genesis 1.2 as a cunning parody of the Babylonian creation from chaos, we might regain the peacemaking Tiamat and expose the warrior. He has occupied the Abrahamic traditions in her absence. "Every type of parody or travesty, every word 'with conditions attached,' with irony, enclosed in intonational quotation marks, every type of indirect word is in a broad sense an intentional hybrid." So Bakhtin: "It is in the nature of every parody to transpose the values of the parodied style, to highlight certain elements while leaving others in the shade: parody is always biased in some direction." (p. 75) Certainly the bias of a tehomic theology, its finite perspective within an interpretive infinity, delights in this dialogical Genesis. Yet it does not pretend to know what the text meant, let alone to know it better than it knew itself. It knows only the "more" of the histories of terror and hope through which we interpret the text; through which the text interprets us back to ourselves.

Some will simply reject the biblical text. Whatever its wisp of parody, it can always reinforce the varieties of matricide. I would fear, however, that in disposing of the texts that have borne the (m)other's traces, we flush out our own future. I do not know how to create–together–a livable future without hovering, oscillating, meditating over the collective potentialities of those plural waters. And in verse 2 after all *ruach* appears neither as a weapon of a cosmic warrior nor as a preemptive Holy Spirit. In its "intentional hybridization" of mythic and Hebrew discourses, the verse annuls Marduk's victory. It reinstates the primal creative sea, not as itself good-natured or personal, yet as the source of the "good" natures in which Elohim delights.

This biblical tehomophilia, happily discovered within a developing third current of exegesis, does not invite romance with the deep. The chaos will not cease to destroy us. Nor will we be born, or born again, from any other matrix. Our interpretations of the deep will dissolve back into the deep; whatever "deep and hidden things" have been revealed, have yet to be interpreted—otherwise, to repeat Bakhtin's phrase for the subversive otherness, tehom translates in and out of an entire "sea of heteroglossia." In the next two chapters, we will explore that sea, as literal sea and as sea of letters, in perhaps its most expansive and windy texts—the first a book of canonical wisdom, the second a canonical North American novel.

7

"RECESSES OF THE DEEP"
Job's comi-cosmic epiphany

It is often very difficult to establish precisely where reverence ends and
ridicule begins.

(M. M. Bakhtin)

I Job's tragic comedy

This chapter claims for a tehomic theology the support of the longest divine monologue of the Bible. I argue that YHWH's speech to Job may be read as an exegetical
iteration of the creation narrative canonized in Genesis 1. The Joban whirlwind
recapitulates, alters and amplifies the P narrative. As P recalls the mythological intertext of the Babylonian cosmogony, so Job 38–41 cites the Genesis creation narrative
(or an ancestral variant–I am not making a chronological argument) as its primary
intertext. This chaosmic citationality suggests a trajectory of texts swallowing texts,
like a series of open-mouthed fish. It effects in Job a marine drama of wildly mixed
genres. Let me suggest that the multidimensional Joban dialogue becomes audible only
through attention to what Bakhtin calls "the entire spectrum of tones–from reverent
acceptance to parodic ridicule."[1] On that polytonal spectrum appears his felicitously
named "sea of heteroglossia." Might we read Job as a creation drama whose full eco-
hermeneutical spectrum has been masked by the "monotone of transcendence"?

   The polytones of Job have posed endless challenges to interpreters. I will borrow
as a starting-point the refreshing hypothesis that "once the poem is set in its full and
final literary context, replete with prologue and epilogue as well as the Elihu
speeches, the most apt and compelling generic designation of the book of Job is
comedy."[2] Christopher Fry put it pithily: "The Book of Job is the great reservoir of
comedy."[3] This comedy would not be a joke but a laughter of resistance, knowingly
captured in my colleague Lynne Westfield's poetry: "Our laughter peels back /
Molten tar of days' scorn."[4] Does tragic rage meld dissonantly in the book of Job with
a defiant humor? If this humor echoes "the common people's creative culture of

laughter," it does so as an uncommonly sophisticated challenge to the dominant piety. "Laughter," writes Bakhtin of the "plane of comic (humorous) representation," pulls its objects close. "Everything that makes us laugh is close at hand, all comical creativity works in a zone of maximal proximity."[5] Does laughter transgress the very transcendence of a distanced Sovereign? But what is there in the rending pathos of Job, let alone the solemn dignity of the creation narrative, to laugh at? Despite its apparently facile resolution, the book of Job stages a scene of suffering, the worse kind of suffering, where loss is compounded by an acute sense of injustice.[6] Indeed there may be no more eloquent single inscription of this kind of suffering (the Korean language gives it a name, "*han*") in literature. A tradition dating back to the fifth century ACE highlights Job's resemblance to Greek tragedy; more recently, Samuel Terrien attributes to Job a new genre, that of "the festal tragedy."[7]

What sort of gallows humor obtains in the face of unjust suffering? A prominent social critic, asked about the humorlessness of the left, insisted dolefully: "But the era is really not funny! Honestly, there is nothing to laugh about."[8] But (honestly) what era *is* funny? Job's any more than ours? Nonetheless, a few critics have highlighted the comic and parodic elements of Job.[9] Biblical comedy in general, and Job in particular, argues William Whedbee, displays a "dual intention." It aims at "both *subversion* of the status quo and *celebration* of life and love—all in the service of transforming perceptions and affirming hope and the possibility of renewal."[10] Comedy in the classic sense enacts a U-shaped movement of fall from happiness, to exaggerated misery, to restoration and affirmation; it deploys the strategies of parody, irony, satire and incongruity; it employs "character types such as boaster, buffoon, and fool." Job mirrors the entire U. Would Job's YHWH in the comic reading then appear as a boaster, Job as a fool, or his comforters as buffoons? And who gets the last laugh? Literally, none other than Leviathan, who "laughs at the rattle of javelins" (Job 41.24, 29). A cruel laughter of nature? Nonetheless, given this particular sea monster's tehomic credentials, we had better pursue this tonal clue.

It is the literary structure of the text of Job that lets it be read as *creation comedy*. The parody is first of all directed at the ur-story, the folksy *inclusio* device that frames the text, and which most folk, having been Sunday-schooled to skip forty of its forty-three chapters, think of as "the story of Job." It tells of the wager with the Satan, "the Accuser" (not so much a personification of evil as supreme Trickster, colleague of YHWH); of Job's loss of everything; of his wife's "Curse God and die." The simple style of the folk narrative lasts only for two chapters. Then come forty chapters of complex, theatrically staged poetry, after which the prose tale picks up again in the last chapter, where all is restored to Job for passing the test of faith. The radical incongruity of style and intention invites a reading of the forty chapters as the Joban poet's parody on the simplistic theology of the folk story itself.

Might we then take the work as an ancient antecedent of the literary genre of *parodia sacra*, the "popular parody" or "travesty" that in Bakhtin's analysis subverted heroic epic (and so provided the prerequisite for the modern novel)? "Laughter destroyed epic distance; it began to investigate man freely and familiarly, to turn him inside out."[11] I showed Genesis 1 already resisting the genre of the epic, with its "single and unified worldview" (ibid., p. 35). All the more so, then, the satiric dialogue of Job. "Parodic intentionality," forged through a mimetic intertextuality, emerged in Bakhtin's account as a medieval European style of subversion, and so *ipso facto* as *theological* subversion. He traces it from Greek through medieval comedy, into the heteroglossia of the modern novel. If such an intentional parody can be spotted at work in Job, whose primary intertext is the already satiric folk story (God gambling with the Satan), then the book offers a Hebrew contribution to the prehistory of the novel.

II Job's dialogized hybrid

The dialogue of Job answers to Bakhtin's notion of a hybrid precisely as "an argument between styles of language," and so "between points of view, each with its own concrete language that cannot be translated into the other."[12] Thus the endless speeches of comfort and exhortation fail to translate into meaning for Job; and the untranslatability of YHWH's big speech into theological concepts poses a profound problem for hermeneutics. Moreover the structure of Job exhibits Bakhtin's definition of parody as "intentional dialogized hybrid." This book enacts the only full instance in the Bible, which is full of dialogue, of the *form* of dialogue set forth as for a play.[13] The bulk of the book unfolds as theatrical dialogue, with Job's mournful and sarcastic demands for a divine hearing interleaved with long declamations by his friends. After a week-long vigil of silent empathy (extraordinary by current consolation standards), they begin to defend YHWH against Job's challenges, demanding that their friend stop asking questions and take responsibility for his suffering. Their speeches slide into a grandiloquent pedantry, Job's satiric rebuttals of which direct the reader's response: "the friends become cruelly and grotesquely comic as they strive with increasing dogmatism to apply their faulty solutions to the wrong problem—and the wrong person" (ibid., p. 234).

> Galling comforters are you all.
> Have windy words a limit?
> What moves you to prattle on?
> I, too, could talk like you.
> If you were in my place,
> I could harangue with words,
> Could shake my head at you.
> I could strengthen you with my mouth.
> My quivering lips would soothe you.
>
> (16.2b–5)

Job's caricatures sustain the tone of dark comedy through to the culmination, and have won him a fan-club of skeptics, anti-authoritarians, clergy-bashers, mystics, and existentialists of all stripes (Blake, Melville, Kokoshka being among the most famous)–yet Calvin, too, wrote a volume of sermons on Job.[14] But it is the advice offered by Job's friends that still circulates as standard Christian piety: the Lord is testing or punishing you; in any case, you deserve what you get. "When you mock, shall no one shame you?" drones Zophar. "Know then that God exacts of you less than your guilt deserves" (11.3b; 6b).

"Another's sacred word," writes Bakhtin, as though describing these earnest speeches, "congeals to the point where it becomes a ridiculous image, the comic carnival mask of a narrow and joyless pedant." Job's resistance, even as comedy, is not to be taken lightly. When he ridicules the theological incoherence, he appeals to a logic of justice, to which the tradition he shares with his friends lends supreme importance: "Even when I cry out, 'Violence!' I am not answered; I call aloud, but there is no justice." From the protest tradition of psalms and prophets, Job voices the most sharply focussed grievance of them all. For he unmasks the contradiction growing in the heart of monotheism: if the God of justice is to be counted all-powerful, that God must be held accountable for all injustice. Indeed the dialogue exposes the terms of a discursive power-imbalance that makes the very unmasking impossible: "There is no umpire between us, who might lay his hand upon us both. / Let him take his rod away from me, and let not dread of him terrify me. Then I would speak without fear of him, for I am not so in myself" (9.33–5). But it is specifically the arguments of the theologian-comforters he deconstructs:

> If indeed you magnify yourselves against me,
> and make my humiliation an argument against me,
> know then that God has put me in the wrong,
> and closes his net around me.

In other words the God in whose name piety blames the victim is the one who *caused* the suffering. Few theologians in the twenty-five centuries since this text have faced up to this opposition between power and goodness. They have largely dissipated the tension with easy mystifications. Were this otherwise, might Christianity have resisted more often than sponsored social injustice?

III Creation in reverse

Job opens with curses. Curses were high-risk performative utterances. He curses his own day of birth. "Let that day be darkness!" At the outset of the dialogue appears the first structural clue that we have to do with a midrash on Genesis 1; indeed, with intense involvement in the chaos of its second verse. In a bitter incantation, Job funnels his death-wish into an entire cosmogony in reverse. The progression of his curse sarcastically mirrors the sequence of events in the creation narrative. Of his own first day he growls, "that day, let there be darkness": a mockery of "Let there be light"–and a self-infantilization that places himself, in negative grandiosity, at the center of the world. As darkness was upon the face of the deep, Job would now "let darkness reclaim it . . ."

"This pattern of reversing the order of creation and returning the universe to primordial chaos and darkness has a prophetic counterpart," writes Habel, referring to Jeremiah's birthday curse.[15] Job's imprecations crescendo in a monstrous incantation:

> Let those curse it who curse the day,
>   those who are skilled to rouse up Leviathan.
>
> (3.8)

But it is Job who is himself enacting the curse and the arousal: if performative utterance is "excitable speech," this is excited rhetoric indeed, challenging the cosmopolitics of creation.[16] It inverts the pacific Genesis 1.21: "And God also created the great sea monsters [*tannin*]."[17] "In rousing Leviathan," argues Habel, "Job is calling up the powers of chaos to destroy the created order and return the night of his creation to the domain of primordial absence."[18] Not unlike Ahab's rousing of another Leviathan, as we shall see, Job rushes headlong and headstrong toward death, calling down chaos upon his world. And these curses presume, indeed they depend upon, the *evil* of the chaos-monster, whom only the warrior YHWH can constrain. "By his power he stilled the Sea; by his understanding he struck down Rahab" (16.12). Indeed Job complains that God treats him like one of these tehomic menaces: "Am I the Sea, or the Dragon, that you set a guard over me?" (7:12). Job's tehomophobic assumption thus mimics the theology of righteous mastery that he is at the same time questioning.

The strategic location of these monstrous allusions supports this reading. Given the leviathanic revelation of Job 42 toward which the poet drives, the monster provides the poet's secret *inclusio* device. In other words, Leviathan has been tucked just inside the obvious frame provided for the story by the folk tale, at the beginning and the end of the long dialogue. The parodic reversal of the very sequence of creation, marked by these "leviathanic allusions" (Melville), structures the entire drama: in the beginning, Job undoes the beginning itself. And in the end, a new beginning becomes strangely possible.

Incongruous inversion, a key *comic* strategy, inflates to *cosmic* proportions. Thus sacred parody–"parodic travesty" indeed–plays itself out as the cosmogonic reversal of a properly ordered creation epic. Is the Joban poet directly parodying Genesis 1? This seems less likely than that the book of Job dwells within the same (post)colonial context as does the P narrative, a culture sharply penetrated by the Mesopotamian war-epics. Indeed if we follow the convention of reading Job as a parable of the suffering of Israel, it would amplify the (post)exilic heteroglossia we already discern in Genesis 1.

At any rate the anti-hero Job has not been granted by his poet a consistent or omniscient voice, but rather a melodramatically honest one. He poses with an unprecedented relentlessness the questions of theodicy, of the "justice" or "justification" of God. Pursuing his stubborn insistence on bringing a lawsuit against God, Job demands with comic pathos that the Lord present a written legal defense. In the comic genre one can expect this self-righteous pestering to get on the nerves of the Almighty. It does. Job gets the chaos he asked for–wind-storm, monsters and all. His initial desire, "to throw all of creation back into primordial chaos," is realized. With a twist. Whereas he summoned with his curses a chaos of death, what answers his call is the chaos of life. The joke is on Job. A suicidal anti-cosmogony turns suddenly–comi-cosmic.

IV The carnival of creation

To the raging question of theodicy (How could a good and all-powerful God permit such injustice?) the voice from the whirlwind replies: *Look at the wild things*. From the vortex storms a detailed, turbulent and impassioned compendium of nonhuman natures. Most readers hear little more than a thundering assertion of divine omnipotence. Levenson, for instance, affirms in Job 38.1–42 a "frigid theocentrism" revealing the chilling truth of "God's inscrutable yet impugnable mastery."[19] Readers numb to the nonhuman life of their own world may have difficulty in feeling the heat of this final poem. When YHWH does actually–against any reasonable biblical expectation–appear as demanded, the tables are turned. The spirit-vortex now questions the questioner.

> Where were you when I laid
> the foundation of the earth?
> Tell me, if you have understanding . . .
> On what were its bases sunk,
> or who laid its cornerstone
> when the morning stars sang together
> and all the heavenly beings shouted for joy?
> (38.4ff.)

The epiphany pulses between impatience at human anthropocentrism, and unabashed glee in a complex, undomesticated universe. The poem soars into what can only be read as its own creation narrative: an emotive expansion of the Genesis sequence, wilder in its rhetoric, at once exasperated and ecstatic. Commentators often read

YHWH as evading Job's questions: "Never really addressing Job's charge of injustice, God changes the subject from ordinary experience to cosmogony."[20] For this reason some modern interpreters infer that the whirlwind sequence was a later emendation. Linguistic analysis has since ruled out that particular solution to this "change of subject."

Indeed rather than evasion we might read here a change of divine subjects: from Job and his friends' almighty anthropomorphism, to the wild spirit of creation. The poem modulates into another key altogether. The divine soliloquy first of all pointedly recapitulates the cosmogonic reversals of Job 4. As in the beginning, now in the end, the sea figures prominently:

> Were you there when I stopped the waters,
> as they issued gushing from the womb?
> When I wrapped the ocean in clouds
> and swaddled the sea in shadows?
> When I closed it in with barriers
> and set its boundaries, saying,
> "Here you may come, but no farther;
> here your proud waves break."[21]

A moving and concise reconfiguration of the images of Genesis 1.2: the ocean here bursts forth in amniotic liquidity, caught like a baby by the midwife and wrapped in the soft darkness. A "frigid mastery of the chaos"? Or an intimate tehomophilia? YHWH does not dilute the mythic danger of the sea and the darkness of origins but liberates them from the mood and meaning of evil. The sea's ferocity is portrayed as the agitation of an infant that requires boundaries for its own protection—not just for the safety of the earth. Habel comments that "the image is deliberately absurd: this violent chaos monster is but an infant, born from a womb, wrapped in baby clothes, placed in a playpen . . ." and nicely notes the parallel to Psalm 104.26, where Leviathan becomes YHWH's "aquatic pet."[22] Yet Habel still conforms to the tradition of reading these metaphors as a display of God's awesome powers of control, noting parallels to Marduk's control of Tiamat. I find the imagery less absurd than adorable in its irony. Might we read the mother/child/infant imagery, even in its masculine bluster, as a ploy to disarm—with farce rather than force—the master paradigm of the warrior/king/creator?

Job had cursed his mother's womb, along with the same morning stars now singing in cosmic harmony: "Let the stars of its dawn be dark . . . because it did not shut the doors of my mother's womb, and hide trouble from my eyes" (Job 3.9a–10). In the final reversal of the reversal, "the womb" has returned, cosmogonically. But whose womb is this, from which "the waters issue gushing"? The Qumran Targum preserves this version of verse 8: "when it gushed from the womb of the deep [*rehem* tehom]" issues with the violence of a writhing neonate from *the deep*, which could erupt again to flood the earth (Genesis 7.11). The distinction of "sea" and "deep" seems to mirror that of Genesis 1.2; its significance is suggested by its echo of Genesis 49.25: *"blessings of the deep that lies beneath, blessings of the breasts and of the womb."*[23] The Joban poet's whimsical infantilization of the sea transforms a private curse into a cosmic blessing. *Rehem tehom* seems, like the contents of Genesis 1.2, to precede the creation; Job does not refer to a creation of either sea or womb. Is this womb "of tehom," as of an anonymous goddess? Or *is* the womb the tehom, more monotheistically? But then whose womb is this, that precedes all creatures? From the perspective of the whirlwind circling like the very *ruach* that pulsed over the deep, how can we avoid the inference that the *rehem* is God's, from whose unfathomable Deep the waters issue? Since goddesses had been *a priori* ruled out (along with cosmic sex and polytheism) the waters stir rather queerly. We would have to say that "His" womb belongs to "His" fecund body. Without fancying the Joban poet a woman, a feminist hermeneutic does not discount such strategically situated, gynomorphic refigurations. Swaddled in the shadows of lost possibility, this tehomophilic countertradition tends to bend its genders, divine and human.

For all its maternal resonance, the countertradition attends to the terror of the chaos. Whimsy rolls into dark poetry:

> Have you entered into the springs of the sea,
> or walked in the recesses of the deep?
> Have the gates of death been revealed to you,
> or have you seen the gates of deep darkness?
> Have you comprehended the expanse of the earth?
> (38.16–18a)

Or in Mitchell's translation–"Have you seen to the edge of the universe?" That astronomical scale, projected as space-time and registered as mortality, here sets an epistemological limit: not a prohibition, but a horizon of what our little body-brains can know. Yet these rhetorical questions give one pause: in some sense Job could answer "Yes"–he of all people had seen the gates of deep darkness; it swallowed his children. The gates, suggestive of the Sumerian myth of the underworld descent of Inanna through seven gates, mark boundaries effected not by exclusion but by finitude.[24] Our "words without knowledge" (Job 38.2) fall like Inanna's garments at the gate. The limits of our knowing, like the limits of our lives, trap us with an often tragic finality. Yet here shadows of ignorance begin to suggest the bottomless mystery not only of death but of life.

The rhetorical questions–"Can you bind the chains of the Pleiades, or loose the cords of Orion?"–do seem to retain a petulant, boastful edge. YHWH's barrage of questions can of course be read as a bullying harangue. The boundaries of human knowledge and agency, which the questions drum in—do you know, could you do—reverberate with astronomical and zoological detail. But what is YHWH's point? "You are ignorant and mortal, human, so shut up"? Or rather: "Be still and *see* all this!"? To me they sound like the fulminations of an artist whose morals have been questioned while her creations get ignored. The artist bursts with frustration at the indifference to the subtle genius of her actual productions, to her stunning, strange universe. *Open your eyes!* Mostly Job gets wind of feral animals:

> Do you know when the mountain goats give birth?
> Do you observe the calving of the deer?
> Can you number the months that they fulfill,
> and do you know the time
> when they give birth,
> when they crouch to give birth to their offspring,
> and are delivered of their young?
>
> (39.1–4)

One imagines the perturbed theologians of ages past meditating on this text, trying to make it yield something of greater supernatural value than the parturative practices of undomesticated animals. Perhaps Job's first response, after several more rounds of this distinctly prescientific zoology spewed from the whirlwind, also registers a throb of ethical, if not spiritual, disappointment: "See, I am of small account; what shall I answer you?" (Right, you are big, you are great, I'll keep my mouth shut. Wild asses? Ostriches? The baby eagles sucking mommy's blood? Aside: If this is the answer, what was my question?)

The whirlwind oracle brims with laughter: not a gentle, reassuring laughter to be sure, but the noisy, defiant laughter of the creatures. "When it spreads its plumes aloft," even the foolish ostrich "laughs at the horse and its rider" (39.18). The horse "laughs at fear." Loving presentation of the wild beasts had been an earmark of Genesis 1, indeed distinguishes the priestly narrative from the *Enuma Elish*, which for all its parallelism features a noticeable absence of animals. While the divine love of the wild does not homogeneously characterize Hebrew scriptures, the Genesis human emerges as the image of God amidst a dense company of other animals.[25]

This billowing life running wild within its ordered ecologies further characterizes the vision as a midrash upon Genesis 1. William Blake depicts exactly this intertextual relation in his engravings of *The Sweet Influences of the Pleiades*: the central picture is of YHWH with arms outstretched in cruciform fashion; beneath him as in a cave Job and his wife (a caring partner, not a raving harridan as in many depictions[26]), and the three friends, listen with wonder; above, a row of androgynous angels anticipate a *belle-époque* chorus line, singing starrily. As though mirroring the graphic format of midrash, in which commentary visually surrounds the Torah, Blake has then engraved

132

4. William Blake, *When the Morning Stars Sang Together* (1825, reprinted 1874), from Illustrations to "The Book of Job." © Tate, London 2002

as a wide frame around this image a summation of Genesis 1 in imagery and text: light, firmament, and land on one side, and great lights, the waters and the earth bringing forth abundantly on the other. And he has inscribed at the bottom a great writhing sea serpent, almost indistinguishable from the waves which lap across the bottom of the page.

V The laughter of Leviathan

"Where were you before I laid the foundation?" (38.4). Tonally it can read like a sneer of sheer power: "Where were *you*? Who are you to speak?" Or like an opening *koan*. The culminating revelation is that of the disproportionately long poem to Leviathan. The "great sea monsters," so unabashedly good in Genesis 1, return in the whirlwind with the splash and crash of the repressed. The divine voice is beside itself with the magnificence of the monster:

> I will not keep silence concerning its limbs,
> or its mighty strength, or its splendid frame.
> Who can strip off its outer garment?
> Who can penetrate its double coat of mail?
> Who can open the doors of its face? . . .
> From its mouth go flaming torches,
> sparks of fire leap out.
> Out of its nostrils comes smoke,
> as from a boiling pot and burning rushes.

And so forth. When YHWH magnifies Leviathan, the very incarnation of the chaos waters, a tehomic theology takes note. To be sure this account cannot make any claim to marine biological prescience—the Leviathan resembles an old-fashioned sea dragon, part whale, part crocodile.[27] Leviathan's breaching causes routine (comi-) cosmic crisis: "When it raises itself up the gods are afraid; at the crashing they are beside themselves." These cowardly gods recall the traitorous grandchildren of Tiamat. Leviathan's scornful invincibility to human assault inspires much of the description: "Clubs are counted as chaff; it laughs at the rattle of javelins" (42.29).

The laughter of Leviathan trumpets the climax of the vision. Yet YHWH does not interpret his own *monstrum*, let alone the relevance of all these nonhuman bodies and beasts to Job's questions. And so we must ask: is this after all a sheer display of force, intended, as many commentators believe, to silence Job's questions? "Yahweh is challenging Job's readiness to stir the destructive forces of chaos" (3.8).[28] Or, "to make such claims is to throw off the yoke of obedience to God, to become like mighty Leviathan, whom alone God can tame."[29] In other words only YHWH the true hero can control the chaos monster—so how dare Job "rouse" either Leviathan or YHWH? The creation sequence can thus be read tehomophobically, as a divine assertion of sheer power over and against Job's (deep) arrogance. The roaring two-monster finale—"Can you thunder with a voice like this?" (40.9)—may be read as a recrudescence of the divine hero myth, defeating Job's existential defiance by a performance of the power that created order out of chaos and continues to discipline the chaos. Thus YHWH would have simply re-reversed the universe, set it right again in the face of Job's chaogenic curses, and so restored His honor in the face of human allegations.[30] Yet contrary to these readings, the text implies no conflict of deity with monster. On the contrary, God seems to delight in Leviathan's fitness to defend itself against all possible attacks. But Leviathan is not shown attacking.

If not a tehomophobic warrior, what about an omnipotent Creator? The latter line of interpretation might seem validated by Job's own confession: "I know you can do all things; no purposes of yours can be thwarted." Von Rad's explanation of the intention of the YHWH oracles typifies the imposition of the *ex nihilo*: "If Job's holding fast to his righteousness was a question put to God, God gives the answer by pointing to the glory of his providence that sustains all his creation. Of course this justice of God cannot be comprehended by man; it can only be adored."[31] I agree that a human concept of justice is being put in its unspeakably immense place, that of creation; I agree that the wisdom of the universe is ultimately adorable. The Joban poet is surely deconstructing an anthropomorphic concept of deity and an anthropocentric construction of "his justice." But the reduction of Job's wild epiphany to a series of orthodox propositions made up of smug theologoumena like "adoration," "glorification," "God's incomprehensible justice," and "his providence" misses its meaning, as though the answer to Job's question is that there is no question.

If this hermeneutical dominology remains the only alternative, I opt for David Robertson's radical reading. God appears therein as nothing more than the loudest voice in the series of blustering speeches of false certainty. He becomes "the friends writ large," adding nothing theologically but the bully power of omnipotence. "God's rhetoric, because Job has armed us against it, convinces us that he is a charlatan God, one who has the power and skill of a god but is a fake at the truly divine task of governing with justice and love."[32] The whirlwind is a windbag; Robertson's Job winks at the audience as he knuckles under. But Robertson misses something. Like the standard interpretations that prop up the charlatan God, he hardly notices the *animals*.

VI Revealing beasts

Most interpreters virtually yawn at the zoological fecundity, the bestial intensity, of the vision. They stand in a long tradition of animal erasure. For instance, in all of Calvin's twenty sermons on Job, he ignores the animals, even the Leviathan.[33] Otherwise, the multiple manifestation of the wild animals registers as at best a passing effect of the Creator's power. A bestial blip. Of the vision's saturation with the chaoid imaginary of watery depths and dragons, of its organization by the motifs of undomesticated nature—they venture little beyond the platitudes of divine power or humanistic revolt. Christian interpreters may appreciate the sun and stars as evidence of omnipotent order. But animals, especially wild ones, have always posed a gamy embarrassment to human dominion.[34] For nonhuman animals do all the procreating and eating that humans do; they resemble us but do not speak. In Job they break silence. The animals approach that "zone of maximal proximity" in laughter.

So what in this zone *does* the divine vortex convey? What if the excessive cosmic and bestial detail is not just medium but message? Have interpretations of Job, looking to the power of the creator rather than to the creation, shown the same obtuseness from which the creator-spirit rouses Job? Do we *yet* care when the antelope calves, or how the wild ass scours the hills for green? Do we consider their lives, their patterns of eating, mating, birthing and moving, so far beneath the dignity of theology, so much less important than human suffering, so much less interesting than human discourse, that we politely skim the poetics of creation? Have we cared so little that we colluded in the rapid discreation of all these carefully crafted species? Might our indifference reflect the cultivated distaste for the *chaos* of creation?

Through parody, I submit, the Joban poet resists a hardening theological anthropomorphism that in the combined context of an urban and exile-prone monotheism was already tending to reduce nonhuman nature to a background effect. It is often suggested that the poet was challenging the deuteronomic account of Israel's history, whereby the people's colonization by neighboring superpowers could be rendered meaningful as divine retribution for the people's sins. This strategy of blaming Israel made God ultimately responsible for all the horrors. In the guise of punishment and test, God became the ruler and eventual micromanager of all history. With every disaster God would have to be re-justified, the people re-blamed.

Did the Joban poet thus resist a double alienation: the loss of the wild integrities of creation and the loss of human justice in history? Does the text not subtly unhinge the causal link between human tragedy and divine causation? According to Carol Newsom the whirlwind blows aside Job's "legal model of rights and faults and his image of God as the great patriarch."[35] Amidst all the suffering of the Hebrew people, the injustices of exile and its aftermath, was this poet worried not just about the suffering as such, not only about its unfairness–but about the deforming effects of the theology of divine retribution? Gutierrez has brought the question of social justice into exegetical relief as Job's own question: "The expectation of rewards that is at the heart of the doctrine of retribution vitiates the entire relationship and plays the demonic role of obstacle on the way to God."[36] Ultimately, then, "Job shows us a way with his vigorous protest, his discovery of concrete commitment to the poor and all who suffer unjustly, his facing up to God and his acknowledgement of the gratuitousness that characterizes God's plan for human history" (ibid., p. 102). While I do not share this belief in a divine "plan" (which belongs after all to the script of omnipotence), I can only underscore Gutierrez' interpretation of God's affirmation of Job's questions as having "spoken of me what is right" (Job 42.7 and 8). Did the poet link demoralization to denaturalization; the loss of promised land to the loss of cosmos?

In other words: perhaps the whirlwind rhapsodizes astronomical bodies, weather and wild animals *because* these resist human dominance. Now that would be quite a startling proto-midrash on Genesis 1.26f., precisely the text most exploited to justify our exploitation of the rest of creation. For on the sixth day, when bi-gendered humankind gets created in the image of God, it receives that ill-fated "dominion": "Be fruitful and multiply, and fill the earth and subdue it; and have dominion over the fish of the sea and over the birds of the air and over every living thing that moves upon the earth" (Genesis 1.26). The current hoard of CEOs and fundamentalists who cite the verse to justify ecological exploitation invariably omit the next verse. "See I have given you every plant yielding seed that is upon the face of all the earth, and every tree with seed in its fruit; you shall have them for food" (1.29). It is a *vegetarian dominion* Elohim has offered.[37] Nor do they quote the climactic verse of Genesis 1: "And to every beast of the earth, and to every bird of the air, and to everything that creeps on the earth, everything that has the breath of life, I have given every green plant for food" (1.30).

In other words we are given what the rest of the animals get. What sort of deflating dominion is this? All that otherwise distinguishes the human from the animal in the priestly narrative, according to Phyllis Trible, is the equality of male and female that designates the *imago dei*.[38] Let me suggest an alternative exegesis of the monster-revelation. As the climax of the recapitulation of the creation, it must be read precisely for its ironic relation to human dominion. I cite the final three verses of the whirlwind panorama, which with indubitably leviathanic levity depict an ancient whale sighting:

> It makes the deep boil like a pot;
> it makes the sea like a pot of ointment.
> It leaves a shining wake behind it;
> one would think the deep to be white-haired.
> On earth it has no equal,
> a creature without fear.
> It surveys everything that is lofty;
> it is king over all that are proud.
>
> (41.31–4)

Thus a vision that had opened with a ludic image of the dread sea as cloud-swaddled neonate now ends with the trope of a harmless old white-haired ocean. Both images poke fun at the cultural tehomophobia. But what of the kingly, fearless Leviathan? Is it not to *be* feared? Or does the assignation of its kingship "over all that are proud" not lock in a bizarre parallelism to Genesis 1.26ff.? The dominion discourse of Genesis derives from the imagery of kingship; unlike the *Enuma Elish*, in which humans are created as servants to the gods, P grants them the freedom and respon-sibility characteristic of divine and human kingship.[39] But Job's "no equal" on earth for Leviathan makes no exception of humans.

Does this midrash of Genesis 1 not only reverse Job's reversal curses, but *revoke human dominion*? Does YHWH annul the specific privilege of our species and sardonically pass it to a monster? Perhaps not so baldly. The final statement implies conditionality: that we lose our special human status when we abuse it. When we mistake dominion for dominance, we fail in our responsibility as caretakers for the earth—*ipso facto* we abdicate "dominion."[40] The Leviathanic tirade, the "awful tauntings in Job" which we will hear in *Moby Dick*, encodes in its parody a more specific warning:

> Will it make a covenant with you to be taken as your servant forever?
> Will you play with it as with a bird,
> or will you put it on leash for your girls?
> Will traders bargain over it?
> Will they divide it up among the merchants?
> Can you fill its skin with harpoons . . . ?

(41.4–7a)

Much has been made of the ludicrousness of the trope of Leviathan as a pet for giggling girls.[41] Little, however, has been said of its *economics*. Like Moby Dick, Leviathan makes a mockery of the whaling industry. The author could not have imagined the current human capacity to annihilate the whales altogether, or to turn the sea into a sewer. But in this deft parody of the ancient world trade and business class, the windy vortex mocks the powers of global commercialization; it puts in question the assumption of the exploitability of the wild life of the world—the "subdue and have dominion" project. The chaos monster does not seek vengeance but respect for its domain. "Who can confront it and be safe—under the whole heaven, who?" In failing to respect the proper dominions of the beasts, humanity also fails to respect their admiring compadre and creator. Our species "pride" emanates from the same anthropocentrism that provoked the deity to cry out "Will you even put me in the wrong? Will you condemn me that you may be justified?" (40.8).

VII Last laughs

Yet YHWH offered no condemnation of Job, the suffering and courageous individual: on the contrary, for his relentless questioning Job received the honor of the longest epiphany. However, Whedbee notes that there is some truth in the friends' worry about Job's arrogance; his demands for God's signed theodicy verge on buffoonery. While the counselors accepted, like most unquestioning theists, the paradox of divine justice and power, Job could no longer abide its hypocrisy. But like his friends, he knew no theological alternative. So he obsessively demanded explanation, pushing the anthropomorphism to its narcissistic limit.

In response the whirlwind offered no defense; it swept away the theo-logic of the complaint. From Job's perspective, innocent suffering had to imply the injustice of God. The divine speeches disclose with poetic bluster and roaring indirection an altogether different perspective. It is as if the shift from legal to cosmogonic discourse delegalized and deprivatized Job's questions. They entered the intense proximity of the *comic* plane–just as they opened into the bottomless expanse of *cosmic* space. It is not Job's own arrogance that is confronted, but rather the arrogance of a species that had learned to trade its sacred dignity against that of the other creatures.

But the whirlwind does not speak only threat. Whedbee festively names its content the "carnival of creation." It invokes a comedically cosmic wonder that moves beyond ridicule to affirmation.[42] Yet it does not lose its parodic edge: the carnival resonates with both the ironic polyglossia of Bakhtin's "carnivalesque" subversions, always a parody of the sacred status quo. But here it is the disorderly deity who brings on the carnival. So I join Whedbee in reading the whirlwind as neither charlatanry nor mastery, but rather as "the unrestrained laughter of a universe filled with bountiful, boundless life" (ibid., p. 252). Still the laughter turns to taunt when we do not join in–not easy to do in the face of lost children. But the tight hope of a universe of controlled outcomes can only block grief and harden hearts. Is *blockage* the problem–rather than a shame-and-blame model of sin? After the epiphany, Job discerns divine agency: he confesses that "nothing can block your purposes." This might be the same old theology of mastery. Or has this purposeful "you" undergone a change of subject during its epiphany? Do these purposes, these "things too wonderful for me, which I did not know," necessarily suggest supernatural intervention or omnipotence? Or do these purposes hint rather at a mystery hidden in full view? Visible only through the eye of the whirlwind? Not a mystery of tidy nature or rational supernature, but a hint of the chaosmos?

It is an ecological activist with an interest in Christian community who has best recognized the wild ecological life of the vision. In a fetching meditation on Job, Bill McKibben hears the voice calling us "overwhelmingly, to joy. To immersion in the fantastic beauty and drama all around us . . . The reason Job matters so much to me is because of the language–the biologically accurate, earthy, juicy, crusty, wild, untamed poetry of God's great speech."[43]

Job, however, sees not just creatures but creator: "but now my eye sees you." Yet there is no trace, no beard or backside, of a personal God who might be thus "seen." What Job "sees" in the vision of God is only the creatures. To "see" God *is* to see the creation. Does this mean that God *is* the creation? Or rather that the creation is God's visible body–*the all that spills forth so chaotically, so creatively, so procreatively* from "the womb"? Divine "purposes" then would suggest the purposefulness of a universe that against all statistical odds yields laws that work, rules of space, time, speed and cohesion through which life continues to complicate itself and emerge undaunted. These are not the purposes of a bully God, a blustering warrior, or a detached omnipotence. Is the only God who can be "seen" amidst the infinities and infinitesimals the one who shares the risks of the creatures, the vulnerabilities of birth, the passions of beauty?

Does Job not in the end address as *you* the spirit who circulates upon the waters, who sports with Leviathan, whose wisdom organizes an immense, teeming and sexy universe?[44] One need not read into the book of Job a systematic process panentheism, in which God's omnipotence is neatly replaced by persuasive goodness, and divine commands by lures. Perhaps such abstractions, however preferable to other anachronisms, flatten the parodic genre. Yet Job already whirls toward an ecological theology of the Whiteheadian sort, in which human becoming looks cramped and cancerous—unless we collude more wisely with the elements, the plants, the beasts and each other. The book of Job was driven by an ethical passion. But the change of divine subject changes the subject of ethics: it *becomes* us. It is not up to God to right our moral wrongs, to fix our injustices and correct our oppressions. That doesn't happen. To depend on God to intervene, to justify "himself," to operate as the just patriarch is to abdicate our own moral responsibility for the earth. Yet this epiphany does not deprive God of agency, or reduce Elohim to an impersonal force of nature: "This new image is one of God as a power for life, balancing the needs of all creatures, not just humans, cherishing freedom, full of fierce love and delight for each thing without regard for its utility, acknowledging the deep interconnectedness of death and life, restraining and nurturing each element in the ecology of all creation." Having thus beautifully summarized the germinal theology of Job, Newsom hardly needs add: "it is a description of God and the world that has strong points of contact with contemporary feminist thought."[45] Indeed this freedom, this delight, seems not accidentally to have marked itself in the concrete and, for its context, unusual behavior of the aftermath: when Job's new daughters are not only given inheritances, but are named—while the sons are not!

Yet even in this hope—for a tehomic countertradition that will lend strength to present struggles—we may tense into the cycle of certainty and disappointment. We may block "your purposes." Unless we laugh with the Leviathan? "Laughter", writes Bakhtin, "is a vital factor in laying down that prerequisite for fearlessness without which it would be impossible to approach the world realistically."[46] In a universe of open-ended indeterminacy, in which our most wounded questions rarely yield direct answers, faith will approximate courage.

Whirlwinds in meteorology are complex chaotic systems that suggest not pure chaos but rather the turbulent emergence of complexity at the edge of chaos. To Job's question: the answer is still blowin' in the wind.

8

"LEVIATHANIC REVELATIONS"
Melville's hermenautical journey

To grope down into the bottom of the sea after them; to have one's hands among the unspeakable foundations, ribs, and very pelvis of the world; this is a fearful thing. What am I that I should essay to hook the nose of this leviathan! The awful tauntings in Job might well appall me.

(Herman Melville, *Moby Dick*)

I Constituents of a chaos

Moby Dick's narrator Ishmael, a schoolteacher after all, proposes to offer a "systematized exhibition of the whale in his broad genera."[1] Before his readers get "lost in the unshored, harborless immensities" of the text, he offers them an encyclopedic review of all known "scientific" texts–and clippings from newspapers, mythology, Plutarch and Genesis–of the whale. Beginning "with cisterns and buckets" of intertext, the novel itself mimics the immense body of a whale, the unbounded expansiveness of sea.[2]

Since "already we are boldly launched upon the deep" Melville dangles before the present theology a great tehomic bait: "a thorough appreciative understanding of the more special leviathanic revelations and allusions of all sorts" (p. 116). But even as he promises this hermeneutical completeness, he teases the reader with a strange synonymity: "The classification of the constituents of a chaos, nothing less is here essayed." He presumes that his readers will fill in the metonymic gap linking "whale" to "chaos." Quite a gap. It bottoms into the "unspeakable foundations," the "very pelvis of the world," in which monstrous vicinity the author inscribes himself groping blindly. The "chaos" signifier cheerfully trumps Melville's own promise of total knowledge. As he concludes his "systematic" cetology, he taunts the ideal of totality: "God keep me from ever completing anything. This whole book is but a draught–nay, but the draught of a draught" (p. 128).

The ever unfinished? The tehomic infinite? As he wrote to Hawthorne, "It is hard to be finite on an infinite subject, and all subjects are infinite."[3] A denial of the finite?

Or to the contrary, an embrace of tragic particularity so profound that it holds the finite creature to its own bottomless incompletion? Melville's humor continually twists the tragic closure of the finite into yet another opening: the infinite play of this language can embrace an intolerable depth of tragedy precisely by holding the subject to its own unfinished story. I argue in this chapter that with Melville we pick up a North American echo, two millennia later, of Job's leviathanic irony. Neither text, whose windy, tragi-comic offense to the proprieties of faith and form has been muffled by canonization, can get enough of the Leviathan. Nor can either finally separate the chaos of whale from the chaos of God: cetology becomes theology. Yet theology has had virtually nothing to say about Melville's oceanic midrash on Job.[4]

II Multitudinous murmurings

With Melville we sail into the waters of the unabashedly indeterminate, where the subject-matter will appear and vanish: the unrepresentable. "There is no white whale as definable essence, as a delineable rendering," comments Glen Mazis; "the total whale exists only in process."[5] The whale itself, like a slippery organ, will elude our grasp. Yet this unspeakability does not stop language. On the contrary, as with the theology of the ineffable (but with more laughter), it produces a nonlinear amplification of writing. Of Leviathan, Melville exclaims: "Unconsciously my chirography expands into placard capitals. Give me a condor's quill! Give me Vesuvius' crater for an inkstand! Friends, hold my arms!" A critic of the period dryly retorts, "Oh that his friends had obeyed that summons! They might have saved society from a huge dose of hyperbolic slang, maudlin sentimentalism, and tragi-comic bubble and squeak."[6] Indeed Melville saw *Moby Dick* widely dismissed as "ravings" fit for "a writ *de lunatico*," and "a monstrous bore" but for the excitement of the chase scenes.[7] But how could Melville's readers have been expected to *get* the tragi-comic joke, i.e. to fill in the virtually endless chain of signifiers flowing from "whale"–to leviathan–Bible–the deep–*tehom*–and "chaos"? Of course what was damned as this "strange, wild, furibund thing" has since been very nearly domesticated, its own nose hooked, as great American novel and Hollywood-worthy boys-at-sea yarn. Yet its embodiment of the subversive-parodic form that Bakhtin attributes to the very genre of the novel, its heteroglossic hybridity, remains audible as a tehomic counterdiscourse.

If the present chapter reads *Moby Dick* as a North American modern midrash on the book of Job, which we just considered as an internal midrash on Genesis 1, we must admit that the novel presents itself more clearly as a commentary on Jonah. "Within this gargantuan novel and these huge folds of whale's flesh," observes biblical scholar Yvonne Sherwood, "are woven distorted images from the book of Jonah– what Father Mapple terms 'one of the smallest strands in the mighty cable of Scripture.'"[8] Given Mapple's foreboding Calvinist homily at the pulpit-prow early in the novel, Jonah's whale as organ of God's inscrutable will thematically predominates.[9] Thus Ishmael returns to write the tale only after his ship has like Jonah's been "shrove" by the great whale. As Father Mapple so mellifluously intones: "And Jonah, bruised and beaten—his ears, like two sea-shells, still multitudinously murmuring of the ocean—Jonah did the Almighty's bidding. And what was that, shipmates? To preach the Truth to the face of Falsehood! That was it!" (p. 50). Given the force of this Truth, the more ambiguous intertext of Job has been far less explored. Yet affinities of structure, tone, and genre, indeed of leviathanic enthusiasm, draw our attention to Melville's Joban allusions.

The sign of the "awful tauntings in Job" presages the novel's climactic scene. Melville clearly has in mind YHWH's rhetorical questions:

> Can you draw out Leviathan with a fishhook,
> or press down its tongue with a cord?
> Can you put a rope in its nose,
> or pierce its jaw with a hook?
>
> (Job 41.1f)

Needless to say, Captain Ahab gave the wrong answer. *Moby Dick*'s epilogue, framing the novel with its narrator Ishmael's survival, is announced by the terse citation: "And I only am escaped alone to tell you—Job." With these words a servant had delivered to Job the news of horrific loss. In the novel, the whirlpool that has just swallowed the Pequod, has now "subsided to a creamy pool." From its center springs the coffin built by Queequeg. So it is as though the sign of the whirlpool reinscribes the entire text within a nonlinear inversion. "One realizes," writes Mazis, "that all has been said from the vantage point of the final swirl of the vortex."[10] The vortex sends Ishmael forward and the reader back to the novel's beginning. Even as it belies the linearity of time, the trope of the spiraling waters inverts life into death and death into life, ship into coffin and coffin into raft. The sign of the vortex mirrors the final, all-encompassing vantage point of the book of Job: the divine whirlwind.

The fact that atmospheric and oceanic vortices pose prime examples of the dynamic systems of chaos is not incidental to a tehomic intertextuality, which describes turbulent orders only much later legible to science. In Mazis' reading, Ahab's desperation for mastery cedes narrative interest, finally, to humble Ishmael, reborn in the coffin from the watery vortex. The Melvillian vortex, which Mazis likens to the vortices of J. M. W. Turner's later paintings, at once expresses and generates a *surface* of turbulent *depth*: "Space and time are two vectors within a more primary depth whose waters are the complexity of competing and often opposing meanings . . . whose mists are the shifting ways in which one can experience and express, and whose sun contains a darkness within its illumination" (ibid.). That "more primary depth" suggests not a monodimensional depth but the chaoid Deleuzian heterogeneity of the "pro/found", the pre-foundational.

III Nebulous transgressions

A contemporary of Melville's captured the analogy to the paintings of Turner: "The climax of the three days' chase after Moby Dick is highly wrought and sternly exciting–but the catastrophe, in its whirl of waters and fancies, resembles one of Turner's later nebulous transgressions in gamboge."[11] Unfortunately the critic means to sink Melville and Turner, not to praise them. Their respective transgressions of the orders of word and image set off a transatlantic resonance of chaos. In an early passage(way) of *Moby Dick* hangs a painting that sounds uncannily like a late Turner. A cold and hungry Ishmael has found hospitality in the Spouter Inn. In its dark hallway he finds "a very large oil-painting, so thoroughly be-smoked, and every way defaced," with "such unaccountable masses of shades and shadows, that at first you almost thought some ambitious young artist, in the time of the New England hags, had endeavored *to delineate chaos bewitched*." His description prophesies the non-representational art of the following century:

> a boggy, soggy, squitchy picture truly, enough to drive a nervous man distracted. Yet there was there a sort of indefinite, half-attained, unimaginable sublimity about it that fairly froze you to it, till you involuntarily took an oath with yourself to find out what that marvelous painting meant. (p. 20)

The painting within the novel: a presentation of the unpresentable? Among known painters Turner alone had–to the consternation of his patrons–plunged into this "indistinctness." Had Melville chanced upon a painting by his tehomic antecedent in art?[12] Melville inscribes on the defaced and dark surface that which soggily resists representation. Kin to what Ruskin called the "dark clue" of Turner's later paintings, an almost invisible, chaotically enchanting abyss *shows* itself.[13] Given the irresolvable metonymic freight of the novel, does Melville paint this "picture" as a disincentive to those who would reduce his subject to a narrative, a moral, a representable meaning?

At the same time, amidst the embrace of that chaos for which, like Turner, Melville would be routinely criticized, he still insists that we discern what is "meant." We are not to forfeit the interpretive task. Indeed both Turner and Melville can be read for their scriptural hermeneutics. David Jasper, a scholar of Hebrew scripture, analyzes the return of biblical themes in Turner's late paintings as "the utterly primal experience recorded in Genesis: 'Let there be light.'" The way the sheer "flux of creative light" passes through Turner's watery matrix may help theology to read the word of Genesis 1.3 less militantly. "The light both blinds and reveals," as Jasper reads it, "suggesting Scripture grasped momentarily as a whole, yet somehow without form, and therefore open to endless interpretation."[14]

5. Joseph Mallord William Turner, *A View of Deal* (1835). Photo: © Nationalmuseum, Sweden.

The infinity of a chaosmic hermeneutic signals again not a dearth but an excess of meaning, a meaning-fullness or meaning-flux released by the refusal of hard lines and clear boundaries. Thus a recent critic writes of the late Turner: "The introduction of chaos into this existing order was part of the process of transformation, chaos not simply as a disorder but as a state of primal indeterminacy that is a prelude to a new social and natural actuality."[15] A transfigural indeterminacy–which disfigures in order to refigure–emanates from the icon of the creative chaos. Thus the painting in the uterine passageway promises to yield upon meditation a certain figuration. Like Turner's late seascapes, it is not a pure abstraction.

> Ever and anon a bright, but, alas, deceptive idea would dart you through.–It's the Black Sea in a midnight gale.–It's the unnatural combat of the four primal elements.–It's a blasted heath.–It's a Hyperborean winter scene.–It's the breaking-up of the ice-bound stream of Time.

Dispersing as quickly as they arise, these mythological associations fold back into the form of the novel itself. The cracking of a frozen temporality eerily confirms Bakhtin's assessment of the temporality of the modern novel: "For the first time in artistic-ideological consciousness, time and the world become historical: they unfold, albeit at first still unclearly and confusedly, *as becoming, as an uninterrupted movement into a real future, as a unified, all-embracing and unconcluded process*."[16] Thus in the medium of Melville's novel, the frozen archetypes, the immobilized stereotypes, the bounded individuals, thaw into an originary flux. As in Job we saw an early dialogic resistance to the heroic epic, in *Moby Dick* the leviathanic laughter again–muted whimsy or wild roar–demonstrates this nonlinear temporality. "Every event, every phenomenon, every thing, every object of artistic representation loses its completedness, its hopelessly finished quality and its immutability that had been so essential to it in the world of the epic 'absolute past,' walled off by an unapproachable boundary from the continuing and unfinished present" (p. 30). If the novel emerged from the subversive medieval genre of the *parodia sacra*, its multilingual hybridizing finds itself in *Moby Dick* stretched into a new scale of multicultural and open-ended temporality. The tehomic "sea of heteroglossia" similarly opens theology into this sense of the infinite as the unoriginate and the inconclusive: the God who might well keep us "from ever completing anything." This deity, like an artist, does not surrender us to chaos but lures us to contemplate the "chaos bewitched." Charmed rather than compelled, we witness an order that to impatient sensibilities may appear as a meaningless or even demonic chaos. "Art transforms chaotic variability into chaoid variety, as in El Greco's black and green-gray conflagration, for example, or Turner's golden conflagration," write Deleuze and Guattari, philosophers of this chaos. "Art struggles with chaos in order to make it sensory."[17]

In the trope of the oil painting, Melville sketches his tehomic hermeneutic. The figure which does finally emerge from its dark vortex not surprisingly signals the significance of his novel and of the submerged tradition we are seeking to resurface: "But stop; does it not bear a faint resemblance to a gigantic fish? even the great leviathan himself?" (p. 20). The leviathanic signifier does not represent but will faintly and irresistibly invoke, provoke, its watery meanings. Melville daubs throughout the novel at the fleeting ontology of his object: "you must needs conclude that the great Leviathan is that one creature in the world which must remain unpainted to the last." But not altogether: "True, one portrait may hit the mark much nearer than another." But "there is no earthly way of finding out precisely what the whale really looks like." And "the only mode in which you can derive even a tolerable idea of his living contour, is by going a-whaling yourself; but by so doing, you run no small risk of being eternally stove and sunk by him" (p. 228). The religion that understandably tries to protect us from the risk has offered us cartoons instead: a God-thing, an evil thing, and a creation full of things, surrounded by nothing.

IV Shadow of divinity

We could of course follow those who simply identify Father Mapple's quite unstereotyped Calvinist sermon as the moral and center of the novel, accommodating an intense darkness in God, even as "Jonah's prodigy of ponderous misery drags him drowning down to sleep."[18] But then we would not need to push off into "the howling infinite," where a theology of leviathanic revelation will remain as elusive and dangerous as the whale, a "shining wake" in language (ibid., p. 161). If the whale was God's organ in Jonah, certainly in the Calvinist Jonah, for Ishmael, "the narrator-turned-cetologist/theologian . . . Godness and whaleness blur" (ibid., p. 158). Decoding the leviathanic surface of the I AM of Exodus 34.23, Ishmael paraphrases the text thus: "I but go skin deep . . . Thou shalt see my back parts, my tail, he seems to say, but my face shall not be seen." From this exodus epiphany of "God in the dark" had emanated negative theology, with its ancient deconstructions of God-language, its God beyond or without being.[19]

The surface of ocean, skin, or text nonetheless bears the cargo of meaning. But if we mean *theologically*–does not the very word, the God-word, threaten to shut down all sense of adventure? Melville, impatient even with the radical transcendentalists and pantheists of his period, offers his own deconstruction: "But it is this Being of the matter; there lies the knot with which we choke ourselves," he wrote in a letter to Hawthorne (anticipating the critique of ontotheology).[20] "As soon as you say Me, a God, a Nature, so soon you jump off from your stool and hang from the beam" (p. 555). These substantiated, stabilized noun-entities strangle the *ruach* of any story. "Take God out of the dictionary," he suggests, "and you would have him in the street." One thinks of the African American "God on the streetz" in a more recent U.S.

manifestation.[21] Yet when religion pretends to "systematized exhibition," it removes us both from the streets and from the deep.

V Truth with malice

What in its evanescence does the white whale signify for Melville? Ishmael explains what it means for the disfigured Captain Ahab. The great whale had taken off Ahab's leg in their first encounter. "Small reason was there to doubt, then, that ever since that almost fatal encounter, Ahab had cherished a wild vindictiveness against the whale, all the more fell for that in his frantic morbidness he at last came to identify with him, not only all his bodily woes, but all his intellectual and spiritual exasperations" (p. 160). That the whale was merely swimming in its habitat, striking back in self-defense, means nothing to proud, "dismasted" Ahab. "The White Whale swam before him as the monomaniac incarnation of all those malicious agencies which some deep men feel eating in them, till they are left living on with half a heart and half a lung" (ibid.). In this prescient account of projection, we observe how all that can be called evil–"the intangible malignancy that has been from the beginning"–gets subliminally funneled into the white whale. For in his vengeful mission, to which he is willing to sacrifice the ship and crew, only a total and personal evil, a devil incarnate, can serve as the adequate target:

> All that most maddens and torments; all that stirs up the lees of things;
> all truth with malice in it; all that cracks the sinews and cakes the brain;
> all the subtle demonisms of life and thought; all evils, to crazy Ahab,
> were visibly personified, and made practically assailable in Moby Dick.
>
> (p. 160)

The Captain excites the crew–including good but pliant Starbuck–to unify under his monomaniacal messianism. Ishmael barely pulls himself free of the mesmerism by which the doomed crew has been gripped. He ponders with pre-Freudian perspicacity "how to their unconscious understandings, also, in some dim, unsuspected way" Moby Dick "might have seemed the gliding great demon of the seas of life." In other words the albino whale has become to Ahab, as Tiamat to Marduk; or Leviathan to the YHWH of Isaiah. This is the YHWH also presumed by Job prior to his epiphany: "By his understanding he smote Rahab" (26.12). Ahab's crew, like Marduk's fellow gods, follow the leader. Melville paints Ahab with a tragic dignity in his Job-like rage, his fury at his own disfiguration, his refusal of the given, his–almost Nietzschean–challenge to or envy of the deity: "Now, then," he tells himself, "be the prophet and the fulfiller one. That's more than ye, ye great gods, ever were" (p. 147). For any constraint on his own self-sufficiency–mirroring as it does a Creator from nothing–assails his freedom.[22]

Here Irigaray's marine reading of a Nietzschean masculinity reverberates with the Ahabian motifs of doomed heroism. "An hour of anxious suspense. The proudest navigators wait and pray . . . And what good is all their seamanship if the sea refuses to submit to it? What good is their language if there is nothing and no one to appeal to? And who will rescue them from the whirlwind sown by their own presumptuousness?"[23] Irigaray offers her own diagnosis of the tehomophobic masculinity, of a transcendence predicated on its mastery of the she/sea. Seeking its vulnerability, its blind spot, through her strategic mimicry, her "disconcerting of language" reveals her as an oracle of the tehomophilic countertradition–however absent as in Melville remain its females.[24] Yet almost like Melville, Irigaray returns the "proudest navigators" to the fluid from which they came: that they might recall "the first 'meeting,' before his thought's beginning," when "she gives–gives herself in the 'form' of fluids."[25] The nautical becomes the natal. Job had cursed that womb. But he finally heard the whirlwind to its speech. Yet Captain Ahab–for whom to hear is to obey–hears no one. "Who's over me? Truth hath no confines" (p. 144). His defiance of transcendent truth represents the modern device for totalizing one's own. Irigaray, dissolving all hermeneutics of mastery, offers this parable:

> The sea shines with a myriad eyes. And none is given any privilege. Even here and now she undoes all perspective. Countless and shifting and merging her depths. And her allure is an icy shroud for the point of view.[26]

The monoperspectival, monomaniacal subject goes under in this polyoptic sea. Like all tormented and self-mastering subjects, Ahab is a wounded creature, whose fury directs itself against another fierce and wounded creature. In that opposition to the Other he mimics it, he merges with the opponent he has created. The whale, jaw carved and impaled by prior attacks, had cut Ahab into a fragment of himself; had revealed fragmentariness itself. Rather than read his amputation as sign–*monstrum*–of the death in life, the finitude carved out by limit and loss, this man, Man, rewrites the already painfully inscribed tehomic body as evil.

VI Animal re/monstration

"'Vengeance on a dumb brute!' cried Starbuck, 'that simply smote thee from blindest instinct! Madness! To be enraged with a dumb thing, Captain Ahab, seems blasphemous'" (p. 144). Moby Dick's defiance seems deliberate, significant, a premeditated revolt: "such seemed the White Whale's infernal aforethought of ferocity, that every dismembering or death that he caused, was not wholly regarded as having been inflicted by an unintelligent agent" (p. 159). It is this specter of animal intelligence that drives Ahab off the deep end. He anoints himself a prophet–"I now prophesy that I shall dismember my dismemberer" (p. 147).

The great whaling captain could hardly be expected to accept defeat at the hands of his prey. Its commercial success legendary, its captains rich, the New England whaling fleet had by now colonized the oceans. The Protestant spirit of capitalism was running high, confirming Man's Dominion over Nature. The Joban intertext allows Melville to challenge the Puritan economics theory summarized in the platitude: "the godly prosper."[27] It is in this context that Melville narrated nature's resistance. Melville could not have predicted the extermination crisis of the twentieth century. Yet *Moby Dick* has been recognized as a precursor to an evolutionary and ecological consciousness; with his detailed cetological exposition, as allegory-resistant as Job's carnivalesque catalog of wild things, he insisted on the irreducible complexity of a particular species.[28] According to one eco-critic and fan, Moby Dick may be, from an evolutionary-biological viewpoint, "the most thoroughly realized animal in all literature."[29]

Yet Ahab surreptitiously gives up on profit in this quest: he represents no petty capitalism. Does he rather embody the proud, vengeful brilliance manning the edges of "man's dominion over nature"? Or does his omnicidal fury disclose more specifically a madness at the edge of western civilization–the ultimately suicidal voracity revealed only lately in the late capitalism, which New England commerce helped to spawn? But if Moby Dick signifies not evil but the wild depth of a creation exploited by modernity and demonized when it resists–how shall we decipher the whale's *whiteness*?

VII The cetology of sex and race

> Melville uses allegorical formations–the white whale, the racially mixed crew, the black-white pairings of male couples, the questing, questioning white male captain who confronts impenetrable whiteness–to investigate and analyze hierarchic difference.
>
> (Toni Morrison, *Playing in the Dark*[30])

In a famous chapter titled "The Whiteness of the Whale," Ishmael offers a detailed phenomenology of the color white itself: for "it was *the whiteness of the whale that above all things appalled me*." After cataloging the convention of identifying white with "whatever is sweet, and honorable, and sublime," he emphasizes that there "yet lurks an elusive something in the innermost idea of this hue," which causes panic, dread, horror–as the white shark, the albatross, the albino, whose "pervading whiteness makes him more strangely hideous than the ugliest abortion"; the shroud, the phantom, "the king of terrors" who "when personified by the evangelist, rides on his pallid horse" (p. 166; my emphasis). Given his context and his known abolitionist views, his contradiction of the color code of white supremacism echoes all the more pointedly.

Might we imagine that he deconstructs the whiteness by which the European

150

immigrants had forged their unity over against those they would color red, black, brown and yellow? In another scene, Ishmael mocks this self-deluding codification: "as though a white man were anything more dignified than a whitewashed Negro" (p. 60) Melville, a firm opponent of slavery, wrote in the postcolonial, antebellum context. But "until the mid-1960's," Carolyn Karcher argues, "there was almost no interest in Melville's racial views, and very little recognition of the prominent place that social criticism occupies in his writing." Her own literary analysis centers on race criticism. "Only since the Civil Rights and anti-Vietnam War movements have forced us to read our national history and literature afresh has it become possible to approach Melville with a different set of questions."[31] Toni Morrison writes thus of Melville: "But to question the very notion of white progress, the very idea of racial superiority, of whiteness as privileged place in the evolutionary ladder of humankind, and to meditate on the fraudulent, self-destroying philosophy of that superiority, to 'pluck it out from under the robes of Senators and Judges,' to drag the 'judge himself to the bar,'–that was dangerous, solitary, radical work." Startling praise for this great white male. "Especially then. Especially now."[32]

"Whiteness," avers Melville, wrapping up his lengthy phenomenology of the ambivalence of whiteness, "is not so much a color as the visible absence of color, and at the same time the concrete of all colors" (p. 169). *Blanc*, blank. ". . . Such a dumb blankness, full of meaning, in a wide landscape of snows–a colorless, all-color of atheism from which we shrink." To make whiteness visible is to learn to read its absent presence: concretely, its racial construction that–until we *see* it–colors my self as white while denying that I have color in the same stroke–truly a colorless all-color. The western dominion over all that can be colored Other has classified the variegated, vivid, dark others–human and nonhuman–of a non-classifiable chaos. And at the same time it identifies as the Selfsame, a whiteness whose disembodied pallor, whose numb aggressions, those must learn, who "learn to be white."

Melville's parody of whiteness kicks off with his characterization of the dark Queequeg. Assigned in Coffin's inn to the same bed, Ishmael reacts with standard race panic: "Why didn't you tell me that that infernal harpooneer was a cannibal?" ("Cannibal" was the going term for Black islanders, implying both their idolatrous and culinary predilections.) The mood turns quickly as Ishmael's respect for Queequeg blossoms. "What's all this fuss I have been making about, thought I to myself–the man's a human being just as I am: he has just as much reason to fear me, as I have to be afraid of him. Better sleep with a sober cannibal than a drunken Christian" (p. 31). Soon they are intimate friends. Overnight, the conventions of racial, sexual and religious propriety get jubilantly overturned: "those same things that would have repelled most others, they were the very magnets that thus drew me. I'll try a pagan friend, thought I, since Christian kindness has proved but hollow courtesy." Queequeg soon pronounces them "married; meaning, in his country's phrase, that we were bosom friends."

Ishmael in turn—after reasoning via the golden rule that if he wishes Queequeg to join him in his good Calvinist worship, he must likewise join Queequeg in his pagan worship—kneels with Queequeg before his portable idol: "do you suppose now Ishmael, that the magnanimous God of heaven and earth—pagans and all included—can possibly be jealous of an insignificant bit of black wood?" Then on the second night, back in bed together, they barely sleep for the joy of their newfound friendship: "Thus then, in our hearts' honeymoon, lay I and Queequeg—a cozy, loving pair" (p. 54). The warm homoeroticism of the scene persists: "Queequeg now and then affectionately throwing his brown tattooed legs over mine, and then drawing them back; so entirely sociable and free and easy were we." Taunting sexual and racial boundaries, luxuriating in their dark interface, Melville brings (te)homophilia to a literary epiphany. The absence of women in his novels might make his novel an odd pick for this feminist theology: indeed the very nauticality of Herman Melville's hermeneutic leaves women on a distant shore. Yet feminists, as in Sena Jeter Naslund's novel *Ahab's Wife* with its passionate hom(m)age, may feel less affronted by Melville's absent women than by their presence elsewhere.[33] That literal absence seems to have afforded him a space free of the leaden patterns of sexuality, a spectrum of ascetic-homoerotic (if not ascertainably homosexual) relations along which he renegotiates masculinity itself.

Melville will not let race alone. Early in the novel, anticipating his pseudoscientific cetology, he parodies the pseudoscience of phrenology, so popular among the white supremacists of his period: "Certain it was his head was phrenologically an excellent one," he gaily avers of Queequeg. "It may seem ridiculous, but it reminded me of General Washington's head, as seen in the popular busts of him. It had the same long regularly graded retreating slope from above the brows, which were likewise very projecting, like two long promontories thickly wooded on top. Queequeg was George Washington cannibalistically developed" (p. 52). In *Moby Dick* the entire fantasy of a white male mastery of the world appears as a doomed "dumb blankness," a whitewashed projection. Does this make the great White Whale the mascot of racism, as Morrison suggests—and Ahab an anti-whiteness hero? I am unwilling to settle for a new demonization of the leviathan. Whiteness, like the whale, is neither good nor evil. I think rather that Melville makes the whale the recipient of the projection of the horrors of whiteness, an ill which great white males had (with a few exceptions like Melville) disavowed. In a culture which openly then and still denigrates darkness as ignorance or sin, the sinister side of whiteness goes unrecognized. Or rather, whiteness becomes sinister *because* it goes unrecognized, unacknowledged in its sociosymbolic construction. So there breaches from the depths the monstrous, unknown Other of our (white) Sameness. We become it. Ahab, suggest Deleuze and Guattari, "has entered into a relationship with Moby Dick that makes him a becoming-whale and forms a compound of sensations that no longer needs anyone: ocean."[34] Ahab perishes pinned as though crucified to his whale-other self.

VIII The colorless all-color

Is it that by its indefiniteness it shadows forth the heartless voids and immensities of the universe, and thus stabs us from behind with the thought of annihilation, when beholding the white depths of the milky way?

(*Moby Dick* p. 169)

The ambivalence of whiteness–and with Melville it remains an undecidable ambiguity,[35] an oscillating, unstable symbolism–stabs us from a theological behind. The divine backside, disclosed as heartless void or luminous abyss, will not settle into any reverse Manichaeanism. The Milky Way was still visible as a great misty arch to most inhabitants of the planet during Melville's time. Astronomy had begun to measure those immensities that have multiplied shockingly ever since. He poses the existential question about our place in all–that *all*, which at once shrinks us to creaturely minuscule and sucks us toward galactic dissipation. The question of our meaning amidst the "heartless voids and immensities" has expanded more or less proportionately to the scales of space. Most theology, still quaintly geocentric, ignores the question. Ecological theologies renarrate the cosmos as the ultimate context for earthlings, the shared address for a cross-creaturely solidarity needed if we are not to render our watery planet uninhabitable. Yet they hardly touch upon the abysmal face of that unsentimental infinity: that "visible absence," or "colorless all-color of atheism from which we shrink" (p. 169).

Noting the "family resemblance between Melville's whiteness and Lacan's Real," Geoffrey Sanborne offers a postcolonial reading of *Moby Dick*. "The conclusion that proceeds from these propositions"–the visible absence of whiteness, the colorlessness of light as the agent of color–"is that the universe is ultimately a visible absence–that the only stable insight is the one between the fact of absence and the illusion of presence."[36] Ahab the colonial purist, cannot tolerate that difference, absence, or gap: the amputation that reveals the illusion. Where Morrison finds in the whiteness a meaningfully present evil, Sanborne inscribes a meaningless absence. I would suggest that neither Melville nor a tehomic theology reduces the universe to an ultimately "visible absence." For within the oscillation of presence and absence, the real and the symbolic, difference breaks out in color. But to abide the oscillation itself is to face the chaos–in its whiteness of all and no color.

Articulating the white noise of chaos, the philosopher of science Michel Serres inscribes in an almost Melvillian flux: "Chaos flows, it flows out, an *Albula*, a white river. I hear a silky white noise, hardly smooth, with little jumping, jolting bits . . . Chaos is nebulous. It does not flow out with a point or a direction, or following some rule, or abiding by some law." Serres shares a bit of Melville's cheerful mockery of scientific codification: "Look how much trouble we have thinking it or seeing it

. . . Our whole classified rationality, all the coding, habits and methods, lead us to speak in externals or negations: outlaw and nonsense."[37] Ahab's consuming crusade against the Other who refused to be appropriated produces the outlaw. Our social codes have thereby blocked genesis, becoming, itself. "I understand finally why death, so often, is its result, its outcome or consequence and why hatred is, so frequently, its driving force. And why rationalism comes under the heading of the sacred, why rationalists are priests, busily ruling out, cleaning up the filth, expelling people, purifying bodies or ideas" (ibid.). So a massed logic of hate–blind to its own irrationality, its own spurting chaos–cannot be understood as a simple projection of darkness, onto an Other. It must contend also with its own white noise, its fear of itself–of the depth and chaos of its own life.

IX Beneath the gaze

To speak of depth, now, is to begin to theologize upon its white skins and its dark faces. "Depth" no longer signifies the identity of an intelligible, spiritual interior, surfaced by a sensory, spatiotemporal exterior. So to continue to engage the quite "external" politics of race, the "external" threat to the carrying capacity of the earth, means in fact to risk this depth. The dualism of surface/depth, outer/inner still continuously rebuilds the wall, which an Ahab-consciousness crashes against: "All visible objects, man, are but as pasteboard masks . . . [S]trike through the mask! How can the prisoner reach outside except by thrusting through the wall? To me, the white whale is that wall, shoved near to me" (p. 144). It is not surprising to hear once again the white male, tragicomically proximate, come "thrusting through." He can no longer abide the play of phenomena, the glittering skin upon which the depth *surfaces*. "The more and the more that he strove to pierce the profundity" the more it "sinks beneath his gaze." (p. 543) Ishmael by contrast does not thrust through but "gropes down"–toward an Other whom he first had feared but now also admires.

The death-drenched depth of tehom does not *break through* the face of the phenomena, the whaling-wall of finite, variegated multiplicity. It is not something lying beneath the surface of appearances, but a nothingsomething breaking *as* every finitude, every wave of becoming. Two conditions keep it hidden: its infinite complexity, which always precedes and exceeds our capacity to know it; and our habits of fear and blankness (*blanc*). But then we are rehearsing for theology a way of thinking, indeed of seeing–Job's vision, or McFague's "attentive eye"–that will not foster epistemic aggression against all that escapes our mastery; that will escape the noose of the sanctified nouns, the controlling representations.

What *is* "Ishmael" that he should hook the nose of this leviathan? One who in the life-buoy coffin "has escaped to tell thee": let the chaos off the hook. Make the unfathomable your fear–and your suicide can become omnicide. Make the untamed universe your enemy–it will blankly oblige.

Part IV

CREATIO EX PROFUNDIS

9

BOTTOMLESS SURFACE

When beginning
bereshit

In the deepest hidden depths, and beyond the horizon, you seek me still. Opening up the limits of what is possible. The scars of the beginning and the end of a story.

(Luce Irigaray[1])

IN THE BEGINNING (*Be-re'shit*): the letter *bet* is the most elevated Crown (*keter*), and therefore this *bet* is larger than all other *bets*. The word "beginning" (*re'shit*) is in fact Wisdom

(*hochmah* Rabbi Isaac[2])

I Beginning difference

Sensitive to initial conditions, the rabbis loved to trace the contours of the first letter. "Why was the world created with a *bet*?" they ask in the *Midrash Rabbah*.[3] Why not with *aleph*? Doesn't B properly follow A? Why unsettle the alpha*bet*ic order of creation? In their arcane liter-alism, they answered: "Just as the *bet* is closed at the sides but open in front . . . you may speculate from the day that days were created, but you may not speculate on what was before that." Open not to the up or the down: this *bet* looks irreversibly *ahead*. It writes creation as spatiotemporal flow. The rabbis thus resist the verticalism of their patristic Christian contemporaries. But when the midrash discourages speculation on the "before"–before "days," before time, before "before" and "after"–would it not quash this present exploration of the deep?

No more than the rabbis does this theology of genesis situate the deep "before" time. When would that be? "There was no then, then," quipped Augustine. Of course for him this "then", without a then meant that prior to time exists the timeless Origin, about which he speculated happily. But the rabbis imagine no such timeless Being. Similarly, a tehomic theology writes of nothing before or outside of time and space. *This* world, *this* spatiotemporal pattern, *this* set of explicate dimensions might have had a big bang of a beginning. But we simply do not know what configurations of spacing and timing precede and transverse our own: even the physics gapes tantalizingly open.[4]

In other words, "beginning" is not synonymous with "origin." Tehom is inscribed not before any beginning, not before the beginning, but *in* it. No "then" without time, no "there" without space: and neither writable "before that" *bet*. But I now presume Rashi's delinearization of the creation of time. For the irreversible flow of time does not entail its linearity: the time of creation moves ahead not along a time-line from a timeless origin "before" but along a flow from beginning. Like writing.

The little letter *bet* spells suggestive spatialities. The *Midrash Rabbah* links "*Bereshit*" (as does Augustine), with the Wisdom of Proverbs 8.22: "The Lord made me *as the beginning* . . ." Hochma/Sophia thus slipped her divine-creaturely masculine-femininity into the future of all beginning. Might the letter *bet* now (only now?) open into a certain unspeakable threshold, open to the front, a gynomorphic aperture "closed due to flooding" even among rabbis–and so still very much *before* us?

This chapter hinges on a conversation with a set of more recent texts, texts one wants to call "original" in their challenge to the ideology of origin. I believe they make possible not just a new reading of *bereshit*, but–within and without theology–of how to begin. Again. Amidst every kind of loss. We will consider questions raised in Edward Said's early *Beginnings*, in relation to the texts of Derrida and Deleuze upon which he depends; and in Whitehead, upon whom Deleuze depends. A membranous Irigarayan tissue will envelop this paper cabal. I want to suggest that the recent distinction of origin from beginning *almost* corresponds to the distinction of the *creatio ex nihilo* from the *creatio ex profundis*. If this book has so far unfolded a self-implicating historical deconstruction, followed by a literary-scriptural hermeneutic, it now initiates a constructive theology of the deep–even as it returns to the texts of the deconstruction itself. To this end it interprets the first semantic unit of the first two verses. In the spirit and to the letter.

II Origin vs. beginning

> Whereas an origin centrally dominates what derives from it, the beginning
> . . . encourages nonlinear development, a logic giving rise to the sort of mul-
> tileveled coherence of dispersion we find in Freud's text, in the texts of
> modern writers, or in Foucault's archeological investigations.
>
> (Edward W. Said[5])

By rescripting the beginning-story as total, the origin came to "dominate what derives from it." *Beginnings* (written "before" Said's postcolonial theory) sets forth the poststructuralist distinction of "beginning" from "origin." Can Said's lucid binary help us to read Genesis as the narrative of a nonlinear beginning rather than of a dominant origin? In such a construction the Genesis narrative would be decon-structing in advance its later submission to the logic of origin. Even the canonical supplementation of Genesis 1 with the second creation myth of the Garden of Eden functions—since their sequences cannot be fused into one—to disperse the mirage of a single origin. We have noted how Rashi's grammatology of *bereshit* resists linearity: the irreversible is not the sequential. But now the indeterminacy of meaning leaks in through current, transdisciplinary understandings of language itself. What would happen if *bereshit* opened into a "multileveled coherence of dispersion"? A dreadful chaos? Answering such deconstructive threats, a current classical theism counters with "an indeterminacy that is not impersonal chaos but infinite interpersonal harmonious order, in which time participates."[6] Thus radical orthodoxy tries to beat poststructuralism at its own game: trading a nice, orderly indeterminacy for a bad chaos. Theology need accordingly not begin again. It rests, it *must* rest, upon its original metanarrative: on "the fact that God *is* the origin of this existence . . ."[7] The ontotheology of origin emits a kind of white noise, an unquestionable continuum *beneath* the textual chaos. "Theology *is* the discourse about the origin of being."[8] I may question these certainties. But frankly, why *would* practicing Jews or Christians want to cast their original foundation upon the waters of deconstruction?

Said disturbingly postulates "the notion of beginning as opposed to origin, the latter *divine*, mythical and privileged, the former *secular*, humanly produced, and ceaselessly re-examined."[9] This is not looking like such a good deal for theology. His resistance to theology here takes crassly oppositional form: "*beginning and beginning-again are historical, whereas origins are divine*." Of course most theologians share the same binary opposition, only in reverse: they affirm origin-as-sacred over against beginning-as-secular. Thus, for example, Wolfhart Pannenberg holds that "the creation of the world is not one of God's historical acts among others, for it is not an act in time and history, if only at their beginning." As with Milbank, an Augustinian concept of the timeless origin of time assures the flow of time itself. "It is the act that constitutes time itself along with all creaturely reality," continues Pannenberg. "The fact that God is the origin of this existence finds expression in the tracing back of the beginning to God."[10]

"Origin" classically subordinates and ontologically precedes "beginning." The distinction of the act of creation from the flow of time need not, of course, imply the entire dualism of a linear history supervised from an abstract eternity. It does, however, secure God's unfettered sovereignty. For Pannenberg the origin underwrites "that which creation by the Word demonstrates, which is the unlimited freedom of the act of creation." This freedom of the Creator "found expression in the formula 'creation out of nothing.'"[11] Or, we wonder, was this idea of freedom as total lack of conditions created *by* the formula?

Inasmuch, however, as Said and Pannenberg reinscribe the same binary of divine origin vs. relative beginning, a tehomic theology differs from both. The secular reversal fails in its self-examination at this point: the secular mimics the myth of origin. Bracketing its more aggressive political secularizations, the *ex nihilo* gesture has iterated throughout the creative countercultures of modernity: in the icon of the original genius, the Schopenhaurian artist, the avant-garde (repeatedly) transcending itself to avoid repetition, to create the new.[12] The purer, the more abstract, the creativity, the more fully it replaces the divine originality, the freedom of a creator *a se*, unconstrained by creaturely interdependencies.

Might we begin (again) with an altered proposition: beginning and beginning-again are historical-secular and *therefore also* mythical/theological; whereas totalizing origins are *onto*theological? The triumphant orthodox synthesis of omnipotence with ontology made possible the *ex nihilo* even as it founded the discourse of the Christian *imperium*. It became common sense for the colonizing, orientalizing civilization whose literatures Said's subsequent works address.[13] The contextual and liberation theologies of the Americas have (prior to postcolonial theory) already shaken that missionary imperialism to its theological foundations. So if we abstain from the modernist dichotomy of secular vs. theological, can theology still benefit from the preference for beginnings?

"Beginnings are a consciously intentional, productive activity whose circumstances include a sense of loss," continues Said. What would loss have to do with the story of the beginnings of the universe? Nothing much, if "the creation" refers to an absolute origin. But any creative activity from which we can draw theological analogies entails loss. Any actualization takes the form of a decision, a choice for this and not some other possibility. The loss may be bland or tragic, but it is inescapable. Thus the medieval philosopher Nachmanides claims that the *bara* of Genesis 1.1—"to create"—means "'to cut away' (*ligzor*) or 'set a boundary' (*velehum gvut nigzar*)."[14] This kabbalism anticipates Whitehead's insight: "Actuality is the decision amid potentiality."[15] "Decision" in "its root sense of 'cutting away'" (*de/cisere*, as "scissors") may or may not involve consciousness; but it always enacts an interdependent agency, a subjectivity that comes to be in the very act of actualization. A cloud of missed possibilities envelops every beginning: it is always *this* beginning, *this* universe and *not* some other. Decision lacks innocence. Around its narrations gather histories of grievance: what possibilities were excluded?

The darkness over the deep precedes the beginning. The cries of loss—*de profundis*—disrupt the confidence of total origin in a secure end. A wound to the text, *vulnus, vulva* of the text, gapes open, *ginan*, at the beginning of the canon. What losses would have encoded themselves in the biblical beginning? If the suffering of colonization and exile drove P to write a new beginning for the people, a recontextualization of their life in space and time, the narrative at minimum lets them grieve productively. It situates them in the only context large enough to contain their sense of displacement: the space-time of the creation. At best, loss morphs into promise. Christianity soon learned to translate loss into pure gain. The creation becomes its chessboard in the ultimate game of win/lose. And first of all it beat and lost its Jews. So in the *creatio ex profundis* Christianity not only confesses this guilt; it mourns the lost Jews and its own lost Jewishness. Perhaps only so can it embrace a nonlinear and relative beginning.

Said further defines the work of beginning as "producing difference." This *différance* signifies no pure alterity or incommensurability. It marks "the interplay between the new and the customary without which (*ex nihilo nihil fit*) a beginning cannot really take place."[16] But then how can one embrace the "interplay between the new and the customary" and at the same time exclude *religious* custom? To what margins of the elite would one need to confine one's "interplay," in order to rule spiritual traditions out of postmodern beginnings? If much theology has already learned to read its own texts as "humanly produced and ceaselessly re-examined," has poststructuralism conversely not also recognized "the limits of a demystification"?[17] A productive interplay hardly has a chance, in other words, if confined to the terms of either the theistic *ex nihilo* or its secular analog: both forfeit their own *preconditions* and thus their own *potentiality*.

If beginning takes place in the interplay between the possible future and the given past, it presupposes always a tangled complexity of relations. These relations remain largely unconscious, dim, unformed. Thus the nexus of relations may be felt as chaos. It sucks us toward its unsettled potentiality, its conflictual difference, or its dissolute undifferentiation. If, however, the chaos is not merely an abstract "before," then it will hold the differential traces of what has already been actual. Chaos is not just prevenient; it is also (as the icons of Leviathan or flood insist) created. In the feedback loop of the new and the given, the tehom comprises a matrix: a between-space in which possibilities *matter*. A place *not differentiated but differential*. Such a *matrix of possibilities* translates the topos of the deep into a place not *before* but *of* beginning.

III Surface vs. the deep

The tehom might evaporate once again if I do not confront the contradiction lurking within this rhetoric of tehom: the impossibility (at least *on the surface*) of a *post-structuralist depth*. I depend upon deconstructive strategies to clear a space for the tehomic hermeneutic. But the pertinent theories discredit "depth" itself. They link depth with origin, with totality, with the identity of the western subject. More recently, Homi Bhabha, effecting a literary-political postcolonialism indebted to Said,[18] blames the "dimension of depth" for "the language of Identity with its sense of reality–a measure of the 'me,' which emerges from an acknowledgement of my inwardness, the depth of my character, the profundity of my person, to mention only a few of those qualities through which we commonly articulate our self-consciousness." Through the perspective of depth as a "vertical dimension" the subject unifies itself through time.[19] Depth thus functions as the very medium of homog-enization, the solvent of difference–the stabilizing site of the "before that."

Similarly, Said had promoted a *"surface espousal."* In this he leans upon Derrida and Deleuze: "For each appeal to the absolute, profound, or transcendent Origin, Deleuze–and this is a methodological principle I support–would oppose in answer an instance of surface, which is the place at which meaning begins."[20] Indeed Gilles Deleuze proclaimed liberation from depth as a veritable gospel: "It is therefore pleasant that good news resounds today: meaning is never principle or origin, it is always something produced. It is not something to be discovered, restored, or re-employed, it is to be produced by new mechanisms. It belongs neither to any height nor to any depth; it is an effect of the surface, inseparable from the surface as its proper dimensions."[21] As depth is to surface, so origin is to beginning. Parodying Paul's "neither heights nor depths," Deleuze sounds like a prophet of postmodern superficiality. As an alternative to deep and original foundations, he effects meaning upon a "plane of immanence." Quite analogously, Derrida sets all signifiers dancing upon the "surface of the text." The return to origins, as discovery or as restoration, produces the illusion of depth, suspiciously subservient to the heights.

If we prefer for theology a self-critical textuality to an authoritative origin, *how can we possibly signify a "new beginning" by affirming the deep?* Will the deep only engulf any fresh discourse of beginnings with the conservatism of origin? (Forgive us our depths . . .) On the other hand, how should we pretend that there is anything revolutionary in the depth-defying gesture? Outside of the rare moments of Augustinian wonder or mystical abandon, "depth" has not been a Christian virtue. (Faith, obedience, charity, chastity, justice–but depth?) On the contrary, the authorities long ago drained the deep of almost all affirmative significance. Only by desacralizing, denying and demonizing those dark waters did meaning condense into the dominant logic. From the *ex nihilo*, meaning thrusts downward, from an original eternity, along a vertical axis: to a surface of reflecting surfaces, the "creation," summoned imperiously from nothing; and–perhaps passing through a soulful interior, aimed at ascent from the surface–"down there" to Augustine's "dark and shameful depths."

So a tehomic theology, stirred up in defense of those denigrated waters, finds itself now at peril on the high seas of theory. Does the "surface espousal" only coat in salty polemics the manly tehomophobia of the opposing orthodoxies? Irigaray, odd one out among poststructuralists, presumably means a Nietzschean-Lacanian discourse theory when she portends: "Delirium of language, the boldest navigators. With their hulls and sails, don't they want to take possession of all depths?"[22] In her metonymic overlay of "woman" and "ocean" she risks essentialism for the sake of these "depths." Her she/sea resists both the stasis of ontology and the delusion of a language of pure surfaces. "And if one casts out of the self anything that might be depth, and if one wishes only for appearances, doesn't this amount, in the end, to letting go of life? Becoming a ghost? And coming back to haunt solid realities" (ibid., p. 63). If students of French theory find themselves priggishly avoiding words like "depth" (along with "world," "reality," "matter" . . .) they had best heed her warning. A surface flux may not comprise a genesis of becoming, so much as a phantom of the *nihil*: another *original* (and therefore repetitive) tehomophobia.

Such postmodern haunting goes beyond theory. In its repressed craving for "solid realities," for "the body," it can produce if Irigaray is right an acquisitive desire. Indeed a predatory economy capitalizes on the vacuum of depth, cramming it with obscene heaps of hardened matter. Feminine body-surfaces gleam profitably upon every available screen and scrim. Despite its academic radicalism, does the "surface espousal" collude with the extrusion across the earth of shiny, late capitalist superficies? If so, we might concur with leftist criticism: "Postmodernism swims, even wallows, in the fragmentary and the chaotic currents of change, as if that is all there is."[23] And yet this denunciation (which not accidentally sounds like radical orthodoxy) also invokes the dread specter of the turbulent waters.

By definition, a tehomic theology cannot exchange its Deep for a discourse of the surface. Yet any rhetoric of profundity may inadvertently reinstate the depth-denying origin. Amidst the contradictions, is some third way at hand? *Does the tensive icon of "the face of the deep" not of itself belie the dichotomy of surface and depth?* Its imagery of depth suggests width more than verticality. So we now investigate whether the language of *depth* necessarily privileges—even in Deleuze or Derrida—a vertical dimension, an origin of transcendence, or the inner life of a masterful subject.

IV The bottomless chessboard

"If all begins with the trace, there is above all no originary trace."[24] *Différance* in this originary Derrida exhibits a peculiar primordiality not unlike that of the preexistent tehom: "*différance*, in a certain and very strange way, [is] 'older' than the ontological difference or than the truth of Being. When it has this age it can be called the play of the trace."[25] Similarly, tehom precedes the ontological difference of a Creator from a creation produced from nothing. Its "age" shows in the intertext—the trace-text—of the mythological Tiamat and her leviathanic brood; and in its nettlesome canonical anteriority to the truth of classical Christianity. As Augustine's "nothing-something" or "nonbeing/being" suggested,[26] the dark difference of tehom within "the beginning" disrupts the origin just by being *always already there*. As such it demands that both creator and creature admit their prior relation to it. Just so the trace of a *différance* that precedes the origin: "[I]t means that the origin did not even disappear, that it was never constituted except reciprocally by a nonorigin, the trace, which thus becomes the origin of the origin."[27]

Without the trace there is no origin; therefore *with* it there is no origin. Derrida hastens to add that "we know that the concept destroys its name and that, if all begins with the trace, there is above all no originary trace." The notion of the nameless name has sucked Derrida irresistibly toward the dark discourse of apophasis.[28] But never does this namelessness name a simple nothing: the originary non-origin has a specific density: it shows itself as "an *originary synthesis not preceded by any absolute simplicity*."[29] That "absolute simplicity" can refer only to the attribute of divine simplicity reserved for the classical deity. With this "originary synthesis" that is therefore no origin at all, Derrida is framing his relation to Husserl's phenomenology: avoiding its presupposition of a "living present" whose synthesis would transcendentally precede and so gather to itself (as a "retention" of a present past) the traces.[30] Such a unifying presence would characterize the "depth perspective" criticized by Bhabha. This originary complexity which is never a pure origin, since it always already carries the traces of a past,[31] bears an untoward resemblance to Whitehead's much earlier notion of becoming.[32] Every existence is an event of becoming, "a novel entity, disjunctively among the many entities which it synthesizes."[33] Whitehead's actual events also presuppose no subject, no consciousness, no transcendental presence; the novel entity synthesizes the effects of the past–but only in the form of "contrasts," for whose operation difference remains irreducible. The standard of contrast replaces that of binary opposition and mere contradiction.[34] Consciousness, if it occurs at all, happens as a flickering product of contrasts. Whitehead repudiates ontological simplicity in favor of a differential pluralism of becoming. For him this process of becoming explicitly replaced the *creatio ex nihilo* with an unbounded process of creativity.[35]

Of course poststructuralism and its *différance* will not "become" the creativity of a process metaphysic. If for a reckless moment, however, we hold together this origin-free cosmology with the grammatology of an originary trace, might they divulge an alternative philosopheme of "the deep"? Such a deep would signify neither an original presence nor a unified consciousness but a layered complexity, a multidimensionality of becoming, in which differences are neither kept separate (as in a clearly bounded dyad of Creator/creature) nor fused (as in a pantheistic substance) but held in contrast. In precise analogy–if not fusion–with Derrida's "originary trace or arche-trace," the origin reveals itself to be a complex, and as such relative/relational, beginning. Tempting as it is, however, let us not too quickly append the name tehom to Derrida's expandable series of "nonsynonymous substitutions"–*différance*, trace, supplement, khora, etc. . . .

At the very site of the primeval trace, just where we thought we caught a taste of salt, we bump into a primary text of the surface espousal: "*There is no maintaining, and no depth to, this bottomless chessboard upon which Being is put into play*." The chessboard, trope of deconstruction itself, connotes endless play upon the surface of the text–itself an overextended trope of all readable, sensorily coded spatio-temporalities. It dissipates the presumed "depth" of ontotheology. If the *ex nihilo* had installed a foundation, a bottom, the "bottomless chessboard" undermines the groundwork of any changeless Being.[36] Does this *différance* with "no depth," however, also checkmate tehom? Must we after all choose between deconstruction and depth? Certainly this is Milbank's "either/or": the depth restored in Christ–or else abysmal relativism.[37] But before I am driven into the arms of a radically orthodox depth-espousal, I must ask: how does the paradoxical figure of the bottomless surface *work*? Surely the *"bottomless"* cannot connote a *flat* or opaque plane. Does this figure perhaps already belie the notion of a surface that could be peeled off its own depth? Perhaps Derrida's chessgame plays in more dimensions than appear—on the face of it.

V Derrida, trace

It is the "play of the trace" that challenges Being, the Same, to a game of perpetual *différance*. Derrida borrows the trace from Emmanuel Levinas, for whom the "exteriority" of the Other as ethical imperative also highlights a certain surface: that of the "face." This face resists the hermeneutics of the "grasp." It defies appropriation by power and imprisonment "in a caricature." The Levinassian face resembles no slick surface of signification. *"The depth that opens in this sensibility modifies the very nature of power."*[38] Depth as the opening of the face: an indispensable tehomic theogram. A depth of opening or a dis/closure of depth subverts the stereotypes by which dominance imprints its order.[39] That depth opens not from a bottom line. It opens irreducibly–bottomlessly. The infinity of the opening counters the closures of totality, identified with the ontological tradition. Thus the depth in the face (*tehom* in the *panim*) appears in Levinas as "the infinite in the finite, the more in the less." "As accomplished by the idea of Infinity, is produced as Desire . . ."[40] We had gleaned a related idea of the *infini*, the unfinished, from Irigaray.[41] At any rate the oxymoron of the bottomless chessboard becomes tehomically legible in the layers of this wider French discourse of infinity.[42] The face breaks up both the deconstructive caricature of depth and the counter-caricature of deconstruction as shallow.

Certain clichés of deconstruction (largely North American side-effects) stress the meaninglessness of anything that cannot be *squarely* situated upon the chessboard of language: the lack of reference to an other, a cosmos, a matter.[43] We may leave that self-nullifying logic to mean nothing. For a tehomic theology, however, the deconstruction of the absolute Logos of the *ex nihilo* yields *an otherness of cosmos bottomlessly preceding and exceeding human language*. That we cannot *grasp* that otherness without caricaturing it—indeed the cartoon of the Creator has been enthroned precisely to master that otherness—does not render it insignificant. The excess and deficiency of significance marks itself as a chaos *vis-à-vis* any totality; it gathers its dimensions here under the sign of the tehom. Biblically it precedes any *logos* and so any cosmos—*bereshit*, God has not yet spoken.

VI Khora, chaos, and the house of hochmah

Early, Derrida had characterized the trace as an "arche-phenomenon of 'memory', which must be thought *before the opposition of nature and culture, animality and humanity*."[44] In other words–contrary to stereotype–this text does not underwrite the privilege of culture over non-human nature, the anthropocentrism that the whirlwind and whirlpool so dramatically challenged.[45] Such fleeting non-dualisms do not make Derrida an ecophilosopher. But if ecology urgently requires the rewriting of *place*, his mysterious archewriting does yield a "spatial" and "sensible" element. Indeed its nondualism implies, surprisingly, a *more biblical cosmology* than that of Levinas' transcendent Other.[46] Derrida returns, however, not to Genesis but to the *locus classicus* of cosmology, to the *Timaeus*, where he retrieves the *khora* of space itself. Khora, Plato's *"triton genos*," the third genre or discursive space, had in Derrida's reading eluded the dualism of the sensible/intelligible for whose service it was postulated.[47] In its spatiality Derrida enfolds the graphic sensibility of the sign; and by the same token, a space that temporizes, a deferral that takes *place*. The "abyssal chasm which would be khora" (ibid., p. 104), the formless matter of form, is figured in the *Timaeus* as receptacle, mother, nurse, imprint-bearer of the creation: matrix indeed. She would be traditionally read as matter before it has received the demiurgic imprint of the forms. Derrida flirts with the matter of her gender. Does he displace the paternal symbolic that (in the first place) fixes this feminine space as passive stuff, to be imprinted, typed, stereotyped? In Derrida's script the platonic forms cede that first place to the anomalous khora. She arises as a subject, a name, a name like that of God in the later Derrida, a name to be saved–"*sauf le nom*." "Who are you, Khora?" (ibid., p. 111). (And you, her contemporary, Tehom?)

As early Jewish and Christian theologians had to wrest their difference from the *Timaeus*, so does Derrida. What relation could we draw by way of this deconstructive, apparently negative path, *of khora to chaos*? Might Derrida's khora support a reading of the primeval chaos as an already always differential spacetime?[48] Depth would not lie below as an interior or undifferentiated potency but would *capacitate* beginning. Khora, similarly, becomes a "site [*lieu*] of politics, politics of sites [*lieux*]." A feminist politics, now resistant to any fixed difference as well as to any indifference to difference, folds in and out of this khoric indeterminacy.[49] The khora opens as "a chasm in the middle of the book, a sort of abyss 'in' which there is an attempt to think or say this abyssal chasm which would be khora, the opening of place 'in' which everything would, at the same time, come to take place."[50] Thus Derrida has his own khoric discourse "*mise en abîme*." (Or in Diane Elam's titular pun: "*Ms. en Abyme*.") The effect resembles an iterating, self-similar chaos: the abyss into which khora is thus thrust, is itself khora. It is noteworthy, however, that Derrida at another moment nervously protects khora from contamination by chaos: "let us not be too hasty about bringing this chasm named khora close to that chaos which also opens the yawning gulf of the abyss." Does this prosthetic separation between chaos and khora symptomatize the postmodern tehomophobia? Or merely acknowledge it? "Let us avoid hurling into it the anthropomorphic form and the pathos of fright. Not in order to install in its place the security of a foundation." Until one has adequately publicized the "friendlier face of chaos" (Pagels) the warning is well taken. The ghost and fear of chaos fuel the dominological orders.

Yet in the adjacent essay Derrida moves to "the edge of nondesire, around the gulf and *chaos of the Khora*."[51] How fortunate for a tehomic theology that Derrida's chaosmic slippage occurs right on the brink of his embrace of negative theology. Here, beyond his concern to protect deconstruction from contamination by the formless depths of the mystical tradition, he discovers Angelus Silesius.

> *The place is the word.*
> The place and the *word* is one, and were the place not
> (of all eternal eternity!) the *word* would not be.[52]

Place *is* Word: the mystic's epigram touches upon a linguisticality of place, or place of language. It echoes a Jewish mysticism in which God is revealed as place, as *Makom*—in whom dwell all creatures. This spatiality of spirit, an articulate space that cannot be opposed to interior depth, has been little thematized in the western tradition. Interpreting the opening midrash upon the *bet* of Genesis 1.1 (Genesis Rabbah), the thirteenth-century Geronese Rabbi Jacob ben Sheshet associates the letter *bet* with "house" (*bayit*):

> The Holy One, blessed be He, is the abode of the universe, and the universe is not His abode. Do not read [the letter *bet*], but rather "house," as is said, "With Wisdom the house will be built." (Proverbs 24.3)[53]

The metonymic links of beginning/house/hochma construct the unspeakable deity itself as the abode of the universe. This is the All-in-God of panentheism.[54] Here the He-God becomes the very *bet* of beginning—the House built by She-Wisdom. As the "architect" of Proverbs 8 she writes the *bet* and so "constructs" the abode—the divinity.[55] Inadvertently prophesying the constructive work of feminist theology, she performs the play of the signifier upon the bottomless surface of the text.

Différance in the present reading would only preclude a depth that occludes its own bottomless regress or its endless signifying surface. Therefore a tehomic genesis need not surrender to the binary of beginning-as-secular-surface vs. origin-as-sacred-depth. For the binary auto-deconstructs. But we have not yet procured from poststructuralism any blessing for the *name* of the Deep.

VII Chaoid variations: Deleuze

Deleuze may bear better news than it had seemed. With Felix Guattari, he unfurls the notion of a "plane of immanence." Another bottomless surface, it provides a certain analogy to the Derridian chessboard. For Deleuze and Guattari, originary theorists of "difference," the plane of immanence comprises a rolling, fractal surface of concepts: "Concepts are like multiple waves, rising and falling, but the plane of immanence is the single wave that rolls them up and unrolls them."[56] If concepts are what a philosopher "creates," the plane comprises their rhythmic interrelations (like the complex self-organizing soliton, a huge wave that keeps its shape for miles). Its differences "emerge on a plane that is able to *crosscut chaotic variability*." How can thought proceed, ask Deleuze and Guattari, "if there are all these layers that sometimes knit together and sometimes separate"? Their answer though meant for philosophy after "God" sketches a method for tehomic theology: "Are we not condemned to attempt to lay out our own plane, without knowing which planes it will cut across? Is this not to reconstitute a sort of chaos? That is why every plane is not only interleaved but holed, letting through the fogs that surround it."[57] Fractal geometry was generating the algorithms of nonlinearity in Paris as they wrote.[58]

Deleuze especially will facilitate the articulation of a tehomic relation of "chaos" to "depth." Unexpectedly–indeed in the same book in which he had proclaimed an end to origin and depth in the name of "difference"–he postulates a second imaginary of depth. Indeed he even sets forth an "*original depth*" (no less tensive a notion than Derrida's "originary trace"). "*Extensity as a whole*," he writes, "*comes from the depths*." In *Difference and Repetition* Deleuze can be described as reconceptualizing the dimensions of the universe. The distinctions of above/below, figure/ground, which define the conventional meaning of "depth," for him "flow from a 'deeper' instance– depth itself, which is not an extension but a pure *implex*." In other words depth is not "a dimension" but the dimensionality out of which the spatiotemporal dimensions unfold. To unfold is to "explicate." What he calls "difference itself" is inexplicable and so unextended. For "its being is *implication*."[59] Explication for Deleuze means actualization of an implicate potency.[60] That which is "pure implex," not yet explicated, is the potentiality he calls "the virtual." His notion of the actualization of the virtual develops as an interpretation of Whitehead's concept of the actualization of the possible.[61] "Difference," from which all else is explicated, thus becomes homologous with the "original depth." "*Depth as the (ultimate and original) heterogeneous dimension is the matrix of all extensity, including its third dimension*." In other words the matrix, or implex, in which extensity or actualization takes place is not an undif- ferentiated stuff but a heterogeneous and thus differential depth: difference itself.

In the Deleuzian cosmography, depth, as the *pro/fond*, comes before (pro) the *fond*, "bottom," "foundation." It occupies the place of difference from which the specific dimensions and actualities of spacetime emanate. "The ground [*fond*] as it appears in a homogenous extensity is notably a projection of something 'deeper' [*profond*]: only the latter may be called *Ungrund* or groundless."[62] (So "ground" need not be simply identified with foundation and dismissed–a more typical deconstructive move–but may divulge instead its dependency upon the prior bottomlessness, or profundity, from which it comes.) Yet the *Ungrund*–like tehom–does not designate a hollow vacuum, an abstract nonbeing or void of relations: rather it remains the place of all relations, all virtualities. This depth defines not a *particular or single* dimension, not the mathematical third dimension, but rather the *intensity* of space–that chaotic potentiality which (try as we might) cannot be kept outside and other.

Here is the Deleuzian gift to a tehomic theology: he freely translates this bottomless place of places as "chaos." Elsewhere, he characterizes the chaos as "milieu."[63] "Chaos", he has written, "is not without its own directional components, which are its own ecstasies" (they explicate, they unfold, ek-stasis). Indeed "what chaos and rhythm have in common is the in-between–between two milieus, rhythm-chaos or the chaosmos." Chaos is thus suggestively defined: "Chaos is not the opposite of rhythm, but the milieu of all milieus" (ibid.). So in the jazzy Deleuzian code, "chaos," "rhythm," milieu of milieus," "implex," "matrix," "groundlessness" and "depth" produce almost interchangeable meanings.

Might that depth of chaos then permit us to map tehom upon the rolling surface of his plane? For the thinking of difference–refracted through the science of chaos–*takes place* upon its face. "[E]very movement passes through the whole of the plane by immediately turning back on and folding itself and also by folding other movements or allowing itself to be folded by them, giving rise to retroactions, connections, and proliferations in the fractalization of this infinitely folded up infinity (variable curvature of the plane)."[64] Thus we may add another French *infini* to the iconography of tehom. The infinitely folded origami of the plane resembles in its virtuality, its potentiality, the "milieu of milieus." But then–as long as the Deleuzian virtual is not mistaken for a seamless unity–it contributes to the tehomic description of a matrix of possibilities.[65] In its almost hallucinogenically multilayered connectivity, the complex Deleuzian surface seems to translate the fluent sur/face of *panim upon tehom*.

For a tehomic discourse, it is only as such a matrix of possibility that chaos becomes *depth*. But this Deep, as I hope has become evident, has little to do with the homogenizing verticalities and interiorities of the depth that come opposed to surface. Rather, read the "heterogeneous depth" in its complexity, indeed its positive chaos, as a liberation of the surfaces from a *homogenizing* depth–from the foundationalism that grounds the orthodoxies of origin, where origin suggests not so much *depth* as *bottom*.

Is the poststructuralist espousal of surface getting in over its own depths? O Bottom, where art thou?

VII Process and chaosmos

It turns out that Deleuze, like Derrida, also returns to the chaos/khora of the *Timaeus*. Indeed Deleuze goes there by way of his reading of Whitehead, in the pivotal chapter of his book on Leibniz and the Baroque, *The Fold*. Deleuze is at pains to affirm an aesthetic dimension of the Baroque—its curls, spirals, labyrinths, drapes, pleats—as a resistance and an alternative to the Cartesian tendencies of the same period. (His fascination with the Baroque resonates at this angle with Derrida's reading of the Baroque Silesius.) It is not often noted that Deleuze depends here, as he marks his relation to Leibniz's notion of the microcosmic event-character of reality, upon Whitehead's concept of interrelated events. Through Whitehead's philosophy of "actual occasions" he rearticulates his own philosophy of becoming: "Events are produced in a chaos, in a chaotic multiplicity, but only on the condition that a sort of screen intervenes." He compares this screen with "a formless elastic membrane, an electromagnetic field, or the receptacle of the *Timaeus*."[66] He then distinguishes Leibniz's monad, which in "its Baroque condition" remains closed to the other monads and thus fully deterministic, from Whitehead's microcosmic event, which is open to the other events. Thus he draws from Whitehead his own argument for the direct and felt connection between contiguous events, and so for the complex indeterminacy of the world constituted by those relations.[67]

His conclusion bears tremendous tehomic weight: "For Whitehead . . . bifurcations, divergences, incompossibilities, and discord belong to the same motley world that can no longer be included in expressive units, but only made or undone according to prehensive units and variable configurations." Whitehead's "prehensions," the "internal relations" by which an entity becomes by "feeling the feelings" of prior events, thus replace the external relations of the crisply bounded monad. "*In a same chaotic world divergent series are endlessly tracing bifurcating paths. It is a 'chaosmos' of the type found in Joyce . . .*" In the chaosmic epiphany, if only for this moment, "God" becomes possible for the anti-theist Deleuze. "Even God desists from being a Being who compares worlds and chooses the richest compossible. He becomes Process."[68]

Thus "the milieu of milieus" permits us to configure the tehomic matrix as a beginning-matrix for a theology of becoming. In the coded rhythms of this thinking, where *Finnegans Wake* merges discordantly with *Process and Reality*, a tehomic theology becomes recognizable—in a bifurcating and diverging sense—as a poststructuralist process theology.

VIII Deep face

> And the sea can shed shimmering scales indefinitely. Her depths peel off into innumerable thin, shining layers . . . And with no end in sight.[69]

In the attempt to route the path of deconstruction through a chaosmic seascape, I have tried to argue for a certain hermeneutical depth *in the face of* the surface—and its espousal. As the depth peels into layers, the face wrinkles into Tehom. Can the textual space of the primeval *bereshit* then host a historicizing, relative and only therefore *profound* notion of beginning? If origin conveys *a vertical mono-dimensionality*, we theologize beginning or begin to theologize from *a fluent multi-dimensionality*. That depth of beginning cross-cuts in theory the "chaotic variability" of a proliferating matrix of tehomic icons: *différance*, creativity, trace, khora, infinity, *complicatio*, multiplicity, the heterogeneous dimension. As *dimensionality* rather than as *a* dimension, the depth enfolds an infinity of virtual finitudes: the creations, the creatures. They *are* not chaos, but the organized explications of its dimensions. "Art is not chaos but a composition of chaos," say Deleuze and Guattari, so that it constitutes "a chaosmos, a composed chaos–neither foreseen nor preconceived."[70] We may readily imagine Elohim's creativity as closer to art than to science. But theology? Scripture, not theology, is appreciated for the many genres of its art forms, its psalms, doxologies, liturgies, dreams and dramas. So then when theology, relieved of its tehomophobia, unfolds scripture, might it sound as much like poetry as proposition? What new beginning–after the authoritative closures, apocalyptic certainties, and lukewarm liberalizations–could we read?

What if we imagine the beginning as frontal opening, as the *bet* of a birth canal, the *B* of the wet bosom? The "crown," *keter*, as the crowning head of the emergent creation? Could its portal of actualization yet dis/close a mother of Wisdom, a matrix of possibilities, a flood of inseparable differences? "In the first 'meeting,' before his thought's beginning, *she* gives–gives herself in the 'form' of fluids."[71] Despite all the losses she starts, *bereshit*, from a creativity that no *logos* of origin has finally mastered. The increasing visibility of this fluid within the work of male theorists may be cause for hope as well as consternation.[72] *Theologoi*, words too old or too new, keep breaking on her surface.

10

THE PLURI-SINGULARITY OF CREATION

Created God
bara elohim

We want a principle, a system, an integration, and we want elements, atoms, numbers. We want them, and we make them. A single God, and identifiable individuals.

(Michel Serres, *Genesis*[1])

If we do not rethink and rebuild the whole scene of representation, the angels will never find a home, never stay anywhere.

(Luce Irigaray, "Belief Itself"[2])

I God creates

God. *Gott*. Its consonants grind like teeth. G-d. Who, saying this name, does not take it in vain? I have hardly been able to write it, to *subject* it to sentences that start "God is," "God does." As though "God" identifies something, some One, rather than, as Meister Eckhart insists, "a non-God, a nonspirit, a nonperson, a nonimage."[3] As though the holy monosyllable might–after dying so many modern deaths, after performing so many gender tricks (the wishful She, the hiccuping S/He, the blustering He)–pull off some liberating new feat of representation. But if we delete the *theos* from theology, what does it leave? A logos alone, a regime of secular monologoi, from which mystery, prophecy and the love that is stronger than death have evaporated? An elite post-theism, which shuns all theologies of social and symbolic struggle?

So I can no longer continue to elude the question: from the topos of the deep, does one confess "God the Creator of Heaven and Earth"? Clearly a tehomic theology does not use "God" as the founding word, "God creates" as its original act and fact. If the *bet* of *bereshit* offered an alternative starting-point, a grammatical shelter for uncertain beginnings, does its offbeat opening perhaps also relocate the identifiable *subject* of theology? In this almost kabbalistic hope, the present chapter sounds out the singular plurality of the next phrase of Genesis. *Bara elohim*.

172

II The elohimic multiple

Retreat momentarily to the desert, to the beginnings of monotheism, which among the Hebrews was gestating slowly, nomadically, uncertainly, amidst a universe of erotic and combative divine multiplicities. Here the god-word still breathes. Whisper: *Elohim*—a flux of syllables, labial, multiple. Its ending marks it stubbornly as a *plural* form of *"eloh;"* here (but not always) it takes the single verb form: *bara*. *"Theos," "deus," "God"* obliterate the traces of this singular Elohimic plural—or rather, of its theological significance. It/they/s/he is hard to identify (let alone to preach). Elohim, like Allah, derives—by way of the little-used Eloah—from the common Semitic term *il* or *el*, both of which occur in the Bible infrequently except "in the purely poetic books of Psalms and Job." This Elohimic tree of names is far wider than YHWH, "the special covenant name of the Israelite national God."[4] Elohim is "an appellative, that is, it can be used of any deity. It is not a personal name, such as Yahweh, el Shaddai, Marduk or Chemosh."[5] Elohim, however, is a common name for the object of the Bible's personal monotheism.

What shall we make of its impersonal plurality? Amidst all the "careful defining, separating and opposing" that accompanies God-naming, this is a "curious slippage," suggest Danna Fewell and David Gunn. "God 'himself' is unsure whether he is plural or singular, echoing the narrator's grammatical confusion of a plural name (elohim, which may or may not be a proper noun!) and a singular verb."[6] Most biblical commentators would manfully protest that the plural form is "used to denote plenitude of might."[7] They read Elohim as an "abstract plural," or "plural of intensity," "suited to the task of summing up the whole of divine power in a personal unity." "Yahweh is not just one individual 'el,' but 'elohim,' the sum of all gods, i.e., Godhead pure and simple, and as such, for Israel at any rate, he rules out all other deities." Thus Walther Eichrodt argues that far from preserving any lingering plurality of gods, the writer of Genesis 1 is said to use the term for the Creator God in order "to protect his cosmogony from any trace of polytheistic thought and at the same time describe the Creator God as the absolute Ruler and the only Being whose will carries any weight."[8] Certainly it is this dominological explanation that has carried weight: the plural signifies all the prior gods YHWH has replaced (or swallowed?); the plural beefs up His Oneness. Thus the exclusive use of the verb *bara* to "designate divine creative activity" can further intensify His singularity: the verb alone is thus expected to carry "the idea both of complete effortlessness and *creatio ex nihilo*."[9] Pure and simple. Theologians, in the meantime, simply skirt this God(s)-talk (as another obsolescent Hebraicism), except perhaps to find Old Testament traces of the Christian trinity.

Registered in the theogram of the plural *Elohim*, however, there remain traces of another interpretation—not of a polytheistic reading but of one which took the residual multiplicity with theological seriousness. Medieval rabbinic commentators were fascinated by the plural form of Elohim. For example, Abraham Ibn Ezra, born in Spain in 1089, poet, grammarian, philosopher and exegete, held that "the noun is plural because its sense makes reference to *the angels*."[10] In verse 20 of the first Genesis narrative, at the moment of the creation of the humans, the plural subjectivity of Elohim gets dramatically reinforced: "let us create . . ." The verb *bara* is here for the first time repeated.[11] But here the plural *Elohim* takes the *plural* verb form. Scholars generally acknowledge a background reference to a divine court or heavenly counsel. Rashi, intriguingly, had found evidence here of "the humility of God." "Since Man was to be in the likeness of the angels and they would be jealous of him, He *consulted* them (*nimlakh*) . . . He *asked permission* of His court" (my emphases). The role of the angels, comments Avivah Gottlieb Zornberg of Rashi's interpretation, "is to suggest a 'many-ness' of viewpoints, a spectrum of opinions, that God has to convince, placate, ultimately to 'receive permission.'"[12] According to Rashi the text itself risks heresy by drawing on the plural verb, with all its pagan reverberations: "In spite of the license given to heretics by this formulation, the text does not restrain itself from teaching the virtue of humility: the great one should consult with, request permission from, the small one. For if the text had said, 'Let Me make man,' we should not have learned He spoke with His angelic court, but merely with Himself." This startling bit of hermeneutical democratization itself "risks heresy" to counter the simple unity of the Aristotelian-Christian God, even as it challenges the dominological tendency of all monotheism.

These grammatological angels raise untoward questions. "The angel of the Lord" pops up at regular intervals in the Hebrew Bible, but is notoriously prone to merge with YHWH himself, so that "YHWH" and "the angel of YHWH" can be used quite interchangeably. The questions become thornier when with Ibn Ezra we spy the angels already inhabiting the first "Elohim created."[13] If the angels are themselves part of the Creator—part of the name Elohim—then how could they have *been* created? Is the Creator a committee? Protestantism has had little patience with this divine complexity. Holy wing of western modernity and hatchery of biblical scholarship, it has rightly suspected these hazy plurals of all manner of vestigial polytheism. Thus it phased out angelology, sophialogy, hagiography and mariology, condensing the tiered multiplicities preserved in Judaism and Catholicism into: "God." And Christ: the one Son of God, eclipsing the many biblical "*bni Elohim.*" And oh yes, the Holy Ghost (though that winged one has always threatened to fly the coop, as the chaotic activity of *ruach elohim* goes to show).[14]

Even though angels were discredited in modernity and downplayed in its religious institutions, popular culture can't get, or *see*, enough of them. The rosy Victorian sentiment for bare-bottomed as well as diaphanously gowned and androgyne guardian angels has yielded to their blockbuster status, starring recently, for example, John Travolta in *Michael*, Michael Landes in *Highway to Heaven*, and, weekly, Della Reed in *Touched by an Angel*. Such angelic luminaries, poignant in their in-between condition, sometimes yearning for human flesh and passion (as portrayed sensitively in *Angels over Berlin*), are conventionally imagined as emissaries, lieutenants or mediators, winging down from the Father enthroned above. But not always. The angelic multiplicity *of God him/her/it/themself* may appear even in a severely mono-theist (and highbrow) setting. I am thinking of the sextet of three male and three female solo voices who perform together the voice of God in Arnold Schoenberg's haunting *Moses und Aaron*: an atonal, bi-gendered pluri-singularity of Elohim.

In his philosophical reading of the Jewish creation tradition, Norbert Samuelson insists on the plurality of entities—not just angels but "thrones," *hochmah* or *torah*, *tohu*, *bohu*, *tehom*, *mayim*—variously presupposed in the reality *before* the creation. "This pre-creation universe is populated by things named in the Genesis account, as well as other entities not explicitly named."[15] He draws upon the angelological rejection of the *ex nihilo* formula. "The verb *'bara'*", had claimed Ibn Ezra, "is singular because its referent is the Holy One." Ibn Ezra "rejects the claim that *BARA* must mean bringing something into existence out of nothing" (ibid., p. 137). To reread the verb—*verbum*, Word as event rather than subject or object—means, it would seem, to revise the doctrine of creation. But in Jewish thought, unlike Christian, the question of the *ex nihilo* had not been nailed shut.[16] Samuelson contrasts Ibn Ezra's reading of the creation to that of the slightly later Nachmanides, for whom the universe before creation was nothing—except "space predisposed to be made into something." Yet such a predisposition belies simple nothingness. Nachmanides interprets Elohim as the "power of the powers of everything." Samuelson reads the latter not as a unifying omnipotence but as a depersonification of Ibn Ezra's angels. They morph into "the first form and matter whose combination produces the four primary elements of earth, water, air and fire."[17] Venturing his own analogue to the medieval philosophical commentaries on the *Genesis Rabbah*, Samuelson refutes the legitimacy of deriving the *ex nihilo* from either the Hebrew or rabbinic heritage. He links the precreation "space" and its medieval "elements" with the material energies of contemporary physics.[18]

These Jewish cosmological alternatives hold open a differential conception of the deity. "Even 'in the beginning' there is God and not-God, thus enabling God, as concept, to be."[19] The not-God within God reinscribes at the same time the many within the one—a move that should not be altogether alien to Christian trinitarians. Does the angelic plurisingularity return today to question the concept of any single, separable individuals—a question readily metabolized in the indeterminacies, multiplicities and infinities of recent science and philosophy?

III The angelic swarm

Let us not, however, too quickly subsume the old angels under a newer science. It could go the other way. For instance, in the form of a dialog between leading

Continental philosophers of science, Bruno Latour attempts to tease out Michel Serres' hermeneutic of chaotic multiples. Serres offers in response a figuration that emerges "at the beginning of the Christian era, taking into account Semitic influences–that of the *multiplicity of angels*." He refers to paintings behind the altars of Rome, "whose backgrounds are filled with wings."[20] Serres opposes this image to that of a conventional Creator, "a single god who is a producer, a radiating source of life like a sun, or a story of the origin of time." He paints a hermeneutical vista "like a heaven filled with angels, obscuring God somewhat." This unscientific epiphany of angels understandably perturbs Latour: "this is not going to clarify things for the public." Besides, he snaps, delivering the *coup de grâce*: "it's not important–this is a *theological* quarrel!" Serres perversely pursues this insignificance: "They are restless, unsystematic (which you find suspect), troublemakers, boisterous, always transmitting, not easily classifiable, since they fluctuate. Making noise, carrying messages, playing music, tracing paths, changing paths . . . Hiding God, revealing God." Now he is on a theological roll, embarrassing Latour further: "This is the transcendental I'm talking about–*the archangelic space-time, the enormous cloud, without clear edges, of angels who pass, a great turbulence of passages. A swarm.* Perhaps what I was writing all along was an angelology" (ibid., p. 118; my emphasis).

The cloud of angels conceals and reveals Serres' philosophy of "the multiple." In distinction from hermeneutics, the angels do not *bring* messages but as the multiple *embody* them. "The angels are the messages; their very body is a message." Therefore "what differentiates angels from Hermes is their multiplicity, their cloud, their whirlwinds. I was about to say their *chaos*, since their collectivity is similar to it. In the reredos in Rome sometimes there are ninety-seven of them, sometimes thirty-two, sometimes twelve–why these numbers? Pure multiplicity" (ibid., p. 119). One sees with new eyes the swarms of angels churning turbulently over the surfaces of Christian art: for instance, El Greco's late *Annunciation*, through whose dramatic chiaroscuro cherub heads proliferate like clusters of grapes, or bubbles, uncannily indistinct for their period, anticipated a much later expressionism–overwhelming the tightened counter-reformation boundaries between the heavenly and earthly spheres; and in the process subverting the canon of representation.

Does this indeterminate multiplicity of angels, cherubs, hosts, perhaps hint at a resignification of the divine it/her/him/theirself? With a tehomic hermeneutic, we read Job's whirlwind, with its chaotic swarms of star, angel and beast, as a midrash on the Genesis creation: the angels of Job, *beni elohim*, echoed the rush and grammar of *ruach elohim*. Might we now begin to reinterpret the "Elohim created" of Genesis 1.1 from the perspective of the verse of chaos? As early as Deleuze and Guattari to philosophize a "positive chaos" from new developments in science, Serres, in his *Genesis*, had written: "Sea, forest, rumor, noise, society, life, works and days, all common multiples; we can hardly say they are objects, yet they require a new way of thinking. I'm trying to think *the multiple as such*."[21]

176

The multiple as such. Both angels and primal elements can thus be read amidst its uncountable swarms: "The increasing deluge, fire, multiplicity always returns. Forest, sea, fire, deluge, figures of the crowd" (ibid., p. 56). Yet when our thought habits press toward unity and division, the multiple is reduced to an aggregate of ones, contained within, adding up or reducing down to a single One: "We want them, and we make them. A single God, and identifiable individuals" (ibid., p. 2f.). But these sub- and super-unities keep dissolving as we approach them. "We've never hit upon truly atomic, ultimate, indivisible terms that were not themselves, once again, composite . . . The bottom always falls out of the quest for the elementary" (ibid., p. 3). The elementary bottoms into the elemental. Simplicity drops into a bottomless complexity. Does the vilified and nilified chaos of Genesis name that very fall? Is the *ex nihilo* the false bottom of theology? At any rate, a tehomic quasi-midrash may now be able to reconcile the two readings suggested by Samuelson of the Elohimic multiple: as angels and as energies.

IV Divining the multiple

If Elohim bottoms into the "power of the powers" of the Nachmanidean elements, its deity would not fall far from Moltmann's "Spirit of life," Pannenberg's divine "field of force," or Cobb's "creative transformation."[22] What if we read "God" not as the separate One–marketed as the only alternative to an older aggregate of separate Ones–but as a distinctive plurisingularity of the text? Such a divine plurisingulart will bear little resemblance to the standard theology of Genesis 1.1, such as: "we are given the barest statement of a sequence of facts resulting from the fiat of the supreme and absolute master of the universe."[23] In itself, however, the text portrays no "absolute mastery." It can just as well suggest an elemental power of creativity, articulate, humble, kenotic, almost democratic, in its delegations; and effusive in its delights.

In further exegetical attestation of this elemental Elohimic multiple, Lynn Bechtel translates "Elohim" as "differentiated unity," appropriate to a "group-orientation" where individuality comes only embedded in collectivity and nature.[24] Within this differential-relational orientation, the "days" of creation would read out as a nonlinear series, rather like Serres' fractal model of time, full of folds, recapitulations and bifurcations: "Basic time, close to chaos, is made up of jolts, of fluctuations, it is not integratable, it cannot congeal either in mass or in class, it can't freeze."[25] The prehuman species would multiply in co-creative collectives; their "swarming" life iterates, amplifies, embodies the angelic host. Creation takes place *within* a fluid interdimensionality; indeed within something like the viscous, insubstantial interdependence of what Serres calls "*relational bodies*." Always already taking body, the creation opens the concept of the incarnation beyond its singularity.

A multiplicity of differences-in-relation, the multiple that as such is the relational, might even thaw open the logic of the Christian trinity. For the most part, its three

177

"persons" sit awkwardly frozen in an exceptionalism that only proves the rule of the One. So first Christianity would have to withdraw from Judaism the stereotype of a legalistic, simplistic monotheism. Judaism has served as foil for the trinitarian dimensionality of its Christian successor. Yet quite apart from the ambiguous status of the (non)creatures of verse 2, the canonic, apocalyptic, midrashic and mystical forms of Judaism have bred magnificent throngs of divine beings: angels, shekhinah, *bni elohim*, thrones, word, torah, hochma/sophia, spirit(s), sephiroth.[26] Crowding and complicating the hermeneutical time-space, the turbulent swarm of godhood has always transgressed any possible boundaries between the One Original Creator and the many derivative creatures.

In this beginning, we hear not just anyone. And not just the One. We hear *the Manyone*. A countless divinity. But the *subject* of creation?

V

> With the Beginning
> the Concealed One who is not known created the palace.
> This palace is called *Elohim*.
> The secret is:
> "With Beginning,   created *Elohim*."
> (Genesis 1.1)
>
>   (*Zohar*[27])

Please read the above blank. The subject of the sentence of creation has been deliberately deleted. Or rather, the kabbalist has pried open a fissure left by the grammar of *bereshit*, exploiting the Hebrew placement of the verb *bara* before *Elohim*, its ostensible subject. So Moses de Leon *changes* the subject.[28] Elohim has been rewritten as the *object* rather than the subject of the act of creation! Nothing fills the gap: it gapes, unspeakably, ungrammatically. Centuries before the deconstruction of "the subject," the western hypersubject, the subject of subjects, quietly drops out. There is no innocence of intention here. The "secret" message is urgently doubled: *Elohim* now signifies a created place, a *palace* (= *binah*, womb)–not "the Creator."[29]

In a certain sense we have seen Elohim deconstructing its own unity from the beginning. For the very ideal of a subject as singular, substantial self-identity belongs to a "scene of representation" foreign to Hebrew discourse. Might we thus imagine that *Zohar*, a text vying with the medieval scholastic tradition, wants to undermine the changeless Subject of western substance metaphysics–that singular One = One of the grammar by which the western subject sentenced its world? At any rate the *Zohar* has with uncanny prescience (in both senses) dislodged the original dominology, or the dominant origin, of western religion. But the secret leaks: the creator is not a subject; the subject is not a creator; the creation has no substantial subject.

Writing Elohim as *effect* of creation, the *Zohar* does not *deny* the proposition that "God creates;" it deconstructs its propositionality. No more does a theology of becoming deny that it is appropriate to worship God as the Creator. Of course I cannot appropriate mystical Judaism (with its textual discipline, specular experience, minority-within-minority cabal, let alone its ethnically distinct patrilineage of interpreters). But I can recognize a kindred attempt to free "God's creation" from cliché. Divinity cascades through kabbalistic iconography into a bi-gendered plurality of ten sephiroth. In its exorbitant hermeneutics, wombs appear, *binah*, among the divine names, secreting innumerable, carefully numbered emanations. Language branches (its graphic trees anticipating fractal scaling) into the multiplicity of names. We encountered *bet* as the first place–crown, *keter*, sephirah of nothingness; and *Wisdom*, concealed here also "with the beginning" as the sephirah *hochmah*.[30] Elohim in the *Zohar* signifies Binah (understanding), the third Sephira, "the womb, the Divine Mother . . . Created being has its source in Her; She is called 'the totality of all individuation' and 'the world that is coming,' constantly coming and flowing."[31]

Does the divine Manyone come again–with flowing anachronism–in the morphology of a famous recent differentiation of "woman" as "neither one nor two, but many"? Such a theology, neither monistic nor dualistic, prepares a pluralism not of many separate ones but of plurisingularities, of interdependent individuations, constantly coming, flowing, *through* one another. Of course borrowed bits of kabbalistic imagery will offer no solution to the problems of feminist theology: *Binah* even as Elohim is not the first or even second manifestation, both of which tend to masculinity. As in most mystical counterdiscourses, the disruption of the patriarchal imaginary by strangely sexed or unsexed icons still privileges a phallic, if feminized, subject-position. "The secret of redemption consists of the female becoming the corona of the male organ."[32] In case Jewish feminist warnings did not already forestall ms/appropriations, Elliot Wolfson's meticulous divulgence of the "secret" of masculine kabbalistic androgyny effectively chills misplaced enthusiasms.[33] But a tehomic theology does not aspire to a new feminist purity, free of patriarchal residues, numb to such heuristically queer, infinitely multiplicative, experiments.

The recapitulative flow of a becoming-feminism depends upon the emancipatory force of sheer plurality. As Judith Butler puts it: "If the regulative fictions of sex and gender are themselves multiply contested sites of meaning, then the very multiplicity of their construction holds out the possibility of a disruption of their univocal posturing."[34] The "univocal posturing" of the creator has always been gendered, as will be any protests against it. At the site of the sex/gender undecidabilities flocks a plurisingularity of contested meanings–angelic, abysmal, confrontive. They seem to be an elohimic subspecies of all that swarm "in the beginning." They will keep the blank open. They will keep the grammar of "God's creation" ambiguous.

VI The unruly deep

> It was always noticed how this name, whose true pronunciation is unknown,
> consists of pure breath . . . while Elohim is the name of the divine effects.[35]

Schelling is here contrasting Elohim to YHWH, the four consonants that can be pronounced only in a rush of expiring air.[36] Could there be some linkage of this notion of Elohim as *effect* to the Elohimic womb-palace of the *Zohar*? If we read Elohim as *effect* of *bara* rather than as its *subject*, might we sneak in through the back door of "the palace"–to the doctrinal question of "God's creation"? Schelling represents the Romantic margin of German philosophy that found guidance in the Kabbalah and acknowledges a debt to the living Judaism. *Of Human Freedom* had invoked (simultaneously with his former room-mate Hegel, but far freer of system) the shocking idea of *God's own becoming*. God's genesis from–what? From "that within God which is not God himself, i.e., in that which is the basis of his existence."[37] The not-God within God? That basis (*Grund*) translates for him as "*das Grundlose*"– the "groundless ground" of both world and God. Its antecedent is the abyss of the kabbalistic *Eyn Sof* and its analog or influence of Boehme's divine *Ungrund*. Thus the radical imaginary of a divinity born from the dark depths–"all birth is a birth out of darkness into light"–required among philosophical Protestants the midwifery of Jewish mysticism.[38]

For Schelling the "groundless" is recognized by its character of "unruliness" and "depth": the precinct of the primal chaos. It is then the "depth" of God that gives birth to God: "*It is in the beginning in God, and is the God-begotten God himself.*"[39] The *bet* of beginning is the house of chaos: thus Elohim precipitates from this bottomless becoming. Becoming is not outside of God nor God outside of becoming. For Schelling "becoming" replaces the idea of "divine immanence" (which he considers too static, "a dead conceptual inclusion" of things in God). All that becomes is *in* God, but not as apples are *in* a basket; perhaps more as they grow *in* a tree. Because all that becomes, becomes *within* God–as *part* of God–God is also becoming. So a primal Other not separate from but within God–*différance* in precisely the sense of the originary non-origin–produces the elohimic effect within language.

To a theology of becoming, this radical genesis *divines* the potentiality of the tehom. Its creativity does not create by itself. By itself it *makes* no difference. Difference itself could remain wrapped in its bottomless layers churning in an eternal undecidability. We know this danger in ourselves. Decision breaks like grace. The great cosmic decision has been traditionally, with justice, named *the creation*; its agency, *the creator*. That which divines the possible also limits the infinite to its multiplying finitudes. The ecission, the cut, of the actual amidst the matrix of the possible makes *something*. It makes it not from nothing but from everything–from the unruly multiple. But "everything" in a state of potentiality is no thing. In this sense at least a tehomic theology can inhabit the *ex nihilo* formula. But it stresses not the empty abysm–the shadow of a lost foundation–but the multiplicity of the no/thing, its chaotic buzz and plenum. Creation signifies not a zap in the void but a decision within a plenary of possibilities. Thus Nachmanides had translated *bara* as "to cut away" (*ligzor*). "The intelligent person will understand what I am alluding to," he winks.[40]

Surely that intelligent person can also name this selective wisdom, this divining difference, "creator of heaven and earth." The creator would be the agency of decision, thus at once of limitation and relation, by which creatures emerge from the creativity. But the creator remains always also in relation–on this the biblical tradition insists. Thus the creator also emerges from the dark depths–this the Bible has not explicated. Whitehead conceives the creator as "the outcome of creativity." Another philosophy of becoming, rendering Elohim as effect? Creativity "is" not creator. Nor is it creature. In the last chapter we drew "*différance*" and "creativity," philosophical first principles inherently resistant to their own status as Origin, into terminological confluence with the Deep. Indeed our Manyone *sounds* suspiciously related to Whitehead's definition of Creativity: "the many become one . . ." But it is not the same. The many-becoming-one means in Whitehead the many-becoming-*many* ones. That creativity gives birth in the present text to the Manyone, in whom difference itself differentiates; who decides (as Barth stresses rightly) *for* the world; whose many ones in turn, for good and ill, make their own decisions, their own differences.

Only in relation to what we call *creation* can what we call *Creator* be signified, i.e. be imagined to exist. "It is as true to say that God creates the world, as that the world creates God."[41] In the reciprocity of influence, both arise as effects of the primal creativity. But Elohim then signifies the effect through whom all causes arise. The creativity is not a cause, not even the First Cause, but rather the condition that conditions all causal processes. The creativity itself does not become; *it makes becoming possible*. We imagine it therefore as the matrix of possibilities. In this tehomic matrix we are always beginning again. We decide; and we fall back into the undecidable. According to this imaginary of bottomless process, the divine decision is made not *for us* but *with and through us*. Amidst the chaosmic committee work of creation, what work remains for a creator to do–aside from its decisive delegations ("let the earth bring forth," etc.)? Can we say with process theology that the creator emits an eros, a "lure to novelty," an "initial aim"–the beginning condition, the "prevenient grace," to which every creature willy-nilly responds? The metaphor works best, I think, if held with hermeneutical lightness. Some respond more *responsibly* than others to the cosmic desire. Committees and democracies make a lot of messes. The creature either responds in creative sensitivity to its own context; or it blocks the flux of its own becoming.

In other words our responses *become* us. They generate our own plurisingular inter-subjectivities–out of the multiples of elemental energies, codes, socialities, ecologies that any moment constellate our cosmoi. Elohim would live among the effects: a becoming God, who inasmuch as we have language for it/them/her/him, is at minimum an irreducible effect of language. But not an effect *ex nihilo*. For this divinity arises out of those unruly depths, over which language catches its breath. The creator, creating, becomes. In singular plurality.

VII Multiplying angels

Do angels number among these transient lures? They would disappear before we can know them. "Guardians of free passage, they cannot be captured, domesticated, even if our purpose is to see ourselves in them."[42] With the help of Serres' "pure multiplicity," we imagined Nachmanides' natural forces and Ibn Ezra's angelic ones reciprocally translating each other, metonymically sliding into each other's semantic fields. Thus theology licenses a continual oscillation between science and poetry. In the next chapter those natural forces will articulate the *tohu vabohu* of chaos science. If the angels flutter closer to an ancient mythopoeic matrix, they are nonetheless messages of this moment, within its turbulence or dissipation of energies. As Irigaray suggests of their fluent bodies and their "different sex," angels always engage with us "face-to-face, even if it is to affront or to assail." The angels "can light up our sight and all our senses but only if we note the moment when they pass by, hear their word and fulfill it, without seeking to show, demonstrate, prove, argue about their coming, their speaking, or appearance" (ibid., p. 43).

When we thus twist and turn the trope of Elohim, will it dissolve kaleidoscopically into its own multiplicity? Into fragments of its language? Into a swarm of angels? My first epiphany took the form of a childhood dream: "*God and his angels*" appeared; they were fields of light pulsating in the dark, a mobile cluster of jazzy Monet-like stars, fluid geometries without human features, asymmetries without representation. They were bringing me the new law. In the dream they had been preceded by a human fireworks display mimicking them in advance. They were the message they delivered.

11

STRANGE ATTRACTIONS

Formless and void
tohu vabohu

It is easy to specify the minimal redundancy, the initial repetition, incipient dawn above the waters of chaos; it is the echo . . . Languages like to articulate it in various ways; tohu-bohu or brouhaha.

(Michel Serres[1])

Science would relinquish all the rational unity to which it aspires for a little piece of chaos that it could explore.

(Gilles Deleuze and Felix Guattari[2])

I Rhyme or reason?

To convey the pre-creation condition, the P poet indulged in an internal rhyme: *tohu vabohu*. This chapter reads its echo-effect. *Tohu-bohu* has even entered the French dictionary as a loanword, meaning hubbub, ruckus, turbulence, a local chaos. *Tohu* connotes biblically the uninhabitable, unformed condition associated with the wilderness of desert,[3] not an abstract nothingness or vacuum, of which the Hebrews had no concept. *Bohu* seems to be related to the Canaanite Baau, "goddess of the primal night, the mother of the first mortals."[4] *Tohu vabohu* remains an indefinable singularity, invented for the sake of its alliteration. "In the beginning is the echo. Background noise, fluctuation, echo."[5] While Serres is thinking more of chaos theory than of the Bible, let us think of both.

William Brown contends that the negativity conveyed by conventional translations of *tohu vabohu*, like "unformed and void," is unwarranted by "the positive description of the condition." Catching P's playful mood, Brown proposes the English compound and farrago "hodgepodge" as a translation.[6] As though to protect the chaos from defamation, a twelfth-century Jewish text similarly cites an ancient etymology to affirm that earth in this state "was *tohu*, something that is astounding (*mathe′*), for it has nothing substantial within it, nor does it possess any form."[7] *Mathe′* connotes wonder. Classical rabbinical commentators, according to Samuelson, "posited that the nothing out of which God created the universe was nothing only in the sense that it was not a thing."[8] He characterizes this no-thing in khoric/chaotic terms as space itself, specifically as "a single, undifferentiated space." Lynn Bechtel translates *tohu vabohu* as: "the earth is differentiated *and* undifferentiated." For "if reality were only undifferentiated, then there would be no reason for Elohim to speak."[9] (Nothing to speak *to*?[10]) Such translations of the no-thingness suggest what Deleuze calls–not compromising the critique of origin but refining it–"a differential and original space and time."[11]

To permit the foreign language of the Hebrew icons its own differentiations, let me suggest that within the sign-matrix of verse 2, "the earth *tohu vabohu*"–in distinction from *elohim*, *tehom*, *ruach*–signifies matter itself, *prima materia*. Thus we consider in this chapter the matrix of possibilities not in itself (in the guise of tehom) but as *materialization*: the stuff of planets, the energy that resists and fuels order, the wildness of wilderness, the *groundlessness* of common ground. Nomadism and exile: the nomadology of the *eretz* itself is a story written after all not for a settled state but for the homeless.[12] So we do not read verse 2 as representing a linear sequence, with the *tohu vabohu* "before" tehom. With Augustine we read the *tohu vabohu* as derivative of the waters; his nothingsomething "differs" from "darkness over the deep," as "corporeal matter before being qualified by any form."[13]

With the help of this "initial repetition," this chapter will fluctuate theologically between biblical and scientific discourses, demarcating a theological "earth," an *eretz tohu vabohu*, which precedes any ground of order, any homeland of being. Difference precedes form, as chaos precedes order, as a poetics of genesis precedes a science of chaos.

The rhyme of genesis precedes its reason.

II Transgressive repetitions

In E. M. Forster's *A Passage to India*, an echo ("ou-boum") in a sacred cave precipitates a crisis in the colonial subject and then in the colony. "But suddenly, at the edge of her mind, Religion appeared, poor little talkative Christianity, and she knew that all its divine words from 'Let there be light' to 'It is finished' only amounted to 'boum.'"[14] In this mocking earth-echo, void of representation, the entire construction of imperial Christian time, space, home, sex and race cave in. The Indian doctor and gracious host to the British ladies, who neatly exemplifies Homi Bhabha's "not white, not quite," becomes the scapegoat of the hysteria. The echo itself performs a kind of "subversive colonial mimicry." No wonder the (Asian) *tohu vabohu* echoing within the Bible itself had to be theologically muffled.

"In every respect, repetition is a transgression," avers Deleuze.[15] We recall that the Genesis text articulated a standpoint amidst geo-political turbulence. Its home-

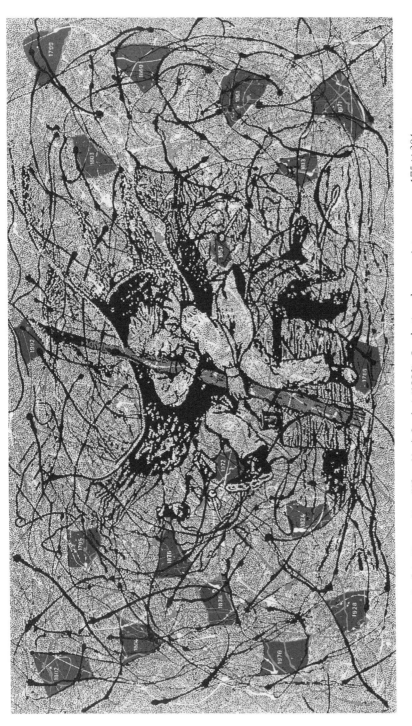

6. Gordon Bennett, *Myth of the Western Man (White Man's Burden)* (1992). Synthetic polymer paint on canvas, 175 × 304cm
Art Gallery of New South Wales
© Gordon Bennett, reproduced with permission
Photo: Christopher Snee for AGNSW

eretz had to be reconstructed under conditions of exile and colonization. Does the order summoned by the creation narrative thus iterate in its chaos the trace of an irretrievable past, the origin that never was? If so, the metaphor of the *eretz tohu vabohu*—the earth before the earth has been "created"—will not be reducible to a naive geocentrism. Might the Hebrew farrago have lent literary form to the experience of a loss-laden and yet productive repetition? And so of a material chaos within which the orders of cosmos rhythmically accrue? Under conditions of acute loss, this *tohu vabohu* signals that every fresh world comes from an initial chaos. The threat of the chaos, in other words, may also purvey—in the creative reinscription of the colonized, at least—the hope of the new. Indeed they may map upon the imposed order the alternative pathways of a transgressive chaosmos.

Might we read the echo-effect of *tohu vabohu* as the minimal gesture of difference—a difference, however, not of separation or opposition but of *repetition*? A repetition is by definition never the "same" as that which it repeats. It is always already other. In its iterations it becomes readable, a code. "Every milieu is coded, a code being defined by periodic repetition."[16] Thus Deleuze and Guattari declare their kinship to "very ancient cosmogonies": "From chaos, *Milieus* and *Rhythms* are born." Any code exists in "a perpetual state of *transcoding*." Thus signs transverse the chaos of heterogeneous space-times through rhythm. In Whitehead's earlier thought, the stability produced by rhythmic repetition replaces the substantial permanence of essence: "*what becomes* involves *repetition* transformed into *novel immediacy*."[17] (If he thus transcoded relativity's energy and Copenhagen's quanta into philosophy, he also influenced the science of Ilya Prigogine's dynamics, which, along with the math of Mandelbrot's fractal iteration, influenced Serres, Deleuze and Guattari.) "*Self-similarity*" is the repetition which takes the place of sameness: *repetition with a difference*.

"I begin again," writes Serres. "A fluctuation appears, it is lost in the desert or the packed-fullness of background noise, either through lack of reference, or through excess of difference." Serres invokes an "initial repetition" where order and disorder interact almost indistinguishably. He then, quite inadvertently, offers a set of possible translations, or transcodings, of *tohu vabohu*: "turbulence is an intermittence of void and plenitude, of lawful determinism and underdetermination . . . an intermittence of being and nothingness."[18] So one might translate Genesis 1.2a as "the *world was void and plenary . . .*" But we need not choose amongst the "hodgepodge" of translations. Let the farrago stand in Hebrew. Its ludic untranslatability reflects—repeats—the character of the chaos itself.

III "Order through fluctuation"

If the chaos is invariably lost in translation, it has nonetheless begun to transcode its rhythmic *nihil aliquid*, its nothingsomething, into the language of science. If *tohu vabohu* may be read as a "double fluctuation, the very first seeding upon the cloud or

7. Homer Wilson Smith, *Mandelbrot Set*. Fractal Images provided by Art Matrix, www.artmatrix.com

the white noise," then already the verse of primal chaos insinuates (in its pre/science) the root principle of chaos theory: amplification through the bifurcating trajectories of extremely unstable systems. But ultimately theology, like science, wonders about the complex and relatively stable systems in which we move, live and get to be. Even when exploring "a little piece of chaos," our mandate remains clear enough: not to trade order for chaos but to construct "order" differently.

An alternative order arises, according to chaos theory, out of *fluctuation*. "Fluctuation" names the very oscillation by which chaos arises, and by which order arises from chaos: hence its doubling. How can this be? Only through what Isabelle Stengers calls a "conceptual upheaval." The pioneering text of Ilya Prigogine with Isabelle Stengers, *Order out of Chaos*, argues that "all systems contain subsystems, which are continually 'fluctuating.' "[19] Fluctuations generate, as demonstrated in any echo, "positive feedback." At a certain point, a fluctuation or a combination of fluctuations may become so powerful, "amplified" through the feedback, that it reaches a "bifurcation point." At this "singular" or "revolutionary" moment, it is "impossible to determine whether the system will disintegrate into "chaos" or entropy, or leap to a new, more differentiated, higher level of "order."

This threshold would come to be known as "*the edge of chaos*;" or with the physicist Per Bak, "*criticality*."[20] Bak investigated the behavior of simulated sand piles. He analyzed how if grains are released in a steady stream, one by one, they perform according to linear, strictly predictable rules. But at a certain point a shift occurs: from predictable linear process to a nonlinear pattern of avalanches, in which all the grains suddenly seem to be "in communication," behaving "like an organism." In chaos theory the "*phase transition*" characterizes this critical point, in which the fluctuations burst into a randomness that might just cause them to dissipate; or that might maintain sensitive interrelations in a relatively stable state–in vortices of wind or water, in cardiac rhythms or mammalian intelligence.[21] Thus chaos and complexity theories now combine to articulate "chaoplexity."

In Prigogine's generative theory, order arises spontaneously out of chaos through a process of "*self-organization*." Chaos for him designates the disruptive, randomizing element of chance, which can be only probabilistically measured in fluctuations.[22] "Self-organization processes in far-from-equilibrium conditions correspond to a delicate interplay between chance and necessity, between fluctuations and deterministic laws."[23] So *fluctuation signifies both the repetitions comprising a chaotic process and the genesis of order*. Prigogine's autocatalytic principle of "order through fluctuations" applies across the spectrum of the natural sciences.[24]

I am invoking the metaphor of "self-organization" as a transcoded theological equivalent to the "order" of creation. Such order maintains itself *within* instability; it corresponds to that third genre which Prigogine has called a "*dissipative structure*."[25] This tensive metaphor answers the challenge of the second law of thermodynamics: how can highly ordered systems such as living organisms evolve in a world in which the sort of irreversible processes they embody lead invariably to an increase in disorder? Prigogine grants that the increase in complexity produces entropy (a greater degree of entropy than the decrease represented by living organisms). But he argues that at the revolutionary bifurcation point—such as the boiling point of water—the system remains irreversible but becomes *nonlinear*. A new structure may occur precisely through the far-from-equilibrium instability, and can maintain itself there (as water passes through a highly unstable point of turbulence into a relatively stable system of boiling bubbles). So complex systems depend upon the chaos from which they arise and to which they contribute: hence they are "dissipative." They do not merely effect transitions to conventional linear systems.

Rather, as Stengers insists, "dissipative structures seem to prolong indefinitely the *fertile instant of the genesis of structures*." A tehomically fertile trope! Such a "dissipative regime" is characterized by its collectivity, which collapses "the distinction between local events and global description." "This is not a reason to mix everything up," Stengers tartly warns: "the fluctuation in itself *does not cause anything*." Fluctuation is incessantly produced in systems peopled by billions of molecules behaving stochastically. What counts in fluctuation is "the specifically kinetic phenomenon of its amplification, the opportunity that this amplification reveals, and what gives way to an intrinsically collective phenomenon." She underscores the dramatic shift in our sense of matter: "We often speak of 'dissipative structures' created by the amplification of a fluctuation to macroscopic dimensions. We are then forgetting the paradox hidden by these words, the conceptual upheaval: a fluctuation was what was by definition insignificant and without consequence; the possibility of its amplification signals the end of the tranquil generalizations of physics."[26] Thus "repetition" peforms its subversion within the precinct of natural science. But the fluctuations of this discourse quickly amplify to include human social structures. Under the tensive symbol of dissipative order, social complexity at every scale oscillates in and out of chaos.

IV At home far from equilibrium

Thermodynamics be damned. Genesis, thank whatever lord may be, has occurred. We all thrive.[27]

Our species nests among a (still) blooming myriad of species. With characteristic color, Stuart Kauffman, the Santa Fe Institute's founding biologist of complexity, asks "the overarching question": "Whence cometh all this bubbling activity, complexity, and *chutzpah*?" Leaping beyond biological bounds, his tehomic answer pulls right up to the edge of cosmogony: "Ultimately, it must be a natural expression of a universe that is not in equilibrium, where instead of the featureless homogeneity of a vessel of gas molecules, there are *differences, potentials, that drive the formation of complexity*." Differences and, or as, potentials: the trace elements of the *tohu vabohu*. "The flash of the Big Bang 15 billion years ago has yielded a universe said to be expanding, perhaps never to fall together in the Big Crunch. It is a nonequilibrium universe filled with *too many* hydrogen and helium atoms compared with the most stable atomic form, iron. It is a universe of galaxies and clusters of galaxies on *many scales*, where none might have formed at all" (ibid., p. 19). In theology we call this nonlinear might-not-have-been "grace."

In the beginning, difference repeats, fluctuates, expands to excess: the *tohu vabohu* always differentiated and undifferentiated. This multi-scalar dimensionality suggests on a cosmic level the tendency for order to irrupt from *within* chaos; to self-organize rather than to depend (like the early Bonhoeffer's "obedient void") upon an external transcendence to impose it. This heterogeneous *tohu vabohu*–science capturing "a bit of the chaos" indeed–provides a welcome analog to the matrix of possibilities. "Here is no mere scientific search. Here is a mystical longing, a sacred core first sought around that small campfire sometime in the past 3 million years" (ibid., p. 20). Such mystical wonder can only annoy the reductionists of lifeless mechanism and evolutionary accident. But it bodes no better for those who possess the simple answer to Kauffman's "whence?": "God, of course." Less than ever does one need a super-natural Creator to supply a transcendent origin for the universe.

In our shockingly expansive, possibly infinite universe–the universe of a hundred billion galaxies, each sporting at least a hundred billion stars–there remains paradoxically *less* space for an omnipotent Person, a Creator *ex nihilo*. But Kauffman's "theory of emergence" does not flatten the creation to a banal continuity. "The vast mystery of biology is that life should have emerged at all, that the order we see should have come to pass." This new scientific sense of the miraculous can only honor the ancient theological questions, even as it probes for new answers. "A theory of emergence would account for the creation of the stunning order out our windows as a natural expression of some underlying laws. It would tell us if we are *at home in the universe, expected in it*, rather than present despite overwhelming odds" (ibid., p. 20; my emphasis). Expected? By whom? Kaufman teeters on the verge of theology. But Christian theology is in no position to play father-knows-best, welcoming the occasional prodigal scientist home.

Rather we confess that long before reductionism reigned, theology worked to evict us from the world.[28] We became "pilgrims on this earth," just passing through this materiality and chaos. To be "at home in the universe" would count as sin, sloth and sensuality, rebellious denial of our true Origin. Tellingly, Prigogine and Stengers, through their reading of Whitehead, recognized the dependence of the colorless, lifeless mechanism that had become the scientific "nature," upon "the Christian nature, stripped of any property that permits man to identify himself with the ancient harmony of natural 'becoming.'"[29] A dominological Christianity had branded any deep sense of belonging within the flux as pagan, irrational–and chaotic. Science superseded and mirrored the ontotheology of timeless truth. "One can speak here of a kind of 'convergence' between the interests of theologians, who held that the world had to acknowledge God's omnipotence by its total submission to Him, and of physicists seeking a world of mathematizable processes" (ibid., p. 49).

Precisely *within* the dissipation of the God of patriarchy, within the very instability of its disruption, we are discerning the self-organization of another discourse of the divine. Insistently pluralist, tuned to the echo of the earth and the scales of the heavens, curious rather than defensive toward the natural sciences, this becoming-theology makes itself at home within complexity. It looks neither for Creator nor for the human creature outside of the ecosocial web of all life. Long-repressed longings for a home within rather than beyond "the world" may be released by this theory of emergence, itself still emerging. But the stabilizing sign of "home" emerges here, paradoxically, within the rhythmic nomadism of far-from-equilibrium dynamics. This is all to the good, for a theological tradition whose Genesis must be thought in proximity to Exodus. If we–a great many of us–do not thrive and belong, we may at least recognize the injustice.

V Holy mater

Being at home as being "expected": an image redolent of pregnancy, nurturance, hospitality. A maternal imaginary appears thus not accidentally–though quite unexpectedly–at one of the rare points where *theology* has received chaos theory. "There could be no self-consciousness and human creativity without living organization, and there could be no such living dissipative systems unless the entropic stream followed its general, irreversible course in time." Arthur Peacocke, Anglican physicist-theologian, is reflecting on Prigogine's theory. "Thus does the apparently decaying, randomizing tendency of the universe provide the necessary and essential matrix (*mot juste!*) for the birth of new forms–new life through death and decay of the old."[30] A tehomic theology recognizes here an epiphany of the matrix of possibilities. Elsewhere Peacocke bears down explicitly on the natal metaphor. He finds the concept of God as Creator "too much dominated by a stress on the externality of God's creative acts. He is pictured as having created something external to himself, just as the male fertilizes the ovum from outside." He briefly experiments with a figuration that eludes any simplistic binary of in/out. "Mammalian females, at least, experience creation within themselves, and the growing embryo resides within the female body. Therefore, female images of the divine are more helpful in this context than male ones."[31] If diverted from a certain biological essentialism, the "within" of the embryo signifies a relation, whose terms cannot be simply divided into same/other, here/there, immanent/transcendent: "We should work with the analogy of God creating the world within herself. *God creates a world that is in principle other than himself, but creates it within herself*" (ibid.; my emphasis).

191

Might such cross-gendered language (which has not yet permeated the rather monosexual science/religion dialogue) help leverage the shift to a becoming that is also a belonging? Philosopher of religion Grace Jantzen, thinking more of ecology than cosmology, puts it this way: "a shift to an imaginary of natality would include a recovery of that kinship with the world" in which our spiritual becoming "is not a matter of escape from the world but of finding it our home."[32] As the embryo is not the *same* as the mother's body, so the world is at no point identical with the deity. The offspring, always differently, iterates the parent: literally and analogically, the birth metaphor dramatizes the repetition of the other in the self and of the self in the other, by which a relationship becomes possible. Semantically kin to Rosemary Ruether's "divine matrix" or "God/ess," the uteral signifier gestates an embryonic chaos. That chaos materializes, bursting wet from the womb (Job 38)—as an already self-organizing potentiality, a chaoplexity.

VI Trickster mom

For some readers, however gendered, the uteral signifier may provoke hysterical sensations of engulfment. Might it not reinscribe the stereotype of a material/chaotic femininity ordered by some invisible masculine Spirit? A feminist might for good reason reject the whole *mater*-complex. One might favor a less exploited figure: "Perhaps the world resists being reduced to mere resource because it is–not mother/matter/mutter–but coyote, a figure for the always problematic, always potent tie of meaning and bodies."[33] Donna Haraway's figure of the trickster not only subverts the grinding exploitation of the feminized earth, but supersedes the maternal altogether. Trickster "makes room for some unsettling possibilities, including a sense of the world's independent sense of humor." We have already watched the Leviathan surface–especially with the help of a Bakhtinian Job–as something of a trickster, alternately playful and cruel. "The Coyote or Trickster, embodied in American Southwest Indian accounts, suggests our situation when we give up mastery, but keep searching for fidelity, knowing all the while we will be hoodwinked" (ibid., p. 199). Fidelity vs. mastery, humor vs. domination: terms for a tehomic theology. Haraway, of course, is not concerned with God but with the "God-trick" of unsituated knowledge.

The unsettling trope of the world-trickster resists any smug resettlement of our "home in the universe"–even as, in Haraway's reading, he [sic] would situate precisely where we *are* in the world. Trickster has, not surprisingly, appeared to help popularize chaos theory. "The clown, trickster, or shape changer becomes the personification of chaos for cultures all over the world."[34] When we attend to the coyote, matter itself takes on the sort of dispersive, differential and irreducible animation that we might have reserved for culture. It ceases to lie flat, to divide into impenetrable atoms, to lie dully outside of ourselves. Glen Mazis makes visible a resemblance between the trickster and the "sensitive interdependence" that generates physical chaos: "interconnection involves a lot of friction and conflict as well as harmony and cooperation, and the Trickster figure demonstrates how these painful and potentially destructive dimensions of existence and community can be suffered through with humor and a sense of play." The tehomic waters glitter upon the surface of this play: "the very idea of humor, which is to become fluid (its roots mean 'to be wet'), to overcome the dryness of life and to allow our normal boundaries to be dissolved," suggests a "frolic," "an animal energy which infuses the world."[35]

Granted, then: the old, abusable symbol of womb/mother or material madonna lacks the naughty glamour of the trickster. But shouldn't we be suspicious of Haraway's supersession of dull she-*mater* by a seductive he-trick? So I suggest that to resist the symbolic reduction of woman to mother, and mother to matter, we circumvent feminist matricide and begin from the bottom up—where matter itself bottoms out into what we might call, crossing its sexes, a *trickster matrix*.

Here appear the unresolved mysteries of dark matter—perhaps three-quarters of the universe composed of this darkness over the deep of space, eccentric in force, countering gravity, truly a force of divergence; here matter might dissolve into countless, infinitesimal, vibrating strings, or membranes; here waves of quantum uncertainty lap into evanescent particles; and strange attractors describe nonlinear, fractal geometries. The trickster matrix gives visible birth as well: in every chaos phenomenon of flux, dynamics, fluctuation, bifurcation; in the way flocks fly, trees branch, solitons swell, populations increase. Every wilderness behemoth or leviathan repeats it.

This matron of matter will not lose the cruel edge of the trickster—who mocks any given meaning—but she may counter its unjust human deployments. If the trickster trope reanimates matter, might the maternal not shamelessly reinvent itself within the emergent chaosmos? As "nature" no longer lies faceless before scientific observation, so "mother" no longer lies like a certainty, a doormat, a Tiamat, beneath her victorious sons and liberated daughters. To admit a maternal figuration of what *matters* is not to reduce femininity to maternity or maternity to body, but to elaborate an earth-embedded code of "bodies that matter."[36] In the *tohu vabohu*, gender itself iterates parodically, repeating sex-roles queerly, sub-versively. Why now, when gender and sex have themselves passed into such a cultural *tohu vabohu*, would we erase the *natality* of nature? Why not let the mother's body—"*la mère qui jouit*"[37]—shift and shimmy. The *mater materializes* differently; or, I fear, *no body will*.

VII Creation from uncertainty

Twenty-six attempts preceded the present genesis, all of which were destined to fail. The world of man [*sic*] has arisen out of the chaotic heart of the preceding debris . . . "Let's hope it works" (*Halway Sheyaamod*), exclaimed God as he created the World, and this hope, which has accompanied all the subsequent history of the world and mankind, has emphasized right from the outset that this history is branded with the mark of radical uncertainty.[38]

A new god-trick? No doubt. But this time the trick is to make ourselves at home within uncertainty. A variety of religious and scientific discourses are evolving their own dissipative stabilities. Stengers places the creative uncertainties of the science of the last hundred years in context: "It is this cultural climate that nourishes and amplifies the discovery of undreamed-of objects, quasars with formidable energies, fascinating black holes, the discovery also, on earth, of the diversity of experiences that nature effects, theoretical discoveries, and finally the problems of instabilities, proliferations, migrations, and structurations." A late modern culture of protest and democratization has facilitated the discursive shift. "At the point where science had shown us an unchanging and pacified nature, we understand that no organization or stability is guaranteed or legitimate, that none can impose itself by right."[39] A transdisciplinary practice of the nonlinear and the uncertain–scientific, aesthetic, coalitional–has in theology stimulated worship of the Spirit that blows where it wills.[40] But Stengers does not romanticize the collective destabilization. "This world that seems to have renounced the security of stable permanent norms is clearly a dangerous and uncertain world." While it can "inspire no blind confidence," she turns–in what seems to be a growing scientific proclivity–to religion. So she cites the above talmudic text, which expresses instead "the feeling of mitigated hope": A far cry from the *creatio ex nihilo*.

When the creation narrative enters thus into midrashic play, the divine itself reveals a trickster face. The *tohu vabohu* of a matter recycled from prior collapses would infect "progressive" theology. Rather than marching forward and abandoning the traditions that have failed us (and which have not?) we recycle. We generate new ones from the debris. The trope of "God's Creation" circulates within "the chaotic heart" of theology. Denuded of omnipotence, linearity, even of His grammatical masculinity, what remains of the work of *ordering*?

VIII Seven days of complex self-organization

We have already observed the symbolic sequence of "seven days" mutate into nonlinearity. It begins to exhibit the principles of critical shift at the edge of–the waters. The creation then reads out not as an imposition of order but as a fractal cascade of indeterminacy and form: a chaosmos eked *tohu vabohu* from the fluctuations. Does the creation then "emerge" in Kauffman's sense? Does it exhibit the character of a complex, *self*-organizing system? When we ignore most of the first chapter of Genesis (bored or blinded by its familiarity), we allow the linear reduction to divine fiat. If Elohim does not, contrary to most readings, unilaterally order a world into existence, Elohim "*lets be*." Thus as discussed earlier divinity "attracts" multitiered cooperation. "God said, 'Let the *earth put forth* vegetation; plants yielding seed etc. . . .' And it was so. The *earth brought forth* vegetation: plants yielding seed of every kind, and trees of every kind bearing fruit with the seed in it." The earth is *agent* of *Elohim's* creation. The same again with the sea: "Let the waters bring forth swarms of living creatures . . ." *Creation takes place as invitation and cooperation*.[41] In a liturgical repetition that overrides the "monotone of transcendence" with the iteration of differences and potentials, the creator lures self-organizing systems out of the fluctuating possibilities. And Elohim saw that it was good. Is this mere self-congratulation? Or spontaneous delight when genesis *works*? What would the mythologem of the Elohim's sabbatical rest mean, after all this work? That God was exhausted from too much exertion? Or that there has come to be so much—to experience? To enjoy and to suffer? The metaphor of "rest" connotes a dimension of divine *passivity*, passion, receptivity, altogether at odds with the classical triumph of the *actus purus*, the purely active, unmoved Mover. As Moltmann notes of classical Christianity: "the resting God, the celebrating God, the God who rejoices over his [sic] creation, receded into the background." I share Moltmann's vision of the "many-faceted community of creation" as place for "the hopes of the alienated . . . that the world should be 'home.'"[42]

Would the divine Sabbath then not support a reciprocity of the divine and the human, and so a vision of the co-creativity of the creatures with the creator—the divine receptivity to the works of earth, of sea, and no doubt of the human too? Not because God is inactive, otiose or defunct, nor because of the deferred "Coming," but because divinity *lures* but does not pre*determine*? So I do not imagine that "being at home in existence" signifies some future Sabbath, when "the relationships between God, human beings and nature lose their tension and are resolved into peace and repose" (ibid., p. 59, n. 30). (Thus Moltmann eschatologically defers the seventh day, correspondent to his *ex nihilo*.) There is no energy without tension—and "energy is pure delight" (William Blake). I suspect that the notion of ultimate "home"—*Heimat*—as stasis, as future cosmic equilibrium, only preserves the ethos of pilgrims on their way to a perfect, timeless world, just passing through this chaotic one. Nor should the icon of God's seventh day rest be sacrificed to the ideal of a final changeless perfection. Rather its genius is to make divinity at home within the rhythmic structures of natural/historical time, even as it structures human work within a sustaining cycle of refreshment. The divine Sabbath suggests an ever-repeating moment of divine internalization; meditative reception, in which the clash and jangle of the universe is absorbed into its widest interpretive context. It would recall Whitehead's "consequent nature of God" in which divinity becomes actual through relation, in which indeed God "repeats" our self-actualizations in Godself. The tensions would be resolved only to be recharged.

The possibility of sustained theological attention to such a cosmic collaborativity evaporated with the tehom. What remained was to read the poetics of creation as "the praises of God's power from the testimonies of nature," denuded of interest in the swarming particularities of the creatures.[43] Thus Calvin attacks the imaginary of the *anima mundi* (an antecedent used by Charles Wesley of panentheism) of the God–world relation as that of a mind that "pervades its members."[44] "As if the universe," he snorts, "which was founded as a spectacle of God's glory, were its own creator!"[45] Does self-organizing complexity represent another version of this self-creation he decries? Is it just another scientific trick to render God superfluous? Calvin with good reason, in the context of a dawning modernity, warns against idolatrous human mimicry of creation, and so against any notion of creaturely self-creation. Yet such creaturely self-creation can only be judged arrogant or impious if it is understood–as Calvin certainly did–as a mimicry of the *creatio ex nihilo*. Scientific autocatalysis makes no such presumption: on the contrary, it signifies emergence as creation from the chaos of prevenient conditions. For a theology of becoming, the divine would indeed pervade those preconditions. It is not the icon of the creator but the spectacular idol of his all-determining power which is thereby made superfluous.

IX The strange attractor

We have brought Elohim into a theological reconnection with the *tohu vabohu* of matter. In the face of the self-organizing complexity of the universe we imagine a creative agency of which Elohim or Creator remain apt, even beautiful, names. So do Word, Logos, Hochmah, or Sophia. Let me offer a tehomophilic figuration. It echoes but does not imitate the confession of "God the Father Almighty, Maker of Heaven and Earth."

Complex systems exhibit the mathematical property called "attractor." When, for example, a marble spins in a bowl, the point at which the marble eventually settles is the point which "attracts" the marble. But in a chaotic system, the attractor is not a point. For the point "moves about along a continuous path in a bounded region that never returns to the same point." Imagine this noncyclical nomadism: "The path of the strange attractor in state space may, in its endless meandering, fill a subspace of the whole space, and this subspace can have a bizarre noninteger fractal dimension. *There is no way we can exactly mathematically construct the geometrical path of such strange attractors*."[46] The attractor is multidimensional, and exists in an infinite dimensional space (the n-dimensional phase space we entered in Lyotard's reading of Augustine). Moreover, motion upon a strange attractor exhibits sensitive dependence on initial conditions. And strange attractors display the paradox of attracting trajectories to *converge* on them while at the same time–because of the butterfly effect–the initially close trajectories *diverge* rapidly (A possible source of Deleuze's "divergent convergence"?) In this way chaos theory enters the astrophysical

8. Homer Wilson Smith, *Lorenz Attractor*. Fractal Images provided by Art Matrix, www.artmatrix.com

calculations of the wildly fluctuating expansion in the seconds after the Big Bang (or Birth)–a strange attractor may account for the rapid divergence, which seems, at different speeds, to be continuing 15 billion years later.[47]

Might we every now and then imagine Elohim as the strange attractor of creation? Attractors function in a mathematical phase space that is dependent on computer simulations; a space perhaps bizarre or chilling to the desires of faith. Nonetheless strange attraction offers an analogy to what Whitehead meant by the Divine Eros, with its "lure" toward actualization. He was thinking as a mathematician in his conception of this "primordial nature of God." Its content is comprised of abstract possibilities, indeed entities "deficient in actuality," which connote a kind of cosmic geometrical/genetic code, his "eternal objects." It acts not by fiat, not by dictate or force, not by an intervening or efficient cause. Here Whitehead's speculation slides out of math into emotion: *mathé*! The action of God is its *relation*–by *feeling and so being felt*, the divine invites the *becoming* of the other; by feeling the becoming of the other, the *divine itself becomes*. The terminological demands of Whitehead's "primordial and consequent natures" aside, might we affirm an *oscillation between divine attraction and divine reception, invitation and sabbath*?

Between the divine "poles," or limit-metaphors, would take place the self-organizing response of the universe: the creature responds to the lure of the creator; the creator responds to the action of the creature. To respond is to become. Without such a reciprocity of genesis, there can be no serious theology of becoming. The "lure for feeling" would be felt as "repetition" of the Other in the self; as the echo of God's desire in the desired creature. But this is the creature emergent from the brouhaha of its world. No other sort of creature exists. Within the chaoplexity of endless fluctuations, an order *emerges*. It reinforces certain differences amidst the endless possible ones. The strange attractor of chaos theory can serve as another figure for the natural law, logos or Torah, that permits genesis at the edge of chaos. It describes a labyrinthine but limiting path–for a path is always a track of decisions–within the ever-incomplete infinite. In such n-dimensional phase-space, theology could find itself right at home. We have practice in imagining iterations (days, generations, ages) of interrelation at different scales–in the fluctuation of psychic, interpersonal, ritual, historical and ecological systems within the system of "the creation." Thus "sensitive dependence upon initial conditions" resonates *naturally* with the icon of the spirit fluctuating in the turbulence.

X Strange manners

If this strange attraction draws to itself the trope of the divine lure, can it also shed light on divine *love*? Unlike the cosmic *eros*, with its mythic bisexual, hybrid and playful atmosphere, the Christian *agape* emits a parental anthropomorphism, a unilateral condescension far removed from the *tohu vabohu* in which the vastly inhuman creation arises. Whitehead did hint at this trickster topos: "The initial aim is the best for that impasse. But if the best be bad, then the ruthlessness of God can be personified as Ate, the goddess of mischief. The chaff is burnt." Usually the trickster's religious forms remain foreign to Christianity, as though love was too serious for such play. But by eliminating the game, did the church lessen cruelty? Or merely lose sight of its own ambiguities? A fictional Hindu (the effect of a certain colonial doubling) comments: "All spirit as well as all matter must participate in salvation, and if practical jokes are banned, the circle is incomplete."[48]

Even the Christian God of love may don the persona of a trickster: "*The fruition of Love is a game / That no one can explain truly.*"[49] Thus the early thirteenth-century Hadewijch dwelt passionately on this unpredictability of divine love. She chose *Minne* (love), "a word of feminine gender and belonging to the language of courtly love," to signify God, Christ, or Divine Love.[50] The Beguine's poetry does not flinch from the feeling of cruelty and randomness provoked by the trickster nature.

> Alas! On dark roads of misery
> Love indeed lets us wander,
> In many an assault, without safety,
> Where she seems to us cruel and hostile;
> And to some she gives, without suffering,
> Her great and multiform joy:
> For us these are truly strange manners,
> But for connoisseurs of Love's free power, they are joy.

This deity does not control and guarantee but "lets us wander"–at our peril. Yet this "multiform joy" passionately echoes the delight of a cosmic "it is good!" It seems not irrelevant to this affective complexity that her divine *Minne* allowed her the feminine personification. The poems of Hadewijch present a rare case of trickster as female, let alone as Christian God.[51]

Strange manners, exercising a strange attraction. The impersonal iterations of the Elohimic manyone have evolved within human language to a high pitch of interpersonality. The sufferings that seem to assault us without rhyme or reason, the miseries whose causes we cannot change, lead us down dark roads indeed. The divinity to whom we cry may collapse into the cause of the torment, or into a mere impersonal fate, a chaos of indifferent nature.

We could lose all sense of humor and home. Or it may be that within the *tohu vabohu* of meaning, within the dark dissipation of a prior confidence, faith, like science, (to repeat) learns to rhyme its reasons.

12

DOCTA IGNORANTIA

Darkness on the face
pne choshekh

But now you put me a question and say: "How might I think of God in Godself, and what is God?" And to this I can only answer thus: "I have no idea." For with your question you have brought me into that same darkness, into that same cloud of unknowing in which I wish you were yourself.

(The Cloud of Unknowing[1]*)*

In the shadows of late night, we talk about the need to see darkness differently.

(bell hooks[2])

I Night visions

A certain Christianity, unfurling towards the light, knew only dread of the dark depths. Its God comes cloaked in light. In the end, when His creation gets terminated, there will be "no more sea" and "no more night." An absolute presence of light, an unwavering God-day, will shine from the lamp that is the lamb. Its neon logic illumines every Sunday School: God called the light "good," so the dark must be "bad." "Just as nothing that is good can come out of tehom, nothing that is good can come out of darkness."[3] The demonization of the dark belongs to the foundational tehomophobia of Christian civilization. So we have not followed the one who "made darkness around him his canopy, thick clouds, a gathering of water" (II Samuel 22.12).

Yet among the deep folds of Christianity, even of a certain orthodoxy, a different interpretive tradition survives. This is the ancient way of the "brilliant dark." Meditating on the "dense darkness" in which YHWH enfolded himself for Moses, Gregory of Nyssa in the fourth century may have first coined the tensive phrase, a trope that deconstructs the opposition of light and dark.[4] It illumines the tradition of negative theology from (Pseudo-)Dionysius in the sixth century, and continues to flicker along a particular rim of Catholic mysticism.[5] The darkness of creation in this

200

tradition has nothing to do with evil. As Meister Eckhart interprets the darkness of Genesis 1.2, it signifies "the hidden things of God; 'above the face of the abyss' meaning above all created reason."[6] The dark, in other words, is none other than that which exceeds our knowledge: the divine itself. When it recurs in the twentieth century, as, for instance, in the title of mystic and civil rights activist Howard Thurman's "anatomy of segregation," *The Luminous Darkness*, it is no casual figure of speech.[7] For western civilization has not innocently worshipped the light. To manufacture the "ontological whiteness" (James Cone) of its subjects—a pallor shining through theological and modern styles of knowledge, regardless of their views of "race"—it has relentlessly, spiritually and materially, de/faced the dark.

This chapter meditates upon an icon of irreducible mystery: *darkness on the face*. It examines the apophatic epistemology of unknowing, with special focus on Nicholas of Cusa; it does this within the context of an enquiry into the iconoclastic force of the luminous dark in general; a force which it tests, in particular, on the singularly pressing case of race construction. Is such a discursive swing too wide, too abrupt? Between the depths of the mystical tradition and the surface of race politics, between the epistemic and the epidermal darkness, do I risk reduction on the one hand and mystification on the other? Let me take the chance, in the interest of an experiment upon the dark surface of the waters. If I fail to hold this mystico-political feedback loop in language, let me at least leave a trace of this hunch: that unless Christianity unblocks *the dark depths* it froze in itself long before "racism" existed, the subliminal habits of whiteness—engrained in liberalism as well as in reaction—will persist. For the "white mythology" of the west emanates from a constitutive fantasy of our virtue, our beauty, our spiritual *light*.[8] It seems to me that merely oppositional discourses have for now run their course, and that indignant strategies of ethical correction will not make up the difference. An unclogging must be effected at the level of that heterogeneous depth, in which multiple causes and effects must be thought together: at a depth of language always already uncertain of itself, apophatic, shadowed.

Let me suggest the following line of argument: a tehomic theology requires the deconstruction of the *light supremacism* of the western spirit. The negativity of theology, with its "cloud of unknowing," marks in the present experiment an overlap between mystical disclosure and prophetic iconoclasm: a negativity—not altogether western—where language itself comes into question. This theology of unknowing thus to present readers seems to perform deconstruction *devant la lettre*.[9] Kevin Hart has put it succinctly: "It is not that deconstruction is a form of negative theology, but that negative theology is a form of deconstruction."[10] So this mystical "darkness" comes now into ethical play not as special spiritual experience but as epistemic strategy. In this reading it is the *iconoclasm* of the luminous dark, not some anachronistically projected *racial intentionality*, which might provide its current social relevance. If the color line can be read (at least in the U.S.A.) as "the limit and constitutive condition for cultural and social life,"[11] then it would not surprisingly run through the topos of "the creation." Nor would those symbolizations be ethically empty, which use the Genesis topography of the dark "above" to subvert the routine subordination of darkness to the light.

"I pray," wrote Dionysius a millennium and a half ago, "that we could come to this darkness so far above light!"[12]

II "In which darkness is infinite light"

According to Genesis, the light–first creature uttered by Elohim–was not created from nothing. Rather it was "separated *from* the darkness." So light is first a part or potential within the darkness-on-the-face. What sort of nondual precreation light does the text thus insinuate? Presumably this initial admixture does not suggest some sort of gray (which would not be "darkness") but rather a black incandescence. In the midst of defining "negative theology," Nicholas of Cusa offers this radical proposition: "this whom it worships as inaccessible light is not light whose opposite is darkness, but is *light, in which darkness is infinite light*."[13] In the icon of the luminous dark, light and dark are not opposites. And the precreation hybrid they form in their inseparability is none other than the God of negative theology. Moreover, this God *is* not. "*For God is not some kind of being*." This is the ontological radicalism established at the edge of the platonic tradition by Dionysius. He set in motion the oscillation of apophatic unknowing and kataphatic affirmations (such as "God is light," "God is good"). The "brilliant darkness of a hidden silence" prayerfully cloaks the "being beyond being" of a God who "is being for whatever is," who "is coming-to-be amid whatever happens;" but who "is not a being," who "was not" and "will not be."[14]

Let us draw the tehomic inference: the God who is not a Being does not exist over against nonbeing, as the opposite of nothing, and so bears little resemblance to the *creator ex nihilo*. As light folds back into the unknowing, so that which "comes into being" folds back into the not-being. Characteristically, the negative tradition dissolves ontology into epistemology: "since *the unknowing of what is beyond being* is something above and beyond speech, mind, or being itself . . ." Thus the paradox of the brilliant dark turns into that of "the knowing ignorance." Yet because the Dionysian scheme nonetheless remains platonic in its celestial hierarchy, its beyond-being or "hyper-essentiality" has been famously suspected of mere ontotheology raised to the highest power.[15] But this very deconstruction, as it turns out, seems irresistibly drawn to the apophasis. For the negative twist within speculative Christian platonism already also anticipates the Heideggerian/Derridean critique of ontotheology–that is, of an uncritical fusion of the platonic Being with the Hebraic Creator. These theologians of negation after all did not offer the truth of a sun beyond the delusions of the cave. They prayed for the darkness beyond the delusions of the sun. They outgrew "God" as the entity mirrored by linguistic propositions and projected by Christian signs of power. Writing their anti-answers between the lines of the most aggressively assertorial religion of all times, they do not so much dispute the classical assertions as engulf them in a chiaroscuro of shadows, silences and self-negations. "Where I would you were yourself."[16] If then Genesis 1 darkly radiates a *chaosmic episteme*, a theology of becoming may depend upon the apophatic gesture for any credibility of affirmation. For it would articulate a faith with which to face uncertainty, not a knowledge with which to eliminate it.

III Language without dominance

> The characteristic experience of faith today is pervaded by *a certain darkness*, emptiness, silence, risk, the cross, akin to the dynamic of apophatic mysticism, even while the drawing near of the sacred is recognized in fragments of healing, beauty, liberation, and love in the human and natural world, understood anew as *luminous*.[17]

The present work recognizes itself in Elizabeth Johnson's coded observation. For her the medieval *via negativa* seems to pry open the theological space—since the Ineffable must be endlessly unnamed and renamed—for "She Who Is." Instead in Dionysius' words what "is rightly nameless and yet has the names of everything that is" cannot (or so feminist theologians presume) forever exclude the names of female or dark bodies.[18] Yet the socially liberating potential of negative theology has remained largely unrealized, often occluded or occulted in a haze of otherworldly transcendence. We must ask how any mystical iconoclasm, preoccupied with divine names, would resist a *socially* oppressive context.

Catholic activist-theologian Dorothee Soelle hears "the silent cry" of mysticism as a call to resistance. Its "topos of ineffability," she suggests, nurtures "a language without dominance." She suggests that it is not in the first chapter of Genesis, nor in the second's work of naming, but rather in the Edenic expulsion—in which a woman is subordinated, an animal demonized, and labor alienated—that "the relationship of dominance is established in the act of naming."[19] Thus she reads all mysticism as "part of the endeavor to escape from this fate of language that serves the exercise of power, control, and possession."

While the classical and medieval mystical discourses rarely address social relations, they articulate a bottomless freedom that in context was judged intolerably dissident.[20] Thus Marguerite de Porete, a twelfth-century Beguine who abandoned feminine habits to wander widely as a teacher, articulated a radical freedom influential of the "classical" mystics, such as Eckhart.[21] "And this soul who has become nothing, thus possesses everything, and so possesses nothing." The kenotic self, rid of ego and its illusions, performs a brazen self-esteem, reminiscent of Buddhism: "Knowing my nothingness I have everything and between nothing and everything there is no room for prayer so I no longer pray." She "meditates" instead. God has "made his secret dwelling place in you," Love tells her. "You bathe in the water of God's love." This tehomic divinity floods the text: "As the water that flows into the sea becomes sea, so does the soul become Love."[22] This proto-theology of becoming flirts dangerously with pantheism, though only a hostile reading would mistake this becoming-in-relation for the being of identity. She flows into God as God flows into her, without ever simply "being" God. Her boundless intimacies with Love seemed incorrigible to the authorities. She was burnt along with her book. Clinging to nothing (but in her case, stubbornly, to her writing), such denizens of the luminous dark resist both dominance and its language.

When the dominological deity is destabilized, so are the coercive practices of His representatives. So the heresiological fervor of Christianity tends to dissipate within the apophatic counterdiscourse. For instance, Dionysius–whose orthodoxy was never questioned, indeed who helped to construct the Eastern ecclesial hierarchy–rebukes a certain "reverent Sosipater," for "denouncing a cult or a point of view which does not seem to be good." He asks him to "cease from the denunciation of others"–and see to improving his own discourse.[23] The potentiality of the apophatic gesture for a resistance to the discourse and practice of dominance remains nonetheless, however, little more than hope and project.[24] Its viability, I believe, lies not in its power to suddenly realize "from within" its own dormant possibilities, but in awakening affinities with movements and politics arising outside of the western Christian discourse; indeed arising in the discourse of the "outside" of materiality, sign, earth and skin.

In the postcolonial writing of the Vietnamese-American-feminist filmmaker and theorist Trinh Minh-ha, for example, there occurs what we might call *a political apophasis*. She collates the nonbinary thinking of the "third term" of Taoism (the "void" which is neither yin nor yang, which is "the interval" between them) with the "third space" of postcolonial theory (which eludes the simple dualism of oppressor/oppressed, of home/exile, of self/other). "What is involved", she writes, "is a state of *alert in-betweenness and 'critical' non-knowingness*, in which the bringing of reflective and cosmic memory to *life*–that is, to the *formlessness of form*–is infinitely more exigent than the attempt to 'express,' to 'judge or evaluate.'" She articulates, not unlike bell hooks, an alternative aesthetic, one that recognizes that "art is political." It counters "the denial of problems of race and gender in the practices of art and of criticism," which "is also the fear to grow and to grope," "to maintain the indeterminacy of art."[25] Theology, like art, is political whether or not it admits it. But the apophatic unknowing would inject uncertainty into the identity politics of most contextual and liberation theologies as well. So the attraction of this chaosmic alternative will be felt only where (among the "multihyphenated" resistances) revolutionary certainties have already crumbled.

The immigrant Trinh Minh-ha's "cosmic memory" insinuates a sentience animating the universe; one that, like the wandering Porete's God, might "dwell within" humans. In its poetic oscillation between formlessness and form, Trinh's Tao provides a profound alternative to the western conquest of darkness and chaos. Her post-colonial theory inhabits the interstitial space of an alternative epistemology. Still, how is it that Trinh's "critical non-knowingness" seems so precisely, across so many worlds, to echo Nicholas of Cusa's "knowing ignorance"?[26] Let us then consider the latter within the discourse of its own arcane—other*wordl*y—terms.

IV The iconoclastic infinite

In Cusa's definition of "negative theology," "darkness is infinite light." "This infinite light always shines in the darkness of our ignorance but the darkness cannot comprehend it." In other words the "darkness of our ignorance" is not a fault or sin. The sin is to deny the darkness: "The theology of negation is so necessary to the theology of affirmation that without it *God would not be worshiped as the infinite God but as creature; and such worship is idolatry*, for it gives to an image that which belongs only to truth itself." In other words the darkness represents the optimum epistemic condition: that of "the learned ignorance." The *knowing* ignorance recognizes any theological certainty as idolatry. Cusa was a German-born polymath who studied Dionysius and Eckhart but became a canon lawyer and conciliarist, eventually a bishop and cardinal, working vigorously for reform within the fifteenth-century church: hardly the portrait of a cloudy, quiescent mystic. On the heels of scholasticism and the brink of Renaissance science, he deconstructs God-talk:

> Pagan: What are you worshiping?
> Christian: God.
> Pagan: Who is the God you worship?
> Christian: I do not know.
> Pagan: How can you so earnestly worship that which you do not know?
> Christian: It is *because* I do not know that I worship.

This is Socratic-Dionysian drama. But Cusa radically extends the unknowing. *Nothing* can be epistemologically mastered. The interlocutor asks: "How, therefore, do I come to know what a human being is, or a stone or anything else I know?" And Cusa responds "You know nothing of these; *you only think you know*." Adding a hint of nominalism to apophasis, he now invokes the *productive* power of language. Our knowledge of these things is not derived from any essence but "from accident, from *a difference* of their ways of operating and their shapes, to which when you discern them, you impose *different names*." In other words it is the play of difference that constructs meanings in language: "For it is a movement in differentiating reason that imposes names." Cusa implies (anticipating Saussure) an arbitrariness in this imposition. Names neither represent nor mirror, but *differentiate*, the real. Thus ignorance and knowledge are no longer opposites within the Cusan epistemology.

Does his *docta ignorantia* then suggest a "third space" comparable to Trinh Minh-ha's critical unknowing? Let me suggest such a space is indeed effected in the cosmological nondualism of his most famous idea, that of the *coincidentia oppositorum*. This "coincidence" resists the dichotomous regimes of a knowledge that separates God from the world, the One from the many, rational light from unknowable dark. And arguably it performs its resistance in the interest not of a neo-platonically undifferentiated totality but of a *differential plenum*: for "this whom it worships as one is all-in-one."[27] This "all" comprises not a homogenizing totality but rather the multiplicity of the universe. "God is not the One withdrawn from the many," as Roland Faber, the Austrian process theologian, interprets Cusa, "but the One who in all multiplicity is not yet distinguished from the many."[28] As the light is not opposed to the dark, so the divine oneness is not opposed to the many but rather contains it; and yet is only *one* as unfolded *into* the many. Thus the One is not identical with All nor separable or separated from All: hence God for Cusa is the "All-in-One." More emphatically than in the Dionysian tradition (and not coincidentally resonant with the Kabbalah) negativity here results not in a hierarchical ladder of transcendence culminating in infinity, but in a full *panentheism*: the third space that resists the Creator/creature dualism as well as the pantheism of which Cusa was (unsuccessfully) accused:

> But everything that actually exists is in God, for God is the actuality of all things . . . Since the universe is contracted in each actually existing thing, it is obvious that God, who is in the universe, is in each thing and each actually existing thing is immediately in God, as is the universe. Therefore, *to say that "each thing is in each thing" is not other than to say that "through all things God is in all things" and that "through all things all are in God."*[29]

God is in each thing, and each thing in God. Cusa adds two extraordinary twists to this classic panentheism: that of the dynamic contracting, or *complicatio* ("enfolding") and *explicatio* ("unfolding") of God and universe into each other; and that of the radical interrelatedness of creatures. For he translates "God is in each thing" into "each thing is in each thing." This latter postulation anticipates Whitehead's "fallacy of simple location," the positive affirmation of which reads: "In a certain sense, everything is everywhere at all times."[30] Thus the negation of knowledge functions to negate substance metaphysics: that is, the epistemology of clearly separable essences. So to *unknow* the certain knowledge of separable things (moving in the opposite direction from the Cartesian modernity that will prevail) is not just to perform a linguistic deconstruction; it is simultaneously to articulate the interdependence of all creatures.

Cusa's subtle panentheism situates difference *in* God. God is thus not "the self-same" of ontotheology; nor is difference derived from the separation of Creator and creature. As Faber interprets Cusa, "the creative non-difference of creativity in all events appears therefore as divine creating and simultaneously as the self-actualization of the creatures." God as "All-in-One" corresponds to another new name: *non aliud*. God *the Not-Other*. This does not mean that God is "the same" as the world. This is not a simple pantheism of "difference-less identity," or "difference-less presence," as Faber argues. Cusa can now situate "the All-in-One as One-in-All, the one as *all-relational*."[31] If the All is the "all-relational," we begin to see how this discourse may resist its own temptation to a mystical de-differentiation, with its corresponding social in*difference*.

In the midst of this relational plenitude, we must not soften the *iconoclasm of the infinite*. While one can argue that his theology moves "beyond positive and negative theology" (ibid.), to acknowledge *relatively* valid god-talk, Cusa unambiguously privileges negation over affirmation. "Sacred ignorance has taught us that God is ineffable; and this is the case because God is infinitely greater than all that can be named; and this is so greatly true that we speak of *God more truly* through remotion and *negation*."[32] This is not the greatness of "oh God, you are so big." Cusa voices a dawning Renaissance sensibility to the scale of the material universe, to its potential infinity and thus its threat to a closed divine order. His divine infinity takes *place*; it *materializes*. Indeed he developed a complex, mathematically generated multiplicity of "infinites."[33] Astronomy today still hovers on the edge between a finite universe whose limits are unknowable, and an ontologically limitless one. The subversive implications of infinity burst into full view in the generation after Cusa, with Giordano Bruno, Dominican friar, mathematical cosmologist, and martyr of early modern science. Bruno elaborated an entire kabbalistic Christian counterdiscourse out of the Cusan *complicatio/implicatio* oscillation. He absorbed the complex interaction of divinity and world emanating from the kabbalistic *Eyn Sof*—understood alternately as First Cause, Nothingness, God, or, literally, the in/finite—and its ten *sephiroth*. Charged with "iconoclasm" for his "*cabala-filosofia-teologia*," Bruno perished in the flames of the Counter-Reformation.[34]

The infinite is the finite name that negates itself. Thus it exercises a bottomless iconoclasm. Infinity subverts all truth-regimes to precisely the extent that they do not first negate themselves, that is, recognize themselves as variously and relatively applicable projections of our finitude. Citing "Rabbi Solomon" (Maimonides) as voicing a consensus of "the wise," Cusa extended his own theological negativity uncompromisingly: "According to this negative theology, in which God is infinite only, *there is then neither Father nor Son nor Holy Spirit*." I am not painting Cusa as a proto-feminist semi-Semite.[35] He does retrieve the traditional Persons, if only as relatively "inadequate" affirmations, necessary to worship. But "according to the theology of negation, nothing other than infinity is found in God." Even the platonic safe haven of "oneness" is here deconstructed: "from the standpoint of infinity, God is neither one nor more than one."[36] While the infinite does not stem from the biblical lexicon, we can only decipher its political potential by way of its kinship to the prophetic tradition of the denunciation of idols. Thus it is not lightly that Cusa borrows the logion of Caesar's coin: without negative theology, he writes, "worship is idolatry, for it gives to an image that which belongs only to truth itself" (ibid., p. 121).

V Secretions of justice

Do more recent theological iconoclasms–according to which God is variously not-man, not-white, not-European, not-ruler, or just not-alive–have anything to do with the arcane infinity of apophasis? Can we after all map a race- and gender-savvy "critical nonknowingness" upon the old "learned ignorance"? Am I stretching the luminous fabric of the dark too thin? Or weaving–as I hope–a versatile postmodern *coincidentia*?

Religious critiques of the oppressive practices usually take place far from mysticism. Yet they make routine use of the tradition of iconoclasm to challenge the idolatry of an exclusive One, for which their constituencies have been subaltern Others. But if a deconstruction of the practice and language of domination arises within the old mystical iconoclasm, then, I am suggesting, the poststructuralist engagement of negative theology becomes useful–though it also bears little resemblance to the populist theologies of protest. For it may help us articulate afresh the radicalism of the older linguistic resistance, without anachronistically overstating its subversive intentions.

How to speak and how not to speak about negative theology? "For a while now," writes Derrida, "I have the impression that it is the idea itself of an identity or a self-interiority of every tradition (the one metaphysics, the one onto-theology, the one phenomenology, the one Christian revelation . . . the one tradition, self-identity in general, the one, etc.) that finds itself contested at its root."[37] Thus Derrida concedes in the negativity of Angelus Silesius something "strangely familiar" to the experience of what is called deconstruction.[38] Rather than a motor of metaphysical oneness, he now finds "an absolute heterogeneity." "Deconstruction has often been defined as the very experience of the (impossible) possibility of the impossible . . . a condition that it shares with the gift, the 'yes,' the 'come,' decision, testimony, the secret . . ."[39] *Sauf le Nom* (unlike the earlier "How Not to Speak") no longer deconstructs the "hyperessentiality" of apophasis. While Derrida here presumes the difference, he shows no further interest in negating its negativity or exposing its ontotheology. Rather, he now attests admiringly to its "critique of ontology, of theology, and of language." Without for a moment becoming any sort of theologian, he stresses its *différance* within the history of theology. Indeed "negative theology is one of the most remarkable manifestations of this self-difference."

This "self-difference," the difference that precedes the origin and so elucidates a tehomic beginning, emits a politics of heterogeneity.[40] Trinh Minh-ha borrows deconstruction even as she delivers (more than will Derrida) on the political promise of difference. "The differences made between entities comprehended as absolute presences–hence the notions of pure origin and true self–are an outgrowth of a dualistic system of thought peculiar to the Occident (the 'onto-theology' which characterizes Western metaphysics.)"[41] She distinguishes this separative difference from "the differences grasped both *between and within* entities," in which " 'I' is, itself, *infinite layers*" (ibid., p. 94).

By tracing this infinite layering within the topos of the deep, within the relational density of its enfolded darkness, may we work to decolonize our corner of "the creation"? If so, we join a long tradition, which, read from its poststructuralist posterior, replaces "God" as the ultimate symbol of this western self-identity with that of a divine self-difference. Derrida solicits the transcontextual possibilities of apophasis: "Negative theology is everywhere, but it is never by itself . . . to say God such as he is, beyond his images, beyond this idol that being can still be, beyond what is said, seen, or known of him." This Derridean "yes" to negative mysticism–after a couple of decades of a more severe "reserve"–seems to betray a secret of its own, a potentiality secreted in the very cracks and obscurities of deconstruction.[42] But of course deconstruction in itself, mystical, poststructuralist, even postcolonial, is inadequate to confront (for instance) the white-faced idols of the global free market. It would need to join forces–through certain strategic decisions amidst its undecidabilities–with the social justice negations and affirmations of the biblical prophetic legacy. For the sake of such coalitions, it seems noteworthy that Derrida makes explicit the positive *ethics* of the infinite: "it is to this end that the negative procedure refuses, denies, rejects all the inadequate attributions. It does *so in the name of a way of truth and in order to hear the name of a just voice*" (ibid., p. 69).

VI Deep as skin

> My sister has skin darker than mine. We think about our skin as a dark room,
> a place of shadows.
>
> (bell hooks[43])

How can I touch upon the face, indeed the *skin*, of this darkness? I cannot enter its room. Here my non-knowingness appears more contextual than mystical. It emits a pale aura of privilege.[44] But the context leaks. The names keep shifting. All the attributions prove inadequate: am I finally "white"–to your "Black"? No, clarifies Thandeka, Euroamerican to African American. Decades of shifts and hyphens cause white-skinned irritation ("Can't they even agree on what they want to be called?"). But one might instead hear in this nomenclatural instability another manifestation of the apophatic depths: "dark revelations", she writes, "of feelings before memory and beyond white."[45] What exceeds *any* names needs *many* names. Names have been inflicted like an order, like a wound, upon those who could be reduced to a dark chaos. That darkness, with its own silences, speeches and self-organizations, struggles toward a new embodiment. A new luminosity. "We talk often about color politics and the way racism has created an aesthetic that wounds us, a way of thinking about beauty that hurts."[46]

Civilization as we know it perpetrates this wound. We may call the wound: "the denigration of the dark." The word "denigration" tells a three-stage story: first it means simply a chemical "process of making or becoming black." Then by the 1800s, according to the *OED*, it takes on the figurative meaning: "blackening of character; defamation;" or "a stain, a black spot." But with a hyphen, *de-nigration* meant the opposite: "unblackening, whitewashing." So a theological denigration of the dark moves a natural association of darkness with blackness to the defamation of blackness as fault, inferiority, stain. But even when Christian cultures recognize racism as sin, they have been quick to whitewash themselves: they go suddenly colorblind, claiming there is after all no difference. Race is just skin-deep, we are all one before God, in Christ, in the light. Light supremacism pierces even the sanctuaries of the sub-altern. I have worshiped with a Black church singing "Wash us in the blood of the lamb, wash us white as snow."[47] Thus those who can never unblacken themselves, even if they try to distinguish their own dark surface from their "inner" light, remain poignantly "not quite/not white." Never bright enough.

Early western modernity systematically encoded ignorance, inferiority and evil as darkness. The "New World," Colon's new creation, was formed out of the darkness beyond the sea, out of subjugated, dark-skinned populations.[48] These others of the *Otro Mondo* were made *knowable* through the color-coding of their bodies. They were appropriated as the objects of a relentlessly confident epistemology. "Early European reading of dark skin posited it as a sign on the surface of the body of a heart unwilling immediately to convert to Christ on hearing the gospel."[49] African skin was translated through the biblical ciphers of "the curse of Ham" or the "mark of Cain." In his reconstruction of Christian theology from the literary remains of Black slave religion, Dwight Hopkins exhumes a catechism written for slaves:

Q.   Who was the first negro?
A.   Cain.
Q.   How did he become so?
A.   The Lord set a black mark upon him.

"Originating from God," comments Hopkins, "the color black then was inscribed on the physical bodies of dark-skinned people as a natural, biological, and genetic inevitability."[50]

The translation of light worship into modern racism required more than Christian sanction. It invoked also that En*light*enment that resisted religious oppression with the higher light of Reason. In *Blackness Visible*, Charles W. Mills exposes a "*Herrenvolk Kantianism*" at odds with the idealized Kant of the academy. "So fundamental is the difference between [the black and white] races of man," wrote Emmanuel Kant, that "it appears to be as great in regard to mental capacities as in color." Thus "a clear proof that what [a Negro] said was stupid" was that "this fellow was quite black from head to foot."[51] The supremacist Enlightenment ethic, infers Mills, "means that moral standing and race, whiteness/personhood/respect and blackness/subpersonhood/disrespect, have been inextricably tied up together for hundreds of years."

"White" personhood absorbs the effects of its own denigration: we who become white become colorless, bodiless. We trade our wintry animal flesh tones for a symbolic white that transfigures us as pure light–in opposition to the black *aliud*. We split from our own bodies even as we split from the human species. Paradoxically the self splits precisely in its refusal of self-difference. Thus "differences are deadened, hidden, denied, or in some way neglected," writes Thandeka of the production of whiteness. "This annihilation of difference can be called the self's civil war."[52] In his Preface to Fanon's *Black Skins, White Masks* Bhabha diagnoses a similarly split self. "The representative figure of such a perversion, I want to suggest, is the image of post-Enlightenment man tethered to, not confronted by, his dark reflection, the shadow of colonized man, that splits his presence, distorts his outline, breaches his boundaries, repeats his actions at a distance, disturbs and divides the very time of his being."[53] As in fractal bifurcation, the split self-identity is repeatedly met, by the "double consciousness" (W. E. B. DuBois)–a self attentive to its own self-difference.[54]

Trying to unknow the certainties that at once order and split the white self, to inhabit again the "infinite layers" of our intersubjectivity, I know this much: without the epistemic shift signaled by a darkened theology, without the specific *depth* of this shift, I no longer know how to live in my own skin.

VII

There is in God (some say)
A deep, but dazzling darkness.[55]

The above treatments of the racialized subject push back neither towards an unsplit subject, the unspilt milk or pure light of presence, nor towards a correspondingly pure, native dark. Might they instead embody in a particular historical context that third space of a light not opposed to darkness?[56] This light respects our bodies. It does not bleach out the colors. It brings "blackness" and "whiteness" into their joint visibility–in which they both radiate into the variegated difference of our disturbed and divided species. Along the full spectrum of luminosities, the multicolors of beauty might become visible–translucent, never transparent, to each other. Self-difference iterates through endless interdependencies. No one, no context, is simply located within the differential plenum. "Each thing is in each thing." But this chaosmos of interconnections only becomes apparent within the love and the discipline of the "knowing ignorance."

The dark will still turn opaque. The unknowability will still turn dangerous. But only the darkness from which light has been extracted, abstracted, takes on a face of "evil." We are not obliged to continue the division. It will only reproduce the twin faces of terror: fear of the dark void and of the white shroud. Under the supreme neon, the black void means *nihilation*, the whiteness becomes *appropriation*. A meaningless abyss and a merciless transparency.

If the denigration of the dark seals the unknown into opacity, perhaps we need a *renigration of the light*. Might we begin "to discover beauty in shadows"?[57] Genesis oscillates between its days and its nights. Shadows penetrate the morning; rays of sun lick the evening. Clouds give us cover. We have so much to renegotiate.

We will never long settle on the truth of a way or the justice of a name. We can, however, learn–as the complicated hybrids of a racy, sexy species–to move more gracefully in the dark. *Is* this darkness and this grace what a tehomic theology would mean by "God"?

"And to this I can only answer thus: 'I have no idea.'"

13

OCEAN OF DIVINITY
Deep

tehom

Deep calls to deep
at the thunder of your floodgates:
all your waves and your billows
have gone over me.

> (Psalm 42.7–8)

Then on the canvas of silence
and on the very shore of time,
she bends over, naked, and naked
regards herself with the face
of water in her words.

> (Marjorie Argosin[1])

I

Darksome deep, dimensionality, womb; *complicatio*, *différance*, *khora*; no/thing and in/finite; milieu of milieus, where what will be, is becoming; a mother chaos tricked by her own wisdom into " creation." A river of names empties into the tehom of language. But would we call the ocean "God"? The silence billows. Its divinity remains "rightly nameless and yet has the names of everything that is."[2] The familiar turns strange. Even the Bible, warns Dionysius, can "seem filled with incredible and contrived fantasy." For, "scripture speaks of God's womb begetting God in a corporeal way; of the divine bosom embracing the Son of God . . . of trees, leaves, flowers, roots, bubbling fountains of water, radiant sources of shining light," etc. He is not complaining about these fleshly, even feminine pulchritudes of language. Surprisingly, he privileges "the incongruities," indeed delights in these juxtapositions of unlike "beauties." Their "dissimilar similarities" thwart the "lazy" certitudes of "positive affirmations." But he wants by the way of negation "to uncover them, to see them in their naked purity."

213

That nakedness, we now suspect, will only mirror us back to ourselves, impure and rippling. And so theology, if it names a godness having "the names of everything that is," is about everything–else. This infinity "flows over," yet is said to stay "full amid the emptying act of differentiation."[3] An impossible act to follow: we *are*, we *make*, its differences. Rarely, utter finitudes that we remain, can we empty gracefully into the fullness; rarely do we feel full enough to let go.

II Tehomic homily A: waves

"Why are you so cowardly? You still don't trust, do you?" (Mark 4.35ff.).[4] So grumbled the one awakened from his nap "on a cushion" in the stern. The wind is howling, "the boat was already filling." He is not annoyed with the sea or the storm, however, but with his tehomophobic friends. Recall that phobia is not just fear, which warns of a danger. Phobia signifies the obsessive reiteration of fear, which cripples the ability to face the fear. We glean from Jesus' irritation that the opposite of faith (*pistis*, "trust") is not doubt, but *cowardice*. Faith here signifies a trust that is kin to courage.[5] It cannot be identified with belief, with knowledge, with any stash of propositions. It does not then expect God to calm the waters *for us*. God "lets us" do it ourselves. *Bear* the fruit, *use* the talent, *heal* the sick, *feed* the hungry, *uncover* the flame, *make* the peace. There may be no life-saver there next time. Those who follow this activating gospel have been variously suspected of Judaizing, gnosticism, Arianism, Pelagianism, atheism, socialism or feminism. Still the tehomic grace left traces all along:

> Don't cry to God / The spring is in you
> Don't block the opening / and it will flow right through. (Silesius)[6]

This do-it-yourself message (is it mystical or activist? can we afford the binary?) has little to do with the self-sufficiency of a lonely ego. Masterful self-enclosure–as surely as cringing dependency–would block the "flow-through." Thus Marduk's ego was produced by the phobia of his comrades. The resultant systems of injustice, compounds of control and greed, enact "sin" from a tehomic perspective. The "original sin" would be first of all a *blockage*: a habitual obstruction of the originary flow.

Since theologians belong among the original sinners, I have in penance diagnosed the *creatio ex nihilo* as the symptom of a systemic obstruction. At the very site of its originative nonorigin, the flow of flows, the ocean of springs, got linguistically frozen. God's omnipotence was accordingly shored up to replace human responsibility for the world, while Christian morality was left to monitor bodily openings and effluvia. An orderly fear of God quietly superseded the dead Jew's tehomic courage. (Do theophobia and tehomophobia then merge?) As for this Jew, the great de-clogging agent, he was rewritten as the one-and-only once-for-all of the settled past. "Christ" was then deployed to restrict divine incarnation to the singularity—thus blocking *out*, keeping outside our finite bodies, the very one to whom we cry?

III Tehomic homily B: deep calls

Why should we not cry? He did, after all—quoting at his worst moment from Psalm 22: "*Eloi, eloi, lama sabachthani*." Perhaps we ought not to generalize from the tortured last words attributed by two of the gospels to a victim of imperial justice. But if we do, must the cry signify either divine amnesia or a final agonizing display of Jesus' humanity? Is it God who "forgets" or "forsakes" Jesus? Or rather an operative *concept* of God—the theogram of central Power who controls all the outcomes? I do not suggest that Jesus held this theology of omnipotence and (at the last minute) noticed its fallacy. Yet the Markan and Matthean versions of the crucifixion encrypt a crisis and contradiction that will beset innumerable Jews and Christians at *their* worst moments. For when faith is most urgently needed, the logic of omnipotence lays upon naked suffering the added burden of godforsakenness.

Do the gospels reinscribe the Joban question? Since we have to do not with a report but with a concise intertext, I suggest we recall (as would Mark's and Matthew's audiences) its psalmic milieu. The citation of 22.1 echoes the great psalm in which "Deep calls to deep": "I say to God, my rock, 'Why have you forgotten me?'" (42.9a).[7] Between the rock and a very hard place, this "I" seems to be going under. So the cry from the cross seems to echo the tehomic call. Psalm 42, we note, neither vilifies the sea nor busts the heads of sea monsters. On the contrary, its Tehom is attributed directly to the divinity: "*your floodgates*," "*your* waves and *your* billows." Are the waves mere instrument, property, or weapon of a controlling—and forsaking—will? The psalm seems to reply: no, not God, but "the enemy oppresses me." The thundering divine waves do not describe the *cause* but rather the *condition* of the suffering. The psalm almost blames God but—like Job in miniature—gets mid-storm a different insight. Indeed in the course of the song itself (in the pleasure of composing?) the psalmist recovers memories. "My soul is cast down within me, therefore I remember you" (42.5b). Memory stirs "hope in God," whom "I shall again praise" (if not just yet), "my help and my God." In other words the poet traces a past and a future *within* the foundering present, and so relaxes the present crisis of divine absence.

An alternative temporality, a stability alien to the classical fantasy of the changeless, apathetic eternity, emerges like a great slippery rock amidst the crashing surf: "By day YHWH commands his steadfast love, and at night YHWH's song is with me" (42.8). Stability *within* the turbulence—such rhythmic continuities as our volatile species can sustain—will come not from an intervening eternity, but from our capacity *to love*. No clinging, clutching dependency, this love, but the root of courage (Latin *cor*, "heart"); we *take heart*. Practiced well, this heartbeat accompanies, I presume, that love that casts out fear. Deleuze and Guattari offer a parable:

A child in the dark, gripped with fear, comforts himself by singing under his breath . . . by singing quietly in the dark . . . The song is like a rough sketch of a calming and stabilizing, calm and stable, center in the heart of chaos . . . Perhaps the child skips as he sings, hastens or slows his pace. But the song itself is already a skip: it jumps from chaos to the beginnings of order in chaos . . .[8]

In the rhythm and the song, the iterations of chaos itself yield the incipient order at the edge of the deep. A theology of becoming negotiates its solidities, its solidarities, *within* the flux. It sketches not disorder but responsive, flexible and *therefore steadfast* forms of self-organization. We gain the courage of our connections.[9] They might not hold. But in the grace of this rhythm and the *divining* of this love, the dark draws music.

IV Droplets: oceans of God

> The abyss that is my soul invokes unceasingly
> The abyss that is my God. Which may the deeper be?
> (Silesius[10])

The call of deep to deep voices, like a tehomic liturgy, the depth at which the self bottoms out. With his koan-like question–itself an echo of Psalm 42–Silesius invokes an ambiguous, far-from-equilibrium self-similarity: the interfluency of "my soul" and "my God," in their utter difference and mirror-play. Silesius summons a related image:

> In a droplet–say how can this be?–
> the whole ocean of God flows into me.[11]

The icon of the divine ocean here reformulates another old conundrum: how can infinity "flow into" the finite? The drop, itself a material instance of fractal theory, suggests a microcosmic iteration of whole in part. One of Silesius' epigrams–themselves droplets of theology–recalls Augustine's sponge:

> God is more in me than if the whole sea
> could in a little sponge wholly contained be.[12]

This saturated metonymy has already suggested the panentheism, not of a stagnant containment of God within world or world within God but of a mutual fluency. But

it then leads to a more radical intuition, one still almost unspeakable in Silesius' era:
that of a divine/human *inter*dependence:

> Myself I must be the sun, whose rays must paint the sea,
> The vast and unhued ocean of all divinity.[13]

The differentiations of the oceanic impersonality here *depend* upon our personal
participation. Where the rays of perception brush the dark face of divinity, drops of
brilliant color condense. Constructivist theories of knowledge are thus succinctly
prophesied.

The oceanic iconography traditionally intimates the infinity of negative theology.
A millennium earlier, John of Damascus stated propositionally: "God is then an ocean
of infinite and therefore undifferentiated substance."[14] Silesius has creaturely
creativity break the depth into its differences. We open its surface. The differentiation
of the deity is its *kenosis*, its outpouring, into the mere droplet of my own existence.
But this self-emptying must be read in its radical negativity: "*Die zarte Gottheit ist
ein Nichts und Uebernichts*."[15] Out of its own nothingness, the creator may well
create–but only *through* creaturely creativity. Not just human creativity, we have
stressed, from the vantage point of our primitive text: the earth and the sea "bring
forth" in response to a permissive invitation. But they produce no idols of themselves.
Unlike theologians. We forget that *we* have *divined* the infinity with our painterly
representations. Then icon becomes idol.

Does the deity of this mystical iconoclasm–heir after all to the metaphysics of
substance–escape the frame of ontotheology? "'God'", comments Derrida on the
Silesian negativity, "'is' the name of this bottomless collapse."[16] *Of Grammatology* had
given the name of *différance* to the "bottomless chessboard." Has its surface here, in
Derrida's reading of Silesius, come into its *depth*? In a similar mood, that of a
deconstruction that flows into the mystical negation, Michel de Certeau writes of
the "scriptural work," the "fable," of theological writing: "The writing of belief, in
its weakness, appears on the ocean of language only to disappear, taken up into the
work of uncovering . . . the movement by which, ceaselessly, they 'come' and 'go.'
According to an expression of the mystics, it is a 'drop in the ocean.'"[17] John Duns
Scotus would later infer from John of Damascus' oceanic God (above) the privilege
of the negative attribute of "infinity;" thus, as in Cusa, of apophatic over kataphatic
theology. Interpreting the apophatic lineage, Roland Faber argues that the metaphor
of God the Ocean must flow "between two abysses [*Abgruenden*]: the danger of a
pantheism and the challenge of a deconstructive critique of God."[18] Faber's double
abyss seems again to echo the calling depths of Psalm 42.

Before a tehomic theology merges "the Deep" of Genesis 1.2 with "the ocean of
divinity," however, and thus "tehom" with "God," let us take account of the double
danger. As to the abyss of deconstruction, is it when "deconstruction" denies the

depth of its own *abîme* that it becomes a threat to theology; when in the interest of an elegant surface it voids both divinity and materiality? In certain appropriations it proclaims its universe linguistically constructed "all the way down." To what bottom? Then indeed it falls short of its own bottomlessness; and of the epistemological radicalism of, for instance, the *docta ignorantia*. Cusa's unknowing cannot be cashed into a knowledge that there *is* nothing outside language. A tehomic theology, at any rate, does not "deconstruct" the creation from nothing by the Word only to perform its postmodern version: *the construction from nothing by language*. Such gleefully shallow constructivism characterizes neither Derrida's nor his religious readers' trajectories. It does, however, mark the point where the *ex nihilo* morphs into *nihilism*.

What of the whirlpool of pantheism, on the other hand? To brand that beleaguered bugaboo of Jewish and Christian orthodoxy a "danger" already reinscribes a bit of familiar heresiology. Nonetheless a tehomic All-in-One is not a pantheism. The temptation of mysticism to a dissolution of difference within the sea of a monistic Presence, has been within theology well countered by the tradition of process panentheism—in which chaos replaces the nihil and in which flux, carefully mediated by forms of stability, permanence and order, remains primary. Between the abysses, Faber identifies the divine ocean within a "process theological heuristic," whereby he proposes a Whiteheadian negative theology.[19] Against the background of Catholic mysticism, he identifies the third space of this divine sea with Whitehead's "creativity," from which both creator and creature emerge as mutual differentiations. I concur. Indeed the metaphor of the divine ocean has been gathering momentum within certain recent theologies of process.[20]

We are drops of an oceanic impersonality. We arch like waves, like porpoises. We buck and turn and paint its surfaces. "It" gets personal. No wonder we get so twisted.

V Droplets: tehomic panentheism

It is as true to say that God creates the World, as that the World creates God. (A. N. Whitehead)[21]

According to this uncertain truth, the co-creativity of creator and creature would then not be limited to divine delegation. Creator and creature create, effect, *each other*; not from a prior nothing but from their shared preconditions. This radical interdependence would take place within the infinite "creativity."[22] But even if we allow Whitehead's category of creativity to interpret the metaphor of the divine ocean, he still sharply distinguishes between the impersonal cosmological flux and a quite personal "divine element in the universe." Might we reserve the term "God," as he does, for a principle of limitation by which the possible becomes actual—and only so actualizes "God"? This would be the "primordial nature" of a wisdom—"the poet of the universe"–by which a *worthier* possibility might be chosen. Would "God" begin to emerge against the bottomless ground of creativity as its difference from itself–from a flux that is in God and yet not the "same" as God? The Jesuit theologian Joseph Bracken has proposed the congenial notion of "divine matrix" as synonym at once for Whitehead's creativity and for the negative "Godhead" or *Gottheit* distinguished by Meister Eckhart from "God."[23]

These convergences of mystical theology with Whiteheadian thought animate a counterdiscourse of creation that we might call *apophatic panentheism*. Panentheism retains what all theism desires: a "Thou" different enough and intimate enough to love and to be loved. Indeed Christian orthodoxy gave birth to the panentheistic vision (however often it seeks to abort its own mystical effects).[24] A theology of becoming flows not just between the waters of nihilism and pantheism (with which it mingles many currents), but also around the rock of classical theism. Let us mark the interstitial strategy of such a tehomic apophasis with the very "*en*" of panentheism. For this little "*en*," "in," does not as one might think designate some clearly lineated space of intersecting substances, let alone of mutual containment–as though the mutual immanence of divinity and world resembles Chinese boxes or intersecting circles. The "*en*" designates an active indeterminacy, a commingling of unpredictable, and yet recapitulatory, self-organizing relations. The "*en*" asserts the difference of divine and cosmic, but at the same time makes it impossible to draw the line. For is not the line always already smudged? The smudge, the flux, "is" the *en*, the overlap, of divinity with world, of world with divinity. Like the sensitive initial condition of the "*bet*," this "in" channels the resonance between "deeps."

Might this "in" of panentheism begin to designate *creation as incarnation*? If the godhead, or rather the godness, "*in" whom unfolds* the universe can be theologized as Tehom, the ocean of divinity, the divinity *who unfolds "in"* the all is called by such biblical names as Elohim, Sophia, Logos, Christ. The all in the divine, the divine in the all: this rhythm of appellations does not name two Gods, or even two Persons. Yet it does echo the trinitarian intuition of complex relationality *immanent* to an impersonal Godhead and personalized in the *oikonomia* of the creation. Their relation to each other, as the final chapter will suggest, can be resignified only through the icon of the oscillating Spirit. So the names Tehom and Elohim may henceforth designate, if not "persons," two *capacities* of an infinite becoming.

A "capacity" signifies–unlike a mere act or force–an ability to receive, and so to give *place* (as a room has a seating "capacity"). In this "capacity" register the tehomic metonyms of place–of khora, or matrix of every becoming. Such capacitation functions not passively, but as an active *capability* for responsive relation. Theologically this means: it is then not that the world is simply *capax dei* (a claim appropriately complicated but unfortunately erased by the Reformation radicalization of sin); but that God is *capax mundi*. Any event, every spacetime of the capacious process of creation, might become readable as a unique, holy and temporary embodiment of the infinite. Each embodiment in a certain sense is granted the grace, the capacity, to create itself. But never from nothing. It may block this capacity: then it will experience the waters as a bottomless threat. But in this capacitation of the creature, the infinity in its indifferent creativity can be imagined to yield place to a difference called "the creator" and a set of differences called "the creation." At the heart of the creation, there takes place always, in endless quantities and qualities of difference, deformation and transformation, the *incarnation*.

VI Messages: incarnation

During low tide, they awaited
the arrival of the child,
or the child similar to the child,
or the child of those
floating in caverns
beneath the sea.
They found
pieces of flesh,
erased by men's wrath,
bearing no messages from the deep.[25]
(Marjorie Agosin[26])

If incarnation is always going on, so is the carnage. Residues of loss drift up opaque, nameless, without even the dignity of crucifixion. Theology–bearing witness, like the Chilean poet Agosin, to systemic iniquity–has gained some liberative clarity: it is "men's wrath," not the wrath of God, which performs the crucifixion. There is no deity who causes the suffering or rescues us from it; no divine life-saver. To incarnate intentionally the Wisdom may in fact heighten the *risk* of crucifixion; but the *aim*, the *lure*, is for new creation. This Sophia accepts no "blood payment;" her justice and her mercy do not organize themselves within the economies of sacrifice. Yet her creativity is not squeamish. Every death is within its capacity. Its births come spattered with blood. Its lives feed on each other. The religions of the book, however, while steeped in the blood of manly slaughter, have been queasy about the blood of life, the life of bodies. Having almost erased tehom from its book, our tradition has helped to rub out the living bodies. We receive back the flesh of faceless surfaces. *Sin los recados de la profundidad.*

No messages, no gospel, of the deep? Has incarnation been trapped in an institution of discarnation? Still, it isn't Jesus or his body who sprang the trap, but (as almost any Jew or Muslim can tell you) the invention of The Incarnation as the God-Man, an exclusive subject to be worshiped rather than an inclusive possibility to be actualized. Did Christianity overshoot its mark? Did it *miss* its own body? Did it miss, despite its theograms of creation, incarnation and resurrection, the *depths* of the body? Irigaray's critique of the standard incarnation comes close to home: "That the growth of life might mean the proliferation, transfiguration, resurrection of bodies in and by their word is intended to remain a veiled or censored message." Irigaray, however, insists on unveiling another message of incarnation: "That the Christic symbol might be decoded as an invitation to become shared flesh, still causes an uproar."[27]

Irigaray's turn to Christ from Nietzsche, Apollo and Dionysus symptomatizes not a christening of poststructuralism but a radicalization of the Christic symbol.[28] An alternative incarnation, this pan-carnation narrates the flesh not as mere matter, extended substance, but as materialization of the possible. Even amidst the obstructions of the Body of Christ–symbol of the shared flesh whose boundaries hardened, producing community by exclusion–the message is getting *delivered*. For if the incarnation is coextensive with the body of the creation, then might not all matter–and not only the baby's skin, the lover's eye, the winter sunrise–exude an incandescence of the deep? "An effusion that goes beyond and stops short of any skin that has been closed back on itself," hints Irigaray. Sin in the Augustinian lineage was well characterized as the *curvatio en se*: the deadening independence of a self closing in on itself, suggestive of systemic blockage though not diagnosed in those terms. Feminism has added the soluble dependence to the catalogue of sin: "curving in" on the other rather than on the self just as surely blocks the wellsprings of the shared body, political or sexual. Salvation in the biblical tradition comes promisingly, if only we could free it from its apocalyptic realism, as a collective, bodily resurrection.

"*The deepest depths of the flesh*, touched, birthed, and without a wound." A *profound* body: a body whose godness is not blocked? Whose soulful effusion is not frozen by lack or shame? I wonder, though, if we need to think this body as quite so pure, so new-born as Irigaray's woundless utopia of the flesh. I suspect rather that the deep flesh, even in its resurrection, will carry the scars. For does its very *profunditas* not consist in a redemptive recapitulation? But *recapitulatio* is not *imitatio* but *complicatio*: a folding-together of our species' gifted and crucifying history. Redemption repeats the past as different. Different from any past that was: but different only "in" the divining love? Even the "tracery of scars"[29] may fade into gentler wrinkles.

VII Practices: birthright

In the very folds of its antiquity the tehomic body throbs with the spirit of beginning: it practices–like Irigaray's revision of the annunciation–"that ability to sense and open up to the most delicate vibration."[30] Not accidentally, it had been an angel, an Elohimic vibration, who delivered the delicate message (*evangelos*) of unwed motherhood. Mary did, according to the gospel, say "yes." Presumably she was given a *choice*–unlike most women who followed. But she was rewritten to be as exceptional (the sexless mother) as her son (the embodied God). If the profound body can be delivered only by way of a practice that honors the becoming of women–those who bear and in growing proportion those who do not–no wonder its delivery has been so painfully deferred.

This sort of natal deconstruction of the *ex nihilo* may, however, have untoward side-effects. Would the tehomic signifier, imagined as infinite womb, not tend to encourage an ecology of unrestricted human multiplication, or an economy of limitless growth? Does the bottomless world-source suggest bottomless *resources*?

To the contrary: what materializes from its matrix, what actualizes, is always and only *limited*. The "procreant urge" of "nature naturing," for example, does not justify among humans–as it does not among other mammals–an unconstrained birthrate as birthright.[31] A genetic urge to reproduce must today be read within the matrix of the hypertrophic forces of overconsumption and overpopulation, which have pushed the planet into an extinction crisis, threatening the survival of our species along with its neighbors. So surely biology, which binds sex to survival, itself demands limits to growth. Genetics subserves genesis. The tehomic womb privileges life within the context of all life–and all life is contextual. Genesis 1 hints that to be human is not *just* to eat and procreate like the other animals (though it is also a lot of that, and with climactic vegetarian gusto in verse 29f.) but also, in the bi-gendered *imago dei*, to accept responsibility for the planet our species already millennia ago was "determined" to take over. The earth's natural, natal, interdependencies require of us as in consequence the *oikumene*, the stewardship, of an economy and ecology serving the "good" of all the other species. Yet we heirs of the text have obeyed "multiply and fill" while mocking the meaning of "dominion," taking as "exploitation" or "annihilation" that which in context can only mean *caretaking* for that divinely loved whole, which only with *all* the species is called "very good."

"Taking birth as the centre of our imaginary", suggests Grace Jantzen, developing Arendt's ethic of natality, "will direct our attention to this world, to our connection, through the maternal continuum, with all others who have been born."[32] Indeed if a tehomic infinite fails to re-embed us in the modest joys of a *finite* birthright, then it too serves the idols. Appropriation and annihilation comprise the twin idols of dominology, the engines by which the denigrated chaos (its peoples, its species) gets reduced either to raw stuff for use, or simply to *nothing*.

So if the mystical tradition now begins to energize struggles for sustainability and justice, its iconoclastic infinity takes on new resonances. As it empties out the divine "properties" it affirms the social democracy of an erotically vibrant chaosmos. The birthright of genesis is then not a right to indiscriminate (re)production. God is not "prolife" but *of life*: the life of the world, the spirit of a chaosmos in which death circulates through every living process, decision always cuts, and choice marks every birth, consciously or spontaneously. At minimum, the human birthright–as opposed to a birth-duty–entails a right to say no to a particular birth.

VIII Deep-end feminism: natal complications

Fluid and flaming as she is, are they not impatient to dry her up? To contain her in some enclosure where she finds her end. (Luce Irigaray)[33]

Still, for the most part, any natal symbolism for creation gets brusquely banished to some archaic past, some banished "before." Not only would a cosmic womb insinuate divine sex, the birth *imago* does not maintain a proper transcendence. The patrilineal Word by contrast could create cleanly, without jeopardizing a difference defined as separation. Even within the doctrinal singularity of the incarnation, even within the person of Jesus, where the natal imaginary bursts annually into the liturgy, an impermeable Chalcedonian boundary keeps the divine nature separate from the human. A wombier divinity, by contrast, would always materialize, mix, mingle and multiply with her offspring.

In the guise of anti-essentialism, anti-biologism, anti-natalism, much feminist discourse shares the impatience "to dry her up." After all, much Christian misogyny still nests comfortably in the sacred maternity of the *theotokos*: womb of God but only human; feminine means to the end of a masculine incarnation. A history of idealizations of maternity has served to keep women in their place, a khora, a milieu designed to refresh men with a brief resort to the origin. (We know all this.) Besides, the tehom does give off an embarrassing scent of she/sea. So not surprisingly female (teho)matriphobia still, indeed in "waves", runs high; we want a clean start and a professional logos; so we essay various forms of feminist *creatio ex nihil*. I nonetheless (or therefore) situate the history of feminist womb-annoyance and womb-avoidance among the tehomic emissions. For the topos of the deep itself de-essentializes any language of sex and gender; its trickster-matrix invokes precisely that which gets *blocked* by the sexual economy of colonized wombs, ruled by a disembodied Word. Surely (post)feminists no more want to reinscribe the matriphobic *nihil* than to revive the tormented Tiamat.

A tehomic theology, writing its *theos* in undisguised mimicry of the masculine imaginary, involves the feminism not of a supersessionist progress-optimism, but of "a wild patience."[34] This admittedly deep-end feminism asks us (not just women) to *bear with* a wide range of wombs, neither censoring nor worshiping their metonymic dis/closures. These do not revert to some *creatio ex utero* but persistently subvert the androcentric symbolic. As long as its transcendent "phallogocentrism" (courteous or violent, lucratively modern or theologically antimodern) runs deeper than law, it continues to requisition every origin. So it must be countered just there, where the origin betrays its dark secret: its deep "down there."

IX Contractions

The icon of the depths contracts readily, iconoclastically, into that of the womb. Recently, Roman Catholic feminist theologians have been the ones to enunciate the imaginary, beyond the mother of God (but no doubt rehearsed by her images), of a mother God (Ruether's God/ess, Johnson's Mother Sophia). But there had been prior intimations in a few male-authored counterdiscourses of creation. Here is Silesius again:

> I have been born of God: this unquestionably
> So just do not ask who might my mother be.[35]

Ironically, the epigram's title answers in advance its evasive question: "Die Gottheit ist meine Mutter." The grammatical femininity of *Gottheit*, as well as its oceanic associations, gives cover to Silesius' startling declaration. But this birth of the self from a maternal Godness inverts itself: the self gives birth to God. Thus echoing Eckhart's "birth of God in the soul," he queries "Why is God born?" This couplet answers: "O incomprehensibility! god got lost / and therefore wants to be born again in me."[36]

The reciprocal birth of God and world is not confined to Christianity. The imaginary of God's birth has certain deep Jewish resonances. Influenced by the tradition of Schelling, Franz Rosenzweig iterates the theme of the theogonic birth. It ramifies into a startling triad: the everlasting *birth of God*; the *birth of the world*; the *birth of the soul*. Different from God's birth in the soul in Eckhart and Silesius, the "birth of God" cannot be confined to the space of human interiority. But then *where* is God born? From what? As a (reborn) Jew he invites no language of womb or goddess. Yet his answer is clear, the allusion to Genesis 1 unreferenced but unmistakable: "*from out of the dark depths.*"[37]

> A secret: for it is not yet manifest to us,
> and cannot be manifest, that this ever-
> lasting birth out of the depth is—
> creation. This becoming mani-
> fest of the everlasting mys-
> tery of creation is that
> ever renewed miracle
> of revelation. We are
> standing at the
> transition—the
> transition from
> the mystery
> into the
> miracle.[38]

His graphic triangle, anticipating the typographic signs of the postmodern, funnels the depths (with no intention to portray a feminine organ) into the surface of a print-icon of birth.

Here is the public "secret": endless birth reveals and conceals the creativity of a creator who is also born. He does not relate this creativity of "the dark depths" to the tehom. But how could that phrase not be alluding to Genesis 1.2b? The young Rosenzweig wrote his book of "secrets" on postcards: sent home, to his mother, from the front, in the First World War. It perpetrates a birth without origin or ends–a cosmographic natality, not the "acosmic" naturalism of *natura naturans*. The uteral triangle suggestively doubles the model of the three-phased birth into a "star of redemption." And indeed this divine birth, because it is "everlasting," going on continuously, cannot be appropriated by the religion of a single, exceptional incarnation.

Such male-authored wombs cannot be simply discounted as reinscriptions of the androcentric symbolic. These insubordinate wombs may count as prophetic, still enfolded possibilities for a deep-end feminism. For once the birth-imaginary goes beyond its confinement to "Mary" or "Israel" or the soul (femininities neatly subordinated to a male God), once it occupies the linguistic locus of divinity itself and, even more improbably, announces an everlasting birth of God–a radical imaginary is at play. These men were no protofeminists; and feminists are not anachronists. But through intentionally gendered readings, these mystical subversions aid in the *conversion* of western religious energies.

Into what? An open, uncertain but sustainable future? The icon of the bottomless womb does not suggest the image of a personal mother, even a sophia or a shekhinah. They must themselves be born. Yet neither does its impersonal dimensionality show the face of an apathetic deity or of an indifferent de-deification. A century later, we still stand at the transition.

X Groans: genesis

The only thing God forces us to do is to become.
(Luce Irigaray[39]

It is in its n-dimensionality, its graphic infinity, that the womb of an open infinity may be brought to *bear* on finite bodies. In its participation in an illimitable universe, a tehomic ecology underscores "the inescapability of limits" (Grace Jantzen). An endless becoming does not signify the unlimited expansion of any entity. Becoming unfolds within the constraining and sustaining contexts enfolding any individual–perhaps even a divine one. Yet limit functions not as container but as skin, permeable membrane, elemental body of mud, water, air and fire. The endless becoming of the

All takes place within a within: that of the milieu of milieus, in which no cost of "growth" can be concealed. Here therefore rests the specific milieu of any creature's creativity. In human form this means that we no longer create as though from an original void. Pastorally, therapeutically, politically: we find ourselves in some densely textured flux, some difficult mix of indeterminacy and constraint. We may feel shame before the chaos in our lives, families, sexualities, movements, ethnicities, drafts, projects. Or we may read this difficult milieu for its freshly emerging order. If we do not try to control what seems out of control, if rather we brood on the fluid face, the *eschaton* between what is too chaotic and what is too limiting, we will discern the specific possibility of the transition. In the inescapable limitation lies the creative *edge*.

Citing Irigaray's notion of becoming-divine, Jantzen adds this important gloss: "the obligation to become divine is not an obligation to become limitless; the quest for infinity would be a renunciation, not a fulfillment, of our gendered, embodied selves."[40] If the language of the *infini* now suggests a finite, skin-enfolded participation in the infinite, why go in quest of it at all? Where is it but here and now, amidst our queerly entangled, decisively limited incarnations? "Divinity in the face of natals is a horizon of becoming, a process of divinity ever new, just as natality is the *possibility of new beginnings*."[41] That horizon has appeared as the edge of chaos: a chaosmic *eschaton*, with no time-line attaching it to an origin.

The tehomic deity remains enmeshed in the vulnerabilities and potentialities of an indeterminate creativity. As Tehom it *is* that process; as deity it is *born from and suckles* that process. So divinity "can never be immune from response to suffering in the face of the natals and of the earth."[42] Not accidentally "the suffering God" emerged as a great trope of the twentieth century, wrested from a hereticized patri-passionism.[43] It is only fair that the father should finally be allowed to suffer at the death of his son; that all fathers might at last take up the cross of their own pain rather than pass it on. But another biblical metaphoricity also pokes through: through creaturely sufferings divinity "gasps for breath" like a "woman in travail" (Isaiah 42.14). No birth is assured.

At the edge of this "process of divinity ever new," beginnings take place not as absolutes but as irreducibles. Not *nova creatio ex nihilo* but *nova creatio ex profundis*. In other words the *creatio ex nihilo* is not needed to defend the contingency and the novelty of beginning. It separated the changeless symbols of "the creation" and "the incarnation," the origin and the climax of the time-line, as singularities–exceptions proving the rule of an immaterial origin.

Creation is always incarnation–and would have been so without the birth of the Nazarene. For Christians, Christ names "the logos as incarnate" (John B. Cobb, Jr) but then precisely as a unique but not exclusive manifestation of the cosmic logos; indeed as the sophia of a universe that infinitely precedes and exceeds Christian or any other *logoi*. And then neither creation nor incarnation expresses a completed process. The spontaneities of actualization (Big Birth, evolutionary leap, psalmic inspiration, social liberation) do not express a unilateral will, gift, or love. If divinity becomes incarnate in endless new forms, the metamorphoses of the creatures cast their effects back upon the divine. The divine and the world form the conditions of each others' becomings. Only, for instance, in the incarnation as the human does this deity get personal. As in the beasts, animal, in the plants, vegetable, in metals, mineral . . . So conversely our becomings–here, now, so circumstantial, so temporary–smack strangely of the infinite.

If we begin ever again not from nothing but *from it all*, *in media res*, any beginning partakes of the irreducible. *Something* may come of it. This should not reassure us. But it may–in the language of the Black church–"make a way out of no way."[44] The force of beginning ripples outward, sometimes with a great splash, sometimes a lighter energy, ever dissipating into–it All. As beginnings disperse they imprint the waves of the future. The becoming remains incalculable in advance and evanescent in the present. It gets causally interconnected only after the fact. It recapitulates, it decides, it flows beyond itself. This becoming-self surges, crashes, expires–dying meaninglessly? Or ebbing into a luminous dark? What would make the difference, the deferred becoming, that has been called "salvation"?

The difference would lie in decision, decision decoupled from the anthropocentric fantasy of a controlling, self-conscious will. Mine or God's. As the wave arches out of the sea of possibility, tracing its unique spiral of history, will it curve back (*curvatio en se*) on itself? Will it try for an impossible permanence and a defining separation? Humans can hardly avoid the attempt. For we have no choice but to make a choice, a "cut," between possibilities. Under the conditions of a systemic blockage, we can hardly muster the courage for decision without fancying ourselves *a se*, self-sufficient, the center of creation. Only to dissolve in defiance or despair. In our difficult differences, we have always been in over our depths. Still, another courage does show its face. As the wave rolls into realization, it may with an uncomfortable passion fold its relations into its future. For in their fluctuations, these relations extend out indefinitely: into that infinite intimacy that may horrify or comfort. They stand forth as particles, as particulars, in their sudden and uncertain differences; they surface and disperse again as waves. Into the ocean of divinity?

In the course of this meditation, Tehom has taken on the names and aura of a certain godness. But it has never been identified with "God," nor with the All; it "is" not *pan* or *theos*. It signifies rather their relation: the topos of creation, where the world surges in its virtuality, in the *complicatio*, or "folding together," the matrix of all relations. The relations, the waves of our possibility, comprise the real potentiality from which we emerge. So tehom, metonym of the divine womb, remains neither God nor not-God but the depth of "God." We do not come to *know* this infinity. Yet we sometimes unblock it in meditation or music, in loss, prayer, love and breath. Its *ruach* breathes with "sighs too deep for words." We do "know that the whole creation has been groaning in labor pains."[45] In waves and drops comes a strange grace: the bottomlessly inhuman contracts again into the site of our becoming.

14

PNEUMATIC FOAM

Spirit vibrating
ruach elohim merahephet

In this in-between, chaos becomes rhythm, not inexorably, but it has a
chance to.

(Deleuze and Guattari[1])

Whose breath subtly suffuses the air, like a vibration sensed by those dis-
traught with love.

(Irigaray[2])

I

. . . and the divine spirit vibrating over the face of the waters . . .

Talk about God: theology has been growing uncertain for centuries. Therein lies its
great opportunity. It partakes little of the optimistic gleam of scientific progress, the
insouciant originality of the arts. When for the sake of that sparkling novelty or that
cultured public, religious thinkers dwell on the "cutting edge," they lose their
traditional constituencies–and *ipso facto*, ironically, the activist potential that
distinguishes *progressive* theology. Inasmuch, however, as we honor the constitutive
accountability of, say, Christian theology to the church, we cannot escape the
dogmatic drag, the vortex of swirling symbols and insecure institutions. This double
bind disorients even the most forward-looking theologies. We tumble off the time-
line of progress.

I did not always recognize this confusion as a gift.

Despite the various fresh winds blowing through seminary, church and temple, I
did not always trust in the birth pangs. I lacked, for instance, one feminist's sense of
glee, as she returned to school "to study the end of God."[3] This long-awaited death
(anticipated after all since Hegel) seemed a bit old. I'd seen Altizer's book displayed
in my local drug store window in Atlanta as a preteen: *The Death of God* blurred with
other adolescent anxieties. As the third Christian millennium slouches forward,

religious terror and counter-terror on the rise, all the avant-garde apocalypses, with their unveilings of God's and other ends, posture rather quaintly. They repeat the supersessionism they mean to supersede.

Perhaps there is nothing to do but *deepen the repetition*. It begins to vibrate. Death, according to one analyst of dreams, is underworld code for depth.[4] Has the death of God, viewed from down under, (un)veiled instead another depth of "God"? Coming not in triumph this time, nor yet in apology, can the God-word find resonance within the gaping between-space, the yawning *ginan*, of so-called postmodernity? Can we inhabit this liminal space of discourse, articulating an edge that does not so much cut as *fold*, complicating rather than separating our divergent times and spaces? "Private and public, past and present, the psyche and the social develop an interstitial intimacy," writes Bhabha of the postcolonial in-between–a positionality which does not so much *fit* as *attract* this becoming-theology. Theologically these interstices iterate into an infinite intimacy. Might we read the in-between of the divine and the world–and so perhaps of the spirit and the waters–as the place of spiritual decolonization, subverting the dispiriting dominologies of antiquity and (post)-modernity? We practice, then, willy-nilly, a theological hybridity, becoming translators of religious tradition and progressive democracy.

In this pneumatic space, the intimacy of the infinite begins to open. It looks (like the *bet* of *bereshit*) *forward*–to a future whose way is measured not in linearities but in irreversibilities: irreducibles of loss, love and insight. Those who tend the clogged texts of spirit, who listen for the surges and the silences, may find–somewhat to their surprise–that they are readier than most to face the future. This hermeneutic capacitates a recapitulation of entire histories; a ritual witness to the unhealed wounds; a joyful work of endless signification. It teaches trust within the cloud of unknowing.

It is not (as some postmodern theisms imply) that Christianity can stand here at its ancient gate, innocent of the aggressions of the West, ready to receive refugees from secular modernity. It may be the case, however, that we who repent the spectacular failure of Christendom to do justice, practice kindness or walk humbly with our God, are ready for new and stranger coalitions. What is hopeful in this? That theology withdraws its legitimation of domination–now that we possess so little power with which to legitimate anything? Nonetheless I believe this weakness bears the risk and the prerequisite of another kind of empowerment. Its hope is quite concrete.

As we stop promising final utopias or transcendent escapes, the discourse and practice of divinity begin to join forces with the chaotic democracies of the becoming-creation. Why not? If we face the shadow in the night–whether we call it Other, angel, Elohim, problem, sibling–we may find ourselves moved by a strange eros. This "wrestling" (*va-ye'avek*), as Rashi comments, "is the way of two people who strain to push each other down to the ground–they embrace and struggle with each other" (*hovko ve-ovko*; Genesis 32.24).[5] Limping into the next day, intimately wounded ("touched in the hollow of the thigh"), the place of this nocturnal struggle has opened up: it is called *Peni'el*. Face of godhood.

The divine attractor traces the oscillations of a wild aesthetic, a beauty neither classical nor stylish. In the struggling networks of its erotic field, we gain not certainty but confidence. We have a chance not just to resist the garish monocultures of the newest empire, but to stir alternative desires. Some who resist nobly, however, do not relay the vibrancy. Let us honor but not emulate them. For without the message of the rhythmic spirit, without the drumbeat and the tides, the good tidings run dry.

It is this spirit, this vibration with moistened wings, to whose topos we finally turn, and have turned all along. So the *ruach elohim* that concludes the verse must also conclude my "draught of a draught." The bottomless deep will not stop opening; the divine manyone will not stop unfolding. But the *ruach* of the "third space," the one whose trace flutters across the *bereshit* of Genesis, the one who broods upon the living waters, can be relied upon to deposit this wad of writing in the next abyss.

Tehom, Elohim, Ruach. In other words, can the third space of spirit provide not just a triadic opening, but a trinitarian dis/closure? Would it support the sort of temporary closure of which the infinity of interpretation admits? Or does "the trinity" already lock down meaning? Does it not almost invariably serve to close God into *His* tripled self-sufficiency rather than to *open* worlds?

II The origami of creation

> We must not view the trinitarian perichoresis as a rigid pattern. We should
> see it as at once the most intense excitement and the absolute rest of the love
> which is the wellspring of everything that lives, the keynote of all reso-
> nances, and the source of the rhythmically dancing and vibrating worlds.
> (Moltmann)[6]

The topos of the Deep has provided the topic of this book. If it were a person or a god it could signify the trinitarian "first person." I would not, however, call it God but *the depth of God*. Ocean of divinity, womb and place-holder of beginnings, it is not Elohim but the first place or *capacity* of genesis. Chaos, as Tehom, the heterogeneous depth of divinity and of world, place of places, forms the first member of a tehomic trinity. Borrowing from Cusa and Bruno, Deleuze cannot resist its formula: "the trinity *complicatio–explicatio–implicatio*." This is a trinity of folds, *plis*, indicating a relationality of intertwining rather than cutting edges. *Complicatio*, "folding together," in Cusa folding of the world in God, signifies "the chaos which contains all."[7]

Anonymously it gives birth to another, "not separate but different" (Tertullian). It can be called the *difference of God*. Its manners are as strange as the universe; yet it enters language as Word, Wisdom, Torah. This second capacity could also be called

231

the *explicatio*: that which "unfolds" what otherwise remains "folded together." To explicate would then mean to *realize*, i.e. at once to *divine* and to *actualize*. It recalls the "divine differentiations" of Dionysius. In its plurisingularity, it designates the "divergent series which lead out and back in" (ibid.)—to the chaos. These pulsations of divergence trace, for instance, the flows of a "run-away universe" and its constants; or the actualizations of the virtual that run a system, community, or self. In the self-organizing process of the world, the oscillation between tehom and elohim, complication and explication, *creates*. "God, therefore, is the enfolding (*complicatio*) of all in the sense that all are in God, and God is the unfolding (*explicatio*) of all in the sense that God is in all" (Cusa).[8] Creation begins—continually—in this relation, this incipient incarnation, at the edge of the waters.

And that relation, the "relation of relations,"[9] may be called by *implication* the *spirit of God*. *Ruach* on the face of the waters: it has provided the pulsing, folding force of a tehomic theology all along. It has ever and again opened the "third space" where Tehom could flow into language and Elohim, by a certain chiastic effect, might listen. The Deleuzian *implicatio* signifies "the differentiator which relates them one to another." Differentiator as connector: thus this spirit will not transcend or obliterate differences; rather differences are intensified precisely by being brought into relation. So the third capacity thus signifies the relationality itself.

Such a definition sounds a lot like the Holy Spirit of the classical trinity: Augustine designated Spirit as *love itself*, the third which binds the first two together as lover and beloved; the *mutuus amor* of Thomas Aquinas. Moltmann lifts this attractive relationalism—which I find troubling in its exceptionalism, not in its self-organizing structure—to the fore: "The existence, the life, and the warp and weft of inter-relationships subsist in the Spirit . . . Everything exists, lives and moves in others, in one another, with one another, for one another, in the cosmic interrelations of the divine Spirit."[10] Elizabeth Johnson radicalizes this subtradition: "Speaking of the Spirit as the power of mutual love proceeding has strong affinities with the model of relationship most prized by feminist thought. Love is the moving power of life," she adds, "that which drives everything that is toward everything else that is."[11] Spirit as the relation of relations relates the divine interdependency to the interdependencies of the world. As a counterdiscourse, in which the divergences are not suppressed within the convergences of theology itself, it breaks the trinity out of its doctrinal self-enclosure in the metaphysics of substance. God the Spirit would then signify not only the "immanent" trinitarian relations, but also an "economic" interdependence of creator and creation, and as such the interrelation of all creatures.

What of the waters (*mayim*) over or with which the spirit vibrates? These waters are distinguished from tehom: no longer tehom, not yet literal ocean (which must be separated out on day "two.")[12] So the *mayim* suggest (analogously to the earth tohu vabohu) the fluidity, the waves, the membranes of energy from which matter forms and stabilizes. The interface of creator and creation is thus *implicated* in material

232

energy: "God's Spirit is life's vibrating, vitalizing field of energy, we are in God, and God is in us . . . God's Spirit is our space for living."[13] This pneumatological materiality, far from effecting a spiritual disembodiment, a flight from the earth, suggests in its very birdiness a dynamism of embodiment: lines of flight *within* the world. Moreover, the etymological connotation of brooding has always emitted the mythical associations of the mother bird laying the world-egg.[14] Despite its precarious biblical legitimacy, the egg has tucked itself into the long history of interpretation—as, for instance, in Hildegard's image of the universe as a cosmic egg.[15] The spirit lays the eggs of matter itself, in the delicate differentiatons of "the waters." A tehomic reading would thus be "grounding the spirit."[16] Such a ground—not to be confused with foundation—firmly embodies our spirit(s) in the shared flesh of our differences: "I will put my Spirit upon him, and he shall proclaim justice" (Matthew 12.18b). The "differentiator" can be said to connect divergent forces to their shared potentiality—i.e. the possibilities that can be realized only in relation: the "I" who cannot become apart from "you." Only as "the Public Person of the Spirit" does the Word of God, or the word "God," speak justice.[17] Justice is *love under conditions of conflict.* If love is the practice of *difference as relation,* love characterizes the spirit. Con/spiring in the differentiation of the universe, this public spirit immerses all becoming-subjects in their *shared* future: not necessarily a reassuring prospect, but a collective process of infinite reciprocations and devastating sensitivities. That process goes on before and after any particular life. Its demanding publicity, however, does not replace or relieve our psychic depth. From the depths we cry . . . and may still in spirit—dance.

Apart from the spirit "brooding o'er the chaos," Tehom remains a sterile possibility and "God" remains mere Word, fleshless abstraction and power code. Only through pneumatology does theology have a prayer. For if the life and breath of divinity is the life and breath of the universe, then only in the "Spirit of Life" can our God-words *address* the mystery. Without this Spirit all our words circulate in a disembodied vacuum. For only in Spirit does Logos have *body*: that of the creation. The universe becomes Sacred Body there where genesis takes *place.* No wonder the Spirit—which abides neither reduction to nor dominance over its manifest body—vibrates at the edge of chaos. There it breathes, contracts, expands, making space, taking flesh, tuning relation to possibility.

III

Shechina
Calling us
From exile
Inside us exiled
Calling us

Home
Home.
(Lynn Gottlieb[18])

The pneumatic oscillation–storm, wind, breath, spirit, who is not some thing sent from a God above, but who "is" whatever is divine–inspires yet another name. *Ruach* becomes *Shekhinah* (from *shakhan*, "to dwell"), the "dwelling" who manifests divine immanence in the context of Jewish exile: "within" for those "without," a presence amidst divine and geographic absence. Shekhinah cannot be expropriated as a synonym for the Christian Holy Spirit or a feminist God/ess; its indwelling was often confined to its people, not to mention their patriarchy. Yet the rabbis drew an unmistakably tehomic analogy between the "confinement of the Shekhinah" and a cave on the sea-shore: "The sea was turbulent and flooded the cave: the cave was filled (with water), yet the sea was in no way diminished."[19] I cannot imagine a more precise picture of the relation between the fragile finitude of our contextual condition and the infinity which rhythmically fills and empties it. The frequent interchangeability of Spirit and Shekhinah in the rabbinic writings also supports the emergence of a non-exclusionary reading of this "dwelling." For "the wings of the Shekhinah" also carries the wider sense of "God's protective presence over all of creation, '*brooding over the face of the water . . . as a dove broods over its nest*'" (T. B. Haggigah 12a).[20]

In the kabbalistic interpretation of Jewish suffering, the Shekhinah became the mythic figure of tragic exile–an exile that ripped *Din*, the sephirah of "strict justice, rigor and divine judgment," from *Hesed*, that of loving kindness, thus fissuring the divine nature. God, already complicated through the explicating differentiations of the bi-gendered sephiroth, becomes a split self. In this way the *Zohar* diagnoses the effects on God of social oppression. In the setting of Jewish-Christian dialog, Michael Lodahl compares this kabbalistic imagery of divine vulnerability with Whitehead's "consequent nature of God," that becoming-divinity actualized only in its suffering and enjoying of the world. He glosses the Shekhinah-Spirit as one who "tragically awaits the response of human beings to the divine flow of energy; or, in process terms, to the divine aims offered to us."[21] The iconography of the exiled Shekhinah and the crisis of the divine *zimsum*–the breaking of the vessels–thus deepens and darkens the intuition of the divine pathos at the chaotic edge of creation.

In the *Zohar* it is the messianic expectation of the day of *tikkun*, the mending of the split, which comprises hope. Does such a hope for a final messianic mending not more closely resemble a linear eschatology than a process open end?[22] However, in Gershom Scholem's reading of Isaac Luria, "the coming of the Messiah means no more than a signature under a document that we ourselves write;" a dream of full presence tragically and perhaps permanently deferred. "A postponed presence," comments Lodahl, considering Derrida. The latter, not untouched by kabbalah, has added his signature to this messianic gap. Indeed he situates hermeneutics itself within the social context of the perennial alien: "the necessity of commentary, like poetic necessity, is the very form of exiled speech."[23] The "presence" or dwelling of this self-differing Shekhinah would never represent a simple or unitary presence, a triumphant repossession, a return to identity. This Spirit offers and takes refuge–among refugee camps and resident aliens, among all homemaking strangers. Far more of them are Palestinian as I write than Jewish. She cannot wash away the moribund history of Abrahamic fratricides. She provides the vulnerable space for negotiation amidst the chaos that mounts in proportion to the attempt to control it. The Other/sibling/angel must be wrestled with as such. Or she is defiled. The Shekhinah, fragmented Dwelling, has been written over and fought over; a mobile home, never quite-being, nor ever not-being, of a *becoming*-Spirit. She might even reverberate in Bhabha's "performance of identity as iteration," the "re-creation of the self" in the resettlement of "the borderline community of migration"[24]–a community in whose suffering and hope the most settled identities are *implicated*. For the pneumatic *implicatio* carries from the beginning this politics of improbable hope: we are implicated one in another.

If her femininity remains traditionally subordinate to the politics of Hebrew manhood, nonetheless the kabbalists took her gender with utmost seriousness.[25] It appears poignantly as the tenth sephira, whose reunion with the masculine deity became the erotic duty of every pious Jew. This would be the *tikkun*: "the unification of the feminine and the masculine within the divine, the Holy One, blessed be He, and the Shekhinah."[26] Unlike the ontotheological patrilineage, this One, He, lacks self-sufficiency. Perhaps this lack will let the future of gender and sex messianically "come." In the present commentary, Shekhinah amplifies the femininity of *ruach/pneuma* herself. She might crack and overflow the vessel of a merely patrilineal bisexuality: "if she became, in the depths of the same, the other of his other."[27] On "her" becoming depends the coming of any Messiah worth waiting for.

IV Deep breathing

Spirit does not come to henpeck the patriarchs. On the "wings of the Shekhinah" her adherents soar far from a present that she has never abandoned. "Crossing back over the borders of their own lives. Flowing back to this side, venturing their breath. Entrusting to the other the very rhythm of their breathing."[28] We practice the enfolding and unfolding of the divine by attending to our breath. We realize bodily the rhythm of the conceptual panentheism. In a great loop, a perichoresis, the caves of identity are filled and emptied by the living waters.

The Deep, the Difference and the Spirit. The *godness* of our depths, our differences, our spirits. Standing at the uterine font, returning it to the *tohu vabohu* of the holy waters: I immerse, dip, write you in the name of: Womb, Word and Wind. Tiamat, Sophia and Shekhinah. Tehom, Elohim, Ruach. All the names, their nouns, their pronouns, mark crossings, breachings, plungings. They dissolve again. They turn to foam.

In the lightness of that foam, the airiness of that breath, *ruach* continues to be mistaken for something like nothing: an immateriality. Spirit has been the agent of sublimation, transparency and escape; God as "pure spirit" gets free of any body; mind as pure spirit does likewise. It was kept suspended *above* the waters. By the Renaissance it could be lampooned by Rabelais, who mocked the pious fantasm of disembodied existence: the inhabitants of "the Island of Ruach," who lived entirely on wind; they ate and drank nothing but wind. "They all die of dropsy and tympanites (swelling of the abdomen caused by air in the intestine). The men perish, farting; the women, pooping. Their immortal souls make their exit from between their buttocks."[29] But if spirit resists its own disembodiment and comes down too close to the chaos of materiality, then, for example, a Barth, as we noted, could ridicule the *ruach* as a queer, fluttering, effeminate thing. The sinuous pulsing upon the waters–waters no longer tehom but *mayim*, materializing, wet, energetic–has not often been richly imagined. It has not had the space.

V The sap of the spirit

The following early thirteenth-century text[30] of the Iyyun Circle deserves therefore to be read closely. It reread the creation narrative as a densely textured process of energy flows. Indeed it unfolds a tehomic cosmogony in dream-like miniature. Perhaps the strange proliferation of its signifiers will seem merely hallucinogenic, another case of the irrationalism of the mystic. Or does it anticipate in its oneiric midrash a creativity that oscillates between energy and matter, light and dark, particle and wave, observer and observed?

> At that moment Moses began to observe the primeval light, the root of all. And he found it to be a darkness composed of two entities stemming from two sources, one flowing with light, the second with darkness.

Moses is not observing something that happened once for all but something in process. These "two entities" inject difference into the origin, and yet preclude any moralizing dichotomy. Indeed he seems to be "seeing" a graphic predecessor for that Cusan light that cannot be opposed to darkness: this "primeval light" is none other than the luminous dark out of which light and dark will gradually be distinguished; a darkness not lying *above* a fluid matrix but written *as* the flux. In its Mosaic counterdiscourse, this dark-light flow defies all denigration:

> Now this flow extends and gushes forth by way of channels, and the flow again becomes weak like a stream, and the stream again becomes minute,

turning into a thread. And in this exiguity it extends and is directed until it becomes small, tiny droplets. These droplets grow and become fragmented entities, and the fragments continue to grow until they burst forth in great strength, mingling and interacting one with another, expanding and conjoining until a sap pours forth from them.

In this mysterious metonymy, the fragments do not resemble shards but rather threads, filaments, displaying a connective rather than dissociative differentiation. This subtle flux, like the Deleuzian series that leads out of the *complicatio* and back in, features a chemistry of drop formation. We recall "*Das Meer in einem Troepflein*"– the whole ocean of divinity condensed in a droplet [Silesius, Book 4, 153]. But the kabbalistic poetry of primal flux also finds an uncanny analogue in a recent application of chaos theory:

> One critical element of drop formation is a filament that forms between the drop and the main source of liquid before it breaks off. This filament effect, which can be more easily observed with honey, has come under scrutiny . . . Starting in the early 90's, theoretical work by Dr. Jens Eggers . . . and experimental work led by Dr. Sidney Nagel . . . demonstrated a surprising characteristic about the pinching off of a drop. The rupture point demonstrates a fractal property called scaling or self-similarity. In essence, the "neck" of the breaking point would look the same–a cascading series of ever-thinning stems. [31]

So then when the kabbalistic drops rupture, grow, mingle and interact at different scales, it is not surprising that a kind of premodern fractal begins to constellate, a strange attractor traced amidst the fragments or fractions of an n-dimensional saturation. The Iyyun Circle continues:

> Now this sap flows and extends and is congealed; and through this coagulation [the drops] are polished, purified, and clarified such that the original fragments that we mentioned are utterly disintegrated. From them come forth a kind of foam which floats on the water, and it transforms everything into a juice, and *from this juice comes forth a wind, that is, the Holy Spirit*. Therefore it is written hintingly, "And the Spirit of God hovered upon the water" (Genesis 1.2). This means that the Spirit grew stronger in holiness and transformed into many blades, each blade transforming into a branch, and each branch transforming into a root from which came forth a myriad of powers, entities, and objects. [my emphasis]

This kabbalistic sensorium can be read as a map of heterogeneous, mutually embedded, far-from-equilibrium processes, bifurcating, iterating, and branching into materialization: into the myriad of powers, entities and objects comprising the creation we inhabit. The grammar of command and obedience has been replaced by an almost cinemographic montage of metamorphosis. Confabulating an evolutionary pathway for the self-organizing complexities by which life itself comes forth, it has inserted itself as a sensuous midrash upon the primary intertext of the present book. Its theological saturation depicts no self-sufficient and discarnate transcendence but a radical incompletion, a streaming infinity. Almost a millennium ago, it teases out of Genesis 1.2 a Spirit that grows, evolving by embodiment.

Unfolding creation from its depths, tracing unpredictable lines of difference, this Spirit connects our depths to our differences. It is of course *our* spirit–not as a possession or a self-possession but as the rhythmic life of all creatures, and only as such the *spiritus creator*. In this "God who is the strength of *all* life,"[32] may we then imagine ourselves, in all the fragmentation and froth of our lives, growing "stronger in holiness"?

*

At any rate the tehomic icons, occasionally breaking into an altered state of signification, take their divinity with a grain of salt. Their trinity may be no more than a device for closure. But their closure may be no more than a trick of dis/closure. We crest, fall, fold down, break. "Sea you return to sea, and rhythm to rhythm."[33] Out of the disintegration foam up other juicy beginnings. You do not own them; they do not disown you. On their faces, read your own. Read the myriad others. Willy-nilly and *tohu vabohu*, they share this Deep. It becomes you. Even more: it *capacitates* its creatures. The *nova creatio ex profundis* requires our entire participation.[34]

In beginning: a plurisingularity of universe, earth echoing chaos, dark deep vibrating with spirit, creates.

NOTES

PRE/FACE

1 Confounding earlier predictions of its slowing and collapse in on itself (the Big Crunch), or even a steady state universe of even expansion, its rate of expansion is itself accelerating. This parallels or replicates something of the initial impulsion of the Big Bang, with its precisely calibrated yet chaotic amplifications. Cf. Timothy Ferris, *The Whole Shebang: A State-of-the-Universe(s) Report* (New York: Simon & Schuster, 1998).

2 Dennis Overbye, in the *New York Times*, *Science Times*, 4 October 2001.

3 Luce Irigaray, *Elemental Passions*, trans. Joanne Collie and Judith Still (New York: Routledge, 1992[1982]), p. 89.

4 In Hebrew, *tehom* carries the meanings "ocean," "deep" and "abyss," related to but not necessarily derived from the Babylonian goddess Tiamat. The Hebrew *tehom*, "ocean," together with the Ugaritic *thm*, the Akkadian *tiamtu*, the Arabic *tihamat* and the Eblaite *ti-a-ma-tum/tiham(a)tum* is a reflection of a common Semitic term, *tiham-*. See David Toshio Tsumura, *The Earth and the Waters in Genesis 1 and 2*, JSOT Sup. 83 (Sheffield: Sheffield Academic Press, 1989), pp. 45–52. In my own theological usage, this term calls upon its depersonified Hebrew meanings, echoing with the range of Semitic and mythic significations. I will no longer treat it as a foreign word. On occasion it may become a proper name, reminiscent of the fact that in Genesis 1.2 it/she functions grammatically without a definite article.

5 F. W. J. Schelling, *The Ages of the World*, trans. Jason M. Wirth (Albany, NY: SUNY Press, 2000), p. 3f.

6 Irigaray, *Elemental Passions*, p. 71.

7 James Joyce, *Finnegans Wake* (New York: Penguin, 1976[1939]), p. 191.

8 Daniel Boyarin, *Dying for God: Martyrdom and the Making of Christianity and Judaism* (Stanford, CA: Stanford University Press, 1999), p. 3. His model lets us "see Judeo-Christianity (not in its modern sense of a homogenized common culture) as a single circulatory system within which discursive elements could move from non-Christian Jews and back again, developing as they moved around the system." ibid., p. 9f.

9 Gregory had been exegetically inspired by Moses' declaration "that he had seen God in the darkness." "This is called darkness by the Scripture, which signifies, as I said, the unknown and unseen." Gregory of Nyssa, *The Life of Moses*, trans. Abraham J. Malherbe and Everett Ferguson (New York/Toronto: Paulist Press, 1978), p. 97.

10 Gilles Deleuze, *Difference and Repetition*, trans. P. Patton (New York: Columbia University Press, 1994[1964]), p. 229.

11 William P. Brown, *The Ethos of the Cosmos: The Genesis of Moral Imagination in the Bible* (Grand Rapids, MI: William B. Eerdmans, 1999), p. 41.

1 MYSTERY OF THE MISSING CHAOS

1 Helene Cixous, *"Coming to Writing" and Other Essays*, ed. Deborah Jenson, trans. Sarah Cornell, Ann Liddle and Susan Sellers (Cambridge, MA: Harvard University Press, 1991), p. 41.

2 Walt Whitman, "Song of Myself," in *Leaves of Grass* (New York: Norton, 1973), p. 30.

3 Double thanks to the brothers Schechter: to Bob for this stanza of Walt Whitman's, to Bruce for the infant twins Sophia and Joshua.

4 The Greek phrase *'ek tou me ontos* ("from that which was not") was translated into Latin as *ex nihilo*, Arabic as *la min shay'*, and Hebrew as *yesh me'ayin*. Cf. H. A. Wolfson, "The Meaning of *Ex Nihilo* in the Church Fathers, Arabic and Hebrew Philosophy, and St. Thomas," in I. Twersky and G. Williams (eds), *Studies in the History of Philosophy and Religion*, Vol. 1 (Cambridge, MA: Harvard University Press, 1973), pp. 207–11. Judaism, for reasons and in cases that will play a formative role throughout the present book, represents of the Abrahamic faiths the least stable *ex nihilo* consensus.

5 John B. Cobb, Jr. and David R. Griffin, *Process Theology: An Introductory Exposition* (Philadelphia, PA: Westminster Press/John Knox Press, 1976), especially pp. 65ff. They offer a "theology of nature" rather than a theology of creation—though one deeply influential upon the present tehomic trajectory. A couple more explicit developments of the *ex nihilo* in process theology (from opposite sides of its theological spectrum) have been released too recently to read seriously for this book. Cf. David R. Griffin, "Creation out of Nothing, Creation out of Chaos, and the Problem of Evil," in *Encountering Evil: Live Options in Theodicy*, 2nd edn, ed. Stephen T. Davis (Philadelphia, PA: Westminster Press/John Knox Press, 2001), pp. 108–44; Thomas Jay Oord has advocated an "open theology" that "embraces the hypothesis that God did not create the world out of absolutely nothing, i.e., *ex nihilo*. The rejection of this ancient Church doctrine may cause some to be puzzled." *Matching Theology and Piety: An Evangelical Process Theology of Love*, PhD dissertation (Claremont Graduate University, 1999), p. 284.

6 Rosemary Ruether in advance and more explicit than most: "Unlike the later orthodox view, the God of Genesis 1 does not create 'out of nothing' but conquers and orders into a cosmos the preexisting watery chaos." *Sexism and God-Talk: Toward a Feminist Theology* (Boston, MA: Beacon Press, 1983), p. 77. See also Karen Baker-Fletcher's brief but profound reflection on "The Wildness of the Waters," in *Sisters of Dust, Sisters of Spirit: Womanist Wordings on God and Creation* (Minneapolis, MN: Augsburg Press/Fortress Press, 1998): "According to Genesis, then, the deep, the darkness, the waters dance in cocreative activity with God" (p. 24).

7 Jon D. Levenson, *Creation and the Persistence of Evil: The Jewish Drama of Divine Omnipotence* (Princeton, NJ: Princeton University Press, 1988), p. 121. Levenson leans on Rashi and Speiser, as will the present argument. I reconstruct in detail the exegetical and hermeneutical case against the *ex nihilo* by numerous scholars since Hermann Gunkel, as well as the attempt to retrieve it by Gerhard von Rad, in Chapter 6.

8 *Saint John Chrysostom 1–17*, trans. Robert C. Hill, in *Fathers of the Church* (Washington, DC: Catholic University of America Press, 1947), pp. 31–2.

9 Nelle Morton, *The Journey Is Home* (Boston, MA: Beacon Press, 1985) will figure in this book's analysis of Augustine, in Chapter 4.

10 "Only half-jokingly known as the Butterfly Effect," the "sensitive dependence on initial conditions" discovered by meteorologist Edward Lorenz, expresses how "tiny differences in input could quickly become overwhelming differences in output: hence the notion that a butterfly stirring the air today in New Jersey can cause an avalanche in the Himalayas next month." cf. James Gleick, *Chaos: Making a New Science* (New York: Penguin, 1987), p. 8. Its repercussions in theology have been cautiously contained, but have produced some serious texts: *Chaos and Complexity: Scientific Perspectives on Divine Action*, ed. Robert John Russell, Nancey Murphy and Arthur R. Peacocke (Vatican City State: Vatican Observator Publications and Berkeley, CA: Center for Theology and the Natural Sciences, 1995). Cf. also an essay by Sjoerd L. Bonting, a biochemist and Anglican priest, "Chaos Theology: A New Approach to the Science–Theology Dialogue," *Zygon*, 345, 2 (June 1999), pp. 323–32. I will not depend upon chaos theory as such–a family of scientific explorations problematically overlapping, indeed by some accounts subsumed in, or superseded by, complexity theory–but upon the resonance of certain indispensable metaphors and insights of the new disciplines of chaos with the present set of theological questions.

11 Cf. Ch. 8.

12 Jacques Derrida, *Of Grammatology*, trans. Gayatri Chakravorti Spivak (Baltimore, MD: Johns Hopkins University Press, 1976[1974]), p. 24.

13 Derrida is interpreting Edmond Jabes' *Book of Questions*, and so "a certain Judaism as the birth and passion of writing": the "*shared* necessity of exegesis, the interpretive imperative, is interpreted differently by the rabbi and the poet." Jacques Derrida, *Writing and Difference*, trans. Alan Bass (Chicago: University of Chicago Press, 1978), pp. 64, 67.

14 Senator Beveridge in 1900, before the fully assembled US Senate. Quote from Kelvin A. Santiago-Valles, "'Subject People' and Colonial Discourses: Economic Transformation and Social Disorder," in *Puerto Rico, 1898–1947* (Albany, NY: SUNY Press, 1932), p. 26; Santiago-Valles is quoting from Claude G. Bowers, *Beveridge and the Progressive Era* (New York: Praeger Publishers, 1932), p. 76. Cited in Mayra Rivera, "Gendered Territories: A Post-Colonial Reading of the US Missionaries Discourse in Puerto-Rico 1898–1920," in Benjamin Valentin (ed.), *Nuevas Vocas/New Voices: Horizons in US Hispanic/Latino(a) Theology* (Cleveland, OH: Pilgrim Press, forthcoming).

15 A bitter harangue against the white liberal Kerner Commission (which had claimed that the race riots of the late 1960s had some social and economic justification), the report is called "a blank check for need, drawn against ability: a blank check for evil, drawn against innocence." It calls for the "virtuous of America" to stop payment on the "carte blanche for chaos drawn against their lives." I cite this rather old-fashioned, Ayn-Rand style of racist exposition just because it makes explicit what I believe is a still widespread identification of whiteness with virtue and talent against blackness as riotous, resentful chaos. Lillian R. Boehme, *Carte Blanche for Chaos* (New Rochelle, NY: Arlington House, 1970), p. 222.

16 Ilya Prigogine and Isabelle Stengers, *Order out of Chaos: Man's New Dialogue with Nature* (New York: Bantam Books, 1984).

17 "Postmodern science–by concerning itself with such things as undecidables, the limits of

precise control, conflicts characterized by incomplete information, '*fracta*,' catastrophes, and pragmatic paradoxes–is theorizing its own evolution as discontinuous, catastrophic, nonrectifiable, and paradoxical." Jean-François Lyotard, *The Postmodern Condition: A Report on Knowledge*, trans. Geoff Bennington and Brian Massumi (Minneapolis, MN: University of Minnesota Press, 1984[1979]), p. 60. Indeed the role of Benoit Mandelbrot's fractals and René Thom's catastrophes, mathematical keys to chaos, in the intellectual life of Paris since the late 1960s has perhaps been underthematized.

18 Alfred North Whitehead, *Process and Reality: An Essay in Cosmology*, ed. David Ray Griffin and Donald Sherburne (New York: New Press, 1978[1929]), p. 43.

19 Emanuel Levinas, *Totality and Infinity; An Essay on Exteriority*, trans. Alphonso Lingis (Pittsburgh, PA: Duquesne University Press, 1967). While I cannot appropriate Levinas' own insistence upon the exteriority of the Other as infinitely Other–which indeed leads him to his own postulation of the *ex nihilo* dogma–nor his accompanying anthropocentrism, I will similarly argue for a depth *not* found already in a contained "within" of the subject. Nor, however, will it be contained in a relation of "absolute exteriority."

20 Claus Westermann, *Creation*, trans. John J. Soullion (Philadelphia, PA: Fortress Press 1974[1971]), p. 42.

21 *Pentateuch with Targum, Onkelos, Haptaroth and Rashi's Commentary: Genesis*, trans. M. Rosenbaum and A. M. Silbermann (New York: Hebrew Publishing Co., 1965), p. 2.

22 ibid. Rashi argues that the noun "beginning" (*reshit*) is in construct form in Genesis 1.1, as in its multiple scriptural parallels. Rashi-guided translations accommodate the subordinate clause dictated by the construct form differently: e.g. (at least in a footnote as alternative reading) thus: "When God began to create . . ." *Holy Bible: New Revised Standard Version with Apocrypha* (Oxford: Oxford University Press, 1989). Occasional minor adjustments in favor of inclusive language may occur, but this edition of the Bible will normally be used unless otherwise indicated.

23 Avivah Gottlieb Zornberg, *The Beginnings of Desire: Reflections on Genesis* (New York: Doubleday Image Books, 1995), p. 4.

24 Among interpreters supportive of the dependent clause hypothesis are E. A. Speiser, *Genesis*, trans. with intro. and notes by him, in the Anchor Bible, Vol. 1 (Garden City, NY: Doubleday, 1964), pp. 12ff.: W. M. Abbott, SJ, Rabbi A. Gilbert, R. L. Hunt and J. C. Swaim, *The Bible Reader: an Interfaith Interpretation. With Notes from Catholic, Protestant, and Jewish Traditions and References to Art, Literature, History, and the Social Problems of Modern Man* (New York: Bruce Publishing, 1969), p. 5. The case for the opposition, which recognizes the threat to the doctrine of *creatio ex nihilo*, is well summarized and attested to in Gerhard F. Hasel, "Recent Translation of Genesis 1:1: A Critical Look," *The Bible Translator*, 22, 4 (October 1971), pp. 154–67. This debate will be discussed at length in Chapter 6.

25 Derrida, *Of Grammatology*, p. 61.

26 See Chapter 9.

27 Cf. also Exodus 20.21. This theophany within "the thick darkness" became the pretext and prooftext of the apophatic tradition in Eastern orthodoxy and later Catholic mysticism. It inspires Gregory of Nyssa's and Pseudo-Dionysius' trope of "the luminous darkness," the subject of this book's Chapter 12.

28 Joyce, *Finnegans Wake*, pp. 118–23.

29 Cf. Philip Kuberski's rich sketch of the "coordinates of a culture and art truly beyond the confines of modernity." He interweaves discussions of the Joycean chaosmos with

an account of the challenge of the "countermodernism, which centers on the idea of a self organizing world." He cites scientists such as Ilya Prigogine, Gregory Bateson, David Bohm, Erich Jantsch, Humberto Maturana and Francisco Varela as among those moving "beyond the asumptions of mechanization and objectivity that guide modern science and technology." *Chaosmos: Literature, Science and Theory* (Albany, NY: SUNY Press, 1994), p. 13.

30 Philippe Sollers, "Joyce and Co.," *TriQuarterly*, 38 (Winter 1977), p. 109.

31 Though I must admit to our pursuing almost altogether independent pathways, I should call attention to the work of Thomas J. J. Altizer, who long precedes the present work in his meditation upon the "epic" importance of James Joyce for Christian theology of beginnings and endings. See especially *Genesis and Apocalyse: A Theological Voyage toward Authentic Christianity* (Louisville, KY: Westminster Press/John Knox Press, 1990).

32 Eco concludes his book with an extraordinary flourish of tehomic revelation: "To make this statement, however, *Finnegans Wake* encloses Chaos within the framework of an apparent Order and thereby places us in the same situation as the apostate Stephen who uses the words of Thomas Aquinas in order to refuse family, country, and church. The only faith that the aesthetics and metaphysics of the Chaosmos leaves us is the faith in Contradiction," Umberto Eco, *The Aesthetics of Chaosmos: The Middle Ages of James Joyce*, trans. Ellen Esrock (Cambridge, MA: Harvard University Press, 1982), p. 87.

33 Cf. Ch. 11; Eco, *Aesthetics of Chaosmos*, p. 87. The present work is indebted to Eco for pointing out the role of the Cusanian category of *coincidentia oppositorum* in *Finnegans Wake*. Also he shows Joyce finding in Cusa "a vision of a polydimensional reality, the infinite possible perspectives of a universal form that can be seen under different visual angles, in endless and complementary profiles" (p. 73). In addition he tracks the powerful influence of Giordano Bruno's Renaissance kabbalism, with its "dialectic of the finite and infinite . . . accomplished only in the ceaseless process of cosmic meta-morphosis. Each being has in itself the seed of future forms that guarantee its infinity. Joyce had read Bruno's *De l'Infinito Universo e Mondi*, and one of the most implicit and explicit axioms of the *Wake* is that of the infinity of worlds, unified by the meta-morphic nature of each word, the willingness of each etymon to immediately become something else and explode in new semantic directions." Eco, *Aesthetics of Chaosmos*, p. 73.

34 Trinh T. Minh-ha, *When the Moon Waxes Red: Representation, Gender and Cultural Politics* (New York: Routledge, 1991), p. 234. Cf. her consistent, if brief, allusions to Taoism as a form of decolonizing language, an Asian apophasis redolent of political meaning: "As our elder Lao Tzu used to say, knowing ignorance is strength, ignoring knowledge is sickness." Trinh T. Minh-ha, *Woman Native Other: Writing Postcoloniality and Feminism* (Bloomington: Indiana University Press, 1989), p. 2.

35 Whitehead, *Process and Reality*, p. 22.

36 ibid., p. 95.

37 Certainly such a conversation is entertained in Catherine Keller with Anne Daniell (eds) *Process and Difference: Between Cosmological and Poststructuralist Postmodernisms* (Albany, NY: SUNY Press, 2002).

38 Jacques Derrida, *On the Name*, ed. Thomas Dutoit, trans. David Wood, John P. Leavey and Ian McLeod (Stanford, CA: Stanford University Press, 1995[1993]), p. 89.

39 How gratifying to read John Caputo making explicit the tehomic link, if only "in a nutshell." Of Derrida's khora, he notes that it is its "indeterminable indeterminacy

which seems rather to fail words, to fall short of word or meaning. In biblical terms, it was perhaps a little more like the chaos over which the spirit of God bent." *Deconstruction in a Nutshell: A Conversation with Jacques Derrida* (New York: Fordham University Press, 1997), p. 96.

40 Derrida, *On the Name*, p. 104.

41 Robert Graves, *The Greek Myths*, Vol. I (Harmondsworth, Mx: Penguin, 1957[1955]), p. 27.

42 *Tao te ching, the New Translation*, ed. Man-ho Kwok, Martin Palmer and Jay Ramsay (New York: Barnes & Noble, 1994, Ch. 4, p. 32.

43 ibid., Ch. 5, p. 34.

44 ibid., Ch. 25, p. 74.

45 Yet creative scholarship by Asian Christian feminists is beginning to effect a distinctive Taoist-Christian hybrid. Cf. Nam Soon Kang Park, *Ideology and Utopia: Taoist and Feminist Theological Responses to the Ideological Structures of Confucianism and Christianity*, PhD dissertation, Drew University, 1993; Jean Hee Kim, *Ecoharmony: An Asian Feminist Theology of Creation*, PhD dissertation, Drew University, 2001. If the present project remains by contrast rather doggedly western in its intertexts, it is not for lack of influence and inspiration by nonbiblical religions but in order to write a *fathomable* body.

46 Ted Hughes' marvelous translation, *Tales from Ovid* (New York: Farrar, Straus, Giroux, 1997), p. 3.

47 John Milton, *Paradise Lost*, Book 1, in *The Annotated Milton: Complete English Poems* (New York: Bantam, 1999), pp. 17–22.

48 Justin, I.10.2; cited in May, *Creatio ex Nihilo*, p. 122. See *Ante-Nicene Fathers*, Vol. 1, ed. Alexander Roberts and James Donaldson (Peabody, MA: Hendrickson, 1994).

49 My historical analysis depends in part upon the defining work of Gerhard May, *Creatio Ex Nihilo: The Doctrine of "Creation out of Nothing" in Early Christian Thought*, trans. A. S. Worrall (Edinburgh: T. & T. Clarke, 1994), p. 179.

50 ibid.

51 ibid., p. 327.

52 Cf. Augustine's line of criticism of the Manichaean teaching concerning the souls confined to the "clod" or bolus of darkness: N. Joseph Torchia, *Creatio ex Nihilo and the Theology of St. Augustine* (New York: Peter Lang, 1999), p. 215, n. 60.

53 *The Confessions of St. Augustine*, trans. John K. Ryan (Garden City, NY: Image/ Doubleday), XII.22; my emphasis. I will depend largely in this book on Ryan's translation, with occasional supplementation by Pine-Coffin.

54 Jürgen Moltmann, *God in Creation: A New Theology of Creation and the Spirit of God*, trans. Margaret Kohl (New York: Harper & Row, 1985), p. 74; my emphasis.

55 ibid., p. 1.

56 ibid., p. 88.

57 Given the fiercely Barthian patrimony of German theology, Moltmann has made significant advances toward feminism, for which we may be grateful. Indeed, he has offered a pointed critique of Barth's own anti-feminist history; cf. his work on Barth's attack on Henriette Visser't Hooft Boddaert.

58 Moltmann, *God in Creation*, p. 87.

59 Moltmann recognizes the proximity of his thought to process theology but repeats the conventional misunderstanding of process theology as unable to "preserve the

fundamental distinction between creation and Creator." Moltmann, *God in Creation*, p. 79. He repeats, too, that all panentheism is incapable of "linking God's immanence in the world with his transcendence in relation to it." ibid., p. 103. If anything, panentheism, in distinction from both classical theism and Spinozist pantheism, heightens the distinction by intensifying relationality.

60 ibid., p. 87.
61 Jürgen Moltmann, *The Crucified God* (New York: Harper & Row, 1974), p. 193.
62 Karl Barth, *Kirchliche Dogmatik,* trans. as *Church Dogmatics*, ed. G. W. Bromiley and T. F. Torrance (Edinburgh: T. & T. Clark, 1936–69). Vol. II, Part 1 (1957); Vol. III, Part 1 (1958), Part 2 (1960); Vol. III, Part 3 (1960), Part 4 (1961). III.3, p. 296.
63 "The mystics do speak of creation out of nothing; in fact, it is one of their favorite formulae. But in their case the orthodoxy of the term conceals a meaning which differs considerably from the original one. This Nothing from which everything has sprung is by no means mere negation . . . For this Nothing comprises a wealth of mystical reality although it cannot be defined. 'Un Dieu defini serait un Dieu fini.' In a word, it signifies the Divine itself, in its most impenetrable guise." Gershom Scholem, *Major Trends in Jewish Mysticism* (New York: Schocken Books, 1946), p. 25. The *Eyn Sof*. Cf. Ch. 11.
64 Barth, *Church Dogmatics*, III.1.105.
65 Irigaray writes here of the Freudian "blind spot." Luce Irigaray, *Speculum of the Other Woman*, trans. Gillian C. Gill (Ithaca, NY: Cornell University Press, 1985), p. 42f.
66 From the hymn to the Holy Spirit by Charles Wesley that forms one of the epigraphs to this book: "and brooding o'er the impregn'd abyss."
67 Cf. Virginia Burrus, *Begotten Not Made: Conceiving Manhood in Late Antiquity* (Stanford, CA: Stanford University Press, 2000) for a definitive analysis of the fourth-century construction of the transcendent manhood of the logos and the concomitant "erasure of the female from representations of divine generativity". ibid., p. 189.
68 Luce Irigaray, *The Forgetting of Air in Martin Heidegger*, trans. Mary Beth Mader (Austin: University of Texas Press, 1999[1983]), p. 178.
69 C. Keller, *Apocalypse Now and Then* (Boston, MA: Beacon Press, 1996), pp. 84–138.
70 Moltmann will himself through the *zimsum* find a more resonant place for the nothing, as the divine contraction, which creates a space for the world–a not-God within God; but he insists on its being "created" in order to maintain, in contrast to the kabbalistic view, a staunch *ex nihilo*. Moltmann relates his reading of the *zimsum* to the contraction theory in Schelling, itself imported from the sixteenth-century Christian kabbalist tradition. *God in Creation*, p. 87.
71 It is precisely in the word of the new, the irreducible, that Moltmann finds the end of things in the beginning. Or rather he finds their future, their hoped-for fulfillment, in the "prereflection of their own true future;" ibid., p. 63, the *regnum gloriae*. The phrase *novo creatio ex nihilo* occurs first in *Theology of Hope* (New York: Harper & Row, 1967). "The horizon of the future" of his earlier work is now filled in and closed along with history itself, in the rhapsodic but by no means open or temporal *regnum gloriae*: cf. C. Keller, "The Last Laugh: A Counter-Apocalyptic Meditation on Moltmann's Coming of God," *Theology Today*, 54, 3 (October 1997), pp. 381–91.
72 Kathryn Tanner makes a persuasive case against the presumption that more immanent notions of divine power show more power to resist political oppression. I agree with her argument that one can uncouple traditional Christian beliefs from "a blind respect for the status quo, support for injustice, and apolitical passivity." Thus there is no empirical contradiction between progressive political activism and the sort of classical,

indeed patriarchal, theological assumptions I am pointing out. Tanner, *The Politics of God: Christian Theologies and Social Justice* (Minneapolis, MN: Fortress Press, 1992), p. 3. So I do not make a causal argument (defeating the *ex nihilo* will lead to less annihilation of the marginalized) but rather a cultural, symbolic one (an alternative to the *ex nihilo* will help some Christians at least to better calibrate their beliefs with their actions). The political effects of a nonsupersessionist transmutation of belief may surprise us, however.

73   Westhelle's analysis accounts for the extreme paucity of reflections on creation in liberation theologies of the Americas; none even in the huge anthology by Ignacio Ellacuria and Jon Sobrino (eds), *Mysterium Liberationis* (Maryknoll, NY: Orbis Books, 1993). The theology of creation, with its cosmological width, has seemed to distract from the urgent sociohistorical needs of the people. The connections between ecology, cosmology and poverty, however, are beginning to be articulated: cf. such as Leonardo Boff, *Ecology & Liberation: A New Paradigm*, trans. John Cumming (Maryknoll, NY: Orbis Books, 1995); Leonardo Boff, *Ecology & Poverty: Cry of the Earth, Cry of the Poor*, ed. L. Boff and Virgil Elizondo (London: SCM Press, 1995).

74   Vitor Westhelle, "Creation Motifs in the Search for a Vital Space: A Latin American Perspective," in Susan B. Thistlethwaite and Mary Potter Engel (eds), *Lift Every Voice: Constructing Christian Theologies from the Underside* (San Francisco: Harper, 1990), p. 131.

75   ibid., p. 134. I have already depended–quite uncritically–upon this rich and concise text for the articulation of a counterapocalyptic theology of place. I find unique and indispensable Westhelle's notion of "vital space," developed precisely in resistance to the conservative theologies of creation, which keep people "in their place" while supporting a status quo that deprives them of their vital space, their land. Cf. Keller, *Apocalypse Now and Then*, pp. 168–72.

76   May, *Creatio ex Nihilo*, pp. 6–8. "That the formulation found in the second book of Maccabees in no way necessitates the thought of the absolute unconditionality of the creation, is also clear from an informative parallel in Xenophon. He says in one place in his *Memorabilia* that parents 'bring forth their children out of non-being.' Naturally that does not mean that the children come to be out of nothing . . ."

77   Westhelle, "Creation Motifs," p. 135.

78   "Liberation theology as a whole has neither taken the side of African Americans as the majority of the poor, excluded, and discriminated, nor tried to see their movements of resistance and religion as equal partners in a dialogue of cultures and religions. Without a recognition and correction of this contradiction, liberation theology leaves untouched a whole tradition of conservative thought and action that systematically negates multiculturalism, polycentrism, ecumenism, and postcolonialism. Therefore, without a recognition and correction of this contradiction, liberation theology runs the risk of remaining in a position that is neither historically relevant, nor postmodern, nor liberating." Josue a. Sathler and Amos Nascimento, "Black Masks on White Faces," in D. Batstone, E. Mendieta, L. A. Lorentzen, and D. N. Hopkins (eds), *Liberation Theologies, Postmodernity, and the Americas* (New York/London: Routledge, 1997), p. 117.

79   See Homi K. Bhabha's nearly classic postcolonial notion: "The ambivalence of colonial authority repeatedly turns from *mimicry*–a difference that is almost nothing but not quite–to menace–a difference that is almost total but not quite." See his *The Location of Culture* (London/New York: Routledge, 1994), p. 91.

80 Eduardo Mendieta, "From Christendom to Polycentric Oikumene," in Batstone *et al.* (eds), *Liberation Theologies*, p. 267.

81 Ivone Gebara, *Longing for Running Water: Ecofeminism and Liberation*, trans. David Mollineaux (Minneapolis, MN: Fortress Press, 1999), p. 47.

82 The metaphor of the "universe as the body of God," developed systematically in McFague's important *The Body of God*, derives from Whiteheadian thought. Cf. Charles Hartshorne's *Omnipotence and Other Theological Mistakes* (Albany, NY: SUNY Press, 1984).

83 Gebara, *Longing*, p. 214.

84 ibid., p. 105; my emphasis.

85 ibid., p. 215. The "new creation" is not in other words to descend from on high like John's New Jerusalem, or from the future as an eschatological guarantee.

86 Marcella Althaus-Reid, *Indecent Theology: Theological Perversions in Sex, Gender and Politics* (London and New York: Routledge, 2001), p. 25. "Political and sexual transgressions are the agenda of carnivals, yet the subject of carnivals, the poor, have been obliterated in Liberation Theology." In the decolonizing world, a carnivalesque chaos resists from below the control of any order: on behalf of a genesis. ibid., p. 23.

87 According to Althaus-Reid, Mies differs from Marx "on the grounds that it is not capitalism which alienates the man–woman relation in society but that on the contrary, capitalism is born from and depends on patriarchy." *Indecent Theology*, p. 171. For Althaus-Reid, this is not simply another monocausal explanation "as in a linear, unique and uniform style of production," but it takes place "in a more complex articulation between patriarchy and race, culture, sexual identities and religion."

88 ibid., p. 92.

89 John Wesley, "Upon our Lord's Sermon on the Mount, III," in *Works*, Vol. 1, ed. Albert Cook Outler (Nashville, TN: Abingdon, 1984–5), pp. 516–17. John Cobb offers an invaluable discussion of this panentheistic element in Wesley's understanding of God's relation to the world, showing the breadth of Wesley's emphasis upon the divine immanence in relation to the latter's remarkable interest in the natural science of his day. John B. Cobb, Jr, *Grace & Responsibility: A Wesleyan Theology for Today* (Nashville, TN: Abingdon, 1995), pp. 50ff.

90 The name of a multimedia oratorio by Philip Glass.

2 "FLOODS OF TRUTH": SEX, LOVE AND LOATHING OF THE DEEP

1 Cf. also Isaiah 51.9–11.

2 W. G. Lambert analyzes the parallel between the psalm's dividing of the sea and Marduk's splitting of Tiamat's carcass. He finds "the case for a battle as a prelude to God's dividing of the cosmic waters unproven in the Psalm, and thus in Genesis 1.2." See Lambert, "A New Look at the Babylonian Background of Genesis," in Richard S. Hess and David Toshio Tsumura (eds), *"I Studied Inscriptions from before the Flood": Ancient Near Eastern, Literary and Linguistic Approaches to Genesis 1–11* (Winona Lake, IN: Eisenbrauns, 1994), p. 105.

3 William P. Brown, *Structure, Role and Ideology in the Hebrew and Greek Texts of Genesis 1:1–2,3*, Society of Biblical Literature Dissertation Series 132 (Atlanta, GA: Scholar's Press, 1993), p. 189.

4 Jon Levenson uses Psalm 74 to clearly distinguish between the serene divine supremacy of the *creatio ex nihilo* doctrine and the biblical *chaoskampf*. He reads in this

battle "*no* indication that the monsters whose demise is there memorialized had come into existence through the creative labors of the psalmist's lord." Rather, he finds here "a myth that speaks of God's total mastery not as something self-evident, unthreatened, and extant from all eternity, but as something won, as something dramatic and exciting." Levenson, *Creation and the Persistence of Evil*, p. 8f. For discussion of Levenson's view of the *chaoskampf* vis-à-vis Genesis 1.2, cf. Ch. 6.

5 Beginning with the aptly named *Creation Versus Chaos: The Reinterpretation of Mythical Symbolism in the Bible* (Philadelphia, PA: Fortress Press, 1987), Bernhard W. Anderson espouses the primacy of the *chaoskampf* and thus the hermeneutical tehomophobia. Yet in the latter book other hints and clues begin to surface in response to Psalm 104 itself: citing in a note James Gleich's *Chaos: Making a New Science* (New York: Viking, 1987), he suggests that not just harmony but "something else about this cosmic order may be consonant with the scientist's perception. This marvelous order is 'contingent'–it is constantly threatened by disorder or 'chaos.' The power of the Creator is evident not only in originating but also in maintaining and sustaining the order of creation" (p. 104). Though Anderson is thus content to ignore the playful tenderness of the psalm's invocation of the chaos monster, he makes another important move. He begins to read ecologically, recognizing the delicate interrelations of the earth's "web of life" as threatened by a chaos produced by "our human lifestyle." *From Creation to New Creation: Old Testament Perspectives* (Minneapolis, MN: Fortress Press, 1994), p. 105.

6 So quips Levenson, p. 17.

7 *Abodah Zarah: Hebrew-English Edition of the Babylonian Talmud*, Vol. 23, trans. A. Mishcon (London: Soncino Press, 1988), p. 3b.

8 Too late for incorporation, I discovered a pertinent juxtaposition of these very psalms in Timothy K. Beal's delightful *Religion and Its Monsters* (London: Routledge, 2002), p. 28f. "When it comes to god and monsters, Psalm 74 shares less with the creation theology of orientation expressed in Psalm 104 and more with the chaos battle motifs of other ancient Near Eastern texts."

9 Heinz Pagels, *The Dreams of Reason: The Computer and the Rise of the Sciences of Complexity* (New York: Simon & Shuster, 1988), p. 83.

10 Brevard S. Childs, *Myth and Reality in the Old Testament*, Studies in Biblical Theology No. 27 (London: SCM Press, 1960), p. 33; cf. also Speiser, *Genesis*, in the Anchor Bible, etc. Grammatically one expects the definite article in the Hebrew.

11 Alexander Heidel, *The Babylonian Genesis: A Complete Translation of All the Published Cuneiform Tablets of the Various Babylonian Creation Stories* (Chicago/London: University of Chicago Press, 1951), I.28, p. 19.

12 ibid., I.37–40, p. 19.

13 ibid., I.41–3, p. 19.

14 I thank MDiv student Betsy Scheuermann for this suspicious suggestion.

15 Daniel Boyarin, *Intertextuality and the Reading of Midrash* (Bloomington: Indiana University Press, 1990), p. 94.

16 Bram Dijkstra, *Idols of Perversity: Fantasies of Feminine Evil in Fin-de-Siècle Culture* (Oxford: Oxford University Press, 1986), p. 264.

17 Joseph Le Conte's "scheme for evolutionary development," cited in ibid., p. 265.

18 Eve Ensler, *The Vagina Monologues* (New York: Villard, 1998), p. 27.

19 ibid., p. 28.

20 Mary Daly, *Pure Lust* (Boston, MA: Beacon Press, 1984), p. 305. See also Ruether, *Sexism and God-talk*, p. 85.

21 Cf. Naomi Schor and Elizabeth Weed, *The Essential Difference* (Bloomington: Indiana University Press, 1994), for a definitive rebuttal of the essentializing terms of the feminist critique of feminist essentialism.

22 See the discussion of Gayatri Spivak's "strategic essentialism" in relation to theological constructivism in Serene Jones' lucid theological deconstruction of the feminist binary of "essentialism" vs. "constructivism" in *Feminist Theory and Christian Theology: Cartographies of Grace* (Minneapolis, MN: Fortress Press, 2000).

23 I have argued in *Apocalypse Now and Then* that the apocalypticism of radical feminism can only be reduced to "essentialism" by an *essentializing* gesture–indeed by a kind of apocalyptic repudiation turned against the (m)other. We might read this epic feminist retrieval of the monstrous mother not as feminine essence but as gender parody. (Cf. Mary McClintock Fulkerson's interoperation of Daly and Ruether in *Changing the Subject: Women's Discourses and Feminist Theology* (Minneapolis, MN: Fortress Press, 1994). At any rate, the women of the second wave did not fail to notice the discreet inscription of the defunct Tiamat within the biblical text (Ruether, Daly, Keller . . .). Indeed the Babylonian myth was otherwise long dead, returned to dust and sand, but for its captivity in the second verse of the Bible.

24 Prigogine and Stengers, *Order from Chaos*.

25 Nietzsche's "song of the night": see *Thus Spoke Zarathustra*, "The world is deep . . . Deeper than day had been aware . . . Deep is its woe . . . Joy–deeper yet than agony." F. W. Nietzsche, *The Portable Nietzsche*, trans. Walter Kaufmann (New York: Viking Press, 1963), p. 339.

26 Irigaray, *Elemental Passions*, p. 13.

27 ibid., p. 15.

28 I neither discredit Irigaray's notion of "gender fidelity," nor join the convention of dismissing her for "essentialism." Yet her refusal of any version of "equality" between the sexes on the basis of "gender difference," indeed the call for "different laws" that protect women's distinct needs, can (especially in conjunction with a disappointing preoccupation with the heterosexual couple) if overgeneralized readily subserve a neo-Victorian doctrine of separate spheres. The difference of genders and the multiplications of styles of sexuality within each gender require, as Irigaray argues, the protection of the specific needs of women, especially regarding reproductive and child support laws. "The Female Gender," in *Sexes and Genealogies*, trans. Gillian Gill (New York: Columbia University Press, 1993), p. 123. But I do not think "gender difference" names the target of sexism any more than "gender homogenization." So gender difference becomes meaningless unless it is empowered by *equality* of right. Equality has never meant simply "sameness."

29 Female figures appear, suggests Ellen Armour, at points where traditional religious boundaries are transgressed–such as (of great relevance to the present project) Derrida's khora, or indeed his Augustine, or Irigaray's swing from "differing woman" to divine femininity. Armour thinks "whitefeminism" through "to its ends" by proposing that "a contested woman as a ground for theorizing and theologizing" offers an invaluable coordination of the radical impulses of deconstruction with the project of contesting "the race-gender divide." Ellen T. Armour, *Deconstruction, Feminist Theology, and the Problem of Difference: Subverting the Race/GenderDivide* (Chicago: University of Chicago Press, 1999), p. 182. Working at an altogether different tangent, yet heading toward a deconstructive and racialized reading of the "darkness" of negative theology (Ch. 12), the present "whitefeminist" theology has affinities with her project. Rather than making race/gender its object, it makes both indelibly but unpredictably constitutive of a wider project.

30 With the exception of John K. Ryan, translators of the *Confessions* usually translate "*ex utero*" as "out of his loins" or otherwise occlude Augustine's queer deployment of the older tradition of the Adamic androgyne.

31 Cf. Ilya Prigogine, *The End of Certainty: Time, Chaos, and the New Laws of Nature* (New York: Free Press, 1996).

32 Augustine, *Confessions*, XII.12.14. Unless otherwise noted, the citations from the *Confessions* will be based on John K. Ryan's translation, *The Confessions of St Augustine*. ibid., p. 314.

33 *City of God*; also *De Gen. et Lit.*; cf. Kathryn Greene-McCreight, *Ad Litteram: How Augustine, Calvin, and Barth Read the "Plain Sense" of Genesis 1–3* (New York: Peter Lang, 1999).

34 Augustine, *Confessions*, III.5. Augustine confesses his initial distaste for the crude narratives of scripture: "To me they seemed quite unworthy of comparison with the stately prose of Cicero because I had too much conceit to accept their simplicity and not enough to penetrate their depths." From Augustine, *Confessions*, trans. R. S. Pine-Coffin (Harmondsworth, Mx: Penguin, 1961), p. 60.

35 Daniel Boyarin has laid out Augustine's discursive coupling of Jewish hermeneutics with carnality itself. He opens *Carnal Israel* with Augustine's *Tractatus adversus Judaeos*: "Behold Israel according to the flesh (I Corinthians 10.18). This we know to be the carnal Israel; but the Jews do not grasp this meaning and as a result they prove themselves indisputably carnal." Boyarin dryly comments: "Augustine knew what he was talking about. There was a difference between Jews and Christians that had to do with the body." He proceeds to affirm that corporeality as the basis of rabbinic anthropology and of the "indeterminacy" and "heterogeneity" of midrashic inter-pretation. Daniel Boyarin, *Carnal Israel: Reading Sex in Talmudic Culture* (Berkeley: University of California Press, 1993), pp. 1, 29, 235.

36 Augustine, *Confessions*, XIII.15, p. 345.

37 John Milbank, Catherine Pickstock and Graham Ward (eds), *Radical Orthodoxy* (London/New York: Routledge, 1999), p. 32.

38 Catherine Pickstock, *After Writing: On the Liturgical Consummation of Philosophy* (Oxford: Blackwell, 1998), p. 110. Pickstock articulates the "third alternative" of radical orthodoxy–between a rationalist humanism and (its own) nihilist deconstruction–with care. "While conceding, with postmodernism, the indeterminacy of all our knowledge and experience of selfhood, it construes this shifting flux as a sign of our dependency on a transcendent source which 'gives' all reality as a mystery, rather than as adducing our suspension over the void." ibid., p. xiii. By thus occluding any "third alternative" between mere nothingness and poststructuralist flux, radical orthodoxy captures thea/theological tendency of deconstruction while, I suspect, projecting the "nihil" of the orthodox *ex nihilo* onto every deconstruction of that *creatio*.

39 Milbank *et al.*, *Radical Orthodoxy*, p. 1f.

40 Cf. J. Wentzel van Huyssteen, *The Shaping of Rationality: Toward Interdisciplinarity in Theology and Science* (Grand Rapids, MI: Eerdmans, 1999), for a superb critique of the "cryptofoundationalism" and the "massive and spectacular fideist claim," especially of John Milbank's version of what is now called radical orthodoxy. The critique is especially helpful because in its commitment to the theology/science interdiscipline it also marks itself off carefully from any facile epistemic relativism; cf. pp. 77, 81.

41 Augustine, *Confessions*, XII.26, p. 327.

42 "While every man tries to understand in Holy Scripture what the author understood

therein, what wrong is there if anyone understand what you, O light of all truthful minds, reveal to [the reader] as true, even if the author he reads did not understand this, since [the author] also understood *a truth, though not this truth?*" (Augustine, *Confessions*, XII.18, p. 320). Augustine, I would argue, has discovered the intentional fallacy. He is so impressed by the ambiguity of the first verses of Genesis that he will not pretend to understand the text as its author may have meant it.

43 "For signs are either literal or figurative . . . Figurative signs occur when that thing which we designate by a literal sign is used to signify something else." Augustine, *On Christian Doctrine*, II.16; see *Ante-Nicene Fathers*, Vol. 1, ed. Roberts and Donaldson.

44 Susan A. Handelman, *Slayers of Moses: The Emergence of Rabbinic Interpretation in Modern Literary Theory* (Albany, NY: SUNY Press, 1982), pp. 120, 119. In a remarkable analysis of the suppression of the divine Word through Greek–and then with Augustine through Roman–allegory, Handelman exposes the Greek and Christian "literalization of the fundamental metaphoricity of things," i.e. with Derrida, the paganism that "literalizes the metaphor" (p. 29); she draws out the striking structural affinities between rabbinic interpretation and Jewish (even avowedly secular) thinkers such as Freud, Lacan and Derrida. Yet she strongly affirms the *creatio ex nihilo* by the Word, as anti-platonic.

45 Derrida's classic critique of the "logocentric" tradition and its transcendental signified attempts to liberate the sign from the binary of "signified" and "signifier," inasmuch as that linguistic dichotomy implies the dualism of the intelligible and the sensible, the timeless and the spatiotemporal. While this early deconstruction of "logocentrism" reflects no serious engagement of the Jewish and Christian sources of the "logos" itself, its attempt to free language from a theology repressive of the trace, repressive of the "originary trace" (which means "there is no originary trace"), will prove indispensable to the present *theological* work (cf. Ch. 9). Derrida, *Of Grammatology*, pp. 6–73.

46 Augustine, *Confessions*, XIII.24, pp. 358–9.

47 ibid., p. 359.

48 ibid., XII.27, p. 328.

49 But not if language itself–its *logos*–now writes us once again "out of this world." That is, a careless appeal to poststructuralism runs the risk of a new enclosure within language, a sufficiency of "the text." It acknowledges the existence of some prelinguistic universe, but with a yawn. Derrida himself denounces the misreading of his work as precluding reference to the world. Cf. John Caputo's excellent documentation of this problematic in *The Prayers and Tears of Jacques Derrida: Religion without Religion* (Bloomington: Indiana University Press, 1997).

50 Much of the use as well as the abuse of Derrida ignores his own rigorous relativizations of his own relativism–"the limits of a demystification." Cf. "Of an Apocalyptic Tone Newly Adapted in Philosophy," in Harold Coward and Toby Foshay (eds), *Derrida and Negative Theology*, trans. John P. Leavy (Albany, NY: SUNY Press, 1992), p. 59. Cf. my own fuller methodological engagement with Derrida in "Eyeing the Apocalypse," in Akma Adams (ed.), *Postmodern Interpretations of the Bible–A Reader* (St. Louis, MO: Chalice Press, 2001), p. 253ff.

3 "TEARS OF ACHAMOTH": THE FATHERS' *EX NIHILO*

1 Irenaeus of Lyons, *Against Heresies*, in *The Writings of Irenaeus*, Vol. 1, ed. Alexander Roberts and James Donaldson (Edinburgh: T. & T. Clark, 1868), Book II.3, p. 145.

2 Luce Irigaray, *Marine Lover of Friederich Nietzsche*, trans. Gillian C. Gill (New York: Columbia University Press, 1991), p. 88.

3 May, *Creatio Ex Nihilo*, p. 178.

4 Irenaeus of Lyons, *Against the Heresies*, Vol. I, trans. Dominic J. Unger (Mahwah, NJ: Paulist Press, 1992), Book 1, p. 30.

5 Prigogine and Stengers, *Order out of Chaos*.

6 Burrus, *Begotten Not Made*, p. 58.

7 P. Fredriksen, "Hysteria and the Gnostic Myth of Creation," *Vigiliae Christianae*, 33 (North-Holland Publishing, 1979), pp. 287–90.

8 May, *Creatio Ex Nihilo*, p. viii. May builds upon a growing repudiation of the long-held assumption that Hellenistic-Jewish theology had formulated any strict sense of *creatio ex nihilo*. He claims that it was H. F. Weiss who first definitively undermined this assumption. *Untersuchungen zur Kosmologie des hellenistischen und palaestinischen Judentums* (Berlin: Akademie-Verlag, 1968).

9 This common intertextual retrojection of the *ex nihilo* was touched upon in the last chapter. "There is here no theoretical disquisition on the nature of the creation process, but a paraenetic reference to God's creative power: the mother of the seven martyrs calls her youngest son to steadfastness by holding before his eyes that God, who has shown his might by creating *the world and mankind 'out of non-being,' will, 'in the time of mercy,' awaken the righteous from death.*"

10 Philo "lacks the decisive basis of the doctrine of the *creatio ex nihilo*, that the biblical conception of God demands that matter also be created" (May, *Creatio Ex Nihilo*, pp. 11, 15).

11 The "second god as personified word or wisdom of God," as *memra* or Sophia, suggests that Logos theology was not the distinguishing mark of Johannine Christianity, but rather situates the author of the fourth gospel among Jews producing versions of Logos theology. Daniel Boyarin, "The Gospel of the Memra: Jewish Binitarianism and the Advent of the Logos; or, Sophia's Choice," Drew Transdisciplinary Theological Colloquium paper (September 2001) (prospective title of collection of papers "Countercreations"), p. 18. Several papers prepared for this symposium enter into the final version of the present chapter.

12 Rudolf Bultmann, *The Gospel of John: A Commentary*, trans. G. R. Beasley-Murray, (Oxford: Blackwell, 1971), p. 38.

13 Romans 4.17, where God "calls into being the things that are not"; and Hebrews 11.13, where "the visible came forth from the invisible."

14 Boyarin, "Gospel of the Memra"; May, *Creatio Ex Nihilo*, p. 126.

15 Justin, *Apol.* I.59.1–5; May refutes the assertion that Justin as a Christian "naturally took it for granted that matter was created by God." *Creatio Ex Nihilo*, p. 122.

16 "The discomfort and ambiguity for Christians and critics alike therefore lies in this hybrid vision of philosophical Christianity." In her persuasive postcolonial reading of Justin, Lyman relates this mimicry to the "not quite not white" of Homi Bhabha's "mimic man." The unsettling power of Justin's "mimicry" of Hellenism while describing Christianity as a transcendent philosophy–almost the same, but not quite–is further reflected in his description of dissent as "heresy." Rebecca Lyman, "The Politics of Passing," Drew Transdisciplinary Theological Colloquium paper (September 2001) ("Countercreations"), p. 16.

17 May, *Creatio Ex Nihilo*, p 150.

18 Marcionite dualism would represent only an aberrant form, rejected by the monistic

mainstream of gnosticism and in current scholarship not even consistently labeled a "gnostic"–in which the preexistent matter was construed as essentially evil.

19 In a recent theological analysis of the problem of evil, viz. *creatio ex nihilo*, drawing on many of the same sources as the present analysis, David Griffin writes: "Thanks to Marcion . . . the idea of uncreated matter became subject to guilt by association, with the result that Christian theologians began attacking the idea of uncreated matter as such." "Creation out of Nothing, Creation out of Chaos, and the Problem of Evil," in *Encountering Evil: Live Options in Theodicy*, 2nd edn, ed. Davis, pp. 108–25 (p. 112).

20 May, *Creatio Ex Nihilo*, p. 148.

21 ibid., p. 179.

22 May is quick to emphasize that this "idiosyncratic creation doctrine of Basilides remained without historical effect;" and that unlike the church emphasis upon divine providential omnipotence, the gnostic form of the *ex nihilo*–Basilides' concept of the creation of a world-seed by the "nonexistent God" the "ineffable ground of all being"–"amounts to a compromise with the doctrine of world creation" (p. 84).

23 Only Tertullian's work against Hermogenes, *Adversus Hermogenem*, is extant. *The Treatise Against Hermogenes*, trans J. H. Waszink (Westminster: Newman Press; London: Longman, Green, 1956).

24 ibid., p. 73.

25 By the same token, the creation from preexistent matter could, in the eccentric Marcionite twist, serve an ever more dualistic grid. "In some gnostic outlines an unformed material principle, sometimes chaos or darkness, is postulated, which in one way or another has a part in the world's origin. But most gnostic theologians are engaged in striving to avoid a dualism of principles." May, *Creatio Ex Nihilo*, p. 40.

26 Tertullian, *Against Hermogenes*, p. 146f.

27 Griffin, "Creation out of Nothing, Creation out of Chaos, and the Problem of Evil," in *Encountering Evil*, ed. Davis, p. 114. For a definitive explication of the problem of theodicy, cf. David Griffin, *God, Power and Evil: A Process Theodicy* (Philadelphia, PA: Westminster Press, 1976).

28 Tertullian, *Against Hermogenes*, p. 85.

29 Irenaeus, *Against the Heresies*, ed. Unger, p. 22; my emphasis.

30 "Arguably, Irenaeus is one of the inventors of heresy, building on Justin's scheme–by gathering all 'other' doctrines under one label of 'heresy' he *produces* the hybrid monster." Personal correspondence, Virginia Burrus.

31 Irenaeus, *Ante-Nicene Christian Library: Translations of the Writings of the Fathers*, ed. Alexander Roberts, Vol. 1 (Edinburgh: T. & T. Clark, 1868), I.31.4, p. 115. Unless otherwise noted, I will henceforth use the Roberts edition.

32 Burrus correspondence.

33 H. von Campenhausen, *Die Enstehung der christlichen Bibel* (Tübingen: Mohr, 1968), pp. 213–44. Augustine would count as the inventor of the Christian *philosophy* of time and history.

34 May, *Creatio Ex Nihilo*, p. 174.

35 H. Paul Santmire, *The Travail of Nature: The Ambiguous Ecological Promise of Christian Theology* (Philadelphia, PA: Fortress Press, 1985), p. 43.

36 Cf. Karl Loewith, *Meaning in History* (Chicago: University of Chicago Press, 1957); also Keller, *Apocalypse Now and Then*.

37 May, *Creatio Ex Nihilo*, p. 164

38 Irenaeus, *Against Heresies*, II.12.3 (p. 155).

39 ibid., Vol. II, Preface (p. 117).

40 "Isn't the anti-depth above all the fear of the 'dirty' gap, full of traces and matters, something that refuses to be the clean *ex-nihilo* void? The abjected depth is a deep which differentiates itself. The strange thing one notices about the sea in Iceland is that the brown/green-dreggy seas are often the most fertile ones (I know that polluted waters are different!). Green and brown opaque waters are full of fish and their food, with the fertile mixture of the warm, tropical sea which has traveled from the Gulf of Mexico and the cold Arctic sea. The clear seas are dead. Haraway's 'dirty ontology' always reminds me of this. The tradition sometimes allows depths in the Godhead but all depths have to be clean of mud and materiality." Sigridur Gudmarsdottir, Lutheran minister and Drew PhD student, in personal correspondence.

41 Irenaeus, *Against Heresies*, II.12.1 (p. 147).

42 ibid., II.13.5 (p. 156). If Irenaeus reads the gnostic allegorical names (like Depth, Grace or Silence, consort of Buthus when it is Father; Mind, Truth, Word, Church, etc.) as though they correspond to literal entities, it is not out of literary naivety– "many parables and allegories have been spoken and can be made to mean many things." *Against the Heresies*, ed. Unger, p. 29f.

43 "and should be contained by no one." Irenaeus, *Against Heresies*, II.1.1 (p. 117).

44 Kathryn Tanner's contextualization of Irenaeus is illumining in this regard; I quote at length since I agree with her analysis, even as I move in another direction: "With Irenaeus, we see something like what I've suggested could be gotten out of Plotinus– the sense that Hellenistic ideas about God's radical transcendence suggest something that most Hellenistic philosophers don't realize–that God is intimately involved with everything. Irenaeus takes Gnostic ideas about divinity as a pleroma–a fullness without limit, the all, what contains everything without itself being contained . . . and argues that they do not suggest what the Gnostics assert–that the first God has nothing very directly to do with this world, that the first God is far off at a distance, that we must escape this world . . . in order to return to that first principle. The argument here is rather simple. If God is this unlimited fullness then nothing really exists outside its direct field of influence and concern, as the Gnostics assume." Kathryn Tanner, "Creation as Mixed Metaphor," Drew Transdisciplinary Theological Colloquium paper (September 2001) ("Countercreations"), p. 10.

45 "Expressed primarily in metaphors of desiring, love-making, and giving birth, Gnostic theological language has sensuous qualities that are striking. This did not escape Irenaeus, who at one point chooses to ridicule Valentinus' sexual vision of making with an equally organic and sensuous language, not from the human but from the vegetative world, envisioning fruit visible, eatable, and delicious." II.5.109. Patricia Cox Miller, *The Poetry of Thought in Late Antiquity: Essays in Imagination and Religion* (Aldershot, Hants: Ashgate, 2001), p. 111f.

46 Irenaeus, *Against Heresies*, II.10.3 (p. 145).

47 ibid., II.11.1 (p. 146).

48 Yet as Kathryn Tanner argues, "the practical resonances of these radicalized claims about God's transcendence and creative agency need have very little to do, therefore, with support for a principle of coercive domination." Irenaeus' intention is to demonstrate God's unobstructed and immediate relation to all things: "God is the measureless context and source for everything; everything is in God's territory, as Irenaeus puts it." "Creation as Mixed Metaphor," p. 10f. I am, however, reading more from the perspective of the continuing effects of this imaginary rather than that of its

formal potentiality, for which the metaphors, affects and effects of the text become incidental. Tanner has systematically developed the case elsewhere for the liberating potentiality of radical transcendence claims. Kathryn Tanner, *The Politics of God: Christian Theologies and Social Justice* (Minneapolis, MN: Fortress Press, 1992).

49 Irenaeus, *Against Heresies*, II.34.4, as cited in May, *Creatio Ex Nihilo*, p. 124.

50 May cites favorably Langerbeck's approval of Irenaeus' transmutation of the Hebrew metaphors with "voluntaristic" traits. *Creatio Ex Nihilo*, p. 174.

51 Julia Kristeva, *Powers of Horror: An Essay on Abjection*, trans. Leon S. Roudiez (New York: Columbia University Press, 1982), p. 12

52 Irenaeus, *Against Heresies*, I.13.2 (p. 51), I.13.6 (p. 54).

53 ibid., I.13.3 (p. 52), I.13.5 (p. 55).

54 This "silliness" becomes a veritable theme of conservative Christians: cf. "Silly Women of the Apocalypse," focussing on the rise of US fundamentalist discourse, in Keller, *Apocalypse Now and Then*, pp. 224ff.

55 Kristeva, *Powers of Horror*, pp. 4, 210, 10. Kristeva draws a profound relation between abjection and the sacred, and specifically emphasizes this abject field of horror as the "ultimate coding of our crises, of our most intimate and most serious apocalypses. Hence its nocturnal power, 'the great darkness' (Angela of Foligno)." We will later consider the mystical darkness in the "light" of tehomophobia. But of present interest is the intensity of the apocalypse paradigm in Irenaeus' salvation history; he precedes the repression of apocalyptic temporality in favor of the Augustinian theology of history. "Such codes are abjection's purification and repression. But the return of their repressed makes up our 'apocalypse,' and that is why we cannot escape the dramatic convulsions of religious crises" (p. 208f.). (As I write, the apocalypses of Christianity, Judaism and Islam are in high dudgeon.)

56 Irenaeus, *Against Heresies*, V.18.3 (p. 105).

57 ibid., V.19.1 (p. 106).

58 Chaos mathematics often uses biological trees as test cases of its post-Euclidean approximations of nature's asymmetries.

59 John Briggs and F. David Peat, *Turbulent Mirror: An Illustrated Guide to Chaos Theory and the Science of Wholeness* (New York: Harper & Row, 1989), p. 145 on Prigogine; my emphasis.

60 Irenaeus, *Against Heresies*, V:33.3.

61 Santmire, *Travail of Nature*, p. 44.

62 Irigaray, *Forgetting of Air*, p. 178.

63 Athanasius, *On the Incarnation (De Incarnatione Verbi Dei). Nicene and PostNicene Fathers of the Christian Church*, Vol. IV, ed. and trans. Philip Schaff and Henry Wace (Grand Rapids, MI: Eerdmans, 1980), II.3.4.

64 Cf. Cox Miller, *Poetry of Thought*.

65 New Oxford RSV.

66 R. P. C. Hanson, *Search for the Christian Doctrine of God* (Edinburgh: T. & T. Clark, 1988), p. 831; Barth as we shall see will bewail Genesis 1.2 a millennium and a half later as a *crux interpretum* (III.1.41; p. 102), requiring exegetical extreme measures (cf. Ch. 5).

67 Burrus, *Begotten Not Made*, p. 44.

68 Derrida, *Of Grammatology*, p. 71. In the context of patristic hermeneutics, in which the creation is always read in the "light" of the prologue of the Gospel of John, Derrida's binaristic privilege of a "pure writing" vs. "logocentric" orality, as reflecting the platonism of the sensible vs. the intelligible and the signifier vs. the signified, the stages

in the Hellenization of the biblical, already Hellenistic/Jewish and Christian logos, admits of no straightforward deployment.

69 Athanasius, *De Incarnatione*, IV.6.
70 ibid., III.3.
71 Burrus, *Begotten*, p. 44.
72 Athanasius, *De Incarnatione*, VI.1–3.
73 ibid., VII.1.
74 Derrida, *Of Grammatology*, p. 71.
75 Burrus, *Begotten*, p. 37.
76 ibid., p. 39.
77 ibid., p. 55.
78 Cited in Althaus-Reid, *Indecent Theology*, p. 87.
79 Athanasius, *De Incarnatione*, IV.5.
80 Judith Butler, *Gender Trouble: Feminism and the Subversion of Identity* (New York/London: Routledge, 1990), p. 3.
81 David Brakke, *Athanasius and the Politics of Asceticism*, Oxford Early Christian Studies (Oxford: Clarendon Press, 1995), p. 168.
82 In this crucial contribution to a counternarrative of creation, Althaus-Reid elaborates: "This Spermatogenesis is the creation of discourses of rationality in the testes (testicles; the place of the divine testimony) of God. From God's testicles, as his divine witnesses, we find a process of auto-dissemination of the Word from which women in Christianity have been excluded." Therefore, she continues, citing Christine Battersby, *Gender and Genius: Towards a Feminist Aesthetics* (London: Women's Press, 1989), p. 50: "God the Father is the scribe of his lonely creational pleasures, for His is the pen/is, the power and the glory." Althaus-Reid, *Indecent Theology*, p. 54.
83 Athanasius, *Christology of the Later Fathers*, Library of Christian Classics, Vol. III, ed. E. R. Hardy (Philadelphia, PA: Westminster Press, 1954), p. 70f; my emphasis.
84 "Simple location" is an instance of the famous "fallacy of misplaced concreteness," whereby an abstraction dissociable from its relations is mistaken for an actuality. Alfred North Whitehead, *Science and the Modern World: Lowell Lectures, 1925* (New York: Free Press, 1967[1925]), pp. 49–51.
85 Athanasius, *Christology*, p. 71.

4 "MOTHER MOST DEAR": AUGUSTINE'S DARK SECRETS

1 Morton, *Journey*, p. 128.
2 Augustine, *Confessions*, XI.2.278.
3 ibid., VII.5.162.
4 Keller, *Apocalypse Now and Then*, p. 28, argues of the *City of God* that its "reduction of all things creaturely to means to the timeless End secures the Western disconnection of spirit from the time rhythms of the earth." I found in this a "sublimation of apocalypse," an "anti-apocalypse precisely as a form of apocalypse;" ibid., p. 102. While I want to maintain a strong distinction between the temporality and sensibility of the *Confessions* and those of the later Augustine, the sublimation as opposed to mere repression of the chaos of beginnings poses a meaningful analogy to the sublimation of the end.
5 Virginia Burrus and I wrote an essay on Augustine: Burrus and Keller, "Confessing Monica," in *Feminist Interpretations of Augustine*, ed. Judith Chelius Stark (Philadelphia, PA: Pennsylvania State University Press, forthcoming).

6 Margaret Miles is disappointed by the transition: "The last books of the *Confessions* are, to me, profoundly sad." In the stylistic shift from autobiography to philosophical and theological essay, she finds expressed a change in Augustine himself. He has become "the converted, institutionalized Augustine," orderly and eager to distance himself from the earlier "chaotic, painful vivid life." This is an invaluable insight into the transition to his later, dominological writings. Yet while she finds herself therefore "less pleasured," I have perversely found great pleasure in tracing the drops of pain and chaos into their cosmological form–perhaps because, unlike Miles, I read his sophialogical quest in contrast to the prohibitive paternalism of the earlier *ex nihilo* arguments; and because I am hooked on the pleasures of theory. Moreover they leave a trail–admittedly more theological–by which we may reconsider the doctrine itself. Margaret Miles, *Desire and Delight: Reading of Augustine's Confessions* (New York: Crossroad, 1992), pp. 126, 130.
7 *Confessions*, III.4; as cited in Burrus/Keller.
8 Morton, *Journey*, p. 128.
9 ibid.; my emphasis.
10 ibid., p. 127.
11 ibid., p. 129.
12 Yet the improvised grammar of "hearing us to speech" became part of the feminist 1980s lexicon; in the search for a logos that would not silence women, Nelle (the life, the friend, the text) was a mentor for me and many, potent in her rough-hewn clarity, her "up from down under" theology reverberating with Black and global liberation. Whatever and however I write depends upon a context transformed by her work: my home institution had been her final one, hangs her portrait and story amidst those of its professing patriarchs, sustains a colorful theological faculty equally comprised of men and women; as to the larger con/text, the critique of the theistic metaphors of masculine privilege (which she was first to teach a course on) opened the floodgates of a theological reformation or transfiguration, which many still decry or ignore–as chaos.
13 Indeed such historical–literal–inscriptions would in his allegorical reading strategy soon count as superficial (literal and Jewish).
14 Hannah Arendt put it thus in her early work on Augustine: "For the more he withdrew into himself and gathered his self from the dispersion and distraction of the world, the more he 'became a question to himself.'" His retreat from the superficial beauties of the creation affords "by no means a simple withdrawal into himself that Augustine opposes to the loss of self in dispersion," but rather "a turning about of the question itself." Hannah Arendt, *Love and Saint Augustine*, ed. (with an interpretive essay) Joanna Vecchiarelli Scoot and Judith Chelius Stark (Chicago: Chicago University Press, 1996), p. 24f. By the fourth and fifth centuries, it was understood that only a few ascetics could become the "great individuals," according to Peter Brown, who face down their own temptations full-time: for the Christians of that time "the power that came from contact with the supernatural was not for everyone to use." This does not make the ascetic personality any less social in *effect*. On the contrary it erects a ladder of social relations that reaches to heaven. This hierarchy became all the more pronounced, according to Peter Brown (see n. 16), as cultural life focussed ever more on the ideal of the great spiritual individual. Augustine inherited almost three centuries of this Stoic and ascetic individualization of spirit. Ascetic interiority, structuring the psyche on the model of hermit and monastery, offered a salutary retreat and a formidable strategy

amidst the multicultural pressures of late antiquity. Athanasius had performed the imago of the holy man, as saint or bishop, playing a daunting mediatorial role–nigh unto that of the Son of God–between the sundered dimensions of the divine and the human. The *ex nihilo* at once stabilized the split and eschatologically overcame it. As Brown continues, "the prolonged 'labors' and the crushing sense of sin that characterized the ascetic life condensed, in the persons of the new ascetic heroes, the privileges and the heavy burdens of an exceptional class of human beings." Before Augustine, a "new spiritual elite of 'friends of God'" had crystallized, to be celebrated by the whole culture.

15 "The Christian bishop, the Christian 'holy man,' the physical remains of the Christian martyr stand out all the more clearly because the upward ceiling of human contact with the divine has come to be drawn more firmly." See Peter Robert Lamont Brown, *The Making of Late Antiquity* (Cambridge, MA: Harvard University Press, 1978), p. 98. Parts of the argument of this chapter were developed in tandem with the jointly written essay: Burrus and Keller, "Confessing Monica."

16 Burrus and Keller, ibid.

17 In the late antique context "friendship" would surely refer to homoerotic bonds. Does Augustine's horror at the "twisted and intricate mass of knots" of his own youthful experimentation suggest that not only the intensity but also the complexity of his own sexuality fuel the force of his self-repudiation? Foucault was writing in anticipation of a project he did not complete. Fragments from his 1980 lectures are cited in Jeremy R. Carrette (ed.), *Michel Foucault, Religion and Culture* (New York: Routledge, 1999), p. 45. This reading of the constitution of the subject continues Foucault's counter-psychoanalytic argument, that desire is not repressed but remade: hence perhaps the attraction, tinged by titillation, of the *Confessions*. Cf. Foucault's last volume of *History of Sexuality*, including his study of eighteenth-century confessional literature. Foucault intended to treat "the role played by hermeneutics and the purifying process of deciphering desire. Divine law, not pagan self-mastery, is the new mode of subjection [*mode d'assujettissement*]." Though Foucault had little to say about Augustine's particular contribution (focussing rather on John Cassian), his hints help to decode the hermeneutical moment of the *Confessions*. In Christian asceticism he seems to recognize the classical antecedent of the internalizing gesture.

18 Burrus and Keller, "Confessing Monica."

19 Andrew P. Morrison, shame theorist, *The Culture of Shame* (New York: Ballantine Books, 1996), p. 13; my emphasis. Shame is an "emotional display of a hidden civil war"; Thandeka, *Learning to be White* (New York: Continuum, 1999), p. 12.

20 Thandeka is the Swahili for "lovable," and was offered her by Bishop Tutu in the 1970s.

21 Thandeka, *Learning to be White*, p. 118.

22 Thandeka concludes that "the shame theology Augustine bequeathed to the Christian West is a doctrine that had made peace with a Roman world of pervasive human suffering framed by a profound sense of personal alienation." ibid., p. 119.

23 It is structured strictly in terms of subjugation: of subjects to emperors, slaves to masters, wives to husbands, and children to parents. Peter Brown, *The Body and Society: Men, Women and Sexual Renunciation in Early Christianity* (New York: Columbia University Press, 1988), pp. 416ff.

24 In the Augustinian establishment of a God who effects unaided all meaningful change, ethical agency freezes. Already in *Confessions* agency compresses into an exhibition of interiority; its contagious fascination with the concupiscent ordinariness of sin only

enmeshes it further in self. So the capacious labyrinths of the African bishop's mind do not allay the suspicion that the theology of shame historically provides little resistance to injustice. More grossly, its tradition actively effects dynamics of projection that, for instance, in the United States construct some as "white" by painting others as "black." The latter not coincidentally appear subject to their own unruly, irrational sensuality, to their "dark and fluid" natures. Ignoring the irony (which would also have been meaningless to Augustine) of his African provenance, *Learning to be White* exposes Augustinian "processes of self-alienation" effectuating racial injustice continents and millennia later. Where and when a tehomic theology uncomfortably finds itself.

25 I would not agree with an account of the *massa perdita*, the Augustinian "lump of perdition," as individualistic. The very originality of the concept means to account for the collective and historical character of the disease, which precisely because of its structural, transgenerational dynamics cannot be mastered by heroic, even ascetic, purity. However, without lumping Augustine's own writing together with its individualistic modern effects, we must agree that the symbol of Adam's sin–in which we are all blameworthy but irresponsible whereas it should have functioned to free us from individual blame for that which deforms us but hold us responsible for our lives nonetheless–functioned as Thandeka suggests, not to make us responsible but to make us unlovable. It legitimated a privatized relationship to God and to difference, which would issue in the modernity of a shamed self and its political dissociations.

26 Cited in Thandeka, *Learning to be White*, p. 108.

27 Irigaray, *Speculum*, p. 318.

28 Augustine, *Confessions*, IX.12, trans. Pine-Coffin, p. 201.

29 ibid., *Confessions*, VIII.12, trans. Pine-Coffin, p. 177.

30 The viscerality of the imagery offers a perfect illustration of Whitehead's "withness of the *body*" (*Process and Reality*, p. 64), indeed of the causal efficacy that he describes as a dark, obscure, visceral prehension, not the "vivid presentation" of "presentational immediacy," i.e. sense perception.

31 "When Augustine represents himself sneaking away from mom on a ship for Rome like Aeneas leaving Dido, this is scarcely I think intended as solely or even primarily a critique of his own behavior–his ambivalent (subversive) inhabiting of classical historiography here as ever conveys a complex message! Unlike Dido she will follow him to Italy, unlike Aeneas he will return to Africa (but without her, crucially). And yet . . . her 'influence' is like a series of near disasters that nonetheless turn out for the best–her refusal to baptize him eventually allows him to claim baptism as his own, her embarrassingly vulgar Christianity leads him, via Ambrose, to the sublimities of platonism, her ambitious arranging of his marriage allows him to find his way to the ascetic life . . . As a child she is a drunkard, her virtue is won in the school of hard-knocks–Augustine's description of her is bizarrely non-encomiastic." Letter from Virginia Burrus, 29 December 2000.

32 Monica not surprisingly had helped to produce her son's shame (laughing, for instance, when he came home in torment from beatings he describes as torture at the hands of teachers; *Confessions*, I.9). Yet he traces sympathetically her own humiliating childhood and marriage. Of course her ability to remain subject to an abusive husband, finally bringing him to conversion, makes her a saint in her son's eyes. Augustine admires her for her submission but also for her courage–and for the protection and the alternative she afforded him. Feminist theology has not and will not come to a simplistic condemnation of Augustine's dominative patriarchy. It lacks the misogynist edge.

33 Cf. John K. Ryan's note of translation in *The Confessions of Augustine*, p. 413.

34 Which we hear of in the words of the psalm: "The heaven of heaven is the Lord's." His "heaven of heaven" is merely a Vulgate Latin translation of the psalmic trope for the "sky as the Lord's."

35 "Out of nothing have they been made by you, not out of yourself, not out of anything not your own, or which previously existed, but out of concreated matter, that is, out of matter simultaneously created by you, since without any intervening time you gave form to its formlessness" (*Confessions*, XIII.33).

36 "God called the firmament Heaven" (Genesis 1.8).

37 He is not the first to work the layers and levels of materialization: the Plotinian philosophical framework highlights the transition from formlessness to form, from potentiality to actuality. Whether or not theologians had gotten on the *ex nihilo* bandwagon, they often understood the biblical chaos as a first stage, a formless matter waiting to be formed. Once the logic of *ex nihilo* had prevailed, it made sense to read the God of Genesis as God creating this "unformed matter" to be the material out of which he would then press the universe. The mainstream tendency by the late second century was to repress it.

38 Cf. Augustine's *transitus* to Whitehead on "transition" between "actual entities" as the prehensions within the chaotic plenum of relations, whereby the past turns into potentiality for the immediate future—not a horror, but certainly a third way neither nothing nor something in terms of substance metaphysics. This is the "fluency whereby the perishing of the process, on the completion of the particular existent, constitutes that existent as an original element in the constitutions of other particular existents elicited by repetitions of process. This kind I have called 'transition.'" Whitehead, *Process and Reality*, p. 210.

39 "This formlessness, this earth invisible and without form, is not numbered among the days. Where there is no form, no order, nothing comes or passes away."

40 Formed "from the very beginning;" while its earth is "invisible and without form." (So the argument from formlessness, which he needs in order to establish this pure and invisible potentiality that distinguishes the first heaven, cancels itself out. He also wants the reader to understand—though he can't quite bring himself to say it, so badly does it jumble the signifiers—that the material sky—the second "heaven"—is derived from the "earth" of "heaven and earth," not from its heaven.)

41 Augustine, *Confessions*, XII.15, trans. Pine-Coffin.

42 Eugene Rogers notes of this passage "that Augustine did not have to have read Freud to mix the yearnings of the spouse and the child that the Bible refuses to separate." While Rogers does not make an explicit link to the confessed homoerotic passion of Augustine's youthful "body," this proposition seems pertinent to its textualization: "Thus Christians have been free with erotic and romantic metaphors, and the eschatology that marries Christians foremost to God before each other could lead to the greatest romantic freedom of expression even, or especially, in such celibates as Augustine." Eugene F. Rogers, Jr, *Sexuality and the Christian Body: Their Way into the Triune God*, Challenges in Contemporary Theology Series (Oxford: Blackwell, 1999), p. 223.

43 Augustine seems intentionally to eroticize the austere Lady Wisdom rather than to summon the intertextual convention of allegorizing the eroticism of the Song of Songs. For a delicious investigation of "The Song of Songs in the History of Sexuality," see Stephen D. Moore, *God's Beauty Parlor: and Other Queer Spaces in and around the Bible* (Stanford, CA: Stanford University Press, 2001), pp. 21–89.

44 The "heaven of heavens" as mother/spouse or upper waters is thus distinguished from the sky, "which was later created between the waters above and the waters below."

45 Irigaray, citing Plotinus in *Speculum*, pp. 168–79.

46 Thandeka on Augustine's theology of shame and its social consequences, *Learning to be White*, pp. 119–21. A paraphragm is a parapet, or outer raised bank. Irigaray, *Speculum*, p. 351.

47 Cf. Marion Grau's ground-breaking analysis of "the hysteric economic male," illumined by her exegesis of "the composite figure of the Rich Young Man/homo economicus," in "Business as Un-usual," in Jon Berquist (ed.), *Strike Terror No More: Theology, Ethics, and the New War* (St. Louis, MO: Chalice, 2002), pp. 24ff.

48 Jean-François Lyotard, *The Confession of Augustine* (Stanford, CA: Stanford University Press), p. 12.

49 Augustine, *Confessions*, VII.5, trans. Pine-Coffin.

50 We must later return to the rare trope of what John of Damascus would call "the ocean of Godhead" (see Chapter 13). For we must ask a question that Augustine and the entire *ex nihilo* tradition was unwilling to pose: if the primordial ocean of Genesis 1.2 signifies the in-finite "stuff" of which the creation materializes, what is its relation to the infinite ocean of deity?

51 See "the fallacy of simple location" in Alfred North Whitehead, *Science and the Modern World: Lowell Lectures, 1925* (New York: Free Press, 1967), a form of "his fallacy of a misplaced concreteness" (Ch. 3).

52 Lyotard, *Confession of Augustine*, p. 10. ". . . what would cut into the latter body, a plane for example, which indeed separates two regions of space, loses this property when inserted into four-dimensional space. Its function becomes that of a line in ours or that of a point in a plane, either of which cut nothing." ibid., pp. 10–11.

53 "Ill, therefore, for themselves do some interpret, saying that by imposition of hands they receive the Holy Ghost and are received into the church": Augustine in *Nicene and PostNicene Fathers*, Vol. I, *On Baptism, vs the Donatists*, XXII.18.

54 Suzanne Seger, unpublished journal, December 1999.

55 Arendt wrote her dissertation on Augustine, *Love and Saint Augustine*, in 1929, and revised it in the 1960s, in the light of her experience, as a German Jew, of the Second World War and its aftermath. Only recently is her Augustinian beginning being taken seriously by those who admire her political philosophy. The recent corrected and revised translation, ed. Scott and Stark, incorporates her later revisions and makes this theological material accessible.

56 Arendt, *Love and Saint Augustine*, p. 147.

57 Hannah Arendt, *The Origins of Totalitarianism* (San Diego: Harcourt Brace, 1979), p. 479 citing *The City of God* (XII.20).

58 Such a politics of free beginnings will have nothing to do with a so-called pro-life politics, no more than it romanticizes the biology or sociality of birth.

59 "These speculations about everlasting Being and the universe are Platonic in origin . . . And the problem of a beginning of the universe, which becomes so perplexing in Augustine, who knows of a definite beginning through the Creator, had been troubling this tradition from its very start." And more pressingly, Augustine's difference from Plato lets Arendt articulate her difference from Heidegger. Arendt, *Love and Saint Augustine*, p. 170.

5 "STERILE WATERS": BARTH'S NOTHINGNESS THAT IS

1 Barth, *Church Dogmatics*, ed. Bromiley and Torrance, III.1.

2 ibid., III.1.106f. Barth here warns against the dark poetry of Novalis, who "proclaimed in inspired language that night is the special friend of man: 'Hast thou too, Dark night, A human heart? What dost thou wrap, Beneath thy mantle, That stirs my soul, with a mighty power unseen?'"

3 Foremost among the poststructuralist Barthians would be: Walter Lowe, *Theology and Difference: The Wound of Reason* (Bloomington: Indiana University Press, 1993); Graham Ward, *Barth, Derrida and the Language of Theology* (Cambridge: Cambridge University Press, 1995); Joerg Rieger, *God and the Excluded: Visions and Blindspots in Contemporary Theology* (Minneapolis, MN: Augsburg Press/Fortress Press, 2001); Isolde Andrews, *Deconstructing Barth: A Study of the Complementary Methods in Karl Barth and Jacques Derrida* (Frankfurt am Main: Peter Lang, 1996); Chris Boesel, *Respecting Difference, Risking Proclamation: Faith, Responsibility and the Tragic Dimensions of Overcoming Supersessionism*, unpublished dissertation, Emory University, 2002.

4 Lowe, *Theology and Difference*, p. 143.

5 cited in ibid., p. 41f.

6 For an incisive, indeed ultimately Christological, critique of the Dionysian/Nietzschean ecstasy cf. Irigaray, *Marine Lover of Friedrich Nietzsche*; cf. also Mary Daly's classic feminist polemic against the Dionysianism of the counterculture, *Gyn/Ecology: the Metaethics of Radical Feminism*, with a New Intergalactic Introduction by the author (Boston, MA: Beacon Press, 1990), pp. 64–5.

7 Serene Jones, "This God which is not One," in C.W. Maggie Kim *et al.* (eds), *Transfigurations: Theology & the French Feminists* (Minneapolis, MN: Augsburg Press/Fortress Press, 1993), p. 130.

8 ibid., p. 132.

9 Susanne Selinger, *Charlotte von Kirschbaum and Karl Barth: A Study in Biography and the History of Theology* (University Park: Pennsylvania State University Press, 1998), p. 132f.

10 For Barth the tension between revelation and veiling, between affirmation and negation, remains lively: "knowing God, we necessarily know His hiddenness" (*Church Dogmatics*, II.1.184/206). Ward reads Barth's combination of "positivist rhetoric and a transcendental epistemology for an apophatic end" as evidence of Barth's "anticipation of all the questions." It lies "in the fact that this negative moment becomes a positive one." Ward, *Barth, Derrida and the Language of Theology*, p. 24. However, I note that the apophatic tradition precisely does not thus cash negations into assertions.

11 Odd how in the attempt to bust modern anthropocentrism, a crass instrumentalism in relation to the creation–an exteriorization performed in purely anthropomorphic terms–takes place. Hence the Barthian Moltmann's ecological critique of Barth's notion of nature as theater is especially valuable; cf. Moltmann, *God in Creation*, pp. 61–2. Barth used Calvin's metaphor of the world as *theatrum gloriae Dei*. Moltmann following Ian Barbour (*God in Creation*, p. 330n), could only accept the metaphor of the stage if "the theatre itself is a part of the play that is being performed. It is impossible if the theatre is declared to be merely the 'setting and background' for the drama" (ibid., p. 62).

12 The "analogy of faith," drawn from Paul's letter to the Romans (*analogian tes pisteos'* [12.6]), becomes in Barth the theological epistemology which relates our words to The Word. For the human ("man") cannot derive from "himself" the knowledge of the

Word, which alone is in fact "true man": it "is not man as such, and not even Christian man, but Jesus Christ, the incarnate Son of the Father, revealed in his cross and resurrection, who is the truth and life of man–the real [*wirkliche*] man, to whom we have to keep if we do not want to speak meaninglessly and futilely" (*Church Dogmatics*, II.1.153/171); cf. also Ward's illuminating discussion, *Barth, Derrida and the Language of Theology*, p.13ff.

13 Cf. Barth, *Church Dogmatics*, III.2.256f., on communication in the mode of I/Thou as "penetration from the sphere of the one into the sphere of the other being": indeed this "intercourse" is defined as unilateral, though it hopes for reciprocity and reception: "Why I cannot be silent but am required to speak is that I necessarily abandon him and leave him to his own devices if I spare myself what is perhaps the thankless venture, and him the unwelcome penetration of his sphere . . . I cannot withhold it, because he encounters me as a man."

14 The "individual being" (again, the trinity, rich in its perichoretic imagery, demon-strates the relationality which attracts many to Barth, but does not alleviate the problem). Having subjugated creation to Christology, as surely as the Old to the New Testament and as Creation to Creator, Barth also adds some surprising rhetoric (sur-prising because of Barth's indisputable leadership in theological resistance to the Third Reich) about "the characteristic Jewish perversion" (*Church Dogmatics*, III.1.46) and "the Jewish element" (in a number of non-Jewish as well as Jewish thinkers, including Troeltsch, all guilty of reading the creation as a process of deification or theosis) (ibid., III.1.47).

15 Barth reads critically but intensively the contemporary existential texts of nothingness, especially those of Sartre and Heidegger (ibid., III.3.334–48).

16 This gender derision calls to mind Lacan's identification of "our God Logos" as the ultimate phallic signifier. Only the male-on-male production of the world by the word can be allowed: this is the ironic constitution of the straightest of heterosexual orders as a "hommosexual" (Irigaray).

17 See Barth's rejection of Teilhard as "gnostic apologist"; cf. Eberhard Busch, *Karl Barth: His life from Letters and Autobiographical Texts*, trans. John Bowden (Philadelphia, PA: Fortress Press, 1976): "Teilhard de Chardin is an almost classic case of Gnosticism, in the context of which the gospel cannot possibly thrive. The reality which is supposed to be manifest and to be believed in is . . . the deity of 'evolution'" (Busch, *Barth*, p. 487).

18 Thus the biblical authors know nothing "of a motherhood of tehom. They give it no such chance" (Barth, *Church Dogmatics*, III.1.105).

19 ibid., III.4.

20 Feminism had found a philosopher in Simone de Beauvoir and thus seemed to him to present a great threat for Christianity, which he pursues at length in one of his huge notes (ibid., 161–3).

21 ibid., II.1.21.

22 His modeling of co-humanity on the male–female relationship shifts and perhaps undermines Buber's idea. Selinger, *Von Kirschbaum and Barth*, p. 134.

23 Catherine Keller, *From a Broken Web: Separation, Sexism and Self* (Boston, MA: Beacon Press, 1986), argues in the company of object relations theorists that a "soluble self" takes place in a feminized symbiosis with the andromorphic "separative self."

24 For a careful, fair-minded assessment of the often criticized and interlinked topoi of Barth's views of "the Jews" and of "gender," with a strong focus on the dependence

of his account of homosexuality on his general theory of the creation of human beings as male and female, cf. Rogers, *Sexuality and the Christian Body*, pp. 140–58.

25 Selinger, *Von Kirschbaum and Barth*, p. 188.

26 ibid., p. 189.

27 Ward finds in these moments "a discourse with a self-ironizing alertness to its own language or textuality" (*Barth, Derrida and the Language of Theology*, p. 242). "This is exactly the form, method and content of Derrida's philosophical discourse, which presents the inability and the inescapable burden of doing philosophy" (ibid., p. 247).

28 ibid., p. 206.

29 Rieger, *God and the Excluded*, p. 144.

30 Barth, *Church Dogmatics*, III.3.77, 103.

31 I do not only hear the dominology of Barth's "*Ordnung*." Its music is undeniable. Specifically he thinks of Mozart, who "has created order for those who have ears to hear." Why does he invoke Mozart on the threshold of the discussion of the Nothingness? "Because in the music of Mozart . . . we have clear and convincing proof that it is a slander on creation to charge it with a share in chaos because it includes a Yes and a No, as though orientated to God on the one side and nothingness on the other" (ibid., 299).

6 "SEA OF HETEROGLOSSIA": RETURN OF THE BIBLICAL CHAOS

1 Daniel Boyarin's translation from *Bereshit Rabbah*, ed. Thedor-Albeck, Vol. 1, p. 3, in Boyarin, *Intertextuality and the Reading of Midrash*, p. 17, n. 52.

2 Friedrich Nietzsche, *The Gay Science*, ed. Bernard Williams, trans. Josefine Nauckhoff, Cambridge Texts in the History of Philosophy (Cambridge, UK: Cambridge University Press, 2001), section 374, p. 240.

3 Homi Bhabha elaborates this notion of "negotiation" within the postcolonial project: "By negotiation I attempt to draw attention to the structure of iteration which informs political movements that attempt to articulate antagonistic and oppositional elements without the redemptive rationality of sublation or transcendence." In other words, this iterative doubling acknowledges "the historical connectedness between the subject and object of critique so that there can be no simplistic, essentialist opposition between ideological miscognition and revolutionary truth," *The Location of Culture*, p. 26.

4 Ward, *Barth, Derrida and the Language of Theology*, p. 174.

5 Irigaray, *Speculum*, p. 135.

6 Gayle L. Orniston and Alan D. Schrift, *Transforming the Hermeneutic Tradition: From Nietzsche to Nancy* (Albany, NY: SUNY Press, 1990), p. 14.

7 Friederich D. E. Schleiermacher, *The Hermeneutics: The Handwritten Manuscripts*, ed. Heinz Kimmerle, trans. J. Duke and J. Forstman (Missoula, MT: Scholar's Press/ American Academy of Religion, 1977), p. 69. Friedrich Schlegel first offered this formulation of the chief principle of hermeneutics, comments Kimmerle (p. 243, n. 4).

8 Hans Georg Gadamer, *Truth and Method* (New York: Crossroads, 1975), pp. 360, 447.

9 In his interpretation of Nietzsche, Derrida finds this hermeneutical project "which is to be enforced for every concept belonging to the system of philosophical decidability" suspended, "disqualified," by writing. *Spurs: Nietzsche's Styles* (Chicago: University of Chicago Press, 1979[1978]), p. 107. Paul Ricoeur would I presume offer a third way. Derrida and Gadamer did attempt a conversation on hermeneutics, in which they failed to come to an understanding. As Gadamer concludes: "Doubtless Derrida thinks—and

I am hoping he will excuse me if I try to understand him—that matters are different when it comes to texts. To him, any word appearing in written form is always already a breach." But for Gadamer, in the movement toward the "fusion of horizons" which Derrida always replaces with a breach, the text, the other, "not only strikes us and deals us a blow but also is supposed to be accepted, albeit with an assent that is the beginning of a long and often repeated effort at understanding." In a tehomically promising move, John Caputo rejoins the dialogue from the Derridean side by arguing for a "radical hermeneutics": "that is why Derrida would not embrace the rhetoric of a fusion of horizons, for it is only in the breach of the horizon that the other manages to gain a hearing." John D. Caputo, *More Radical Hermeneutics: On Not Knowing Who We Are* (Bloomington/Indianapolis: Indiana University Press, 2000), p. 58.

10 Friedrich Nietzsche, *On the Genealogy of Morals*, ed. and trans. Walter Kaufmann (New York: Vintage, 1967), 3rd essay, section 12, p. 119; my emphasis.

11 [III:116–21] Heidel, *The Babylonian Genesis*, p. 35; translation of these lines uncertain.

12 For a summary of and an argument against the widely held presumption since Gunkel that the Hebrew tehom "has its mythological background in the ancient Babylonian goddess Tiamat," cf. Tsumura, *The Earth and the Waters in Genesis 1 and 2*, pp. 45–52. Tsumura's contention, even could it be "proven" to represent an important refutation of a long-standing tradition, would only nuance the theo-cultural movement of the present argument.

13 Gerhard von Rad, *Genesis*, trans. John H. Marks, Old Testament Library (London: SCM Press, 1961[1949]), p. 48.

14 Albright challenges Gunkel's identification of the wind with Marduk's weapon. W. F. Albright, "Contributions to Biblical Archaeology and Philology," *Journal of Biblical Literature*, 43 (1924), p. 368 and n. 10.

15 [IV:45–6] Heidel, *The Babylonian Genesis*, p. 38.

16 [IV:98–101] ibid., p. 40.

17 As Australian ecofeminist theologian Anne Frances Elvey notes, "Through her 'mouth' she has been impregnated by the Evil Wind with the seed of her own death . . . life emerges from the dead body of Tiamat, a body and a life now circumscribed and marked by the male Marduk to the jubilation of his father[s]." Anne Elvey, "The Pregnant Body: Questions of Representation from the Worlds of Ancient Sumer to Second Temple Judaism and Early Christianity," in Constant J. Mews and Kate Rigby (eds), *Ecology, Gender and the Sacred* (Clayton, Vic.: Centre for Studies in Religion and Theology, Monash University, 1999), p. 15.

18 [II:110–11] Heidel, *The Babylonian Genesis*, p. 29.

19 Keller, *From a Broken Web*, pp. 80–5.

20 Von Rad, *Genesis*, p. 47.

21 ibid., p. 63.

22 ibid. Here von Rad seems to be in close proximity with Barth's "nothingness," which has no autonomous existence, but only an existence for faith—as the negated (im)possibility of creation. Cf. above Ch. 5.

23 [VII:132–4] Heidel, *The Babylonian Genesis*, p. 59.

24 [III:73] ibid., p. 33.

25 Boyarin, *Intertextuality*, p. 94.

26 Michaela Bauks, *Die Welt am Anfang: Zum Verhaeltnis von Vorwelt und Weltenstehung in Genesis 1 und in der altorientalischen Literatur* (Dusseldorf: Neukirchener Verlag, 1997), p. 9; my translation.

27 Von Rad, *Genesis*, p. 62.

28 Bauks, *Die Welt am Anfang*, p. 52, offers a helpful contextualization of von Rad's biblical theology as a refusal of the conventional modern separation of theology from historical/critical studies.

29 Von Rad, *Genesis*, p. 62.

30 Westermann, *Creation*, p. 42.

31 Von Rad, *Genesis*, p. 62.

32 Brevard S. Childs discusses Eichrodt's imputation of *ex nihilo* to *bara* and F. C. Rust's objection to the argument; see Rust's *Nature and Man in Biblical Thought* (London: Lutterworth Press, 1953), pp. 33ff. Childs inclines to agree with Eichrodt and von Rad; see his *Myth and Reality in the Old Testament*, p. 41. We discussed in Ch. 1 Moltmann's deployment of this strategic reading of *bara* as proof of the *ex nihilo*.

33 Heidel argues from the Hebrew *bereshit* for the *ex nihilo*–precisely the opposite of Rashi's argument from the construct state of "beginning" and its lack of article. So he takes the classical route of saying: "the initial verse of Genesis . . . designates heaven and earth as first created out of nothing in a rude state but in their essential or basic form." Heidel, *The Babylonian Genesis*, p. 91. Heidel's important translation of *The Babylonian Genesis* seems, strangely, to have been commissioned for the express purpose of defending the *ex nihilo* against the mythological threat; at least I would not know how else to read his acknowledgement of a research subvention from the Lutheran Church's Missouri Synod (a denomination committed to biblical inerrancy and the other fundamentals); ibid., p. vi.

34 For the other major exegetical defense of the *creatio ex nihilo* in Genesis 1, see Walther Eichrodt, "In the Beginning: A Contribution to the Interpretation of the First Word of the Bible," in Bernhard W. Anderson and Walter Harrelson (eds), *Israel's Prophetic Heritage: Essays in Honor of James Muilenburg* (New York: Harper & Row, 1962), pp. 1–10.

35 Bernard Batto, *Slaying the Dragon: Mythmaking in the Biblical Tradition* (Louisville, MO: John Knox Press, 1992), p. 85.

36 Anderson, *From Creation to New Creation*, p. 199.

37 Cf. Paul Hanson, *The Dawn of the Apocalyptic*, rev. ed. (Philadelphia, PA: Fortress Press, 1979). Cf. my own reading of the emergence of the apocalypse pattern, with reference to the Book of Revelation's metamorphosis of the prophetic antecedents: Keller, *Apocalypse*, pp. 1–34ff.

38 Levenson, *Creation and the Persistence of Evil*, p. 121; my emphasis.

39 Anderson offers an eco-friendly reading of Psalm 104 as–nonetheless–expressive of the *chaoskampf*. He reads YHWH's "rebuke" of the waters, who "took to flight" at the thunderous command of the Creator, as the achievement of natural harmony through a primordial battle. Anderson, *From Creation to New Creation*, p. 87.

40 Rashi (and those who revive his interpretation) argues that because *bereshit* lacks the definite article, it stands in the construct state; and that Genesis 1.2 would have to begin with *vattehi ha-ares* (instead of the actual *we-ha-ares hayetha*) if verse 1 were an independent sentence. *Pentateuch with Targum, Onkelos, Haptaroth and Rashi's Commentary*, ed. Rosenbaum and Silbermann. One finds early receptions within modern biblical scholarship of Rashi's moves; cf. especially E. Schrader, *Studied zur Kritik und Erklaerung der biblischen Urgeschichte* (Zurich: 1863), pp. 43–7; J M, P. Smith, in the *American Journal of Semitic Languages and Literatures*, XLIV (1927/23), pp. 108–10.

41 W. F. Albright finds in this parallelism to the *Enuma Elish* (*enuma* in Babylonian and *ud-da* in Sumerian both mean "on the day that" or simply "when" and thus like *bereshit* initiate a subordinate clause) "the most obvious and clear-cut illustration of ultimate dependence on Mesopotamia in the Old Testament account of the Creation." *Journal of Biblical Literature*, LXII (1943), p. 369. Speiser protests that the Hebrew narrator should have chosen *beyom* rather than *bereshit*, for an exact analog. Speiser, *Genesis*, pp. 3–13. The counter-arguments run in Albright's direction: because P does not *exactly* parallel the Mesopotamian texts, therefore *no* significant relation exists; the *ex nihilo* can be imputed to the text, because it does not contradict it.

42 For a compact statement of the case against the innovation, associated preeminently with Albright and Westermann, cf. Hasel, "Recent Translations of Genesis 1:1," pp. 154–66.

43 *Pentateuch with Targum, Onkelos, Haptaroth and Rashi's Commentary*, ed. Rosenbaum and Silbermann, p. 2f.; my emphasis.

44 Zornberg, *The Beginning of Desire: Reflections on Genesis*, p. 4.

45 Elazar Touitou reads Rashi's commentary in the context of the crusaders' conquest of Jerusalem for Christ, as undermining the Jewish God and making Jews vulnerable to Christian conversion; so Rashi's argument against sequence cuts the text off from the rampant Gentile cosmological speculation; and also allows his midrash on the movement of the *ruach* on the waters as "the royal throne stands in the air and is moved over the face of the waters by God's breath and his word"–to rule out an identification of *ruach elohim* with the Holy Spirit. This argument, which would play all too well into Barth's hand, cf. Ch. 4, exhibits at least the layered conflictuality which history seams into this intertext. Elazar Touitou, "Rashi and His School: The Exegesis of the Halakhic Part of the Pentateuch in the Context of the Judaeo-Christian Controversy," in R. Albert, Y. Friedman and S. Schwarzfuchs (eds), *Medieval Studies: In Honour of Avrom Saltman* (Ramat Gan: Bar Ilan University Press, 1995), pp. 231–52.

46 Speiser, *Genesis*, p. 11.

47 "Though its prefatory function is paralleled in Mesopotamia, attempts to show that Genesis 1 is directly dependent on Enuma Elish cannot be judged successful," writes Richard Clifford. He criticizes Speiser for simply adopting Heidel's chart of the sequence of acts in Enuma Elish and Genesis 1, assuming that it proved borrowing. R. J. Clifford, "Creation Accounts in the Ancient Near East and in the Bible," *Catholic Biblical Quarterly Monograph Series*, 26 (Washington, DC: Catholic Biblical Association of America, 1994), p. 140. He notes that Heidel "is more cautious than Speiser, concluding that 'the whole question must still be left open'" (p. 139). But one can read this scholarly debate quite differently: Heidel in fact is polemically determined to prove that the "differences between Enuma Elish and Genesis 1:1–2:3 'make all similarities shrink into utter insignificance.' For God speaks, and it is done; he commands, and it stands fast." "Moreover, a comparison of the Babylonian creation story with the first chapter of Genesis makes the sublime character of the latter stand out in even bolder relief." In other words the fact that Heidel traced out the parallels *at all* indicates, given his dogmatic perspective, their strength: the first three are the most pertinent to us (though the columns contain five more):

(1) *Enuma Elish*: divine spirit and cosmic matter are coexistent and coeternal//
     Genesis: divine spirit creates cosmic matter and exists independently of it [but not
     vice versa]

(2) primeval chaos: Tiamat enveloped in darkness//the earth is a desolate waste, with darkness covering the deep (tehom)

(3) light emanating from the gods//light is created.

Heidel, *The Babylonian Genesis*, p. 129; used by Speiser, *Genesis*, p. 9f.; discussed by Clifford, "Creation Accounts in the Ancient Near East and in the Bible," p. 140. We can, however, avoid making incautious claims of direct borrowing while acknowledging a parallelism of which the priestly author may have been conscious; but such parallelism might indicate neither simple dependence nor simple opposition, not an irrelevance but rather a parodic divergence.

48 Westermann, *Creation*, p. 42.

49 Brown uses the "*figura etymologica* constructions" to analyze how the word for "produces" is related to that for what it produces in all three cases of the co-creativity. Juxtaposing Genesis 1 with the *Timaeus*, he finds startling similarities in their understandings of "the process of creation as a result of God's working with the powers inherent in the primordial materials. Nowhere within the series of creative events does divine intelligence subvert the natural sequence or replace the natural powers." William P. Brown, "Divine Act and the Art of Persuasion in Genesis 1," in *History and Interpretation: Essays in Honour of John H. Hayes*, ed. M. P. Graham *et al.*, *Journal for the Study of the Old Testament*, Supplement Series 173. He presents the full case in *Structure, Role, and Ideology in the Hebrew and Greek Texts of Genesis 1:1–2:3*, p. 93. Brown finds Elohim if anything *more* rhetorically graceful than the platonic demiurge in his exhortations of the elements "to yield up their appropriate products (vegetation, sea creatures, etc)." Brown is not operating in a theological vacuum; he refers substantively to Michael Welker, who had written his *Habilitationsschrift* on Whitehead's concept of God. The rather oceanic influence of the process theological "lure" makes itself felt here, through the indirection of a hermeneutical and rhetorical analysis.

50 Brown, *The Ethos of the Cosmos*, p. 47.

51 I do not mean to imply, of course, that conservative or evangelical proponents of the *ex nihilo* doctrine necessarily oppose scientific teachings of creation and evolution. On the contrary, Lutheran theologian Ted Peters has done much to advance the dialogue of science and theology from his classical Christian point of view. Cf. the essays in Ted Peters (ed.), *Cosmos as Creation: Theology and Science in Consonance* (Nashville, TN: Abingdon, 1989). See especially Peters' well-argued "Cosmos as Creation" for a reading of the Big Bang through biblical hermeneutics, and in defense of the *ex nihilo* faith; pp. 45–110. Walter Brueggemann, *Genesis: A Bible Commentary for the Teaching of Preaching* (Atlanta, GA: John Knox Press, 1982).

52 This is Hasel's approach: he thinks that the creation account of Genesis 1 serves as an anti-mythological polemic, establishing the superior power of the Hebrew Creator. G. F. Hasel, "The Polemic Nature of the Genesis Cosmology," *Evangelical Quarterly*, 46 (1974), pp. 81–102. Such a view is in line with Barth's exegesis, but bases itself in the comparative materials. Tsumura leans in this direction as well, stressing that "tohu vabohu has nothing to do with primeval chaos," but rather the earth in a bare state, to be "inhabited by animals and humankind by God's fiats." "Genesis and Ancient Near Eastern Stories of Creation and Flood," in Hess and Tsumura, *I Studied Inscriptions from before the Flood*, p. 33.

53 Susan Niditch notes the relation of tehom to Tiamat, and comments wryly (against the theomachic exegesis) that "the Israelite author who has provided the opening chapter

of the Bible wants none of the uncertainty of this battle motif . . . If his account lacks a matriarchal goddess, it also does not present the creation of the world as dependent on her death." "Genesis," in *The Women's Bible Commentary*, ed. Carol A. Newsom and Sharon H. Ringe (London: SPCK, 1992; Louisville, MO: Westminster Press/John Knox Press, 1992), p. 13. I suppose we are thanking Elohim for a blessing of omission. Of course when Tsumura enunciates the absence of a Tiamat-femininity in Genesis 1, another register is unmistakable: "One thing is clear with regard to the religious nature of the creation story of Genesis: in Genesis 1 and 2 no female deity exists or is involved in producing the cosmos and humanity. This is unique among ancient creation stories that treat of deities having personality." From this viewpoint it is not the absence of divine war or matricide but of *divine woman* that marks the Hebrew difference. Tsumura, "Genesis," in *The Earth and the Waters*, p. 32.

54 Boyarin, *Intertextuality*, p. 41.
55 Daniel Boyarin's translation from *Bereshit Rabbah*, ed. Thedor-Albeck, Vol. 1, p. 3, in Boyarin, *Intertextuality*, p. 17, n. 52.
56 We will find this motif resurgent in Job's whirlwind Leviathan, in the next chapter, which will for us function as a key intertext in the midrashic inflection of the present project. This tehomic animation will for our own hermeneutical construction both exemplify and expand Bakhtin's concept of "interanimation," as linked with his concept of the "intentional hybrid" and thus generative of Kristeva's notion of the intertext in the first place.
57 Boyarin argues that "what marks the rabbinic culture is its heterogeneity," a heterogeneity "founded on an underlying unity, the interpretation of human being as fundamentally, essentially corporeal." D. Boyarin, *Carnal Israel: Reading Sex in Talmudic Culture*, p. 29. Boyarin is not here proposing a talmudic metanarrative but marking the difference between the specific forms of rabbinic male dominance, which he does not fail to expose, and the misogyny derived from Hellenistic Jewish or Christian society. This rabbinic privileging of the body as the seat of human animation–rather than the soul–marked the Jew as carnal, material, literal, and so as the chaotic waste of a biblical religion converted to Hellenism. The implications for the primal matter, from which the Holy Spirit had increasingly to be distanced, seem evident–as does the reason that it is more among Jewish thinkers such as Rashi, Bin Ezra, and recently Levenson and Speiser that we find a critical mass of resistance to the *ex nihilo*.
58 Boyarin, *Intertextuality*, p. 101; my emphasis.
59 Cf. the Jewish male as caricatured in nineteenth-century Europe as feminine, "sissy," even gay, in Daniel Boyarin, *Unheroic Conduct: The Rise of Heterosexuality and the Invention of the Jewish Man* (Berkeley/London: University of California Press, 1997).
60 Nietzsche, *The Gay Science*, section 374.
61 Cf. Isabelle Stengers' phrase regarding Whitehead's theory of truth. Keller and Daniell, *Process and Difference*, pp. 235–56.

7 "RECESSES OF THE DEEP": JOB'S COMI-COSMIC EPIPHANY

1 M. M. Bakhtin, *The Dialogic Imagination: Four Essays*, ed. Michael Holquist, trans. Caryl Emerson and Michael Holquist (Austin: University of Texas Press, 1981), p. 77.
2 Christopher Fry, "Comedy," in Robert W. Corrigan (ed.), *Comedy: Meaning and Form* (San Francisco: Chandler, 1965), p. 15.

3   J. William Whedbee, *The Bible and the Comic Vision* (Cambridge, UK: Cambridge University Press, 1998), p. 223.

4   N. Lynne Westfield, "Unencumbered Self (For my *Dear Sisters'* Literary Group)," in *Dear Sisters: A Womanist Practice of Hospitality* (Cleveland: Pilgrim Press, 2001), p. 43. Dr. Westfield's poetry is part of her multimedia strategy for the raced and gendered scene of religious education.

5   Bakhtin, *The Dialogic Imagination*, p. 23.

6   See Gustavo Gutierrez, *On Job-God talk and the Suffering of the Innocent* (Maryknoll, NY: Orbis, 1987).

7   Samuel Terrien, "The Yahweh Speeches and Job's Responses," *Review and Expositor*, 58 (1971), p. 507. Cf. other proponents of tragic exegesis; Bill Whedbee (*The Bible and the Comic Vision*, p. 222f.) notes the early position of Theodore of Mopsuestia, and the extreme view of H. M. Kallen, who argued for an explicit dependence of the Joban poet on Euripides: Kallen, *The Book of Job as a Greek Tragedy/Restored* (New York: Moffat, Yard, 1918).

8   So Pierre Bourdieu responded to Gunther Grass in "A Dialogue," *The Nation* (3 July 2000), p. 260.

9   Whedbee, who first argued for "The Comedy of Job" in *Semeia*, 7 (1977), recapitulates the comic interpretations of both Christopher Fry and Northrop Frye (in Corrigan, *Comedy: Meaning and Form*); and in biblical studies see the work of J. C. McLelland, *The Clown and the Crocodile* (Richmond: John Knox Press, 1991), which sets Job in the context of comedy, as well as Bruce Zuckerman's focus on Job's parody, in *Job the Silent: A Study in Historical Counterpoint* (New York: Oxford University Press, 1991).

10 Whedbee, *The Bible and the Comic Vision*, p. 226; my emphasis.

11 Bakhtin, *The Dialogic Imagination*, p. 35.

12 ibid., p. 76.

13 Genesis 18, the drama of the visitation of the "three men" to Abraham and Sarah– including the comic relief of her laughter–comes close to such a dialogical format (I thank my colleague Dana Fewell for this observation). Indeed Genesis brims with comic, ironic and satiric elements. Cf. the not-quite-heroes such as "He laughs" Isaac; Jacob the trickster. Whedbee, *The Bible and the Comic Vision*, pp. 15–125.

14 Calvin, however, represents that wing of the tradition that had no problems with divine omnipotence; as David Ray Griffin has demonstrated, the Reformers solve the puzzle of theodicy by quietly deleting any human sense of divine beneficence and thus protecting the attribute of omnipotence (through such constructs as majesty, glory, providence and predestination). See his *God, Power and Evil: A Process Theodicy*, pp. 116–30.

15 In the vision of Jeremiah 4.23–6; "In the design of Job's curse, however, it is his personal origin rather than Israel's fate which is made contemporaneous with the primordial through the ritual act of execration." Norman C. Habel, *The Book of Job: A Commentary* (Philadelphia, PA: Westminster Press, 1985), p. 104.

16 The phrase is Judith Butler's, whose description of our linguistic vulnerability suggests the "possibility for a counter-speech, a kind of talking-back," not inapplicable to Job's performance. *Excitable Speech: A Politics of the Performative* (New York/London: Routledge, 1997), p. 15.

17 Fishbane cites an Aramaic parallel: "I enchant you with the adjuration of Yam, and the spell of Leviathan the serpent." Cited in Habel, *The Book of Job*, p. 160.

18 Habel, *The Book of Job*, p. 108f.

19 Levenson, *Creation and the Persistence of Evil*, p. 156.

20 ibid., p. 155.

21 This is Stephen Mitchell's translation.

22 Habel, *The Book of Job*, p. 538.

23 Pope agrees with the womb allusion. See *Job*, ed. and trans. Marvin H. Pope, in the Anchor Bible (Garden City, NY: Doubleday, 1973), p. 293.

24 Habel draws the analogy to the Sumerian myth of the goddess' descent to the underworld. *The Book of Job*, p. 340.

25 Isaiah features wild animals in his messianic vision, but domesticated animals for the peaceable kingdom, the lion lying like a good Genesis 1 vegetarian with the lamb; whereas Ezekiel uses undomesticated animals and plants strictly as symbols of disobedience and chaos, and envisions only useful ones, such as edible fish, in his eschatology–the temple vision which modeled John's New Jerusalem. Cf. Keller, "Eyeing the Apocalypse."

26 Cf. Terrien of Blake's depiction of Job's wife: "The artist persists in placing woman on a par with man"–in contrast to the art history of depictions of Job's anonymous wife as the derisive harpy or, in Kokoschka's poster for his play *Hiob* (*Job: A Drama*), a woman "resembling a living corpse" who "clutches with her claw-like fingers the body of a dying man already flayed." Samuel Terrien, *The Iconography of Job through the Centuries: Artists as Biblical Interpreters* (University Park: Pennsylvania State University Press, 1996), p. 233.

27 A *crocowhale*, quipped Jason Starr. Behemoth, the earth monster-hippopotamus, who gets described at comparable length just before, partakes also of this mythic character– unlike the quite fastidious naturalism of the creatures described in the previous two chapters.

28 Thus Habel (relying on a questionable translation of the ambiguous 41.1–4 as God's "silencing of Leviathan," whereas the Hebrew can also be read as "Who can stand before the Leviathan?"–not "before YHWH"), *The Book of Job*, p. 570.

29 Levenson, *Creation and the Persistence of Evil*, p. 156.

30 The poet does show-case the nonhuman energies with not just predatory but warlike imagery; and in particular Leviathan's power is displayed within the context of the tradition of theomachy. These readings conform to the warrior hermeneutic (cf. Ch. 5).

31 Gerhard von Rad, *Old Testament Theology*, Vol. I, *The Theology of Israel's Historical Traditions*, trans. D. M. G. Stalker (New York: Harper, 1962), p. 417.

32 David Robertson, "The Book of Job: A Literary Study," *Soundings*, 56 (1973), pp. 462ff.

33 Not that Calvin fails to make edifying use of the whirlwind: "Here God persists in mocking the foolish presumption of men, when they think they have so much subtlety in them that they can dispute and plead against Him." To his congregation he booms: "Let us learn to keep our mouths shut. For why is it that we immediately open our mouths to vomit up what is unknown to us?" Although this is far from the spirit of apophatic mysticism, nonetheless something of the dark edge of that spirit's negativity "flows" through here. Jean Calvin, *Sermons from Job*, selected and trans. Leroy Nixon (Grand Rapids, MI: Eerdmans, 1952), p. 300.

34 Cf. Carol Adams' extensive work on Christian reification of animals and its relation to misogyny: *The Sexual Politics of Meat: A Feminist Vegetarian Critical Theory* (New York: Continuum, 1990).

35 Carol A. Newsom, "Job," in Newsom and Ringe, *The Women's Bible Commentary*, p. 136.

36 Gutierrez, *On Job-God-talk*, p. 5.

37 David J. A. Clines, "A Vegetarian Reading, Job 1–20," *World Biblical Commentary*, Vol. 17 (Dallas, TX: Word Books, 1989).

38 "Whereas the sea, air, and land animals are broken down into various species, each 'according to their kinds' (RSV), no comparable divisions are indicated for the human creatures. Yet only for them, not for any of the animals, is sexuality designated as male and female (I.27). Moreover, this specific reference pertains not to procreation but to the image of God." While Phyllis Trible's optimistic reading has its challengers even among feminist exegetes (Bird, Clines), its "clues" remain indispensable. See Phyllis Trible, *God and the Rhetoric of Sexuality* (Philadelphia, PA: Fortress Press, 1976).

39 In the Babylonian account, "man [*sic*] was made to be the servant of the gods, to be a kind of breadwinner of his divine masters, and to be the builder and caretaker of their sanctuaries. In the initial chapter of Genesis man was to be the lord of the earth, the sea, and the air." Heidel, *The Babylonian Genesis*, p. 121. If one can bracket Heidel's exultant ethnocentrism and anthropocentrism, the contrast does bear witness to a potentially subversive difference: that human beings are in one case created to be mere underlings, in the other endowed with "dominion" like gods. In other words we can read the royal imaginary as a fanfare not to "man's superiority over the beasts" but to human freedom–which includes responsibility for the beasts.

40 The managerial function of "stewardship" became inevitable, long before Genesis and Job were composed, probably with the spread of plough agriculture. According to such ecologians as Wes Jackson and John Cobb, as well as environmental philosopher J. Baird Callicott, "the fall" is best situated "some twelve thousand years ago, with the dawn of plow agriculture." Jay B. McDaniel lucidly summarizes and advances this line of thinking in *With Roots and Wings: Christianity in an Age of Ecology and Dialogue* (Maryknoll, NY: Orbis, 1995), p. 123.

41 Habel, *The Book of Job*, p. 73.

42 So Whedbee carefully distinguishes his own reading from that of David Robertson, who has the Joban poet exposing a "charlatan God, one who has the power and skill of a god but is a fake at the truly divine task of governing with justice and love." Robertson, "The Book of Job," p. 464, reduces epiphany to irony and laughter to ridicule. Whedbee, *The Bible and the Comic Vision*, pp. 246ff.

43 Bill McKibben, *The Comforting Whirlwind: God, Job, and the Scale of Creation* (Grand Rapids, MI: Eerdmans, 1994), p. 54.

44 Without any discussion of Job's whirlwind, L. J. Tessier writes pertinently: "I believe that there are clues in the nature of the erotic bond between sexuality and spirituality itself, and that some of these clues relate to wilderness–to chaos–which takes us back into the whirldwind." L. J. Tessier, *Dancing after the Whirlwind: Feminist Reflections on Sex, Denial and Spiritual Transformation* (Boston, MA: Beacon Press, 1997), p. 19.

45 Newsom, "Job," p. 136.

46 Bakhtin, *The Dialogic Imagination*, p. 23.

8 "LEVIATHANIC REVELATIONS": MELVILLE'S HERMENAUTICAL JOURNEY

1 Herman Melville, *Moby-Dick: An Authoritative Text*, with reviews and letters by Melville, analogues and sources, criticism; ed. Harrison Hayford and Herschel Parker, Norton Critical Editions (New York: W. W. Norton, 1967), p. 116.

2 Yvonne Sherwood, writing with Melvillian glee, offers a lovely excursus on the literary form and biblical motifs of Moby Dick: "The gargantuan novel *Moby Dick* is obsessed with, and modeled on, the body of the whale." While she focusses on the history of effects not of Job but of Jonah, her reading (to which I came at the end) shares a Bakhtinian sense of Melville's intertextuality: "Motifs from the biblical text float overtly on the surface, as in Mapple's sonorous sermon . . . but also materialize in a more submerged, carnivalized form, like images distorted under water." Yvonne Sherwood, *A Biblical Text and its Afterlives: The Survival of Jonah in Western Culture* (Cambridge, UK: Cambridge University Press, 2000), p. 153.

3 Letter from Melville to Hawthorne, reprinted from *The Literary World*, 17 and 24 August 1850; in Melville, *Moby Dick*, ed. Hayford and Parker, p. 551.

4 Biblical and literary critics have had more to say on the confluence of cetology with theology in *Moby Dick*. Analyzing Ishmael's cetological taxonomy for its "blasphemous meanings," T. Walter Herbert, Jr, shows how Melville sets the "tauntings" in relation to orthodox Calvinists. "The leviathan in Job was an image not only of God's power but of his transcendent mystery, an image proposed to humble man's pride of knowledge." *Moby Dick and Calvinism: A World Dismantled* (New Brunswick, NJ: Rutgers University Press, 1977), p. 133. See Larry J. Kreitzer's refreshing analysis of *Moby Dick* in literature and the movies, in *The Old Testament in Fiction and Film: On Reversing the Hermeneutical Flow* (Sheffield: Sheffield University Press, 1994), pp. 49–93.

5 Glen A. Mazis, "'Modern Depths,' Painting, and the Novel: Turner, Melville, and the Interstices," *Soundings*, LXX, 1/2 (Spring/Summer 1987), pp. 121–43.

6 William Harrison Ainsworth, "American Authorship, No. 4: Herman Melville," *New Monthly Magazine* [London], 98 (July 1853), pp. 307–8; in Melville, *Moby Dick*, ed. Hayford and Parker, p. 619.

7 Anonymous reviewer, *The Southern Quarterly Review* (January 1852), p. 262; in Melville, *Moby Dick*, ed. Hayford and Parker, p. 618.

8 Sherwood, *A Biblical Text and its Afterlives*, p. 153.

9 For an account of the role of the figure of Jonah in the novel, see Nathalia Wright, *Melville's Use of the Bible* (Durham, NC: Duke University Press, 1949), pp. 82–96. Melville seems to defend the traditional religious view that Jonah was literally swallowed by the whale. Of this posture Kreitzer notes: "most scholars agree that Melville is actually making a tongue-in-cheek criticism of such orthodox defenders of the literalness of the story of Jonah's encounter with the whale" (p. 58).

10 Mazis, "'Modern Depths,'" p. 142.

11 Ainsworth, "American Authorship, No. 4," p. 621. "Gamboge" is a yellow pigment.

12 When a purchaser complained to Turner's agent about a painting's indistinctness, Turner retorted: "You should tell him that indistinctness is my forte." Cited in David Jasper, "J. M. W. Turner: Interpreter of the Bible," in J. Cheryl Exum and Stephen D. Moore (eds), *Biblical Studies/Cultural Studies: The Third Sheffield Colloquium* (Sheffield: Sheffield Academic Press, 1998), p. 301.

13 The famous art critic John Ruskin read in the later paintings what he considered Turner's "tragic insight, so little understood by his contemporaries." ibid., p. 312.

14 Jasper is thinking especially of paintings like *The Angel Standing in the Sun* and the *Deluge* canvasses. ibid., p. 313.

15 Within the context of an apocalyptic imaginary, art historian Jonathan Crary finds Turner's art related to "the poetry and imagery of William Blake." What he says of Turner applies to Melville: "Turner's art is one of the crucial sites within modernity

where an aspiration to expand radically the limits of sensory experience parallels the convulsive unfolding of social, political and technological change": *J. M. W. Turner: The Sun is God* (Liverpool: the Tate, 2000), p. 25.

16 Bakhtin, *The Dialogic Imagination*, p. 30.

17 Gilles Deleuze and Felix Guattari, *What is Philosophy?*, trans. Hugh Tomlinson and Graham Burchell (New York: Columbia University Press, 1994[1991]), p. 205.

18 Newton Arvin; cf. Sherwood's critique in *A Biblical Text and its Afterlives*, p. 157.

19 To be developed in Chapter 12.

20 Interpreters not privy to the continental problematization of "Being" and thus to Melville's prescient critique of ontotheology, cannot make sense of Melville's deconstructive gesture. "Is this a mistaken reading of Melville? Perhaps Julian Hawthorne's transcription is an error for Melville's 'Being that matters' or 'Being that maddens.'" Critical annotation, Melville, *Moby Dick*, ed. Hayford and Parker, p. 555.

21 Karen Baker-Fletcher and Garth Kasimu Baker-Fletcher, *My Sister My Brother: Womanist and Xodus God-Talk* (Maryknoll, NY: Orbis, 1997), p. 54. The "streetz" (as Rappers call and spell it) are a visible place for exploring God-talk.

22 "Cursed be that mortal interindebtedness which will not do away with ledgers. I would be free as air: and I'm down in the whole world's books." The idea of pure independence has become "an insanity" with Ahab, argues the definitive biography of Melville. "The thought of dependence in any form is a torment." Because he cannot imaginatively or ethically accept his dependencies upon the whole world, Ahab, comments Arvin, "gets not independence but isolation: and, since he is after all human, it is unendurable." Newton Arvin, *Herman Melville* (New York: Sloane Press, 1950), p. 178. Of course a tehomic theology suggests that such aseity would be unendurable and delusional in a God as well.

23 Irigaray, *Marine Lover*, p. 49.

24 One might as a feminist find Melville's all-male worlds less sexist than most male portraits of women. Ahab's dismasted masculinity may not portend the end of the phallus. But amidst the ecstatic descriptions of the sensuous golden sperm of the whale— "Squeeze! squeeze! squeeze! All the morning long; I squeezed that sperm till I myself almost melted into it . . . and I found myself unwittingly squeezing my co-labourers' hands in it" (p. 348)–of Ishmael's relation to Queequeg, of the "woman's look" of the sky and the "man-like sea" in "the Symphony" (p. 442), Melville melts down the stereotypes of heterosexism—even as Irigaray's sexual difference risks reinstating it in the interest of the oceanic femininity.

25 In Irigaray's allusion to the Heideggerian "*es gibt*", the given or gift embodies itself first of all in the amniotic membrane that the transcendent masculine, the captain, the hero, staunchly forgets. "This gift without measure remains undemonstrated." Irigaray, *The Forgetting of Air in Martin Heidegger*, p. 32.

26 Irigaray, *Marine Lover*, p. 47.

27 Deleuze and Guattari, *What is Philosophy?*, p. 169.

28 T. Hugh Crawford, "Networking the (Non)Human: Moby-Dick, Matthew Fontaine Maury, and Bruno Latour," *Configurations*, 5, 1 (1997), pp. 1–21 (Johns Hopkins University Press).

29 Glen A. Love, "Ecocriticism and Science: Toward Consilience?" *New Literary History*, 30, 3 (1999), pp. 561–76 (University of Virginia). Another critic points out that eight years before Darwin's achievement, *Moby Dick* implicitly predicts that "humanity will not be able to destroy the Moby dicks of the world without psychic and actual damage

to itself." Marian Scholtmeijer, *Animal Victims in Modern Fiction: From Sanctity to Sacrifice* (Toronto: University of Toronto Press, 1993), p. 51.

30 Toni Morrison, *Playing in the Dark* (Cambridge, MA: Harvard University Press, 1992), p. 69.

31 Carolyn Karcher, *Shadow over the Promised Land: Slavery, Race, and Violence in Melville's America* (Baton Rouge: Louisiana State University Press, 1980), pp. ix–x. See also Valerie Babb's discussion, "Of Whales and Whiteness," in *Whiteness Visible: The Meaning of Whiteness in American Literature and Culture* (New York: New York University Press, 1998), pp. 89–117.

32 Toni Morrison, "Unspeakable Things Unspoken: The Afro-American Presence in American Literature," *Michigan Quarterly Review*, 28, 1 (1989), pp. 1–34 (18). I would not want to resort to her construction of Ahab as white antiracist hero, and Moby Dick as the demonic symbol of white supremacism–rather I understand him to bear Ahab's unconscious projection of that demon. I will explore further the theological question of whiteness as "light supremacism" in Chapter 12.

33 Since Melville's time, women have inscribed ourselves in the open ironies of public and publishable adventure. Sena Jeter Naslund has quite literally written us into *Moby Dick*, in *Ahab's Wife, or, the Star-gazer: a Novel* (New York: HarperCollins, 2000). An irrepressible young protagonist disguises herself as a boy for the shipboard journey into chaos, and eventually–through a densely citational tangle of relations, relations evidently but not entirely anachronistic in their explorations of race, gender and sexuality–inscribes her voice as writer into the proximity of Melville himself. Yet in its mimetic play with *Moby Dick*, everything comes out differently. The *différance* of gender amplifies into its own midrashic enormity, with whales as innocent victims, tragedy firmly grieved and replaced by a hybrid little community–perhaps too nicely feminist but so engagingly utopian. She stands in a long lineage of tehomophilic intertext. *Ahab's Wife* swallows *Moby Dick*, which swallowed the books of Jonah and Job, which latter swallowed Genesis 1, which swallowed the *Enuma Elish*–and we have yet to see what theology, what feminism, what monstrous compound of both and neither, gets vomited, still resisting its own vocation, upon the beach of text.

34 Deleuze and Guattari, *What is Philosophy?*, p. 169. "We are not in the world, we become with the world; we become by contemplating it. Everything is vision, becoming. We become universes. Becoming animal, plant, molecular, becoming zero." And so Ahab becomes that which he hates, for his affect betrays him to his object.

35 Sherwood continues: "At one point (and for a whole chapter in fact) 'Ishmael' engages in a lengthy speculation on 'whiteness' in the manner of a French literary theorist; and then snapping out of his proto-Derridean reverie on the abyss, he takes his own temperature, apologizes that he must be sickening for a fever, and shifts to a more earthy kind of contemplation–of whale balls for breakfast." Sherwood, *A Biblical Text and its Afterlives*, p. 155.

36 Geoffrey Sanborne, *The Sign of the Cannibal: Melville and the Making of Postcolonial Reader* (Durham, NC/London: Duke University Press, 1998), p. 158.

37 Michel Serres, *Genesis*, trans. Geneviève James and James Nielson (Ann Arbor: University of Michigan Press, 1995), p. 98.

9 BOTTOMLESS SURFACE: IN BEGINNING

1 Irigaray, *Elemental Passions*, p. 97.

2 Rabbi Isaac, "The Process of Emanation," in *The Early Kabbalah*, ed. Joseph Dan, trans. Ronald Kiener (New York/Mahwah: Paulist Press, 1986), p. 80.

3 *Midrash Rabbah*, Vol. 1, *Genesis*, trans. Rabbi H. Freedman (Oxford: Oxford University Press, 1977), p. 9.

4 According to Prigogine, the Nobel laureate of chaos, "time precedes existence." Prigogine, in collaboration with Stengers, *The End of Certainty*, p. 163. He disputes not only the Newtonian universal flow of time, but also the tendency of most physicists, including Einstein, to postulate the priority of eternity and hence of time-reversibility. We have no data as to what precedes or does not precede the Big Bang. Prigogine thus speculates that the Big Bang is "an irreversible process par excellence." There would have been an irreversible phase transition from a pre-universe that we call the "quantum vacuum." Admitting that "we are dangerously close to science fiction," he argues that "irreversible processes associated with dynamical processes have probably played a decisive role in the birth of our universe. From our perspective, time is eternal" (ibid., p. 166). Is Prigogine violating the rabbinic prohibition? *Au contraire*: he does not speculate about before the beginning, because it does not comprise an absolute origin, with a then or there about which one might speculate. Physics may begin to corroborate Prigogine's theory. A recent *Scientific American* reports on emerging theories, influenced by string theory, that deny an absolute beginning to time and space. "Singularities are the toxic waste of cosmology," begins the article. "Last fall cosmologists Paul Steinhardt of Princeton University and Neil Turok of the University of Cambridge . . . proposed that the big bang is not a one-of-a-kind event but part of a recurring cycle. 'What we're motivated by string theory to believe is that the big bang is not what we've always thought–a beginning of space and time, where temperature and energy diverge,' Steinhardt says. 'Rather it is a transition between the current expanding phase and a preexisting contracting phase.'" George Musser, "Been There, Done That: The Big Bang May Not Have Been a Singular Event," *Scientific American*, 286, 3 (March 2002), pp. 25–6. Thanks to Thomas Oord for this tip.

5 Edward W. Said, *Beginnings: Intention and Method* (New York: Columbia University Press, 1985 [Basic Books, 1975]), p. 372f.

6 Milbank, Pickstock and Ward, "Introduction," in *Radical Orthodoxy*, p. 1. Milbank *et al.* make a consistent case for the classical version of *ex nihilo* theology as the only alternative to "nihilism." ibid., p. 4.

7 Wolfhart Pannenberg, *Systematic Theology*, Vol. 2, trans. Geoffrey W. Bromiley (Grand Rapids, MI: Wm B. Eerdmans, 1994), p. 42.

8 Philip Blond, "Introduction: Theology Before Philosophy," in *Post-Secular Philosophy: Between Philosophy and Theology*, ed. P. Blond (London/New York: Routledge, 1998), p. 12.

9 Said, *Beginnings*, p. xiii; my emphasis.

10 Pannenberg, *Systematic Theology*.

11 Pannenberg alludes then to the conventional prooftexts: II Maccabees 7.28; cf. Romans 4.17; Hebrews 11.3 (p. 13); cf. esp. May's refutations of the arguments for any of these texts as evidence of a biblical or Hellenistic Jewish *ex nihilo* doctrine, discussed in Chapters 1, 3.

12 Cf. Morris Berman, *Coming to Our Senses: Body and Spirit in the Hidden History of the West*

(Seattle: Seattle Writers' Guild, 1998), for an affecting challenge to the counter-orthodoxy of absolute originality in western artistic modernity.

13 Yet Said arguably gains traction for his important political writings, from *Orientalism* onwards, in *Beginnings*, and indeed from his affirmation in the conclusion of Vico's *New Science*. Closely linked to the kabbalistic-mystical countertraditions of the Renaissance, Vico accomplishes a historicizing "shift from divine originality to human beginning" (p. 372). Yet precisely in his incipient secularism, Vico surely represents not a one-way exit from the theological heritage but its self-critical edge.

14 The clue comes with a wink to the reader: "The intelligent person will understand what I am alluding to." T. M. Rudavsky, *Time Matters: Time, Creation and Cosmology in Medieval Jewish Philosophy* (Albany, NY: SUNY Press, 2000), p. 6.

15 Whitehead, *Process and Reality*, p. 43.

16 Said, *Beginnings*, p. xvii.

17 "No doubt one can think—I do—that this demystification must be led as far as possible, and the task is not modest. It is interminable, because no one can exhaust the overdeterminations and indeterminations of the apocalyptic stratagems." Derrida, "Of an Apocalyptic Tone Newly Adapted in Philosophy," in *Derrida and Negative Theology*, ed. Coward and Foshay, p. 59. But then the immodesty of the task requires precisely the modesty of the limit—the limit to the "end of . . ." and thus by implication to the deconstruction as such. This poststructuralist sense of a bottomless–infinite–critique that is itself finite has often been missed. Perhaps I am missing it. But its significance both for origins and endings lies close to the heart of the tehomic countercreation, which is the other side of a counterapocalypse. Cf. my reading of this point from Derrida, in Keller, "Eyeing the Apocalypse," in Adams (ed.), *Postmodern Interpretations of the Bible*, pp. 272–5.

18 Positioning Derridean postmodernism as a deconstruction "of the concept, the authority, and the assumed primacy of the category of the West" (p. 19), Robert Taylor maps the contributions of Bhabha and Said upon this poststructural postmodernity. His interrogation of Said's later repudiation of poststructuralism as "textualism" (p. 137) helps to keep these positionalities circulating. Robert Young, *White Mythologies: Writing History and the West* (London: Routledge, 1990).

19 Bhabha offers the case of John Locke's criteria for the continuity of consciousness (in the absence of traditional substance metaphysics, I would note): "as far as this consciousness can be extended backwards to any past action or thought, so far reaches the identity of that person." Thus for Locke depth as this retroactive unification, or backwards synthesis, unites according to Locke "those distant actions into the same person." Needless to say, Locke—who does not himself here claim "depth"—privileges a homogeneous linearity of time. So the depth which Bhabha imputes to this temporality characterizes the monodimensional "before" or "above" or "below" (like that shunned by the *Midrash Rabbah*). Bhabha, however, does not question this reading of depth, though he does suggest alternative temporalities of difference. Bhabha, *The Location of Culture*, p. 48f.

20 Said, *Beginnings*, p. 377.

21 Deleuze, *Difference and Repetition*, cited in Said, *Beginnings*, p. 377.

22 Irigaray, *Marine Lover of Friedrich Nietzsche*, p. 48.

23 David Harvey, *The Condition of Postmodernity: An Enquiry into the Origins of Cultural Change* (Oxford, UK/Cambridge, MA: Blackwell, 1989), p. 44.

24 Derrida, *Of Grammatology*, p. 61.

25 Jacques Derrida, "Différance," in *Margins of Philosophy*, trans. Alan Bass (Chicago: University of Chicago Press, 1988), p. 22. The "ontological difference" refers to the Heideggerian distinction of "Being" from "beings."

26 Augustine, *Confessions*, XII.6.

27 Derrida, *Of Grammatology*, p. 61.

28 Cf. Kevin Hart, for a definitive discussion of the relation between Derrida and Christian mysticism; also of negative theology as a form of deconstruction. *The Trespass of the Sign: Deconstruction, Theology and Philosophy* (New York: Fordham University Press, 2000), pp. 183–93. Cf. also my Ch. 12.

29 Derrida, *Of Grammatology*, p. 62.

30 "Therefore the concept of trace is incompatible with the concept of the becoming-past of what has been present." Derrida, *Margins of Philosophy*, p. 2.

31 ". . . that has never been present." Derrida, ibid., p. 23.

32 For a methodological discussion of the promise and problem of any "originary synthesis" of Whiteheadian cosmology with poststructuralist theory, cf. my Introduction and my chapter "Process and Chaosmos: The Whiteheadian Fold in the Discourse of Difference" in *Process and Difference*, Keller and Daniell (eds).

33 Whitehead, *Process and Reality*, p. 21. Whitehead's first principle, "Creativity," is defined as "the many become one and are increased by one." That increase is in fact a pluralization, a differentiation, by which the many are uniquely "synthesized" into each momentary event of becoming. Each spatiotemporal moment of genesis, or actual entity, is "a novel entity, disjunctively among the many entities which it synthesizes." *Process and Reality*, p. 21. Thus the "actual entity is the real concrescence of many potentials." Such becoming-concrete in the event of becoming entails a synthesis—temporary and complex, that is, in which the differences of the potentials actualized are not dissolved into unity but held in contrast.

34 "Contrast" refers to the convergence within a single experience of divergent, mutually irreducible Others. For Whitehead, however, "contrast elicits depth, and only shallow experience is possible when there is a lack of patterned contrast." *Process and Reality*, p. 114.

35 For Whitehead "order is a social product." Therefore he finds Plato's *Timaeus* closer to "modern evolution" than Newton's *Scholium*. "In the *Timaeus* the origin of the present universe is traced back to an aboriginal disorder, chaotic according to our ideals. Plato's notion has puzzled critics who are obsessed with the Semitic theory of a wholly transcendent God creating out of nothing an accidental universe." The present writer is puzzled by the persistence of this stereotype of "Semitism." Whitehead found no lure to hermeneutics in the Hebrew text. He blithely dismissed Genesis 1 in a footnote as "too primitive to bear upon this point." *Process and Reality*, pp. 93–5.

36 Derrida, *Margins of Philosophy*, p. 22.

37 John Milbank suggests that "we trust the depth, and appearance as the gift of depth, and history as the restoration of the loss of this depth in Christ." The implications for transdisciplinarity are dire: hence it is indeed for radical orthodoxy an either/or: philosophy (Western or Eastern) as a purely autonomous discipline, or theology; Herod or the magi, Pilate or the God-man." Milbank, "Knowledge: The Theological Critique of Philosophy," in Milbank, Pickstock and Ward (eds), *Radical Orthodoxy*, p. 32

38 Levinas, *Totality and Infinity*, p. 198

39 US contextual theologies live by resistance to the stereotypes ordering the Others–the

chaos of women, Blacks, Hispanics, Asians, gays, lesbians–and so may benefit from this Levinassian depth. Cf. Edith Wyschogrod, *Saints and Postmodernism: Revisioning Moral Philosophy* (Chicago: University of Chicago Press, 1990) and Grace Jantzen, *Becoming Divine*; they may help a reader of Levinas to negotiate the tensions between his work and that of the social movements.

40 Levinas, *Totality and Infinity*, p. 50.

41 Cf. Irigaray's incantatory rendition of Levinas in "The Fecundity of the Caress: A Reading of Levinas, *Totality and Infinity*, Phenomenology of Eros," in *An Ethics of Sexual Difference* (Ithaca, NY: Cornell University Press, 1993[1984]), pp. 185ff.

42 Derrida in *Of Grammatology*, p. 72, seems to resist any "infinitism" as Spinozist and logocentric, but would not identify the monist infinity with that of Nietzsche's infinity of interpretations, let alone the open *infini* of Levinas and Irigaray.

43 John Caputo offers an effective and snappy rebuttal to this line of criticism, i.e. of Derrida's "linguisticism," in Caputo, *Deconstruction in a Nutshell*, p. 104.

44 Derrida, *Of Grammatology*, p. 70; my emphasis.

45 See Chapter 7.

46 Levinas confesses an explicit version of the creation *ex nihilo*–in opposition to the ontology that I have argued founds within Christianity the *ex nihilo* doctrine (*Totality and Infinity*, p. 293). Because he identifies any "synthesis" with totality, he substitutes–in the move which alienates his work from the relationalisms of feminist theology–"separation" for any residue of ontology. "To affirm origin from nothing by creation is to contest the prior community of all things within eternity, from which philosophical thought, guided by ontology, makes things arise as from a common matrix" (p. 203). I am indeed proposing such a common matrix, and so must dispute the ethical superiority of this "separation resistant to synthesis." The ontological tradition has in fact rigorously and aggressively perpetrated separation–between Eternity and time, infinity and the finite, Creator and creatures–and thus achieved the very totalism he pits infinity against. What produces the synthetic unities he criticizes but the aggressive separations he seems to avow? "My" consciousness or "my" community can manufacture its internal unity only by postulating the gulf between itself and the Other. The tehomic matrix would not comprise a prior community of things within eternity except by a "fallacy of misplaced concreteness" (Whitehead). Community and its syntheses are a function of actuality not potentiality. But of course the difference which for us links trace/difference/tehom does not express "the absolute gap which transcendence implies." I do not know if one can meaningfully "separate" Levinas' face of the infinite from his appeal to a transcendent, *ex nihilo*, origin. But I hope it is clear that my recourse to certain indispensable Levinassian metaphors remains minimal.

47 Derrida, "Khora," in *On the Name*, ed. Dutoit, p. 91.

48 For helpful resistance to the identification with pure undifferentiation of khora and primal chaos in the Middle Eastern mythologies, including Tiamat/Tehom, cf. Edward Casey, *Getting Back into Place: Toward a Renewed Understanding of the Place-World* (Bloomington: Indiana University Press, 1993) and *The Fate of Place: A Philosophical History* (Berkeley: University of California Press, 1997).

49 Cf. Diane Elam's discussion of the debate on Derrida's relation and use to feminism, *Feminism and Deconstruction: Ms. en Abyme* (London: Routledge, 1994), esp. pp. 27ff. "The cognitive abyss of sexual difference is where we are, before we know where it is we are," she avers, responding sympathetically to Derrida's interest in a non-binary "sexual otherwise." ibid., p. 58.

50 Derrida, *On the Name*, p. 104.

51 Derrida, "Khora," p. 83; my emphasis.

52 Cited in Derrida, "*Sauf Le Nom*," in *On the Name*, p. 57.

53 Jacob ben Sheshet of Gerona, "The Book of Faith and Reliance," in *The Early Kabbalah*, p. 126.

54 Why not vice versa–the God-in-All? Did the latter represent the common belief the kabbalist wished to deconstruct: the anthropomorphism of a personal Creator entering His creation and moving around, as man in his house?

55 Cf. Elliot R. Wolfson, *Circle in the Square: Studies in the Use of Gender in Kabbalistic Symbolism* (Albany, NY: SUNY Press, 1995) to forestall any facile feminist appropriations of kabbalistic imagery of the feminine. Cf. more discussion in my Chapters 10 and 14.

56 Deleuze and Guattari, *What is Philosophy?*, p. 36.

57 ibid., p. 207; my emphasis. Also p. 51.

58 Benoit Mandelbrot (fractal geometry) and René Thom (mathematics of catastrophe) dot the footnotes of Deleuze and Guattari.

59 *Implicatio, explicatio, complicatio*: in a way which will have paramount importance for the final chapters of this book, Deleuze borrows these terms from Nicholas of Cusa, via his careful reader, Giordano Bruno. To "explicate" is to fold out, to "implicate" is to *fold in* and to "complicate" is to *fold together*. Cf. esp. Gilles Deleuze, *The Fold: Leibniz and the Baroque*, trans. Tom Conley (Minneapolis, MN: University of Minnesota Press, 1993[1988]).

60 For a convergence of Deleuzian explication with the quantum physicist David Bohm's "implicate order," cf. Timothy S. Murphy, "Quantum Ontology: A Virtual Mechanics of Becoming," in Eleanor Kaufman and Kevin Jon Heller (eds), *Deleuze and Guattari: New Mappings in Politics, Philosophy, and Culture* (Minneapolis/London: University of Minnesota Press, 1998), pp. 211–19. Murphy, however, does not mention the fact that the dyad *implicatio/explicatio*, which I read as derived in Deleuze from Cusa via Bruno, comes from the same lineage in Bohm, who became the notorious mystic of quantum mechanics.

61 Deleuze, *The Fold*, pp. 98ff.

62 Deleuze, *Difference and Repetition*, pp. 229; my emphasis.

63 Gilles Deleuze and Felix Guattari, *A Thousand Plateaus: Capitalism and Schizophrenia*, trans. Brian Massumi (Minneapolis, MN: University of Minnesota Press, 1987[1980]), p. 313.

64 Deleuze and Guattari, *What is Philosophy?*, p. 39.

65 For objections to Deleuze's notion of the virtual, which target his strong Bergsonism, cf. Constantin V. Boundas, "Deleuze–Bergson: an Ontology of the Virtual," in *Deleuze: A Critical Reader*, ed. Paul Patton (Oxford: Blackwell, 1996), p. 98. Boundas alludes to Edith Wyschogrod's critique as the "objection of the seamless plenum." He argues rightly that such seamless unity cannot be found in Deleuze's differential milieux. As her protest against any ontological interconnectedness or matrix derived from her reading of Levinas, this tension (between difference as differentiation of a matrix and difference as absolute and transcendent gap) infects the present discussion.

66 But chaos as such remains "an abstraction," he claims, "because it is inseparable from a screen that makes something–something rather than nothing–emerge from it." He is working from Leibniz via Whitehead to his own construction here, as though along a single trajectory, dubbing Whitehead as the latest "successor, or diadoche" of the school. "Chaos would be a pure Many, a purely disjunctive diversity, while the

something is a One, not a pregiven unity, but instead the indefinite article that designates a certain singularity." Deleuze, *The Fold*, p. 76.

67 For a discussion of the relation of Deleuze and Whitehead, see Keller, "Process and Chaosmos," in Keller and Daniell, *Process and Difference*, pp. 55–7; also "A Whiteheadian Chaosmos? Process Philosophy from a Deleuzean Perspective," in ibid., pp. 191–208 (this warns against, in effect, what I am doing–theologizing Deleuze); and Roland Faber, "De-Ontologizing God: Levinas, Deleuze and Whitehead," in ibid., pp. 209–34. See also Roland Faber, "The Infinte Movement of Evanescence: The Pythagorean Puzzle in Deleuze, Whitehead and Plato," *American Journal of Theology and Philosophy*, 21, 2 (May 2000), pp. 171–99.

68 Deleuze, *The Fold*, p. 81.

69 Irigaray, *Marine Lover*, p. 46.

70 Deleuze and Guattari, *What is Philosophy?*, p. 205.

71 Irigaray, *Forgetting of Air*, p. 32.

72 For a fruitful convergence of Irigarayan and Deleuzian approaches to the embodied fluidity of becoming, cf. Tamsin Lorraine, *Irigaray and Deleuze: Experiments in Visceral Philosophy* (Ithaca, NY: Cornell University Press, 1999).

10 THE PLURI-SINGULARITY OF CREATION: CREATED GOD

1 Serres, *Genesis*, p. 2f.

2 Irigaray, "Belief Itself," in *Sexes and Genealogies*, p. 42.

3 Meister Eckhart, Sermon 83: *Renovamini spiritu* (Ep 4:23). "So be silent," says Eckhart (speaking right to me and fellow theologians), "and do not chatter about God; for when you do chatter about him you are telling lies and sinning." *German Works. Meister Eckhart: The Essential Sermons, Commentaries, Treatises, and Defense*, trans. Edmund Colledge and Bernard McGinn (Mahwah, NY: Paulist Press, 1981), p. 207f.

4 Walther Eichrodt, *Theology of the Old Testament*, trans. J. A. Baker (Philadelphia, PA: Westminster Press, 1961), p. 178.

5 Gordon Werham, *Biblical Commentary on Genesis* (Waco, TX: Word Books, 1987), p. 15.

6 Fewell and Gunn transcribe thus: "Then God(s) [or 'divinity'] said [sing.] 'let us make humankind in our image, after our likeness' . . . So God(s) created [sing.] humankind in his own image, in the image of God(s) he created him, male and female he created them . . ." Significantly, they add: "the slippage extends from the God(s) to the human(s) created in his/their image. While humankind is one (him/it) it is also plural–male and female (them)." Danna Nolan Fewell and David M. Gunn, *Gender, Power, & Promise: The Subject of the Bible's First Story* (Nashville, TN: Abingdon, 1993), p. 23.

7 According to a standard Jewish commentary on verse 1, "Elohim is the general designation of the Divine Being in the Bible, as the fountain and source of all things. *Elohi* is a plural form, which is often used in Hebrew to denote plenitude of might. Here it indicates that God comprehends and unifies all the forces of eternity and infinity." Thus it can say of "created" that "the Hebrew word is in the singular, thus precluding any idea that its subject, Elohim, is to be understood in a plural sense." *The Pentateuch and Haftorahs: Hebrew Text with English Translation and Commentary*, ed. J. H. Hertz (London: Soncino Press, 1988), p. 2.

8 Eichrodt, *Theology of the Old Testament*, p. 186.

9 Von Rad, *Genesis*, p. 47.

10 Ibn Ezra's Commentary on the Pentateuch, along with other medieval commentaries, becomes a key resource for Samuelson's Jewish philosophical reading of "creation." Norbert Samuelson, *Judaism and the Doctrine of Creation* (Cambridge, UK: Cambridge University Press, 1994), p. 137.

11 The rare *bara* occurs also in Genesis 32 and I Samuel 28.13.

12 Zornberg, *The Beginnings of Desire*, p. 4f.

13 Ibn Ezra differs, for instance, from Rashi, who has the angels created on the second day. ibid., p. 5.

14 Eichrodt notes in connection with the plural of *elohim* that the angels are called *bene elohim* ("sons of God") in Genesis 6.2, 4, Job 1.6, etc., in which *bene* "is not to be taken in a genealogical sense, but as an expression connoting 'congruence' or 'belonging together'. Analogous is the use of *ruach elohim* to mean the 'spirit of divinity'" (Genesis 41.38f.). Eichrodt, *Theology*, p. 186, n. 2.

15 Samuelson, *Judaism and the Doctrine of Creation*, p. 133.

16 The *Midrash Rabbah: Genesis* early opposed any notion of a preexistent chaos, redolent as it still was of an animate or pagan Other. While the *ex nihilo* position took hold in Judaism as a reaction against gnosticism (and no doubt a determination not to be outmaneuvered by the Christian God's omnipotence), rabbinic teachings—reacting in part against the style of hellenistic exegesis consolidated in the church—did not take the form of doctrinal exposition. Likening the notion of creation from chaos to that of a monarch building a "palace on a site of sewers, dunghills, and garbage" and so discrediting it, the text has R. Huna argue: "If the matter were not written, it would be impossible to say it, viz., GOD CREATED HEAVEN AND EARTH; out of what? Out of NOW THE EARTH WAS TOHU AND BOHU (1.2)." Chap. 5.1, p. 2f. "Three cosmological traditions can be distinguished among the rabbinic texts, according to creation from an eternal matter, creation *ex nihilo*, and emanation theory." Rudavsky, *Time Matters*, p. 5. Cf. also Samuelson's analysis of the multiple Hebrew and Latin variations on the theme of "out of nothing." *Judaism and the Doctrine of Creation*, pp. 101ff.

17 Samuelson, *Judaism and the Doctrine of Creation*, p. 141.

18 ibid., pp. 206–40. Finding in contemporary astrophysics a more radical notion of creation from nothing than in "the Jewish dogma of creation," he suggests that while there is extensive congruence between the classic Jewish teaching and physics, the latter "fails to capture the sense in which this nothing is a motion towards something." ibid., p. 240. According to Nobel winner Ilya Prigogine, Big Bang theorists overreach their own data when they imply a creation from nothing. He argues for the possibility of "an irreversible process transforming gravitation into matter," claiming that the Minkowsky vacuum, the starting point for such transformations, "does not *describe creation ex nihilo*." There would for him be no basis for inferring that there was a time before any temporality. *The End of Certainty*, p. 179.

19 Stephen Moore, in personal correspondence, February 2002.

20 Michel Serres with Bruno Latour, *Conversations on Science, Culture, and Time*, trans. Roxanne Lapidus (Ann Arbor: Michigan University Press, 1995), p. 118.

21 Serres, *Genesis*, p. 6; my emphasis.

22 "As a field of force, the creative working of the Spirit of God is linked to time and space in its sphere of operations," suggests Pannenberg. Yet in order to preserve the purity of origin, he separates this pneumatological and eschatological function of the Holy Spirit from the "creative speaking of God by which the dynamic of his Spirit becomes

the origin of the specific creaturely reality." Pannenberg, *Systematic Theology*, Vol. 2, p. 110. Pannenberg deploys modern energy physics to reinterpret the creativity of the Spirit as involving "an element of indeterminacy," and of "the event of information" as constituting the transition to an independent form of "creaturely operation." Yet (unlike Samuelson, for instance, let alone process theologians, who similarly draw upon astrophysics at the heart of their theology) he means thereby to vouchsafe the *ex nihilo* formula.

23 Speiser, *Genesis*, pp. 8–9.

24 Lynn Bechtel, unpublished manuscript, "Genesis 1.1–2.4a Revisited: The Perpetuation of What Is", p. 6.

25 Serres, *Genesis*, p. 100.

26 I and III Enoch are especially rich in angelology.

27 *Zohar: The Book of Enlightenment* (Mahwah, NY: Paulist Press, 1983), p. 50.

28 We are indebted to Mary McClintock Fulkerson's *Changing the Subject* for this bottomless pun, as well as for the theological and indeed feminist reverberations (the latter inaudible within de Leon or other medieval mystical writings) of a challenge to the western Christian subject-structure.

29 Daniel Chanan Matt offers these helpful notes on the above text from the *Zohar*: "*The secret is*: The Zohar offers its mystical reading of the first words of Genesis. The . . . subject of the verse, Elohim, 'God,' follows the verb, 'created.' The Zohar insists on reading the words in the exact order they appear and thereby transforms Elohim into the object; cf. Megillah 9a. This means that there is now no subject, but that is perfect because the true subject of emanation cannot be named. For the Zohar the words no longer mean: 'In the Beginning God created,' but rather: 'With Beginning by means of the point of Wisdom the Ineffable Source created *Elohim* the palace of *Binah*." Notes to pp. 50, 210.

30 *Zohar*, p. 34.

31 ibid. "*Elohim*: a divine name meaning 'God' or 'gods.' Here the name signifies Binah, the Divine Mother who gives birth to the seven lower sephirot; cf. *Zohar* 1.3b, 15b." ibid., p. 210.

32 The Infinite, the *Eyn Sof* from which the gender binaries of the divine emanate, remains according to Elliot Wolfson "entirely masculine." Ultimately the female is subsumed in what he calls "the mythic complex of the androgynous phallus" (p. xiii). (But even the masculine deconstruction of the hermaphroditic, sliding masculinity need not close down the opening of sites of symbolic gender difference.) Wolfson, *Circle in the Square*, p. 120f.

33 Cf. Judith Plaskow, *Standing Again at Sinai: Judaism from a Feminist Perspective* (San Francisco: Harper & Row, 1990). For further discussion of Jewish feminist relations to mysticism, see Ch. 14. For a discussion of parallel problems in Christianity, see Grace M. Jantzen, *Power, Gender and Christian Mysticism* (Cambridge, UK: Cambridge University Press, 1995).

34 Butler, *Gender Trouble*, p. 32.

35 Schelling, *The Ages of the World*, p. 52. Schelling was influenced by Kabbalah, both in its Jewish and its Christian modes. Moreover he defends the importance of the Hebrew Torah as living text rather fiercely for his context: "But what particularly hinders teachers from reaching this whole is the almost improper disregard and neglect of the Old Testament in which they (not to speak of those who give it up altogether) only hold as essential what is repeated in the New Testament . . . Only the singular

lightning flashes that strike from the clouds of the Old Testament illuminate the darkness of primordial times, the first and the oldest relationships with the divine essence itself." ibid., p. 51.

36 I thank Rabbi Arthur Waskow for first making me aware of this ancient reading of the unspeakable tetragrammaton as a set of consonants literally unpronounceable except as sheer breath.

37 Friedrich Wilhelm Joseph von Schelling, *Of Human Freedom*, trans. James Gutmann (Chicago: Open Court, 1936), p. 33.

38 The intuition of a becoming-God echoes Eckhart's "birth of God from the soul." It nonetheless diverges from Eckhart's still more platonic self-identity of God. Cf. Aran Gare on Schelling, *Process and Difference*, pp. 31–54. Schelling's figure of the God-begotten God, significantly, does not make reference to Christ.

39 Schelling, *Of Human Freedom*, p. 35.

40 Rudavsky, *Time Matters*, p. 6.

41 Whitehead, *Process and Reality*, p. 348.

42 Irigaray, "Belief Itself," p. 42.

11 STRANGE ATTRACTIONS: FORMLESS AND VOID

1 Serres, *Genesis*, p. 118.

2 Deleuze and Guattari, *What is Philosophy?*, p. 205.

3 Westermann divides the uses of *tohu* in the Hebrew text into three categories: "desert" (Deuteronomy 32.10; Job 6.18; 12.24; Psalm 107.40); "devastation" (Isaiah 24.10; 34.11; Jeremiah 4.23); and "nothingness" (I Samuel 12.21; Isaiah 29.21; 40.17; etc.). William Brown disagrees with the latter category, and sifts its nuances into varieties of "unhabitability" and "uselessness." See his *Structure, Role and Ideology in the Hebrew and Greek Texts of Genesis 1:1–2:3*, p. 74.

4 Umberto Cassuto, *A Commentary on the Book of Genesis*, Part I, trans. Israel Abrahams (Jerusalem: Magnes Press, the Hebrew University, 1961), p. 22.

5 Serres, *Genesis*, p. 119.

6 Brown, *Structure, Role and Ideology*, p. 74. He borrows this suggestion from Sasson.

7 Rabbi Isaac the Blind in *The Early Kabbalah*, p. 80. This interpretation is already found in the *Midrash Rabbah*, Genesis 2: "Therefore, AND THE EARTH WAS TOHU AND BOHU (BEWILDERED AND ASTONISHED)" [caps in text]. *The Early Kabbalah*, p. 16.

8 Samuelson, *Judaism and the Doctrine of Creation*, p. 226.

9 Lynn Bechtel argues that the text tries "to construct concepts that attempt to differentiate undifferentiated reality, while subtly demonstrating that conceptual abstraction and reality do not match." With Speiser she classifies the rhyme as a "hendiadys" noting that the traditional translation "ignores the oppositional structure of a hendiadys and makes the two words virtually the same." "Genesis 1.1–2.4 Revisited," unpublished ms. Like Brown, she is arguing against the negative reading that simply amplifies *tohu* as unhabitable waste. But Brown, like Sasson, argues (*contra* Speiser, Westermann and Wenham) that this is not a hendiadys or a merismus, "since neither designation takes account of the alliterative quality of the phrase." Brown, *Structure, Role and Ideology*, p. 74.

10 Westermann salutes this presumed irrationality of the text: "A command without addresses has no meaning. The Creation command which runs through the first chapter of the Bible is beyond our understanding." *Creation*, p. 12.

11 Deleuze, *Difference and Repetition*, p. 50.

12 Luise Schottroff helpfully contextualizes the narrative. "The story of creation is addressed to these deported Jewish farmers and craftsmen in the country of the Babylonian lords. These writings from the Priestly Code are an attempt to provide a people in misery with a new order and comprehensive cult, a structure which make a home for the homeless and deported in a manifest relationship to God." "The Creation Narrative: Genesis 1.1–2.4a," in *A Feminist Companion to Genesis*, ed. Athalya Brenner (Sheffield: Sheffield Academic Press, 1997[1993]), p. 25.

13 Augustine, *Confessions*, XII.15, 17.

14 E. M. Forster, *A Passage to India* (New York: Grosset & Dunlap, 1924), p. 150.

15 Deleuze, *Difference and Repetition*, p. 3.

16 Deleuze and Guattari, *A Thousand Plateaus*, p. 313.

17 Whitehead will identify that repetition with the form of relation he calls "prehension" and the equivalent form of fluency he calls "transition" (p. 210). On his behalf we identified that transition with the notion of "transition" we found in Augustine, as the amorphic flux between forms. It may be a contribution of the twentieth-century antisubstantialist philosophies to recognize in transition the dynamism not of mere disorder, but of repetition-with-a-difference. It is repetition that creates continuity once the ontotheological framework of continuity has been dissolved into events of becoming, that is, as Whitehead puts it, "there is a becoming of continuity, not a continuity of becoming." Whitehead, *Process and Reality*, p. 35. For their pertinent discussions of Whitehead, see Prigogine and Stengers, *Order out of Chaos*, pp. 93–6; and also Prigogine, *End of Certainty*.

18 Serres, *Genesis*, p. 119.

19 Prigogine and Stengers, *Order out of Chaos*, pp. 4, 6.

20 Chaos theory does not in itself explain complexity, argues Bak. "However, precisely at the 'critical' point where the transition to chaos occurs, there is complex behavior . . . The complex state is at the border between predictable periodic behavior and unpredictable chaos." Per Bak, *How Nature Works: The Science of Self-Organized Criticality* (New York: Springer-Verlag, 1996), p. 30f. See also M. Mitchell Waldrop, *Complexity: The Emerging Science at the Edge of Order and Chaos* (New York: Touchstone/Simon & Schuster, 1992), pp. 198–240.

21 The implicit crisis of criticality reflects what is called a "resonance"–as when a third body attracts a second one from its proper orbit (Poincare's many-body problem). Such cosmological bifurcations express not the loss but the (downright adulterous) excess of relation. See Briggs and Peat, *The Turbulent Mirror*, p. 27.

22 Chaos, like quantum indeterminacy, is usually viewed as an epistemological limitation, a limitation in principle of what we can know. The possibility that it indicates an ontological open-endedness in the system can by the same token not be excluded. Yet the concept of "deterministic chaos" signals the difference between nonlinearity and indeterminacy. Chaos, according to Lorenz, is "behavior that is deterministic, or is nearly so if it occurs in a tangible system that possesses a slight amount of randomness, but does not look deterministic." Edward Lorenz, *The Essence of Chaos* (Seattle: University of Washington Press, 1993), p. 8. Thus Bak makes a strong distinction between chaos and complexity; the latter occurs only at the point of criticality, between simple, unpredictable chaos and periodic predictable behavior. "Simple chaotic systems cannot produce a spatial fractal structure like the coast of Norway." Bak, *How Nature Works*. Murray Gell-Mann, a Nobel laureate in physics, points to the

problem, still unsolved, of "quantum unpredictability and the classical chaotic kind." Initial results suggest that "it is useful to regard chaos as a mechanism that can amplify to macroscopic levels the indeterminacy inherent in quantum mechanics." Murray Gell-Mann, *The Quark and the Jaguar: Adventures in the Simple and the Complex* (New York: W. H. Freeman, 1994), p. 27.

23 Prigogine and Stengers, *Order out of Chaos*, p. 176.

24 In an example not irrelevant to–but not defining of–the present meditation, fluctuations play a critical role in the attempt to theorize the initial inflation after the so-called Big Bang.

25 The trope of dissipation resonates suspiciously well in its French with the slightly poststructuralist sense of dispersion or dissemination discussed earlier. It is worth noting that Prigogine's co-author, the philosopher and physicist Stengers, draws her methodology from both Deleuze and Whitehead. Cf. Stengers, "Beyond Conversation: The Risk of Peace," in Keller and Daniell (eds) *Process and Difference*, pp. 235–56. For the relation of Deleuze and Guattari to Prigogine and Stengers, cf. Bruno Bosteels, "From Text to Territory," in *Deleuze and Guattari: New Mappings in Politics, Philosophy and Culture*, ed. Eleanor Kaufman and Kevin Jon Heller (Minneapolis, MN: University of Minnesota Press, 1998). Timothy S. Murphy claims that "Prigogine has named Deleuze one of the contemporary thinkers in whom he has 'found inspiration' for his work on self-organizing complex systems, such as living organisms." "Quantum Ontology," p. 212.

26 Stengers, *Power and Invention: Situating Science* (Minneapolis, MN: University of Minnesota Press, 1997), p. 71; my emphasis.

27 Stuart Kauffman, *At Home in the Universe: The Search for Laws of Self-Organization and Complexity* (New York: Oxford University Press, 1995), p. 10.

28 Cf. Sallie McFague, *The Body of God: An Ecological Theology* (Minneapolis, MN: Fortress Press, 1993).

29 Prigogine and Stengers, *Order out of Chaos*, p. 51.

30 Russell, Murphy and Peacocke (eds), *Chaos and Complexity*, p. 143.

31 Arthur Peacocke, "Theology and Science Today," in *Cosmos as Creation: Theology and Science in Consonance*, ed. Ted Peters (Nashville, TN: Abingdon, 1989), p. 36.

32 Grace M. Jantzen, *Becoming Divine: Towards a Feminist Philosophy of Religion* (Bloomington: Indiana University Press, 1999), p. 151f.

33 Donna J. Haraway, *Simians, Cyborgs and Women: The Reinvention of Nature* (New York: Routledge, 1991), p. 201.

34 Briggs and Peat write perhaps the most inviting popularizations of chaos theory along aesthetic lines. "Though he is the 'epitome of the principle of disorder,' the trickster is also identified as the bringer of culture, the creator of order, a shaman or 'super-shaman.' The trickster is the wily survivor, the mischievous underdog who defies convention, subverts the system, breaks down the power structure, and gives birth to new ideas. He is the fox in some traditions, the raven or coyote in others. He is Br'er Rabbit who knows his way around the briar patch. He is Hermes the shape-shifter . . ." John Briggs and F. David Peat, *Seven Life Lessons of Chaos: Timeless Wisdom from the Science of Change* (New York: HarperCollins, 1999), p. 9f. In what they confabulate as "a joke by the cosmic trickster" Briggs and Peat suggest that "chaotic wholeness now celebrates the very phenomena that were dismissed as 'messy' and 'accidental' in the mechanical paradigm" (ibid., p. 157). By chaotic wholeness they mean the recapitulation of the whole within each fractal iteration, indeed paradoxically the "missing information"–the

unpredictable difference–is the whole within each fractal iteration; in its untotalizing nonlinear openness. So: "think of missing information as the trickster of chaos theory" (ibid., p. 172).

35 Glen A. Mazis, *Earthbodies: Rediscovering Our Planetary Senses* (Albany, NY: SUNY Press, 2002), pp. 196–8.

36 To know the significance of something is to know how and why it matters, where "to matter" means at once "to materialize" and "to mean." Judith Butler, *Bodies that Matter: On the Discursive Limits of "Sex"* (New York: Routledge, 1993), p. 32. Materialization, unlike the inert, nonsignifying matter of both materialism and idealism, means active and multidimensional embodiment.

37 "*La mère qui jouit*" ("the mother who takes pleasure") encodes Julia Kristeva's maternal *jouissance* in Jean Graybeal, *Language and "The Feminine" in Nietzsche and Heidegger* (Bloomington: Indiana University Press, 1990).

38 A. Neher, "Vision du temps et de l'histoire dans la culture juive," in *Les cultures et le temps* (Paris: Payot, 1975), p. 179, quoted in Prigogine and Stengers, *Order out of Chaos*, p. 313.

39 Stengers, *Power and Invention: Situating Science*, p. 58.

40 In the master metaphor of his important pneumatology, Hodgson likens theology to sailing, thus linking the tehomic icons: "It is in contact with powerful, fluid elements, symbolized by wind and water, over which it has little control and by which it is drawn and driven toward mysterious goals." Peter Hodgson, *Winds of the Spirit: A Constructive Christian Theology* (Louisville, KY: Westminster Press/John Knox Press, 1994), p. 3.

41 William P. Brown's lovely proposition, that God works "*per collaborationi*" more than *ex nihilo*, addresses this process. Thus "creation is enlisted and coordinated not only by divine activity but also by particular elements at God's behest. These include earth, water, and light, the basic domains or elements of earthly life from the Priestly purview." Brown, *The Ethos of the Cosmos*, p. 40f.

42 Moltmann, *God in Creation*, p. 5f. Yet for Moltmann, differently from a theology of endless becoming, the Sabbath rest of God is deferred until the messianic end of time, as the "eternal hope that it will be created anew as the 'world without end.'" Indeed unfortunately this eschatological hope for him precisely motivates *creatio ex nihilo* to begin with. The Sabbath of creation thus homologizes the "*novo creatio ex nihilo*."

43 Co-creativity will from this viewpoint always appear to be idolatry–the matrix of divine/world overlap can only appear as pantheism from a Calvinist vantage-point (not quite so of the patristic writers, not so of Augustine).

44 "God is in all things, and . . . we are to see the Creator in the glass of every creature . . . we should use and look upon nothing as separate from God, which indeed is a kind of practical Atheism": John Wesley's third sermon, "Upon Our Lord's Sermon on the Mount," as cited in Cobb, *Grace and Responsibility: A Wesleyan Theology for Today*, p. 50.

45 Calvin prefers to read the creation poetry of the Bible as "the praises of God's power from the testimonies of nature," "divine the source of those life-seeds" within Virgil's invocation of the *anima mundi*. John Calvin, *Institutes of the Christian Religion*, ed. John T. McNeill, trans. Ford Lewis Battles, the Library of Christian Classics XX (Philadelphia, PA: Westminster Press, 1975), p. 59. His beef is especially with the renaissance of pagan elements during his time in forms of Christian mysticism (such as we see in Cusa's divine One-in-All).

46 My emphasis. Further: "In this case the point in state space moves about along a continuous path in a bounded region that never returns to the same point . . . The

crucial feature of these strange paths . . . is that if you examine two nearby paths in state space and follow them along, they rapidly diverge, moving far apart. This behavior reflects the sensitivity of the chaotic solution on the choice of initial data. A tiny difference in the initial data, corresponding to nearby paths in state space, is quickly amplified. The other attractors do not have this property. Hence if we know the initial state of a system (only approximately, which is all that we can achieve), this knowledge has no predictive value when there is a strange attractor present, because the future orbit depends so sensitively on our choice of the initial state. Strange attractors, an endless path in the abstract state space, are rather beautiful geometrical objects. They can be constructed using computers and viewed on a video screen. The path of the strange attractor in state space may, in its endless meandering, fill a subspace of the whole space, and this subspace can have a bizarre noninteger fractal dimension. There is no way we can exactly mathematically construct the geometrical path of such strange attractors; there are no equations that precisely describe them, as we can often find for other attractors." Pagels, *The Dreams of Reason*, p. 79.

47 For a lucid discussion of the "spasm of *exponential* expansion" (in the 10–34 [to the negative 34th power] second before *linear* expansion took over the Big Bang), and, more radically, of Andrei Linde's cosmology of "chaotic inflation," see Ferris, *The Whole Shebang*, p. 229. According to Linde's hypothesis, our universe balloons out of a prior one like a bubble. The "maternal spacetime is chaotic in that it contains scalar fields of all possible parameters." ibid., p. 259.

48 "By sacrificing good taste, this worship achieved what Christianity has shirked: the inclusion of merriment." Forster, *Passage to India*, p. 289; Professor Godbole, in the closing Temple scene.

49 *Hadewijch: The Complete Works* (Mahwah, NY: Paulist Press, 1980), p. 245.

50 See notes on Van Mierlo and Axters vs. De Paepe in the introduction to *Hadewijch*; ibid., p. 8.

51 For a trickster figure in the Bible, see Camp's imaginative exegesis of Hochma as bifurcation of the Strange Woman. Claudia V. Camp, *Wise, Strange and Holy: The Strange Woman and the Making of the Bible* (Sheffield, UK: Sheffield Academic Press, 2000). For a trickster theology, cf. Marion Grau's ecofeminist development of a "trickster economy," *Miraculous Exchanges: A Constructive Theology of Salvific Economies*, Drew University, PhD dissertation, 2001. See also her use of the trickster economy in response to 11 September 2001, in *Strike Terror No More*, pp. 24ff.

12 *DOCTA IGNORANTIA*: DARKNESS ON THE FACE

1 *The Cloud of Unknowing*, ed. James Walsh (Mahwah, NY: Paulist Press, 1981), p. 130; translation adjusted for clarity.

2 bell hooks, "An Aesthetic of Blackness," in *Yearning: Race, Gender and Cultural Politics* (Boston, MA: South End Press, 1990), p. 113.

3 Barth, *Church Dogmatics*, III.1.106. "God's relation to this magnitude is one of victory over darkness . . . Even the intransigent statement of Isaiah 45.7 cannot be adduced to prove the opposite: 'I am the Lord, and there is none else. I form the light and create darkness. I make peace and create evil. I am the Lord that doeth all these things.'" Compare to Thurman's use of Psalm 139, below.

4 Gregory of Nyssa, *Life of Moses*, p. 95. The formulation refers actually to "John the sublime, who penetrated into the luminous darkness" (*en to lampro gnopho*).

5 Denys Turner, *The Darkness of God: Negativity in Christian Mysticism* (Cambridge/New York: Cambridge University Press, 1995). As to the argument that from the fourth century, orthodoxy and apophaticism are closely identified, V. Lossky, *The Mystical Theology of the Eastern Church* (London: James Clarke, 1957), Ch. 2.

6 *Meister Eckhart: The Essential Sermons, Commentaries, Treatises and Defense*, p. 45.

7 Thurman opens with a prologue comprised of a citation from a student's description of his experience as a deep-sea diver, as he moves "to a depth of water that cannot be penetrated by light above the surface. It is dark, foreboding and eerie. The diver's immediate reaction is apt to be one of fear and sometimes a sudden spasm of panic that soon passes. As he drops deeper and deeper into the abyss, slowly his eyes begin to pick up the luminous quality of the darkness; what was fear is relaxed and he moves into the lower region with confidence and peculiar vision." Letting this text stand without comment, and giving in the course of the book no indication that he is aware of the old mystical "luminous dark" tradition, he does, however, cite Psalm 139.11f. Howard Thurman, *The Luminous Darkness: A Personal Interpretation of the Anatomy of Segregation and the Ground of Hope* (New York: Harper & Row, 1965).

8 Robert Young develops Derrida's phrase in *White Mythologies: Writing History and the West*.

9 It was the tradition of Eastern Orthodoxy, the Christianity of the Greek-speaking fathers, to which came the Cappadocians, and then of course Dionysius (for whom I am dropping, as is becoming conventional, the misleading designation "Pseudo"). And further east, far prior to Christianity, other traditions had developed their own profoundly apophatic insights: the sunyata of Buddhism, the "Tao which cannot be named" in China. The divine nothingness of negative theology approximates more closely to these Asian varieties of nothingness than to the *nihil* negated by the classical *ex nihilo* (even as presupposed by the mystics). For convergences and divergences between the Asian ways of negation and the deconstructive reading of Western apophasis, see Coward and Foshay (eds) *Derrida and Negative Theology*.

10 Hart, *The Trespass of the Sign: Deconstruction, Theology, and Philosophy*, p. 186. One imagines that Hart's delicate reading of "the God effect that shimmers along the edges" (ibid., p. 284) of Derrida's readings of theology (especially in "Circumfession") has helped to lure Derrida to the more affirmative readings of negative theology in evidence in more recent texts, such as *Sauf le Nom*.

11 Du Bois predicted over a century ago that the problem of the twentieth century would be the problem of the color line, a claim which in retrospect deserves prophetic accreditation and pluralist complication. Samira Kawash's reading is helpful: "The color line is not simply a limit to thought or action that can be recognized and traversed. The stubborn persistence of the color line in representation and experience is not a problem of false consciousness or anachronistic thinking; rather it indicates the power and continuity of the cognitive, discursive and institutional workings of the color line as simultaneously the limit and constitutive condition for cultural and social life." Samira Kawash, *Dislocating the Color Line: Identity, Hybridity and Singularity in African-American Literature* (Stanford, CA: Stanford University Press, 1997), p. 6.

12 *Pseudo-Dionysius: The Complete Works* (Mahwah, NY: Paulist Press, 1987), p. 138.

13 "De Docta Ignorantia," in *Nicholas of Cusa: Selected Spiritual Writings* (Mahwah, NY: Paulist Press, 1997), p. 125f.

14 *Pseudo-Dionysius*, pp. 95, 135; my emphasis.

15 Derrida presents his deconstruction of apophasis not as denunciation but as askesis:

"I had to forbid myself to write in the register of 'negative theology,' because I was aware of this movement toward hyperessentiality, beyond Being." The "onto-theological reappropriation always remains possible–and doubtless inevitable insofar as one speaks, precisely, in the element of logic and onto-theological grammar"–as did Dionysius and other mystics both within and without the forms of neo-platonism sanctified by orthodoxy. But Derrida left the future of this past tense of his own abstinence open: "It remains a question, and this is why I return to it again" (p. 79). Jacques Derrida, "How Not to Speak: Denials," in *Derrida and Negative Theology*.

16 *Meister Eckhart: The Essential Sermons*, p. 208.

17 Without ever foregrounding an argument for negative theology, this *magnum opus* of Catholic (and catholic) feminist systematic theology stresses the interplay of *via positiva* and *via negativa* in Aquinas of *She Who Is*. Thus Elizabeth Johnson opens the space within the tradition for her trinity of female names: Spirit Sophia, Mother Sophia, Jesus Sophia: a case for "strategic essentialism" in feminist theology if ever there was one! E. Johnson, *She Who Is: The Mystery of God in Feminist Theological Discourse* (New York: Crossroads, 1992). (Cf. Serene Jones' application of Spivak's indispensable phrase, in *Feminist Theory for Theology*.)

18 The Divine Names, in *Pseudo-Dionysius: The Complete Works*, p. 49.

19 Dorothee Soelle, *The Silent Cry: Mysticism and Resistance* (Minneapolis, MN: Fortress Press, 2001), p. 62.

20 In addition to Soelle, cf. Leonardo Boff; an early essay by Matthew Fox, "Meister Eckhart and Karl Marx: The Mystic as Political Theologian" and Segundo Galilea, "Liberation as an Encounter with Politics," in Richard Woods (ed.), *Understanding Mysticism* (Garden City, NY: Image Books, 1980), also Don Cupitt, "The Politics of Mysticism," in his *Mysticism after Modernity* (Oxford: Blackwell, 1998). In my *Apocalypse Now and Then* I traced in some detail the sources of Joachim of Fiore's mystical-apocalyptic visions and their metamorphoses into what Marxist philosopher Ernst Bloch considered the fountain of all western revolutionary movements.

21 Cf. Bernard McGinn (ed.), *Meister Eckhart and the Beguine Mystics: Hadewijch of Brabant, Mechthild of Magdeburg, and Marguerite Porete* (New York: Continuum, 1994); see also Soelle, *The Silent Cry*, pp. 118–24.

22 *A Mirror for Simple Souls: The Mystical Work of Marguerite Porete*, ed. and trans. Charles Crawford (New York: Crossroads, 1990), pp. 86, 118.

23 ". . . for it could happen that the one hidden truth could escape both you and others in the midst of falsehoods and appearances. What is not red does not have to be white." *Pseudo-Dionysius*, p. 266. In other words, just because he recognizes a mistake doesn't mean he recognizes the truth.

24 Cusa, similarly, articulated in relation to Islam–even as its armies threatened Christendom–a surprisingly ecumenical, nearly pluralist, assessment. On principle, at least, the self-critique entailed by the epistemic iconoclasm inhibits the denunciation of others, the production of heretics, infidels, inferiors. I am not making an empirical case for the ethical effects of the history of mysticism, however; adherents of the negative way, such as St. John of the Cross, sometimes participated in extreme anti-Judaism and sexism. Yet I agree with Soelle that the impressive activist *vita* of twentieth-century mystics is not incidental to their understanding of religious language. See especially her chapter on the "Mysticism of Liberation," in *The Silent Cry*, pp. 279–98.

25 Trinh T. Minh-ha, *When the Moon Waxes Red*, pp. 234, 232; her emphasis.

26 "Dialogue on the Hidden God," in *Nicholas of Cusa*, p. 209.

27 *Nicholas of Cusa*, p. 121.

28 Attentive to the poststructuralist suspicion of the discourse of oneness, Roland Faber interprets Cusa's "God as the absolute One" as a sign of radical nondualism. "'Gottesmeer'–Versuch ueber die Ununterschiedenheit Gottes," in his *Leben in Fuelle: Skizzen zur christlichen Spiritualitaet. Festschrift fuer Prf. Dr. Weismayer zu seinem 65. Geburtstag* (Muenster: LIT, 2001), p. 80. "Weil aber solche 'Einheit' keine Vielheit 'ausser' sich haben kann, also *im Gegensatz* zum Einssein der Gegensaetze in Einem, muss dieses Eine auch gegenueber dem Vielen *nichtdifferent sein*."

29 "De Docta Ignorantia," in *Nicholas of Cusa*, p. 140.

30 Whitehead, *Science of the Modern World*, p. 91.

31 Faber, "Gottesmeer," p. 90. This "*non aliud*" reveals itself as "the ground of all identity and difference (from each other and with God). Difference and Identity disclose themselves now as an event *in* God." ibid. Here Faber's own larger constructive theology shines through: he finds in Cusa's panentheism an important precursor for his own reading of Whitehead's panentheism as the basis for a postmodern negative theology. Cf. Roland Faber, *Prozesstheologie: zu ihrer Wuerdigung und kritischen Erneuerung* (Mainz: Matthias-Gruenewald-Verlag, 2000). Also Faber, "Gottesmeer," p. 82.

32 *Nicholas of Cusa*, p. 126.

33 For instance, as inference from his notion of God the infinite contracted in all finite things he unfolds the notion of the universe as "privately infinite" yet not, as matter, capable of "being extended to infinity." *Nicholas of Cusa*, p. 131.

34 The charges were precisely iconoclasm, Arianism and the possession of heretical books (mostly it seems of Erasmus)–the *Eyn Sof* as the infinite, the kabbalistic pervasion of Bruno's thought "*l'ensofico universo*" becomes in this work "*idumenti*," "garments"–which I take to be analogous to Cusa's "contractions" of the infinite into the finite; and which according to de Leon-Jones "render better the concept of an infinite universe and an infinite divine Intellect." Karen Silvia de Leon-Jones, *Giordano Bruno and the Kabbalah* (New Haven, CT: Yale University Press, 1997), p. 37.

35 Those disturbed by the sex/gender manipulations of divinity might take the negative traditions more seriously. Johnson's appeal to the apophatic tradition necessarily and to powerful strategic effect remains secondary to her invocations of Aquinas' principle of analogy. Indeed feminist theology has been preoccupied with both a negative project (usually not linked explicitly to apophasis) of exposing the idolatry of merely masculine God-talk, and the generation of an affirmative feminine symbolism of the divine. But even the most radical edges of the Christian tradition will remain a source of ambivalence for feminist theology. For an astute feminist deconstruction of the gendered language of the mystical tradition itself, see Grace M. Jantzen, *Power, Gender and Christian Mysticism* (Cambridge, UK: Cambridge University Press, 1995).

36 *Nicholas of Cusa*, p. 126.

37 Jacques Derrida, "Sauf le Nom," in *On the Name* (Stanford, CA: Stanford University Press, 1993), p. 71. After Derrida's "How Not to Speak: Denials," there has followed a lively and growing debate on the relation of deconstruction to negative theology. See in addition to Hart, *Trespass of the Sign*, Mark C. Taylor, "Denegating God," *Critical Inquiry*, 20 (1994), pp. 7–14; Charles Winquist, *Epiphanies of Darkness: Deconstruction in Theology* (Philadelphia, PA: Fortress Press, 1986). Multiple writings by John D. Caputo, esp. *The Prayers and Tears of Jacques Derrida*, pp. 1–68. John D. Caputo and Michael J. Scanlon (eds), *God, the Gift, and Postmodernism* (Bloomington: Indiana University Press, 1999), pp. 20–47.

38 Derrida, "Sauf le Nom," p. 43.

39 Indeed of "the proposition, of the verb 'be' in the third person indicative and of everything that, in the determination of the essence, depends on this mood, this time and this person." ibid., p. 49.

40 Perhaps coincidentally it is another feminist reader of Derrida, in this case one also strongly drawn to Irigaray, and even more to the point of this chapter, one who reads for racial marks, who emphasizes the difference between the deconstructive abyss and a mere void. Writing of Derrida's metaphor of hymen/veil–a nonsynonymous substitution for khora, trace and co., Ellen Armour admits that "there is an abyssal quality to this mimetic economy, but it is the abyss of a set of many-sided mirrors bouncing reflections off one another to infinity; it is not a dark, empty hole of nothingness." *Deconstruction, Feminist Theory and the Problem of Difference*, p. 78.

41 Trinh T. Minh-ha, *Woman, Native, Other*, p. 90.

42 Derrida, "Sauf le Nom," p. 63.

43 hooks, "Aesthetics of Blackness," p. 113.

44 The oppression, the liberation and the decolonization of human beings racialized as "black," "dark" or "colored" function differently than they do for women (or gay men or Jews) racialized as "white." And for women or gay men of color, the iterative amplification of the effects of subjugation has been well thematized by Womanist theologians as the "multidimensionality of oppression" (Kelley Brown Douglas). If the struggles of Euro-American feminism with the traditional divine affirmations are by now familiar, those against racism have operated on a criss-crossing but different religious axis, in the face of a yet more devastating trajectory of social, institutional and economic hegemony. The root symbolism of light vs. darkness remains yet to be fully–and multi-dimensionally–examined.

45 Thandeka, *Learning to be White*, p. 1.

46 hooks, "Aesthetics of Blackness," p. 113.

47 An older more revealing version: "Awake from guilty nature's sleep, / And Christ shall give you light, / Cast all your sins into the deep. / And was the Aethiop white."/ C. Wesley, "O For a Thousand Tongues to Sing".

48 See my *Apocalypse*, on "De/Colon/Izing Spaces," Ch. IV.

49 Jim Perkinson argues: "Dark skin signified a 'black' heart," in his unpublished paper on white witchcraft theory of religion: "Between Unconsciously White and Mythically Black: Desire Demasked, Vitality Revisioned (Or, Which Witch is Witch?)." Jim Perkinson, Marygrove College, 11.12.01.

50 Dwight N. Hopkins, *Down, Up and Over: Slave Religion and Black Theology* (Minneapolis, MN: Augsburg/Fortress Press, 2000), p. 89f.

51 Mills interprets this early essay in light of a later, developed one, "On the Different Races of Man" (1775), as a "classic hereditarian, antienvironmentalist account of innate racial difference that essentially anticipates post-Darwinian 'scientific' racism." Charles W. Mills, *Blackness Visible: Essays on Philosophy and Race* (Ithaca, NY/London: Cornell University Press, 1998), p. 73.

52 Thandeka: "When the remains–that is, the lack of self-coherency and integration–of this self demolition process are discovered by the conscious self, this self, seeing its own brokenness, feels shame." *Learning to be White*, p. 108. Thandeka depends in her analysis upon Heinz Kohut and Daniel Stern rather than Lacan–which only makes this intersection with Bhabha's reading of Fanon on race more promising. Her work offers an original analysis of "the pervasive child abuse practices, racial indoctrination

programs, and class exploitation strategies of Euro-American communities that impair their members' abilities to relate wholeheartedly to others. Our critical investigation thus helps us to make sense of the pervasive racial and class fears found in so many Euro-Americans today: shame. They feel white shame because the persons who ostensibly loved and respected them the most actually abused them and justified it in the name of race, money, and God" (p. 134).

53 Homi Bhabha, in Frantz Fanon, *Black Skin, White Masks*, trans. Charles Lam Markmann (New York: Grove Press, 1968), pp. xiv–xv. Also Young, *White Mythologies*, p. 153, on the ambivalence of Bhabha.

54 Charles Long reads double consciousness of the oppressed as "indicative of the structure of a modern consciousness that must come to terms with the facts of this [colonial] epoch." Charles Long, "Towards Post-Colonial Method in the Study of Religion," *Religious Studies News*, 10, 2 (May 1995), p. 5.

55 Henry Vaughan (1622–95), Welsh poet, country doctor, from his poem "The Night," lines 49–50.

56 Of course the postcolonial "third space" of "hybridity" does not provide an answer to oppression; nor does postcolonial theory smoothly fit the conditions of racialized injustice in the United States. Cf. Kawash, *Dislocating the Color Line*.

57 Tanizaki, cited in bell hooks, "Aesthetic of Blackness," p. 113.

13 OCEAN OF DIVINITY: DEEP

1 Marjorie Agosin, "Idioms," in *Sargazo/Sargasso: Poems*, trans. Cola Franzen (Fredonia, NY: White Pine Press, 1993), p. 29.

2 *Pseudo-Dionysius: The Complete Works*, p. 56.

3 ibid., pp. 150, 66.

4 The Gospel of Mark, in *The Complete Gospels*, annotated Scholars version, ed. Robert J. Miller (San Francisco: Harper, 1994), p. 23; *ti deiloi este*: "*delos*" has the sense not just of "fear" but of timidity, fearfulness or cowardice.

5 It is not that a tehomic faith lacks a cognitive dimension. On the contrary, its quest and construction of knowledge are endless. Anselm's definition of theology as "faith seeking understanding" implies after all that faith, to be faith, is always seeking; that there is no point at which the Christian would possess that understanding. The more one does understand, the more there is to understand: the more the darkness glows in its infinity. Faith as trustful courage is an endless process. I am of course indebted to the spirit if not to the ontology of Paul Tillich's classic redefinition of faith in terms of courage, in *The Courage to Be* (New Haven, CT: Yale University Press, 1952).

6 I.55. *Du darfst an Gott nicht schrein / Der Brunquell ist in dir; Stopfst du den Ausgang nicht / Er fluesse fuer und fuer.* Angelus Silesius, *Der Himmel ist in dir: Von der Seelenlust mystischer Froemmigkeit* (Zurich: Benziger Verlag, 1986), p. 55; my translation.

7 Both psalms of lament, 42 and 22, express despair in the face of some mortal illness, compounded by the humiliation of mocking enemies: "he committed his cause to the LORD; let him deliver him" (22.8).

8 Deleuze and Guattari, *Thousand Plateaus*, p. 211.

9 A theme developed as part of the relationalism of Keller, *From a Broken Web*, drawn from its quite early feminist reading of *Enuma Elish* as constitutive western matricide.

10 I.68. Angelus Silesius, *The Cherubinic Wanderer* (Mahwah, NY: Paulist Press, 1986), p. 42.

11 IV.153. *Sag an, wie geht es zu, wenn ein Troepfelein / In mich, das ganze Meer, Gott ganz und gar fleusst ein?* Angelus Silesius, *Cherubinischer Wandersmann* (Einsiedeln: Johannes Verlag, 1980), p. 38; my translation.

12 *Gott is noch mehr in mir, als wann das gantze meer / In einem kleinem Schwamm gantz and beysammen waer.*

13 I:115. Silesius, *The Cherubinic Wanderer*, p. 44.

14 As cited in Faber, "Gottesmeer."

15 I.111. Silesius, *Der Himmel ist in dir*, p. 58.

16 Derrida, *On the Name*, p. 55.

17 *The Certeau Reader*, ed. Graham Ward (Oxford: Blackwell, 2000), p. 237.

18 Faber, "Gottesmeer," p. 64.

19 Faber, *Processtheologie: Zu ihrer Wuerdigung und kritischen Erneuerung*, p. 441. I find myself close to much of Faber's analysis, though wary–at least in English–of his trope of divine in/difference (*Ununterschiedenheit Gottes*), which may collapse into an apatheia he certainly does not intend, but which of course lurks within the transcendent platonism of even the most attractive mystical counterdiscourses.

20 Jay McDaniel develops a richly ecological version of the ocean image of God, using an ocean–fish analogy to explicate process panentheism. Indeed in this context he notes that this model "is not creation out of nothing but rather creation out of chaos," associating the chaos with "a creative energy within God that God cannot manipulate but can lure into various forms of order and novelty relative to the situations at hand." McDaniel, *With Roots and Wings*, p. 102f. See also for a pastorally rich use of the divine ocean metaphor, Marjorie Suchocki, *In God's Presence: Theological Reflections on Prayer* (St. Louis, MO: Chalice Press, 1996), p. 125; and Rita Nakashima Brock concludes her pioneering feminist Christology with a parable of Jesus "like the whitecap on a wave." "In thinking that a single person, a savior, or even one group can save us, we mistake the crest of a wave for the vast sea churning beneath it." *Journeys by Heart: A Christology of Erotic Power* (New York: Crossroads, 1994), p. 105.

21 Whitehead, *Process and Reality*, p. 348.

22 "Creativity," in *Process and Reality* translates the "substantial activity" of Whitehead's *Science and the Modern World* (a de-essentialization of the Greek sense of substance and a rereading of Spinoza) by which "the many become one and are increased by one": the "category of the ultimate" which is *not* God but God's everlasting source.

23 Joseph Bracken, *The Divine Matrix: Creativity as Link between East and West* (Maryknoll, NY: Orbis 1995). The divine *Ungrund* of Schelling, influenced by Eckhart's notion of the Godhead, lends itself to comparison with the groundless cosmic activity of Whitehead's Creativity. Joseph Bracken has collated these concepts, systematically linking them–with scholarly care for their differences–with the intuitions of Sunyata and Tao as well. While I have usually avoided the grounding metaphysical language, I agree with his exegesis of Whitehead's panentheism: "creativity and the extensive continuum are located within God in the sense that they together constitute in the first place the divine nature or the ground of the divine being" (ibid., p. 59). Moreover the affinity between his own name for creativity–"the Divine Matrix"–and the matrix of possibilities here nicknamed Tehom, is unmistakable.

24 Evidenced in this text by Gregory of Nyssa, Irenaeus, Athanasius and Augustine, as well as Cusa or Silesius. That vision has been reborn in recent theologies of radical embodiment, which neither defend nor nihilate the orthodox antecedents–in this text represented especially in the works of Cobb and Griffin, Charles Hartshorne, Sallie McFague, Leonardo Boff, or Ivone Gebara.

25 *la profundidad*.
26 Agosin, "Orphan Girls," in *Sargazo / Sargasso: Poems*, p. 31.
27 Irigaray, *Marine Lover*, p. 170.
28 Tamsin Lorraine's reading of this move in *Marine Lover*, as it is not theologically motivated, provides an illumining transcription: "If the virgin-mother is reduced to a sensory-substrate, if the father–son relationship is reified and referred to a distant realm, if Christ is set up as an idol of incarnation, these things have been done in keeping with the narrative from Dionysus and Apollo–a narrative Irigaray insists is premised on the denial of the feminine and the refusal to acknowledge sexual difference." *Irigaray and Deleuze*, p. 59.
29 Irigaray, *Elemental Passions*, p. 101.
30 Irigaray, *Marine Lover*, p. 176.
31 cf. C. Keller, "Chosen Persons and the Green Ecumenacy: A Possible Christian Response to the Population Apocalypse," in David Hallman (ed.), *Ecotheology: Voices from North and South* (Geneva: WCC, 1994; Maryknoll, NY: Orbis Books, 1994), pp. 300–11.
32 Jantzen, *Becoming Divine: Towards a Feminist Philosophy of Religion*, p. 151.
33 Irigaray, *Marine Lover*, p. 48.
34 Adrienne Rich, *A Wild Patience Has Taken Me this Far* (New York/London: Norton, 1981), p. 8.
35 "*Auss Gott bin ich gebohrn: ists ohne deuteley; / So frage mich nur nicht wer meine Mutter sey . . .*" Silesius, *Der Himmel Ist in Dir*, p. 94 (Book 2, no. 245); my translation.
36 "*O Unbegreiflichkeit! Gott hat sich selbst verlorn, / Drum will er widerum in mir sein neugeborn.*" ibid., p. 70 (Book 1, no. 201); my translation.
37 Rosenzweig's star is composed of triangles, the first of which he *literally* blocks out in print, like a graphic artist of midrash.
38 Franz Rosenzweig, *The Star of Redemption*, trans. William W. Hallo (New York: Holt, Rinehart & Winston, 1970[1921]), p. 90. Rosenzweig's affinity to negative theology sets the stage for the Star: "Of God we know nothing. But this ignorance is ignorance of God" (ibid., p. 23).
39 "The only task, the only obligation laid upon us is: to become divine men and women, to become perfectly, to refuse to allow parts of ourselves to shrivel and die that have the potential for growth and fulfillment." Irigaray, *Sexes and Genealogies*, p. 68.
40 Jantzen, *Becoming Divine*, p. 155.
41 ibid., p. 254; my emphasis.
42 ibid.
43 Whitehead, Heschel, Cobb, Moltmann, Johnson.
44 Cf. Delores Williams' powerful invocation of this symbol in her Womanist theology of survival in the "wilderness." *Sisters in the Wilderness: The Challenge of Womanist God-Talk* (Maryknoll, NY: Orbis, 1993), p. 234.
45 Romans 8.22; 26.

14 PNEUMATIC FOAM: SPIRIT VIBRATING

1 Deleuze and Guattari, *A Thousand Plateaus*, p. 313.
2 Luce Irigaray, *Forgetting of Air*, p. 177.
3 "What will happen to God in His last years?" she wondered. "And who or what will replace Him?" Naomi Goldenberg, *Changing of the Gods: Feminism & the End of Traditional Religions* (Boston, MA: Beacon, 1979), p. 4. In this little classic of radical feminism in

religion, Goldenberg, a psychologist of religion, prophetically disagreed with reformers that "improving the position of women is a minor alteration in Judeo-Christian doctrine." I would suspect that decades later she would not consider her questions yet answered–or perhaps answerable.

4 James Hillman, *The Dream and the Underworld* (New York: Harper & Row, 1979). Perhaps it is not coincidental that Hillman in his psychological polytheism was a powerful influence for Naomi Goldenberg.

5 Zornberg, *The Beginnings of Desire*, p. 234.

6 Moltmann, *God in Creation*, p. 16.

7 Deleuze, *Difference and Repetition*, p. 123.

8 *Nicholas of Cusa: Selected Spiritual Writings*, p. 135.

9 The relation of relations emerges in my *Apocalypse Now and Then* in the concluding chapter on the spirit (a structural iteration that for some reason became inevitable).

10 Moltmann, *God in Creation*, p. 11.

11 Johnson, *She Who Is*, p. 143.

12 It suggests a relation to the literal ocean analogous to the relation of the pre-creation "earth tohu vabohu" to the literal earth (tehom is to mayim as tohu vabohu is to earth).

13 Jürgen Moltmann, *The Spirit of Life: A Universal Affirmation* (Minneapolis, MN: Fortress Press, 1992), p. 161.

14 Concerning the verb *merahephet*, Cassuto notes that "many modern exegetes render the word, on the basis of one of the senses of the root in Syriac, 'brooding' (like a bird brooding over its eggs) and see here a reference to the idea of the World-Egg, which is found in the cosmogonies of several peoples, including the Canaanites." He notes, however, that the biblical context makes this association odd, since "the waters of the deep are not an egg or anything resembling one." Also the verb does not have the connotation of "brooding" in Hebrew. He prefers "flutter." *Commentary on Genesis*, p. 24f. Not surprisingly, feminist scholar Luise Schottroff is quite content to read "the brooding mother-bird with fluttering wings" as "God's quickening breath, his [sic] invigorating and supportive spirit. Furthermore, God's spirit is neither masculine nor neuter, but feminine." "The Creation Narrative: Genesis 1.1–2.4a," p. 25.

15 Cf. *Scivias* (I.1.3) cited and contextualized in relation to alternative accounts of creation, in Constant Mews, "The World Soul and the Cosmic Egg: Some Counter Discourses of Creation from the Twelfth Century," unpublished conference presentation Counterdiscourse of Creation, Drew University, September 2001.

16 Sharon Betcher, *Getting Grounded: Spirit Incarnate and the Kindling of Livelihood*, Drew University, PhD dissertation, 1998. Her developing pneumatological corpus "is an attempt to pick up the traces of a religious hope that stays honest to corporeality–that knows how to traverse the tears in a tragic, transient, sentient nature–a religious hope that does not abandon its basic trust in life when proportions are ruptured, when causal relations are suspended, when chaos exceeds control." Sharon V. Betcher, "Wisdom to Make the World Go On: On Disability and the Cultural Delegitimation of Suffering," *Word and World Supplement Series*, 4 (2000), pp. 87–97 (p. 87).

17 Michael Welker, *God the Spirit*, trans. John Hoffmeyer (Minneapolis, MN: Fortress Press, 1994).

18 Lynn Gottlieb, "Speaking into the Silence," *Response*, 41–2 (Fall–Winter 1982), pp. 23, 27.

19 So the Shekhinah is argued by Rabbi Joshua of Sikhnin in the name of Rabbi Levi to be

not a mere creation of God but "none other than God," according to Urbach, who traces this debate throughout Jewish medieval interpretations of the Shekhinah. "The omnipresence of God-Shekhinah is one of the primary postulates." Thus "the wings of the Shekhinah" suggests this full deity: "God, or the Shekhinah, spreads His wings over Israel 'As an eagle that stirreth up her nest, hovereth over her young'" (Deuteronomy 32.11). Ephraim E. Urbach, *The Sages: Their Concepts and Beliefs*, trans. Israel Abrahams (Jerusalem: Magnes Press, 1979), p. 46f.

20 Michael E. Lodahl, *Shekhinah/Spirit: Divine Presence in Jewish and Christian Religion* (Mahwah, NY: Paulist Press, 1992), p. 57

21 ibid., p. 92; I tend also to locate the spirit as CNG and the aim as second person/capacity/logos/sophia. Lodahl rightly echoes a frequent critique of process theology. Whereas "process theologians, on the whole, maintain a basic confidence in God's capacity to weave a world of harmony and beauty even out of the worst of our sufferings," he notes, a reception of the kabbalistic myth "poses the question of whether the process vision either of human sin or of divine vulnerability is radical enough." "What effects might human sin, senseless suffering, and radical evil be exercising upon God?"

22 David Tracy reads the Jewish "fragments of the divine" as hints of a resistance to totality, not identical with but intersecting the texts of the postmodern; he locates the divine shards "theologically as saturated and auratic bearers of infinity and sacred hope." In "Fragments: the Spiritual Situation of Our Time," in Caputo and Scanlon (eds), *God, the Gift and Postmodernism*, pp. 170–9 (p. 173).

23 Derrida, *Writing and Difference*, pp. 108ff.

24 Bhabha, *The Location of Culture*, p. 9.

25 Judith Plaskow assesses a variety of Jewish feminist strategies as well as the difference between mainline and mystical Judaism, presenting both liabilities and possibilities of the Shekhinah's divine femininity. "Female images that might balance the prevailing male metaphors exist in Judaism, but—except in the marginalized mystical tradition—they must be ferreted out as a tiny minority strand." They "have had virtually no impact on the dominant image of God." Yet she notes that Jewish feminists "turned early on to the one developed image Judaism has to offer–the image of the Shekhinah as the indwelling presence of God. While in the Talmud and midrash the Shekhinah represented the manifest presence of God without any suggestion that this presence was female, in kabbalism the Shekhinah became a feminine element in God alongside the masculine 'Holy One, Blessed be He.'" *Standing Again at Sinai: Judaism from a Feminist Perspective*, p. 138. Plaskow affirms the nonhierarchical imaginary of immanence that the Shekhinah represents as well as its mystical development in the "holy marriage," "the reunion of God and his Shekhinah, as the very meaning of mystical redemption" (ibid., p. 188). While the terms remain clearly androcentric, nonetheless she finds this sex-positive vision promising, accompanied as it is with thirteenth-century arguments for a respectful and caring sexual relationship of husband to wife (ibid., p. 189).

26 Elliot R. Wolfson, *Along the Path: Studies in Kabbalistic Myth, Symbolism, and Hermeneutics* (Albany, NY: SUNY Press, 1995), p. 108.

27 Derrida on Levinas, "At This Very Moment in This Work," trans. Ruben Berezdivin, in *A Derrida Reader: Between the Blinds*, ed. Peggy Kamuf (New York: Columbia University Press, 1991), p. 438; the essay is from Jacques Derrida, *Psyché: Inventions de l'Autre* (Paris: Galilée, 1987), where Derrida takes Levinas to task for his androcentrism.

28 Irigaray, *The Forgetting of Air*, p. 177.

29 François Rabelais, *The Five Books of Gargantua and Pantagruel*, in *The Complete Works of Rabelais*, trans. Jacques LeClerq (New York: Random House, 1944), pp. 614–15.

30 "The Fountain of Wisdom," one of the few texts yet published of the "Iyyun Circle" of Jewish mystics; the circle is so called because of its most famous work, the brief Sefer ha-'Iyyun ("Book of Contemplation"). These early thirteenth-century texts do not partake of the sources or the theosophical symbolism of the Kabbalah (such as the ten sephiroth) but would later be conjoined with classical kabbalistic symbolism. See *The Early Kabbalah*.

31 *New York Times*, Science Section, 6 March 2001.

32 Here where the New Creation in the face of finitude means the renewal, not the replacement, of "heaven and earth," I want the echo of this womanist poetics of Genesis: "To return to the dust, to the waters, to the winds is also to return to Spirit because Spirit is present in life. We humans belong to them. They are our mothers, our fathers, the source of our humanness, spirit and body . . . We are called into a vision of New Creation, a moment by moment, day by day, generation by generation process of earthly and spiritual renewal." Karen Baker-Fletcher, *Sisters of Dust, Sisters of Spirit: Womanist Wordings on God and Creation* (Minneapolis, MN: Augsburg Press/Fortress Press, 1998), pp. 125, 127.

33 Cixous, *"Coming to Writing" and Other Essays*, p. 57.

34 A last note, in case the book has proved inconclusive: the *creatio ex nihilo* is to the counternarrative of *creatio ex profundis* as the supernatural New Creation is to the counterapocalyptic *nova creatio ex profundis*.

INDEX